Indians
of the Pacific Northwest

Indians

of the Pacific Northwest

From the Coming of the White Man to the Present Day

VINE DELORIA JR.

FOREWORD BY BILLY FRANK JR.
AFTERWORD BY STEVE PAVLIK

FULCRUM
GOLDEN, COLORADO

FOREWORD

▲ ▲ ▲ ▲ ▲ ▲ ▲ ▲

BILLY FRANK JR.

I don't even remember when I first met Vine. It might have been when he was with the National Congress of American Indians in 1969. Or it might have been when he came up to the Northwest to teach at Western Washington University in 1970. But it seems as if I had always known him. It seems like he was always there fighting for us. Vine was always on the front lines.

Vine was a big part of our fight to win our fishing rights. He protected us. Whenever we got in trouble exercising our sovereign rights, we would call him and he would help. He would give speeches, testify on our behalf, and once he appeared on *The Dick Cavett Show* telling our story. He helped us win the Boldt decision.

After the Boldt decision, the commercial fishermen tried to undersell the Indian fishermen. Also, the State of Washington passed a law that steelhead could not be sold in the state, so we had no market for our salmon and our steelhead. We called Vine, who was in New York at the time. Vine found us a good market for our fish with the Mafia at the Fulton Fish Market in New York City. We butchered our fish at Frank's Landing at the mouth of the Nisqually River, boxed them, and took them right to Sea-Tac airport to send back East.

Another time we were in Portland, Oregon, hauling cigarettes to our smoke shop at Frank's Landing. The Department of

Revenue stopped us and confiscated our cigarettes and our truck. We had paid federal taxes on those cigarettes, but not state taxes. We called Vine. He sent us money and told us how to contact a judge and get an injunction. We did that, and we won. We got our cigarettes home, thanks to Vine. We used that money to support our fishing rights struggle. Vine was always on call to help us.

Vine used to hold traditional knowledge conferences. We had conferences on the animals, on the stars. I always attended those conferences. One year, he held his conference at Frank's Landing. We held it at the powwow grounds, at the Wa He Lut School. He brought us together, and we talked about giants and little people. We never recorded it, but I remember it just like it was today. We opened with a prayer and a ceremony. There were about a hundred of us there, all in a circle holding hands. It was a powerful thing, a sacred thing. That's what Vine did—he brought us together.

The last time I talked to Vine was at the final traditional knowledge conference held in Albuquerque, New Mexico, in 2005. Vine was sick then and couldn't come personally, so he telephoned us. We put him on the loudspeaker, and he talked to us. He passed away not long after that. Vine may be gone now, but in reality he is always with us. Wherever we go, Vine is still there—still watching over us every day. We continue to fight for our rights, and he continues to fight with us. One of the ways that Vine remains with us and helps in our fight is through his books and other writings.

Vine was our historian. I have always read Vine's books and they have helped me set my own course. He wrote the truth. He tried to rectify all the lies that were told about Indians. We have twenty-nine tribes in the State of Washington, and nobody knows our true story. Our own children don't know our true story. This is why *Indians of the Pacific Northwest* is so important. After more than thirty years, it is still the best book about the history of our people and what we went through, how we survived. It is a book that everyone should read. But most importantly, it is a book that needs to be read by our own people, and especially our young people.

CHAPTER ONE

▲ ▲ ▲ ▲ ▲ ▲ ▲ ▲

When I was first elected to the directorship of the National Congress of American Indians, I was introduced to the tribes of the Pacific Northwest, particularly those tribes that live in and around the Puget Sound area. The Makahs, who live on Cape Flattery, one of the northern peninsulas of Washington State, told me how a Spanish expedition in the late 1700s had invaded their lands and built a fort. The Makahs bided their time, cleverly captured the fort one morning, and sent the Spanish fleeing for their boats, leaving behind cannons, guns, and all manner of goods. While the name of Juan de Fuca was given to the strait between the lands of the Makahs and Vancouver Island, the lands and waters remained in the hands of the Indians for some time afterward.

The chief complaint of the Indians of the Pacific Northwest when they would come to the national Indian political conventions would be that the whites, particularly the officials of the fish and game departments of Washington State, were violating their treaties and harassing the Indian fishermen. I grew up in South Dakota, a member of the Sioux tribe, and when we talked about fish in that country we were talking about something approximately six inches long that you were sometimes lucky to get out of a creek in midsummer. So I could never figure out just what the problem was in Washington State, and the idea of people complaining because they couldn't go fishing seemed a little absurd to me at the time.

But the coastal tribes kept after the rest of us. They would compare the salmon with the buffalo, telling us how the salmon was to them what the buffalo had been to the Plains tribes. It was, we all agreed, ridiculous to compare a tiny fish with the magnificent animal that had provided us with food, clothing, weapons, and other articles of our culture. We were polite but firm and tried to press on to larger and more important topics of discussion that affected Indians all over the nation.

Finally, perhaps in some despair over the stupidity of this Plains Indian they were trying to educate, the Pacific Northwest tribes invited me to come to Washington State and attend a meeting on Indian problems. I was eager to get out and meet the people of the different tribes, and so I accepted and flew to Seattle. A car picked me up, and we went to the state capital, Olympia, where the Indians were having a banquet with their congressman, Lloyd Meeds, who has spent his time in Congress working hard with the tribes to resolve some of their problems.

There were nearly fifty Indians at the banquet, and, of course, salmon was served. Everyone ate his fill of the delicious meal, and after the ceremonies and speeches one of the Indians took me to the kitchen to see the remains of the salmon that had provided us with our meal. I was confronted with the skeletal remains of a gigantic fish, far surpassing in size the tiny catfish of my youth. When I learned that this one salmon had fed the entire banquet, I came to understand why the salmon was so important to these people.

Over the next decade I kept in close touch with the tribes of the Puget Sound area and came to know many of their leaders very well, as friends and as fellow workers. They were always courteous, hospitable, and generous, often sending me smoked salmon when their delegations came east. I developed a special admiration for the tribes because they had persevered against incredible odds over the past century and were quite often betrayed by the federal officials who were supposed to help them.

I found that the more I learned about the people of the Pacific Northwest and their history, the more I wanted to learn. In 1970, I moved to upper Puget Sound to teach at Western Washington State College, in Bellingham, which was a mere twelve miles from the Lummi reservation. In the year and a half that I lived in the Northwest, only a half mile from the reservation, I learned much more about the tribes of the area. It always puzzled me that so little was known about these exciting people, who had developed a very sophisticated fishing technology centuries before the coming of the white man and who had successfully maintained their fishing culture even a century after they had been overwhelmed by the settlers.

To my knowledge, no adequate history of these tribes has ever been written. Most studies on Indian life in the Pacific Northwest have concentrated on the tribes farther north, in British Columbia, such as the Kwakiutl and the Nootka. These tribes, who live in what is now Canada, had a ceremony known as the potlatch, in which they gave away immense amounts of goods as a means of determining their social status and wealth, somewhat in the same manner as the very rich in today's society tend to create foundations to distribute their wealth. This Indian practice fascinated the early scholars who visited the area, and they tended to overemphasize the custom in their scholarly works, completely overlooking the other facets of Indian life that made the people of the area so interesting. Today when you look at a book on the Indians of the Pacific Northwest, chances are that you will find a great deal on the Kwakiutl and the Nootka but very little on the Lummi, the Makah, the Skagit, or the Nooksack, and certainly only the slightest mention of the Chehalis, the Nisqually, or the Chinook. Yet these tribes have a history well worth learning.

It is perhaps best to start with a description of their lands, for the manner in which these different tribes adapted to their lands pretty much determined how their social and political customs, and certainly their great economic wealth, came about. So we will concentrate on the area from the Canadian border along the west side of the Cascade mountain range, down to the Columbia River, and south of that river a little way into the Willamette Valley.

The Cascades form a giant barrier on the West Coast, catching the rains and winds from the Pacific, which blow constantly inland. In prehistoric times, the volcanoes of the

Cascade were active, and some of the larger ones still smoke. Mount Baker, the largest of the far-northern mountains, formed part of the eastern border of the area, and within sight of its large snowfield lived the Lummi, Nooksack, Samish, and Semiahmoo around the Bellingham Bay area. To the south lived the Skagits, Swinomish, and Snohomish, near Whidbey Island and the Skagit Valley floodplains.

The Seattle area was settled by a number of small villages of Indians who fished the Green, White, Puyallup, and Nisqually rivers, and from that multitude of villages have come the Duwamish, Nisqually, Puyallup, and other tribes of today. The Nisqually ranged around the southern end of Puget Sound, near present-day Tacoma and Olympia. Beside them on the west, extending on around the western shore of Puget Sound, were the Squaxins and the Suquamish. On Cape Flattery lived the Makahs, and south of them along the coast were the Hohs, the Quileutes, the Queets, the Quinaults, and finally, along the Oregon coasts, the Chinooks.

Separating the lands of the coast tribes from the lands of the Puget Sound tribes were the majestic Olympic Mountains and the giant rain forest that blankets their slopes. Mount Rainier and other high mountains had their own glaciers and snowfields, which, along with the rain forests, ensured that the whole area west of the Cascades was interlaced with rivers, streams, and creeks of all sizes, fed in the fall and winter by the incessant rains from the ocean and in the summer by the melting of the snows. The White River, for example, was so called because of the color of the water as it came down the slopes of Mount Rainier. Other rivers seemed to change color as the seasons changed and the water shifted from melted snow to seasonal rain and back again.

Most of the mountains had special names given to them by the Indians who lived near them. Mount Rainier, for example, which figured prominently in their folklore, was called Dahkobeed by the Duwamish, Tacobud by the Nisqually, and Takkobad by the Puyallups. The Lummi name for Mount Baker, Komo Kulshan, meant "the great white watcher"; the mountain was said to watch over the people. Some of the Indian stories seemed ridiculous to the early settlers, especially those that accounted for the earliest geologic changes, but modern discoveries bear out the story line of the old Indian legends very well.

One old story told of the days when the eastern part of Washington was a gigantic lake and there was no Columbia River. The coyote, who was generally helpful to the people, realized that if there was no river the salmon could not come up into the lake, and the people would starve. So he made a hole in the mountains, and water began to drain from the lake into the ocean, forming the Columbia. Soon the salmon came, and the people were fed. For a while, a stone bridge existed where the coyote had dug through the Cascades, and people could cross the Columbia on this bridge. But eventually, during an earthquake, the bridge collapsed, forming the cascades of the Columbia, and the people had to use boats to cross the river. The funny thing is that new mapping techniques via satellite seem to indicate that a large lake did once exist in eastern Washington and that a channel eventually was formed that is now the Columbia River.

So completely did the rivers dominate the region that there were practically no trails through the dense forests at all. The Indians all traveled on the rivers, and except for the tribes that lived far inland on the slopes of the mountains (called horse Indians by the water peoples), everyone lived by the water and used canoes to get around. As the rivers were so important, it was natural that the people would keep track of each other according to river systems or drainages. The suffix -amish, which is found on many of the tribal names, for example Swinomish, Stilaguamish, Snohomish, Suquamish, Duwamish, and others, indicates that they are the "people of" a certain river system.

The Puget Sound area was one of the most heavily populated areas north of Mexico City before the coming of the white man. There was no formal tribal organization among the different groups, as was the case farther east and south. The rigid social system of the Pueblo villages, for example, and the highly developed clan system of the Iroquois were entirely foreign to this land. Rather, the people lived almost everywhere in very small groups. The average village consisted of one and perhaps as many as three long houses, comfortably containing from four to six families. They were usually constructed at river junctions or along favorite fishing sites such as a falls, or cascade, of a river.

The unusual aspect of Puget Sound life was that most of the villages had both summer houses, which were comparable to modern summer cabins, and winter houses at the more settled village from which the people generally took their name. Winter, though dreary and very rainy, was the time for the most important religious ceremonies, with the one exception of the first-salmon ceremony, observed at the beginning of the salmon runs, in spring. When not involved in their religious rituals, the Indians spent their time making needed household goods and fishing. The steelhead trout, which returns to the streams in winter, provided them with fresh meat, and food preserved during the previous summer further supplemented their diet.

Spring, summer, and early fall were devoted to fishing, gathering berries, and preparing for the winter. Many families wandered far over the islands that dotted Puget Sound and the upper-straits waters. The Lummis scattered all over the San Juan Islands in their reef-netting activities, the Makahs went far out to sea to hunt whales, and other tribes spread throughout the region in search of berries, camas roots, and other delicacies of the table. In the summertime there were many large gatherings of people from the various villages. It was a time for large feasts and visiting. Marriages were arranged and business transacted between families of different villages. Summer for the Indians resembled vacation time today in the Pacific Northwest. Everyone tried to get away to a quiet place to relax and engage in frequent celebrations.

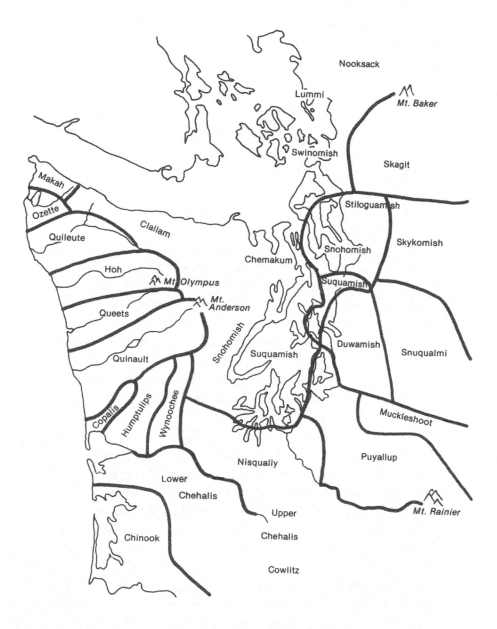

The traditional lands of the tribes of western Washington prior to the arrival of the white man.

This comparison between modern life and the life of the Indians before the coming of the white man is more than apt. One might have characterized the region as being completely suburbanized during the summer because of the variety of fishing sites used by the different families. Fishing stations were hereditary, for the most part, and some tribes appeared to specialize in the catching and preparation of certain species of salmon while others concentrated their efforts on another species. People would even share the lengths of streams, and so sophisticated was their taste that many said they could tell, from one bite of the food, exactly what stream a fish had come from and which group of Indians had prepared it.

Depending upon the type of salmon caught and the weather conditions prevailing, salmon could be prepared in any number of ways. Sometimes it was smoked, other times, with a good dry wind, it was cured by wind-drying. Sun-drying was risky because of the high humidity. The salmon eggs, considered a great winter delicacy, were also dried and smoked.

Fish was not the only food of the people, although it certainly was the major item on the menu. The larger land animals—deer, elk, and bear—were very important. These animals tended to live on the many small prairies and foothills of the Cascades. All the tribes hunted them, particularly in the wintertime. An extensive trade between the inland people and the coastal tribes, extending sometimes across the Cascades to the eastern part of Washington, was based on the exchange of dried or smoked salmon for buffalo, antelope, and other meat delicacies.

Mountain goat meat was considered a treat among many of the tribes, and they were happy to trade their fish for it. Strangely enough, the absolutely best salmon was considered to be that of the Yakimas, who lived across the Cascades on the Columbia. The Puget Sound people, who had more salmon than they knew what to do with, often traveled across the snowy Cascades to trade for salmon that had come up the Columbia to the famous Celilo Falls of the Yakimas. Celilo Falls, unfortunately, is no more. After the Second World War, dams for generating electrical power were built on the Columbia, and the famous fishing site was flooded.

The women and girls gathered shellfish such as clams, oysters, and crabs, the best crabs, of course, being those of Dungeness Bay, which was in the land of the Clallams. They also gathered the camas root, similar to a potato, and a seemingly infinite variety of berries. Years after white settlement, Indian women had at their disposal more than two hundred recipes for preparing and combining food staples such as salmon, berries, and camas roots and other vegetables.

With such a taste for delicacies, it was no wonder that the peoples of the Puget Sound area developed a very extensive trading system. With five species of salmon alone, oil from seals, whales, and dogfish, and a variety of other fish and foods, the trading for various commodities became quite complicated.

The sockeye salmon, for example, did not run in any of the streams on the Strait of Juan de Fuca, the area where the Makahs and the Clallams lived. But it did run on the western coast, south of Cape Flattery, in the Ozette River. Thus trade for sockeye developed. The Makahs did not have sufficient cedar of suitable quality for either houses or canoes, so they traded with the Nootkas on Vancouver Island for cedar canoes and planks. What did they use for trading purposes? Whale and seal oil, dried herring roe, which formed a type of caviar, and other products that could be obtained only in the Pacific Ocean and required very large canoes made only by the Nootkas.

The western Indians sold slaves (people they had captured in war), haikwa (a precious seashell), dried clams, and camas roots to the tribes in the mountains and farther inland in exchange for mountain sheep wool, porcupine quills, embroidery, and particularly for a certain kind of grass from which they made delicate threads for sewing. The peoples who lived on the western slopes of the Cascades brought mountain goat meat to the Makahs and traded it for whale meat and oil. The Makahs, in turn, traded the meat for red ochre, used for paint and cosmetics, and found only in Quileute territory. When one considers the complex number of trades among tribal groups in the days before the white man came, then it is possible to

understand how the Indians of the area welcomed the fur traders, the first non-Indians to come among them.

One can also understand how the hostility between the
Indians and the later settlers arose. The people who followed
the traders and trappers were primarily farmers, who did not
enjoy a trade fair and the endless dickering for bargains that
always accompanied trading. For the Indian, trade, besides
being profitable, was just plain fun and provided an exciting
opportunity to visit other peoples. Because the food and other
trade items were so plentiful, people had to become specialists in order to produce goods for trade. One could not simply smoke salmon because everyone did. Rather, the different
villages had to develop specialty items that would be coveted
by other tribes in order to participate in the trade. So no one
grew very rich and no one was very poor. It was a system that
worked out well for all.

CHAPTER TWO

▲ ▲ ▲ ▲ ▲ ▲ ▲ ▲

The picture of a Native paradise in the Pacific Northwest is not the whole story, however, and one only begins to learn of the complexity of pre-Columbian Indian life with an understanding of Indian technology. Unfortunately, except for a few scholarly studies on Indian house-building and fishing techniques (the latter based on a system of twig fences, called weirs, scattered throughout the streams), there has been little investigation of the real technology by which the Puget Sound Indians gained their livelihood.

Imagine, if you will, being placed in a land where a great variety of salmon filled each and every river, where ducks and geese filled the evening sky, where berries literally dripped from the bushes at harvest time, and where crabs, clams, mussels, and oysters abounded. One's first inclination would be to fish, hunt, and gather as much food as possible, but the real question would be *how* to gather this food as efficiently as possible and how to preserve it. In developing techniques for catching fish, preserving berries, and cooking shellfish, the Indians of the area were supreme. In order to understand the development of Indian skills, let us examine the great variety of techniques they used to gather food and imagine ourselves carefully observing the clever use of every resource in hunting and fishing.

First, there were at least five different kinds of fishing, distinguished by the nature of the water in which the fish lived. There were freshwater lakes; freshwater streams and creeks that drained into the various inlets and bays on the sound and the straits; the waters of the shallow bays and estuaries, basically the tideland flats; the inlets and the sound itself, which were considerably deeper and broader bodies of water than the shallow bays; and finally there were the ocean and the large straits, virtually boundless in length and depth.

Shellfish such as clams and oysters could be collected in the shallow bays and on the beaches. At the appropriate times, the women and girls of the villages turned out to harvest these shellfish, drying some of them for the winter but generally preparing a gigantic feast of fresh clams or oysters. Crabs were harvested in the same way, but these shellfish tended to be concentrated along the northern end of the Olympic Peninsula. Crabs were usually plentiful in the spring and were difficult to preserve, so they provided only a seasonal treat.

Salmon-fishing techniques varied greatly, according to the nature of the water system. On freshwater lakes, the object would be to catch the fish before they entered deep waters. The Indians would therefore station themselves at the outlet of the lake (i.e., where the river or stream drained it) and either spear or gaff the salmon. (A gaff is an implement about six feet long with a hook at the end.) There was little effort to use baited hooks; the trick was to spear a fish and haul it aboard in one swift, continuous motion. Some people used nets, and when the salmon were arriving at the lake in large quantities, during the spawning season, they might literally herd large numbers of them to the shores, where they could be taken.

The technique of impounding fish was generally used in the tideland areas, however, because of the action of the tides. Fish would come into the secluded and narrow parts of bays during high tide, and the people would build large pens while the water was still high. When the tide went out, the fish would be trapped inside the pens. Sometimes with the smaller varieties, such as smelts or candlefish, impoundment was the only practical way to catch a large number quickly.

The most famous fishing techniques were those developed for use in freshwater streams and creeks that drained into the inlets. The salmon spent an average of three years at sea and returned to their spawning grounds and gravel beds in the freshwater streams in the mountains. Large weirs, usually community property, were built across the rivers to catch the returning salmon. Weirs varied with the width of the stream, but generally they would consist of three tripods embedded in the stream bed with brush fences between the stakes, which trapped the salmon as they swam upstream.

Once the salmon were trapped behind the weirs, the people used dip nets to take the salmon. While the weir was community property, the dip-netting platforms were privately owned by families, and one had to ask permission of the owners to use them. All the facilities for curing the fish were also privately owned. This peculiar distinction between community ownership of the means of catching the fish and family ownership of the means of preserving the fish was misunderstood for decades by lawyers involved in fishing-rights cases. They used to insist that because Indians shared the weirs, they had no concept of individual property rights. But if one had no means to preserve the fish once it was caught, fishing was of little value, and the houses for curing the fish and the drying racks were individually owned.

On freshwater streams and creeks the Indians used gill nets as well. The gill nets were large nets designed to catch fish of a certain size. The openings of the mesh in the net would allow small fish to pass through it with ease, but it would snare the gills of larger fish when they tried to force their way past the net. The nets would be set in a river for hours at a time and then pulled to shore filled with fish. Generally these nets were not placed across the entire river but, rather, on alternating sides of the river every several hundred yards so that some fish could get through the nets and up the river to spawn.

In the northern part of the inland waters near the Straits of Georgia, the Lummi developed a unique kind of fishing aptly called reef netting. They would take two canoes, extend a large net between them, and anchor it on the floor of the bay or passage where the salmon would be coming. As the salmon began to swim into the camouflaged net, they would believe that the floor of the bay was shifting upward. The salmon would swim upward with the incline of the net, and at a certain point the head fisherman would shout—a signal to raise the net, thus trapping the fish.

The head fisherman was vitally important in this type of fishing, because he had to tell from the movement of the water how far into the net the majority of the fish had come. If the net was raised too soon, the salmon would be frightened and swim away. If it was raised too late, the salmon would be able to swim over the net, or they would have been able to detect the net in front of them and rapidly swim around it.

With such split-second timing necessary, the leader of the fishing expedition had to have an almost mystical sense about the salmon, the water, the nets, the current of the water, and his men's ability to raise the net quickly. Reef-net fishing required an incredible sense of timing and an intimate knowledge of all the factors that affected fish life. Leadership on a reef-netting expedition was so intuitive that those men who had continued success as reef netters were considered to be possessed of a supernatural ability and religious powers over the salmon.

When the white men came to the Straits of Georgia and tried to learn reef netting, they were unable to catch any salmon, and many quit in disgust when the salmon would not come into their nets. Eventually they learned how to camouflage their nets in the Lummi manner, but they never learned that special, mystical sense that the old Lummi fishermen had about the timing of the catch. The salmon never spoke to them as they had spoken to the Lummi reef netters.

Reef-netting sites were the most prized inland fishing grounds because the catch was generally sockeye salmon, considered a delicacy by all the tribes of the region. Catching sockeye meant that the Lummis could trade extensively with the other tribes for desirable goods, especially for the whale and seal oil and the meats of the coastal tribes. Reef net ownership has proved a great aid in scholarly interpretation of the treaties. By comparing the owners of reef-netting locations with signatures on the treaties, it can be determined if the Indians understood that they were giving up fishing rights. No Indian would sign any document that took away his reef-netting site, and so when we see the signatures of reef net site owners on treaties we know that they were promised freedom in their reef netting.

Besides reef netting, the people of the sound and the straits also developed trolling, long-lining, jigging, and set-lining techniques for fishing. In all these methods, the Indians relied upon their cleverness in designing nets and hooks for fishing that would coincide with the manner in which the salmon could most efficiently be taken. Since the salmon, in preparation for spawning, do not eat once they have entered fresh water, it was ridiculous to use hooks in the manner we do today. When the white men came into the area and saw the Indians fishing without bait, it was a great surprise to them, and they were even more shocked when they learned that the Indians had relatively good luck despite the lack of bait.

In the ocean and the large straits, fishing was a wholly different matter. Nets were not as important, because the people were out after larger game—whales, seals, sea otters, and the like—and both skill and technique were much different. The Makahs of Cape Flattery, the whalers of the Northwest, caught few salmon but many halibut in their coastal waters. The whaling canoes would go from twelve to twenty miles offshore to hunt the large mammals with harpoons. The canoes, although very large, were tiny beside the gigantic whales, and so the trick was to harpoon the whale while preventing him from sounding and breaking loose from the harpoon. Seal bladders, used for floats, were attached to the whale once the harpoon had been thrust into it, thus preventing the giant mammal from diving.

The Makahs used a combination of floats to tire the whale. As more and more floats were attached to it, the whale lost some of its agility, since it became increasingly difficult to swim while dragging so many floats. With a number of canoes surrounding the whale, the Indians guided it toward the shore, where they could finish killing it and butcher it. It was a rare occasion when the Makahs lost a whale, because they did not try to kill it immediately but, rather, used its strength to take it back to a more convenient place.

Again, with whaling, like reef netting, the leader of the expedition had to be a very exceptional person in order to lead a successful hunt. Especially among the Makahs, the chief whalers were people of great religious powers who knew the whales and seals and sang songs encouraging them to come and provide food for the people. Songs were highly prized and were passed down in the families from father to son as the most important heirlooms. There could be no greater insult or thievery than to steal a song from a family, and whenever someone tried to do that it created a big crisis in the tribe. One may scoff at the place of religion in the whaling activities of the Makahs, but the fact remains that they were able to beach the giant animals with tools and boats that one would have considered totally inadequate for such activity. We can only conclude that with their songs and equipment, the Makahs had devised an activity that was partially spiritual and partially economic.

What surprised the white men when they came to understand the Makah whalers was the fact that they had portioned off areas of the ocean into exclusive family plots. These areas were owned as property, passed down from father to son. People had heard of dividing the lands by constructing fences and setting up boundaries but no one had even dreamed it possible to divide the ocean. But the Makahs did it. They would sight from the various landmarks on the shore and establish where lines would intersect if drawn on a map. A Makah could take his canoe almost out of sight of land, and by sighting to the different outstanding landmarks such as points of land, high mountains, or river entrances, he could tell exactly where his family's whaling area was. No one used a compass or other device to mark out the areas, because from the time each boy was old enough to ride in the canoes he was taught where the fishing areas were and who owned them.

The Chinooks who lived along the Columbia River had a unique manner of catching fish in the large river. They would construct a net some five hundred feet long and nearly fifteen feet in depth that would be placed in the river, going nearly all the way across in some places. As the salmon run began, they would gradually pull the net around to catch the fish and then ease it toward the shore. When they reached shallow water, the fishermen would go into the net with mallets and clubs, killing the fish and throwing them up on the shore. This technique involved many men and was useful only when there was a large run of salmon on the river, but in the Columbia especially the salmon runs in the old days were incredibly large, and so the device worked very well.

Perhaps the most exciting type of fishing done by the Indians of the region was flounder fishing. The flounder, a flat fish that tends to rest on the bottom of mudflats, loved those along the sound. The Indian fishermen would simply wade into the mudflats until they stepped on a flounder, and then they would stand on the fish long enough to spear it with a sharp stick. The method sounds simple, but the sight of a hundred Indians all standing in mudflats jabbing sharp sticks at their feet was enough to frighten the whites who watched them. It was difficult to believe that the Indians rarely speared their own feet with all this frenzied activity, since the spectacle was one of continuous motion amid the muddiest water in the region.

With such an intimate relationship between the people and the fish, it is not surprising that the chief religious ceremony of the Indians of the area was the first-salmon ceremony, at the beginning of a salmon run. During congressional hearings on fishing in 1964, Frank Wright, then chairman of the Puyallup tribe, described the first-salmon ceremony of his tribe:

> Since salmon was 80 to 90 percent of their diet the Puyallup Indians held a cultural festival or religious ceremony in honor of the salmon. At this ceremony they barbecued the first salmon of the run over an open fire. It was then parceled out to all, in small morsels or portions so all could participate. Doing this, all bones were saved intact. Then, in a torchbearing, dancing, chanting, and singing

procession they proceeded to the river, where they cast
the skeleton of the salmon into the stream with its head
pointing upstream, symbolic of a spawning salmon, so the
run of salmon would return a thousandfold.

The various tribal ceremonies were variations of this basic ceremony. The Indians universally cut the salmon lengthwise and
not crosswise, for fear that the salmon would get insulted and
never return to the stream. Perhaps there was some wisdom in
this belief, since the cut lengthwise of a large salmon is much
cleaner and easier than a crosswise cut.

Barbecuing the salmon was almost universal among the
tribes also. Even when the whites came into the region, the Indians refused to sell the first run of salmon to them for fear that
they would boil the fish rather than barbecue or broil it. The
religious nature of this ceremony is well defined, because the
usual manner of preparing the salmon was by boiling in a large
box using heated stones to provide the heat for cooking. But by
barbecuing, the spirit of the salmon was allowed to rise with the
smoke of the fire and observe the thankfulness of the people.

When the first white men came to the Puget Sound area,
they saw at certain points along the shore a series of tall poles
and wondered what purpose they served. They were greatly
surprised when they were told that the Indians used them to
hunt ducks and other waterfowl. At night, the Indians would
spread large nets across these poles, and at a given signal they
would come out of the darkness along the shore carrying
lighted torches and yelling. The birds, frightened by the noise
and lights, would fly off, enmeshing themselves in the net and
falling to the ground. Quickly the Indians would gather them
as they lay stunned by their encounter with the net, and the
harvest would be complete. It was a unique way to hunt birds
and depended, of course, upon a perennial surplus of birds.

The upland tribes who lived in the foothills of the Cascades employed a similar method to hunt deer and elk. They
would hunt at night using torches of pine heavily daubed with
pitch. Coming on a deer or elk, the sudden light of the torch

would startle the animal, causing it to freeze long enough for the hunters to get a clear shot at it. It seems ironic that the Indians were the first jacklighters of deer, in view of the discredit that the practice receives today among hunters.

The Indian technology extended to woodworking also, and in this art the Indians of the Pacific Northwest may have been unsurpassed. The lands of the Puget Sound area have a great deal of western red cedar, a unique type of wood that, though easily split, has great tensile strength. The bark of the tree consists of two distinct layers, and the soft, downy inner layer was used instead of cotton or wool for pillows, weaving materials, and other domestic purposes. Indian women were very skillful in shredding the bark into thread-size strips for weaving and sewing, and many of the clothes they wore were of woven cedar bark.

Much of the wood used in houses and for domestic utensils was of cedar, although other species of trees were often used for their specific, desirable properties. Cooking vessels were generally cedar boxes made watertight. The cedar would be split into an appropriate shape, steamed until it was somewhat flexible, shaped, fastened with wooden pegs, and then allowed to dry. In drying, the wood would contract and close together, making the pot or kettle entirely waterproof.

The bows used by hunters were taken from living trees, and expert bowmakers would spend hours walking in the forest looking for a tree with the proper bend in its grain to make a good bow. Usually the yew or another hardwood was chosen for the bow because of its great flexibility and strength. A glue was made from the skin of the dog salmon, and decorations were attached to the bow, making it not only a very powerful weapon but a work of art. This glue, one of the greatest natural adhesives known, could also be used to mend split or broken weapons.

Canoes varied in length from five or six feet for a river canoe used for ferrying to fifty or more feet for a large oceangoing canoe for whaling. The whaling canoes were very sleek and designed for fast, silent travel over the waves. They were made of hollowed cedar logs with the outsides burned to eliminate the splinters. They were then sanded down, using the skin of the dogfish, or shark, if available; a series of curved grooves were made along the length of the canoe outside. These were designed to turn aside waves in a sequence and were considered an engineering triumph by everyone who saw them.

Cargo canoes were somewhat shorter and much broader than oceangoing canoes. As the canoe was being hollowed out, boiling water was placed in it and the whole frame was stretched out to a width of nearly six feet. The finished canoe could carry a great deal of material, and wooden boxes for carrying goods were made with slanting sides to enable them to fit almost exactly into the canoe bottoms. Indian canoes were probably the first container ships in the world.

When I was teaching at Western Washington State College, I encouraged students to visit the reservations and learn what they could from the old Indians. One student became very well acquainted with an old Yakima man, and the old man told him a story about the making of the large canoes.

It seems that in some of the tribes, ownership of a canoe was a religious responsibility, and in order to become a canoe owner a young man would have to fast and meditate in the wilderness for many days. He was taught to sing a certain song as he walked through the woods, asking a tree to bless him with the ownership of a canoe.

If the prayers of the young man were answered, a tree would choose him to be a canoe owner and it would sing back to him. Then the young man would make a camp at the bottom of the tree and stay there to learn all the responsibilities of canoe ownership. When the tree was satisfied that the young man was worthy of having a canoe, it would teach him how to fell it and how to trim its branches. Then the tree would teach the young man a special song, and as the young man returned to his village singing the song, the tree would follow him down the mountainside to the village, where it would be made into a canoe.

The legend seems hard to believe, but the technique of making a fifty-foot canoe lends credence to it. A lot of the western red cedar of which the canoes were made grew miles from the shores where the villages were. The Indians did not have saws or axes or indeed any metal tools whatsoever. They also lacked horses or oxen to drag the large tree from the mountains to the beach and roads over which a tree fifty feet long could be brought. When one considers today that modern loggers sometimes have to use helicopters to get the same cedar logs out of the mountains, the story of how Indians got their canoes takes on added significance. I am still not sure about the actual process of getting the large trees to the beach, but it seems to me that the Indian story is as viable an explanation as any other I have heard.

CHAPTER THREE

▲ ▲ ▲ ▲ ▲ ▲ ▲ ▲

The paradise of the Indians of the Northwest might have lasted forever were it not for the strange belief held by the Europeans that a Northwest Passage existed somewhere in North America that would allow an all-season route to the Orient. In the latter decades of the eighteenth century, expeditions were first sent out in search of this mythical passage, and many efforts concentrated on the Pacific Northwest, with the idea that ships could sail eastward to the Great Lakes, the Saint Lawrence River, or Hudson Bay.

Authorities disagree on which expedition should be credited with the first contact with the Natives of the northern Pacific Coast. Captain James Cook's third voyage landed at Nootka Sound, in what is now British Columbia. The sailors traded some of their goods for sea otter pelts, and when they arrived in China they discovered that the Chinese prized these furs above any others they had seen. The urge for discovery ebbed when others learned of the fantastic profits that such a trade made possible, and the Pacific Northwest became the target of many additional expeditions.

Cook's expedition had little effect on the Puget Sound tribes, of course; their first indication of the presence of white men in the area must have been when a smallpox plague swept through the Puget Sound area in 1782, decimating many of the villages. Though the sickness was unknown among the tribes of the area, they had no reason to suspect that it had come from Europeans and tended to view it as a normal but frightening course of events. Disease was to sweep through the area at least twice more before 1850, leaving the Native populations reduced by nearly 80 percent.

The next expedition to the coast landed south of Puget Sound, on the Columbia, and was headed by Captain Gray, an American, in 1788. The ship wandered along the Oregon coast, stopping at various places to trade for furs and map the various bays and inlets. John Hoskins, one of Gray's officers, remarked on the hospitality of the Chinooks of the Columbia River area:

> I was received at my landing by an old chief who conducted me with Mr. Smith [another officer] to his house; seated us by a good fire; offered us to eat and drink of the best the house afforded; which was dried fish of various sorts, roasted clams and mussels. Water was our drink, handed in a wooden box with a large sea clam shell to drink out of; the chief's son attended me, opened my clams, roasted my fish, and did various other kinds of offices in which he was pleased to engage. After this entertainment we were greeted with two songs, in which was frequently repeated the words, "Wakush Tiyee a winna" or "Welcome traveling chief."

Such hospitality by the Chinooks did little good, however, for while the chief was busy entertaining the officers of the ship *Columbia*, the crew proceeded to kill one of the tribesmen, and the ship had to flee from the area. The first experience of the Indians with the Americans, whom they came to call Bostons because every ship seemed to be from Boston, left a distinct dislike among them for Americans.

The Spanish arrived in the Strait of Juan de Fuca area a few years later, when an expedition under Quimper landed at Clallam Bay. The following year, 1791, the Juan Francisco de Eliza expedition explored most of the inland waters, but people are still not certain whether the Spanish were looking for possible mission sites or preparing to enter the sea otter trade in earnest. By 1792, the Oregon coast was being visited by a steady Boston trade, and some twenty-five ships cruised the coast looking for canoes of

Natives with furs for exchange. The Puget Sound area was still undiscovered, however, and the tribes there, although they had heard of the strange, bearded men with white skins, had not yet encountered the newcomers.

With all the ships sailing around the Columbia River and Strait of Juan de Fuca in 1792, only one expedition took the time to name any of the landmarks, but that expedition, headed by Captain George Vancouver of England, made up for the rest in this respect. He named the large island across from Cape Flattery for himself, of course, and then, beginning approximately at the present-day American-Canadian border, named numerous natural features for his friends. The volcano that guarded the north for the Lummis, Komo Kulshan, became Mount Baker, after his third lieutenant; the bay at its shore became Bellingham Bay; and the large island south of the area was christened Whidbey, after another lieutenant. As the expedition proceeded southward, the sound got the name of the second lieutenant, Peter Puget, and the large inlet west of the present Seattle-Tacoma region became Hood Canal, after Lord Hood. Tacobud, the sacred mountain of the Nisqually, was given the name of Mount Rainier after an English rear admiral who had been a friend of Vancouver's. The Indians, of course, were not impressed with the European terminology and continued to call the waters, islands, and mountains by their proper names.

Along with the sea otter trade, an inland trade for beaver pelts began when the malcontents of Canada's famous Hudson's Bay Company formed their own Northwest Company and sent David Thompson overland to the Pacific in search of pelts for Europe's hatmakers. By 1789, men from the Northwest Company were arriving on the Pacific Coast and beginning to establish trading posts with the Indians of the northern interior near the present Spokane area. Thompson was regarded as one of the foremost geographers of American history, because he laboriously recorded every possible feature he could map in his various journeys in western Canada. But his treatment of the Indians should provide him with even more fame, for he was one of the most honest men ever to deal with Indians, refusing to provide them with rum when trading and always ensuring that they received a fair deal.

David Thompson's charisma was felt by both whites and Indians, and while his business partners demanded that he make a profit on his transactions, he was noted for his willingness to assist both whites and Indians in their hardships. One of the tribes in the Fraser River area looked upon Thompson as something of a god, and this admiration was to cause him some trouble. On one of his journeys he purchased canoes for a trip down one of the rivers that led to the Strait of Georgia. The tribes promptly provided him with the canoes and wished him a good voyage. He and his party did not get very far, because the river was treacherous and nearly impossible to float on due to its rocks and rapids. When Thompson complained to the tribes about allowing him to travel down the river, they explained with a great deal of sincerity that while *they* were afraid to take a canoe down the river, they regarded him as so much better than themselves that they knew he could descend the river with ease!

With the coming of the Northwest Company, activity along the trading routes of the Puget Sound area greatly increased. The exchange of salmon and other foods—particularly the whale oil of the Makahs—was stimulated by the wealth flowing into the region from the commerce in sea otter and beaver pelts. As a result, the tribes began to adapt their style of living to their newfound riches.

But there were disadvantages to the trade also. The Yuku-ltas, a tribe that lived on the coast far to the north, received guns fairly early in the trading days, and they began making raids in the Puget Sound area for furs and slaves. The old custom of taking slaves as a result of tribal conflicts escalated into the practice of taking slaves as a means of acquiring wealth, and wars between the tribes of the Puget Sound area and the Canadian tribes increased enormously. The raids became so bad that, as late as the 1840s, the tribes of the area had stockades for protection against the Canadian tribes. The early settlers perpetuated this warfare so that the tribes of lower Puget Sound would act as their sentries in case anyone, white or Indian, became hostile.

The sea otter trade declined in the Washington and Oregon areas because of the rapid harvesting of the little animal, and the ships quickly shifted their trade to Alaskan waters. The furs were shipped from the Pacific Northwest to Hawaii and China, where they were exchanged for goods bound for Boston and other eastern ports. As a result of this trade triangle, many Hawaiians came to live and work at trading posts on the Pacific Coast, and when the trade declined, they took jobs farther inland with the Northwest Company and the Hudson's Bay Company.

Simon Fraser, one of the partners of the Northwest Company, established a number of forts in the British Columbia region. Between 1805 and 1808, forts Saint James, McLeod, Fraser, and George were all built, tilting the balance of trade to the Canadians and providing the British Columbia tribes with additional goods to use in trade and war with the Puget Sound tribes. One of the features of this expanded trade was the development of an annual fair held by the Puget Sound tribes at Bajada Point. Each year, the tribes would gather for feasting, serious trading, and a general good time, and it was probably this annual event that set the pattern for the later extravagant potlatches that were recorded by scholars in the last decades of the past century.

The inland fur trade developed into a tidal wave in the second decade of the nineteenth century. John Jacob Astor, an American fur merchant, sent a company of traders out in 1811. They built Fort Astoria at the mouth of the Columbia and began a brisk trade in furs. The same year, David Thompson descended the Columbia from its point of origin in British Columbia and was astounded to discover the Astorians happily entrenched on the river when he paddled up in his canoe.

The Astor company was just beginning to make an impact on trading patterns in the Pacific Northwest when word of the impending war between the United States and Great Britain reached the coast. In what will probably go down as one of the craftiest business moves in history, Astor sold his trade and fort to the Northwest Company a couple of days before a British warship arrived to inform everyone that war was under way. The Indians much preferred the British to the Bostons, who often took advantage of them and used whiskey to cheat them out of their furs, so Astor's move made sense in every way. It is doubtful if the American post could have withstood a prolonged British and Indian siege.

Following the War of 1812, the European nations began a withdrawal of claims to the Pacific Northwest. In 1818, the United States and Great Britain made a ten-year agreement that citizens of either country could settle in the Oregon country, as the region was called, without impairing the claims of either country. The agreement was slanted heavily in favor of the Americans, since the British saw the territory in terms of the fur trade while the Americans looked to eventual settlement of the region. In 1819, Spain withdrew all her claims to the Columbia River drainage, and in 1824–25, the Russians surrendered their claims to the area, leaving Great Britain and the United States as the sole contenders.

Almost as if the British anticipated a long-term competition with the Americans, they began to consolidate their efforts in the Pacific Northwest. In 1821, the Northwest Company and the Hudson's Bay Company merged their operations on the coast, and Dr. John McLoughlin was appointed as chief factor of their trading operations in the Columbia Basin. When the American traders returned to the area, in 1824, they discovered that the British had things very well organized under McLoughlin.

Even with all this activity, the Puget Sound tribes were not directly affected by the whites. The British concentrated their efforts in the Vancouver and Columbia River areas and encouraged settlers to settle south of the Columbia, in the Willamette Valley, thus leaving the Puget Sound region and the northern coast virtually intact under the control of the various Indian villages.

It is somewhat misleading, however, to refer to the Hudson's Bay operations as British, because people of all racial backgrounds worked for the company. Among the most numerous employees of the Hudson's Bay Company were the French Canadians of Quebec, who formed the backbone of the regular service group. Many of these people were of mixed French and Indian blood, and they lived more as Indians than as whites. A great many employees were Iroquois—primarily Mohawks from the Caughnawaga reservation, near Montreal—who, for the most part, were Catholic. It is said that the first time the Indians of Puget Sound encountered the Iroquois, they were astounded to hear them singing Christian hymns to mark their rhythm in paddling their canoes.

As noted above, the old sea otter trade had resulted in the migration of many Hawaiians to the Pacific Northwest. A great number of these people worked for the Hudson's Bay Company. While they had a great deal of difficulty in paddling the cumbersome cedar canoes, they were invaluable in the bay and inlet waters, which were more like the waters of their homelands. It was this amalgamation of races that distinguished the British operations from the American traders. The Americans tended to be mostly whites, contemptuous of the Indians of the area and interested only in a quick profit. The British sought a well-regulated trade and eventually settled at the trading posts.

To see just how cosmopolitan the Hudson's Bay crews were we have only to look at the composition of Ross's Hudson's Bay expedition to the Columbia in 1823. It had two Americans, seventeen Canadians, five half-breeds of an undetermined tribe, twelve Iroquois (probably Mohawks), two Abnaki Indians from Maine, two Nipissings from the East, one Soulteau from the Canadian plains, two Crees from the eastern slope of the Canadian Rockies, one Chinook from the Columbia River region, two Spokanes from the headwaters of the Columbia, three Flatheads from the Montana area, two Kalispels (a tribe that lived between the Spokanes and the Flatheads), one Palouse from eastern Oregon, and one Snake slave from the eastern Oregon area. All told, the expedition had nineteen men of white blood and thirty-four Indians.

The influence of the Indians working for Hudson's Bay became most pronounced after Ignace La Mousse, sometimes called "Big Ignace," settled in 1812 among the Flatheads of the interior. An Iroquois Catholic from Caughnawaga and former employee of the Hudson's Bay Company, La Mousse was a fervent practitioner of his faith who often spoke to his Flathead friends about the Christian holy book, in which all knowledge is contained.

The Flatheads and the Nez Percés pondered this mystery for many years and finally decided to send a delegation to the East to get a copy of the book. In 1831, a group of Flatheads and Nez Percés arrived at Saint Louis demanding a copy of the sacred writings of the white men. It may have been the most unfortunate voyage in Indian history, for the sight of Indians from the Far West seeking information about the Christian religion inspired a dramatic missionary movement among both Protestants and Catholics that was to destroy the solitude in which the Indians of the Pacific Coast lived.

The tribes on Puget Sound had no knowledge, of course, of the Flathead visit to Saint Louis and not an inkling of the dozens of missionaries girding themselves for the trip to the Oregon country. They were busy expanding their trade with the British, who had established Fort Langley on the Fraser River in British Columbia in 1827 and Fort Nisqually near present-day Olympia, Washington, in 1833, and an extensive direct trade with the tribes of the inland waters was developing rapidly. The British encouraged the Indians to raise vegetables for trade with the various posts, and the potato was introduced by the Fort Langley traders soon after the fort was built. Thereafter the tribes cultivated vegetables as well as various shellfish beds for sale to the Hudson's Bay Company.

The chief trading commodity of the Hudson's Bay Company was the famous blanket that made it unnecessary for the Indian women to spend long hours threading cedar bark for their fibers. Almost overnight the blanket became not only a symbol of wealth but the actual measure of wealth, just as the dollar measures wealth today. Canoes, guns, knives, kettles, axes, horses, and any other items that could be traded were valued at a certain number of blankets. On the eastern side of the Cascades, where the fur trade was still fairly lively, the value was figured in beaver skins, so that a gun might be worth fifty beaver skins at the Colville trading post and thirty-five Hudson's Bay blankets at Fort Nisqually.

Not only did the blankets change the way of life of the Indians, but the manner of dress was changed drastically by the British company. Smoke-tanned hides were unknown before the coming of the whites. When the Hudson's Bay traders showed the Indians how to tan hides using that process, the costume of many of the inland tribes changed from the cedar-bark clothes they had formerly worn to the new, frontiersman leather-and-skins costume. From about the middle of the 1820s on, it was very difficult to distinguish the Indians from the traders in either dress or background, since everyone dressed alike and a great many Indians were employed by the company in one capacity or another.

For a twenty-year period, from 1820 to 1840, the Indians and the "King George" men lived in comparative peace and harmony in the Puget Sound-British Columbia region. The British always went out of their way to ensure justice to the Indians and treated them with fairness even in legal matters. If an Indian harmed a white man, he was promptly called to account, but if a white man harmed an Indian, he was called before the same officer and given the same sentence for the offense that the Indian would have gotten. Such evenhanded justice endeared the British to the Indians, and they developed a great loyalty to the British.

As the number of whites in the area increased, the resulting expansion of trade caused the Indians to become specialists in commercial matters. The Makahs, who had used to trade whale meat for salmon, and halibut for ready-made canoes from the Nootkas, now concentrated their efforts on producing oil from whales, seals, candlefish, and dogfish for use as machine oil. They made long voyages to Forts Nisqually and

Langley to trade their oil, the availability of which resulted in the establishment of sawmills. These in turn required more settlers and offered additional jobs to Indians willing to live near the forts and work for a wage.

Perhaps the only indication of change during the third and fourth decades of the century was the gradual shift, on the part of the Hudson's Bay post at Fort Vancouver, on the Columbia, from collecting furs to providing implements and other necessities for incoming settlers. This shift occurred at a time when smallpox and measles were sweeping through the Chinook tribe, which controlled the banks of the Columbia River. There had been nearly one hundred thousand Indians in the Pacific coastal regions in 1800, but by the 1840s fewer than half that number were left. Their absence, of course, left miles and miles of lands unoccupied, thus encouraging the whites to expand their settlements into the various tributary valleys of the Columbia.

The Hudson's Bay Company followed this trend of moving into areas of comparatively sparse Indian occupancy and in 1838 formed the Puget Sound Agricultural Company, which began farming and ranching operations in the Puget Sound region. Dr. John McLoughlin, the factor supervising the Columbia River operations for the company, had more than one thousand head of cattle, besides hundreds of heads of hogs, sheep, horses, and oxen by 1838 and developed a large business exporting dairy products to the Russians in Alaska as a sideline to the company's fur-trading functions.

The Puget Sound Indians were prosperous, happily adapting their traditional way of life to accommodate the white man's new and exciting technology, while the Hudson's Bay Company came to control practically the whole northern Pacific Coast. There were, in 1839, a mere 151 Americans living on the coast, and if one would have been asked to guess which nation would eventually own the area, all bets would have been placed on Great Britain. But the missionaries were yet to be heard from.

CHAPTER FOUR

▲ ▲ ▲ ▲ ▲ ▲ ▲ ▲

The arrival of the Indian delegation in Saint Louis, as we have seen, created a considerable stir among the Christian churches. Missionary ventures were at a low ebb because of the lack of success of previous efforts among the tribes of the Mississippi valley. But now, with a definite call from the heathen for help, the churches were galvanized into action. In 1835, Jason Lee was sent by the Methodists as a missionary to the Flatheads. He spent a short time with this tribe and when his efforts were not immediately fruitful moved from the western slope of the Rockies to the Willamette Valley, near the Oregon coast, where he established a new mission.

The American Board of Commissioners of Foreign Missions sent Dr. Marcus Whitman to the Wallawalla country the year after Lee arrived in the Flathead country, and the famous missionary began his short-lived career as a Protestant leader in the Northwest. The competition between the Methodists and the Presbyterians, of which Whitman was the representative, was sparked by the appearance of two Jesuits, Fathers François Blanchet and Modeste Demers, in 1838. A ghastly war of religious intolerance began between the Protestants and the Catholics, with occasional sniping between the two Protestant representatives during periods of relative calm. The dazed Indians were baffled that the three groups appeared to be talking about the same God but hated each other with a passion beyond the understanding of mere humans.

Intratribal religious conflict ensued wherever the missionaries had been, and the process of trading converts back and forth among the three groups as the puzzled Indians tried to choose a winner reduced the credibility of the church ventures to naught. The Hudson's Bay people looked on with horror as they saw the peace of their empire shattered by a devastating religious competition.

Whitman was intolerant of Indian beliefs as well as Catholic beliefs and seemed to have an inflexible personality that refused to consider the practical realities of living in a strange land. His visionary bent resulted in the Great Migration, which he may have created singlehandedly. Feeling that the United States should eventually control the Oregon country, Whitman sent reports back to the United States urging a massive migration of people to Oregon, and in 1843 nearly a thousand settlers heeded his pleas and marched over the famous Oregon Trail to the new country.

In spite of his failure to make friends with either Indians or local whites, Whitman continued his efforts both to Christianize the neighboring tribes and to get the Oregon country settled. He might have eventually become one of the statesmen of the territory if events had not combined against him in 1847. During the summer, a severe epidemic of measles hit the camp of the influential chief of the Wallawallas, Peopeo Moxmox, and nearly half the camp died from the sickness. The rumor spread among the Indians that Whitman was poisoning them, and in November of 1847 the Cayuses attacked his mission and killed some of the people, taking the rest as prisoners held for ransom. Some of the employees of the Hudson's Bay Company interceded with the tribe and ransomed the captives, but the Americans used the incident to attack Indian villages in the Oregon country indiscriminately, infuriating both the Indians of the region and the British settlers who had lived at peace with the Indians for nearly half a century.

Because of the previous presidential election, however, the chain of events was not in the hands of local people. James K. Polk had campaigned on the platform of "Fifty-four forty or Fight," a slogan that meant that the British had to cede most of British Columbia to the United States or face the prospect of war in the Pacific Northwest. As a result of the hawkish campaign in the East, the boundary of the Oregon country had been established at the forty-ninth parallel the year before the attack on Whitman's mission. The Hudson's Bay Company found itself in a state of limbo, with its status as a landowner and probable citizen still undefined. Congress did not take any action to establish Oregon as an American territory until 1848, so no one in the area knew what laws pertained or who should govern the region.

The American attitude toward the Indians was clear and in direct opposition to the former policy of the British. While the Americans claimed to recognize the Indian title to their lands, the United States did so only to make giant land purchases possible and to move the Indians to remote reservations, away from the line of settlement. The British policy had been to recognize Indian lands and waters and to set aside these lands as places in which Indians could live. They did not restrict the Indians to these small reserves, for any Indian who wished to live off the reserves had merely to settle and record his claim, and it was recognized by the British authorities.

Even the American missionaries failed to understand that the best way to get along with the Indians was to treat them as equals. Many felt that the demise of the Indian was a fore-ordained event and that their only task was to ease the pain with which the Indians declined. There was no recognition that laws should protect the Indians or offer them a share in the coming development of the region. Elkanah Walker, one of the missionaries of early Oregon, offered this justification for his religious activities:

> It seems the only way they can be saved from being destroyed from the face of the earth is by their yielding to the control of the whites, and nothing will induce them to do this but a cordial reception of the gospel, and how can this be done without the labors of the Christian missionary.

Their concern was not so much with saving the Indians' souls as with rendering them helpless to the control of the whites. It

is no wonder that resentments against missionaries still exist
in Indian communities today.

Immigration nearly ceased in 1849, when everyone went
to California to mine gold, but the following year Congress
provided an incentive for settlers in the Oregon country. The
Oregon Donation Act was passed, which allowed new settlers
to claim a total of 640 acres for a man and wife in homesteading
the Oregon Territory. Although no formal, recognized claim
on the territory had been made, the US government was giving
away thousands of acres of land still inhabited by Indians.

Some people in Congress were aware of this injustice,
and so, in 1850, the Indian Treaty Act was passed, requiring
the United States to get formal agreements to land cessions by
the tribes of the Northwest Coast. The act also required that
the Indians be moved to remote areas of eastern Oregon, away
from the Willamette Valley and other fertile areas where there
would likely be white settlement.

Anson Dart was appointed to get the treaty concessions
from the Oregon tribes, and in 1851 he began to make the rounds
of the Chinook villages on the southern bank of the Columbia,
seeking to make agreements with the tribes. The Chinooks had
suffered the most from the intrusions of the whites over the previous half century. When Lewis and Clark visited the Columbia
in 1805, the Chinooks were the largest tribe on the coast, total-
ing in excess of sixteen thousand people. The great epidemic of
1829, called ague fever (though it was probably measles), killed
four fifths of the tribe, and the remnant in 1851 was scattered
along the various streams of Oregon, living in very small groups
and fearful for their future.

Even the older settlers, who had known happier times
when whites and Indians lived peacefully together, felt sad upon
seeing the Chinooks' struggle for survival, and perhaps it was
this sentiment that changed Dart's mind from his original purpose. He signed some thirteen treaties with the Chinooks and
Tillamooks that made provisions for them to keep small tracts
of land in their traditional homelands instead of moving them
away to eastern Oregon, which had little to recommend it.

Congress refused to ratify Dart's treaties, because they were not in conformity with the Treaty Act. Dart's letter of transmittal to the commissioner of Indian Affairs submitting the treaties and arguing for their ratification is worth quoting, because it shows that he did everything possible to help the tribes keep some of their lands. Yet he recognized, as many of them did, that their situation was at best precarious.

"It is necessary to inform you," Dart began, "that the habits and customs of these fishing Indians are unlike those of any other part of our domain. It is characteristic with them to be industrious. Almost without exception, I have found them anxious to work at employment at common labor and willing too, to work at prices much below that demanded by the whites. The Indians make all the rails used in fencing, and at this time do the boating upon the rivers: In consideration, therefore, of their usefulness as labourers in the settlements, it was believed to be far better for the Country that they should not be removed from the settled portion of Oregon if it were possible to do so."

The argument that the Indians could easily adjust to the new patterns of settlement and even make a contribution to the territory did not have much effect on the policymakers in the East, as is so often the case in Indian affairs. Dart's second argument contained all the pathos of mankind's experiences when one people has replaced another with great rapidity.

"The poor Indians are fully aware of the rapidity with which, as a people, they are wasting away," Dart wrote. "[O]n this account they could not be persuaded to fix a time, beyond ten years to receive all of their money and pay for their lands, saying that they should not live beyond that period." The Chinooks and the Tillamooks, then, did not expect to survive longer than ten years and so did not want annuities after that point. If a more dismal view of the future ever existed, one would wonder what it might have been! Dart reluctantly agreed with the Indians' estimate, noting, "I cannot but admit that there is great probability that only a few years will pass ere they will all lie side by side with their Fathers and Braves— the tribe or tribes extinct."

Dart illustrated the extreme conditions of two of the tribes of the lands north of the Columbia by remarking, "the only males . . . are the two signers to the treaty; there are however several females—women and children yet living." These tribes lived on Shoalwater Bay and Dart described the lands as bordering those of the Chehalis and Cowlitz, tribes that were later to figure prominently in the history of Puget Sound.

The wave of settlers could not be stemmed, however, even by such reasonable men as Anson Dart. More and more Americans poured into Oregon Territory and, using the provisions of the Oregon Donation Act, began invading the Puget Sound area with impunity. Even the Hudson's Bay Company was cheated out of its lands and properties when many of its claims were disallowed because of the outcry of the new settlers. When it finally left the American territory, the British company received little more than a token payment for its holdings. Even Dr. John McLoughlin, the former factor for the company during the preceding two and a half decades, who had helped the various waves of new settlers by loaning them seeds and tools and helping them choose lands, was cheated out of his personal property. McLoughlin's declaration of his intent to become an American citizen, which should have acted to safeguard his property, was overridden by the popular demand of the new settlers for the confiscation of British property and its subsequent appropriation by Americans. McLoughlin died a pauper, in no better shape than the Chinooks and Tillamooks with whom he had spent most of his adult life.

The degree of inundation experienced by the Indians in the Pacific Northwest can be illustrated by some of the tentative census figures for those times. In 1839, as we have seen, there were only 151 Americans in the whole area. By 1850, some five hundred Americans lived in the Puget Sound area, and two years later more than two thousand lived there. Settlement was not systematic, nor was it based on surveys of public lands. People simply arrived on the scene and started building. If there were Indians or previous settlers on the spot, they were promptly run off under one pretext or another. Lawlessness and thievery dominated the area.

News traveled fast in the Pacific Northwest, and the tribes on Puget Sound and in the eastern portions of Oregon and Washington were terrified at the prospect of more whites coming into their lands. In 1852, word arrived among the tribes about the massacres of many Indian villages in California by the miners, and all braced themselves for the expected onslaught from the intruders.

The tribes east and south of Puget Sound and the Columbia were in a much better position to confront the invasion. Across the mountains were the Yakimas, Cayuses, Nez Percés, and Wallawallas, all fairly large tribes able to mount a concerted attack if threatened. In the southern part of Oregon were the Klamaths and the Modocs, who were valiant warriors and occupied a sufficiently large area of land to be feared by other tribes and whites alike. Conflict was inevitable, and throughout the 1850s, in spite of numerous treaties signed with these tribes, there was intermittent warfare. The little villages in Puget Sound and the Willamette Valley were often attacked by whites, who feared all Indians and used the distant wars as excuses to clear Indian territories altogether.

The situation grew so intense that even Congress could no longer ignore the state of confusion in the Northwest. In March of 1853, Washington Territory was created and a new governor appointed to bring order out of the existing chaos. He was directed to sign treaties with the tribes of the new territory and to survey a new route for a transcontinental railroad across the northern part of the United States. In this tripartite role as governor, Indian agent, and railroad surveyor, Isaac Ingalls Stevens came to Washington Territory in 1853 determined to develop the country as rapidly as possible and, with this development, to foster his own career as a leading political figure in the United States.

Stevens knew nothing about the Indians of the area and had little knowledge of the history of the white settlement of the coast. The old politeness and formality that had marked the relations between the English and the Indians were swept aside as mere foolishness, and this violation of accepted norms of civilized behavior was perhaps one of the most objectionable things Stevens represented. He never dressed up for conferences with Indians and seemed to regard all his meetings as necessary annoyances to his central task of taming the West.

When some of the experienced settlers in the Puget Sound area saw the type of governor they had, they tried to make him understand the problems facing the territory. E. A. Starling, the Indian agent for Puget Sound, offered suggestions for the Indian treaties that Stevens was preparing to negotiate. "I would recommend," he wrote, "that when treaties are made with these tribes, their future homes be all included in one reservation—each tribe having the extent of its reservation marked off—and their fishing grounds be granted them; and over the reservation, that the law regulating trade and intercourse with the Indians, and any other law relating thereto, be extended with full force." Starling saw clearly that if the culture and rights of the Indians were not protected, trouble was sure to follow.

But Stevens understood neither Indians nor their culture. In 1854, he prepared to begin treaty negotiations with the tribes of the Pacific Coast and Puget Sound, thus bringing to an end their nearly half century of relative isolation from the inroads of white settlement. The Lummis, Makahs, Nisqually, Puyallups, Quinaults, Skagits, Swinomish, Duwamish, and other fishing tribes had avoided the fur trade and the early settlements, because the whites tended to go either south of them to Oregon or north of them to British Columbia. They had nonetheless developed a substantial commerce. The Makahs, for example, had sold twenty thousand gallons of whale and fish oil for the sawmills of Olympia in 1852 and were the chief source of machine oil for the entire coast.

But it was almost as if the tribes were destined to suffer the depredations of a half century in several years. The year 1853 marked the last year of relative freedom the tribes of the Northwest were ever to know.

CHAPTER FIVE

▲ ▲ ▲ ▲ ▲ ▲ ▲ ▲

As we have seen, fishing and its related activities were the heart of the Puget Sound and coastal Indians' culture. They had successfully joined the trading activities of the Hudson's Bay Company by providing foods, canoes, and oils to the trading posts. As the Americans came into the area, the tribes continued to provide foods and oils, thereby becoming essential to the initial success of the white settlers.

Had the tribes been able to continue their fishing activities, they would undoubtedly have become a strong force in the development of Washington Territory. But government policy dictated two major changes in Indian life. The first change to be made was the concentration of as many villages as possible on one reservation, which would be isolated from the rest of the settlements and directed by an agent chosen because of his political influence and beholden not to the Indians but to his sponsor in Washington, DC. The second major change was that federal policy envisioned turning all Indians into farmers. All Indians, without exception, had to learn farming whether they lived in an arid Arizona desert or in a massive cedar forest on the Quinault River, because the theory of history accepted by American society at that time said that man evolves from a hunter and gatherer to a farmer and therefore all Indians were expected to conform to the theory.

Almost all subsequent conflicts between whites and Indians in western Washington Territory and Washington State have stemmed from the failure or refusal of the United States to fulfill its commitments as promised by Isaac Stevens while signing treaties with the tribes in 1854–56. It is important, therefore, to examine carefully the promises of the treaties in order to understand the Indians' present-day appeals for rights guaranteed them in a dreadful bargaining session.

A small steamer was chartered to take the treaty-making party around the region of Puget Sound and the straits because the time was late and the expected rains and storms of December and January made travel by canoe or horseback almost impossible. The first treaty was negotiated and signed on December 26, 1854, and seemed to set the pattern by which the other treaties would be designed. The tribes of the Tacoma-Olympia region were called together at Medicine Creek, which is about halfway between the two settlements, and the treaty took its name from that site.

One of the controversial aspects of the Pacific Coast treaties was the language in which the treaty was explained to the Indians. Stevens insisted on using the old trade jargon called the Chinook jargon, which consisted of fewer than three hundred words, including some Indian words, English, and French phrases. Chinook jargon was initially used during the early days of fur trading, when the fur traders of the Hudson's Bay Company included people of all nationalities, and communication between groups of traders and trappers was restricted to frantic arm waving and a few phrases symbolizing goods and needs.

Owen Bush, one of Stevens's staff who attended the treaty session, was disgusted at the requirement that Chinook be used to explain the provisions of the treaty. When he was asked to fight against the Indians a couple of years later, he refused and explained his refusal as follows:

> I could talk the Indian languages, but Stevens did not seem to want anyone to interpret in their own tongue, and had that done in Chinook. Of course it was utterly impossible to explain the treaties to them in Chinook. Stevens wanted me to go into the war but I wouldn't do it. I know it was his bad management that brought on the war, and I wouldn't raise a gun against those people who had always been so kind to us when we were weak and needy.

Other old settlers testified that Stevens was less than a model representative of the United States. Ezra Meeker, an old settler in the Puget Sound area who wrote a book on his pioneer experiences, remarked years afterward, "Governor Stevens was intoxicated and unfit for transacting business while making these treaties."

The treaty of Medicine Creek set aside three small reservations for the Nisqually, Steilacooms, Puyallups, Squawskins, Squiaitl, S'Homamish, and other tribes. Stevens's original plan was to place all the Indians in a temporary reservation until they could be permanently located on farming land in a remote section of the territory. But the Indian representatives, particularly Leschi of the Nisqually, refused to budge from their traditional fishing stations, and so the three smaller reservations were created. The Squawskins (known today as Squaxins) received a small island in the Hood's Canal region, the Nisqually got a rocky and barren tract of land away from their traditional fishing sites, and the Puyallups got the south side of Commencement Bay, which is now the city of Tacoma.

The Indians refused to surrender their traditional fishing grounds, and with good reason. They had developed an extensive trade with the whites in salmon and other foods and saw their place in the territory as an important one. Stevens seemed to recognize the importance of the Indian fishing, since he allowed the Indians to keep their fishing sites as part of a planned role for the Indians in the future of the territory. In a letter to George Manypenny, then commissioner of Indian affairs, Stevens commented on the provision allowing Indians to keep their fishing sites:

> It may be here observed that their mode of taking fish differs so essentially from that of the whites that it will not interfere with the latter. They catch salmon with spears in deep water and not with seines or weirs.

Stevens's knowledge of the Indian method of fishing was no more accurate than his understanding of the territory he had been sent to govern. As we have seen, there was extensive use of weirs and seines by the Indians, and they really controlled almost all the fishing then done in the territory. *The Columbian*, a newspaper published in the little settlement of Olympia, had commented the year before:

> What little has been done in the business of securing the salmon, has been done solely by the Indians, through their crude method, and slender appliances, and that their lazy and worthless habits prevent a sufficient bestowal of time and attention, in furnishing any considerable quantity for export, beyond their own necessities, and what is required for present home consumption.

The failure of the Indian fisheries was not their control of the trade in fish but the fact, according to the paper, that they were not efficiently making a business out of it.

There were two interpretations of the fishing controversy even at the negotiations on the treaty, and the Indians secured a special article in the treaty to cover their rights to traditional grounds for fishing. The article has been the center of conflict in the intervening century and a quarter and is probably the single most familiar treaty provision in the nation:

> *Article Three.* The right of taking fish, at all usual and accustomed grounds and stations, is further secured to said Indians in common with all citizens of the Territory, and of erecting temporary houses for the purpose of curing, together with the privilege of hunting, gathering roots and berries, and pasturing their horses on open and unclaimed lands: Provided, however, that they shall not take shellfish from any beds staked or cultivated by citizens.

Articles of the same or nearly identical wording were placed in all the treaties negotiated by Stevens during the next two years, and almost all of them have proved controversial in their interpretation. At the time the treaties were signed, however,

the whites did little fishing of note, and the intent of the white
negotiators was to respond to the Indian demand for the preservation of their fishing grounds.

Following the Medicine Creek treaty, the Stevens party
went to Mucklteoh, or Point Elliott, where they met the largest
delegation of Indians on the western slope of the Cascades. The
tribes from the Canadian border south to the Seattle area were
called together at Mucklteoh, and the chief Indian spokesman
at that conference seems to have been Chief Seattle, who was
regarded as the leader of both the Duwamish and the Suquamish peoples.

The Mucklteoh treaty set aside a number of reservations,
which have continued until the present; the most famous of
these has been the Lummi reservation near the present city of
Bellingham. Perhaps the most important feature of this treaty
was that it was a valiant effort to get all the Indians of the area
together on the three reservations established under the treaty,
an effort that nonetheless failed. In the region immediately
east of the Puget Sound shoreline lived a number of mountain
tribes that did little fishing but were known as horse Indians,
because they had access to horses. They acted as middlemen
in the extensive trade that had developed between the Puget
Sound tribes and the larger tribes across the Cascades, in eastern Washington.

Though Stevens expected the horse Indians to come to the
new reservations, they had little intention of doing so, and even
as late as the First World War, small groups of these Indians
had not yet decided to live on the reservations but continued to
live in the woods along the western slope of the Cascades. So
controversial was this proposal to consolidate all the tribes on
the reservations that another one, the Muckleshoot, had to be
established away from the water for the tribes who were used
to living on the prairies and uplands.

Mucklteoh was signed in early January, and by the end
of the month the Stevens party was sailing along the northern shore of the Strait of Juan de Fuca to the curiously named
Hahdskus, or Point No Point, where they were to meet the

S'Klallams and Skokomish. Again the same basic provisions were set out, including fishing rights and the establishment of small reservations. The treaty of Point No Point was signed on January 26, 1855, and a week later the party arrived at Neah Bay to negotiate a treaty with the Makahs.

The Makahs differed from the other tribes of the region in that they were primarily whalers and traders and thus greatly concerned about their whaling rights. The Makahs were providing almost all the oil used for logging and other activities of the white settlers and also had a virtual monopoly on the halibut trade in the region. They therefore had a great deal to lose from any cessions of fishing rights. The curious aspect of this treaty was that Stevens wanted to show a clear purchase of the lands he had designated as belonging to the Makahs, while the Indians were worried about preserving their ocean properties.

The Makahs had developed a sophisticated property law regarding their beaches. These were very precisely divided among the prominent tribal families. Each Makah house owner claimed not only a section of the beach but also any material that happened to float ashore on his property. Old men who could no longer go whaling spent their days propped up against a wooden backrest, chatting with their cronies while waiting for something to float in on their section of the beach.

Not only did Stevens fail to understand the complex nature of Makah beach ownership, but he promised the Indians more rights than the United States could reasonably guarantee. Stevens told the Makah chiefs that he did not want to stop their whaling but would see that the government sent them oil kettles and fishing apparatus to make their fishing even more efficient. "The Great Father," he noted, "knows what whalers you are, how you go far to sea to take whales. He will send you barrels in which to put your oil, kettles to dry it out, lines and implements to fish with."

In the case of the Makahs, therefore, both Stevens and the Indians felt that the treaty would guarantee the special rights of the tribe. The article securing fishing privileges, Article Four, was essentially the same as the other treaties except that it read: "The right of taking fish and of whaling or sealing at usual and accustomed grounds and stations . . ." The "stations" of the Makahs, however, were patches of ocean marked by their special method of sighting intersecting landmarks from their boats far out to sea. The complications of this treaty provision would become apparent many years later.

After the treaty of Neah Bay, things seemed to dissolve for both the Indians and Stevens. A gathering of Indians was convened on the Quinault River, and the Quinaults and Quileutes signed their treaty on July 1, 1855, but the treaty commission wanted to get all the tribes who lived as far south as the Columbia under the Quinault treaty, and the southern tribes, the Cowlitz, the Chehalis, and the Chinooks, refused to sign the treaty. It was kept open until the following January, and a few more Indians signed it, but the large land area of southwestern Washington State was never formally ceded by the Indians to the United States.

All five of the treaties had promised educational services, annuity goods, and access to fishing, while restricting Indian trade to the Americans. Each treaty forbade the Indians to go to Vancouver Island to trade with the Canadians, because the local whites had much need of the Indian trade and because the government wished to limit the great influence the British still held with the Indians. The lands of the area west of the Cascades were declared cleared of Indian title, but in fact they would not be cleared until the treaties could be formally ratified, an event that did not occur for several years. In the meantime, Stevens made a grievous mistake; perhaps it was not even a mistake, but a deliberate effort to spur a conflict. At any rate, after signing five peace treaties with the tribes of the Pacific Northwest, Stevens promptly triggered the only Indian war in Puget Sound history.

Isaac Stevens and Joel Palmer, superintendent of Indian affairs for Oregon, went to the eastern tribes of the region to get treaties of land cession from them. The situation among the Cayuses, Yakimas, Nez Percés, Wallawallas, and other tribes who lived between the Cascades and the Rockies was desperate because of the discovery of gold in the Idaho region and the subsequent rush of miners into the Indian lands. Many of the Indian leaders across the mountains refused to sign the treaties, and the spirit of war hovered over the deliberations. Yet, because of the friendship of Peopeo Moxmox and other respected leaders, Stevens was able to secure agreements with the tribes. Large reservations were set aside for the tribes and they were expected to move onto them within two years after the treaties were signed.

The settlers all over the area were waiting to invade the remaining Indian lands now that the treaties were signed, and the two Indian superintendents gave them their opportunity. They signed a joint article in the June 23, 1855, issue of the Oregon *Weekly Times* announcing the signing of the treaties in highly misleading terms:

> By an express provision of the treaty the country embraced in these cessions and not included in the reservation is open to settlement, excepting that the Indians are secured in the possession of their buildings and implements till removal to the reservation.

The effect of such a statement was electrifying, and settlers began claiming lands whether there were Indians on them or not. While the proclamation had originally referred to the lands of the eastern slope of the Cascades, the whites living in the Puget Sound area saw no reason to be left out of the general land rush, and soon the little Indian settlements on the inland waters were overrun with white squatters.

Only the sparsity of whites in the Puget Sound area saved the tribes from total extinction. There were simply more Indians than whites. Yet the situation rapidly deteriorated, particularly among the Nisqually, who had been given a reservation far from their traditional fishing grounds and unfit for anything, even horse grazing. By the end of 1855, matters had come to a head, and the chief of the Nisqually decided on a course of action.

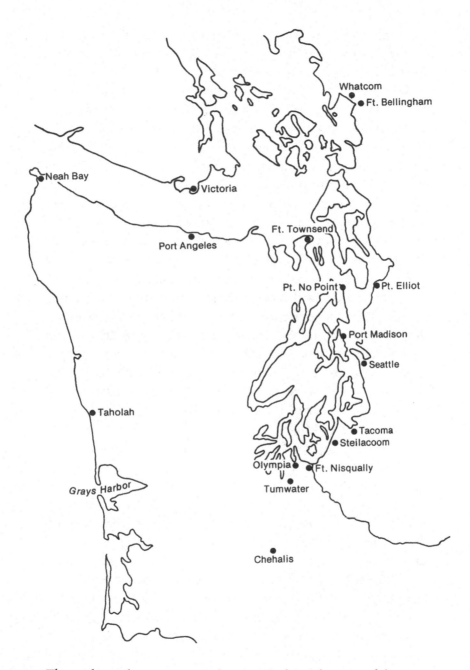

The early settlements in Washington State at the time of the signing of the treaties purchasing the Indian lands and guaranteeing perpetual fishing rights to the Indians, 1854.

On January 26, 1856, Leschi and the Nisqually with some allies from other tribes attacked the little settlement of Seattle and were giving the settlers a very difficult time when warships in the harbor began shelling the Indian positions. As with other Indian efforts to repel the whites, friendly Indians informed on the Indian forces, thus dooming their own people to failure. The war, which curiously became known as the Yakima war because of the simultaneous conflict east of the mountains by the Yakimas under their great chief Kamiakin, lasted about three years and became a conflict of sporadic ambushes and skirmishes that accomplished very little for either side.

Had Stevens returned to Puget Sound promptly on hearing about the Indian troubles, things might have worked out differently. Perhaps he feared the political backlash of the settlers, for he exercised little leadership in getting the Indians and the whites together to resolve the problem of land squatting. Instead of acting as a leader for peace, Stevens encouraged the fight against the Indians by organizing "volunteer" companies, i.e., groups of bandits who scourged the Indian villages. General John Wool, commander of the Army Department of the Pacific, condemned the use of the Oregon and Washington volunteers, remarking:

> Their net result was to turn friendly and neutral Indians
> into hostiles.

A heated conflict ensued, between Stevens and Palmer on the one hand and Wool and the army on the other, over the causes of the Indian troubles and the use of volunteers to calm the Indians. Wool argued that disbandment of the volunteers would stop them from provoking the Indians and thus restore peace. Stevens and Palmer were excited over the political benefits that the war would give their careers, remembering perhaps "Old Tippecanoe" and other Indian fighters who had once occupied the White House.

The Indian effort collapsed, of course, because with a few exceptions there were no strong ties among groups of Indians that would cause them to see the conflict as a direct threat to themselves. Leschi fled to the Yakimas following the disaster at Seattle; he was betrayed by his Indian friends, found guilty of murder in two swift trials, and eventually hanged as a renegade. Numerous appeals by white settlers who had known the Indian side of the story did not budge the new settlers, who had just had their first taste of Indian war, minor though it was, and who saw vengeance as the only way to teach the Indians about civilization.

About the only positive result of the conflict was the establishment of the Muckleshoot reservation near present-day Auburn, Washington, and the reestablishment of the Nisqually reservation on lands more favorable to their fishing economy. Some historians saw the war as the last resistance of the Indians in the Northwest, but the simple fact remains that there had been no significant controversy during the previous half century because the Indians and the whites had worked together in harmony. It was only after a great influx of whites onto the Indian lands, through Stevens's and Palmer's urging, that the pattern of life on the coastal lands was disrupted and conflict ensued between the two peoples.

CHAPTER SIX

▲ ▲ ▲ ▲ ▲ ▲ ▲ ▲

The brief war between the Indians and the settlers served to hasten settlement in some of the outlying areas of the territory. During the war, the older, long-established settlers built twenty-two blockhouses for protection, but some of these were designed to protect both Indians and whites against the intrusions of the tribes from British Columbia who took advantage of the hostilities in the Puget Sound area to raid both Indian and white settlements. The volunteers built another thirty-five blockhouses during their short time under arms, and the regular army built four blockhouses, so that by 1856 the area was dotted with sixty-one fortifications. Around these blockhouses many settlements were later to develop.

For the most part the war did not drastically disrupt life either for the Indians or for the whites. Outside of those tribes actually engaged in hostilities, most of the outlying villages were so remote that some did not know that a war was being conducted and the others had only vaguely heard of the troubles across the sound. Thus it was that in many places in the territory there was no animosity between Indians and whites, and trade between the two continued to develop. Probably the only change was the movement of some of the smaller villages from their traditional homes on the rivers to the new reservations. A new style of life quickly developed for these people, and it would be well to visualize how they now began to live.

The largest of the new reservations were Tulalip and Muckleshoot. On both of these, people from both the tidelands and the mountain foothills settled. At first there was some difficulty in adjusting to the new life. The old villages had been very small groupings of families, while the new reservations had several thousand Indians living on them. The closeness of the different families became unbearable for many of the people, and they began to wander off to find other places to live.

This new life was particularly difficult for the mountain people. As we have seen, they had been used to a different kind of fishing in the freshwater streams and lakes, and they did not take to the idea of fishing in bays and inlets. In time they went to the agents and complained that they couldn't make a living on the new reservations, and many of them were allowed to go back to their old homes. Though the treaties had set aside only a fixed number of reservations, the agents found it necessary to establish several new ones for the different groups who refused to be concentrated on the larger tracts of land.

In the midst of the confusion caused by the setting up of new reservations without orders from Washington, a big controversy arose over whether the new Muckleshoot reservation was under the agent at Tulalip or the agent at Nisqually. The reservation had been provided for under the Medicine Creek treaty, the only treaty to have been ratified by Congress before the beginning of the war. This placed it under the jurisdiction of the agent at Nisqually. But it was actually established within the boundaries set by the more recent Point Elliott treaty, and so the agent at Tulalip felt the reservation should come under his control.

This confusion worked to the advantage of some of the tribes of the southwestern part of the territory who had not signed a treaty in 1854 or 1855. Isaac Stevens had visited Grays Harbor in 1855, following his successful negotiations with the Makahs and Quinaults of the Pacific Coast, with the idea of getting the Chinook and Chehalis tribes occupying the southwestern quarter of Washington Territory to agree to his treaty terms. But he reckoned without the strong attachment of the Chinooks to their fishing grounds. The tribes refused to sign the treaty when they discovered that it gave the president the right to move them away from their lands to a large reservation. "That little creek," one of the Chinooks declared, was the only place he ever cared for, and the treaty was not signed.

If the officials in Washington realized that much of the state had not legally been cleared of its Indian title, they made no effort to inform the agents in the field about what they were doing to correct the situation. The Indian agent at Puyallup, in writing his annual report in 1876, rather crossly noted that he had discovered a new Indian reservation that the officials in Washington had established in 1866 on Shoalwater Bay. But, he insisted,

> its existence as an Indian reservation was unknown to any officer of the Indian Bureau in this Territory till I accidentally discovered it a short time before the abolishment of my office as superintendent of Indian Affairs of this Territory, and my visit to it last month was the first visit ever made to it by any officer of the Indian Bureau.

It remains a mystery how the government in Washington could set aside an Indian reservation without informing its officials that such a reservation existed, let alone how a reservation could be in existence for ten years before being discovered. But such mistakes were commonplace in the years when the reservations were being established.

We can easily imagine the early reservation settlements in Washington Territory from the descriptions found in the annual reports of the Indian agents. For the most part, the small villages of the old days were abandoned in favor of much larger villages that featured houses made in the white man's way, for single families, not for several families. Little log cabins dotted the lands surrounding the government agencies where the Indians could collect the annuities promised them in the treaties. An agent lived at the largest village on each reservation; he might be a farmer or a schoolteacher, but he was responsible for everything that happened there.

The little agency towns were usually designed according to the new white settlement patterns, with streets and sometimes a common grazing ground for the horses and cattle. Generally a schoolhouse was the most prominent feature of the new village because of the treaty provisions for the education of

Indian children. This schoolhouse would generally have dormitories for children who lived far from the village; on the Tulalip agency, for example, the children of many of the smaller reservations such as the Lummi and Swinomish came to stay and attend school. Each school would have a complete farm as part of its program if at all possible. This farm would include dairy cattle, fruit trees, and numerous smaller sheds and storehouses for supplies and machinery.

The first task of the new agents would be to instruct the adult Indians in farming their lands, because farming was regarded as the best means of ensuring civilization of the Indians. The agents' reports during the 1850s and 1860s are very interesting because they reflect an unbounded enthusiasm for the achievements of the Indians in farming. But in the later years, after the agents had been working several decades to teach the Indians farming, the reports begin to reflect a great discouragement at the Indians' meager progress.

The answer to this strange puzzle is very easy to understand. The tribes, as we have seen, were traditionally fisher folk, and they loved the life of fishing more than any other. Their farming efforts were largely undertaken to please their new agents, and thus they accomplished just about what they figured would satisfy the strange white man, who insisted that they plant vegetables and grains when common sense told them such things would never grow in so wet a climate. On most reservations, the Indians spent nearly as much time fishing as they always had, except that with their farming duties they had to work a little harder, since farming took a great deal of time during the spring and early summer.

Sometimes the agents recognized the great difficulty in trying to make the Indians farm, and they resented the federal policy as much as the Indians did. The agent at Tulalip, for example, in his annual report of 1879, made the following observation on the lands of the northern reservations:

> The land on the Tulalip, Madison and Swinomish is of
> such a poor quality that it affords but little encouragement

to the Indians to follow farming as a business, for with
the exception of a few small swails or marshes it is high
and gravelly, and thickly covered with a dense growth of
fir, cedars, and spruce. It requires an immense amount of
labor to clear a few acres, and even when in a fit condition
for planting the yield is so small that it is truly discourag-
ing, and would tax the continuity of a more industrious
and determined people than the Indians.

But in spite of the agents' protests, government policy dictated
that all the Indians be farmers, and so every effort was made to
transform them even if their lands were unsuitable.

So determined was the government in Washington that
the Indians be farmers that the commissioner of Indian affairs
required every agent to list the accomplishments of the Indians
of his reservation every year in order that some comparisons
could be made about the readiness of the Indians to accept
the ways of the white man. The following paragraph is taken
directly from the agent's report on the Puyallup reservation in
1876 and shows just how detailed these reports were.

Over a hundred and twenty Indians have taken homesteads on this reservation, mostly of 40 acre lots, and they
have among them all 715 acres under cultivation, as follows: 139 acres of oats; 47 acres of wheat; 95 acres of potatoes; 85 acres of peas, turnips, cabbage & s; 199 acres of
timothy meadow; 16 acres of corn; 134 acres of cleared
pasturelands. About one-seventh of these lands have been
reduced to cultivation within the last year. The Indians of
that reservation also own 220 horses, 224 cattle, 60 hogs,
and 26 wagons, and all have more or less farming-imple-
ments. The oats, wheat, potatoes, pease, and corn have
been more or less injured and cut short by the great amount
of wet weather during the last year, and the potatoe-crop
has been largely destroyed by the rot. A few of the Indians
have made some money by the sale of saw-logs from their
claims, and others by the sale of cottonwood bolts.

Perhaps it never occurred to the agents, facing each year with optimism, that their annual reports when viewed over a twenty- or a thirty-year period, had the same tone and recorded the same dismal results. There would be a listing of the different crops being planted each year with the concluding sentence of the report generally noting that wet weather had destroyed the crops and that the Indians had also fished, worked the lumber camps, or worked for the local white farmers to earn their living that year. What was happening was that the Indians were really living as fishermen and supplementing their income by part-time jobs in commercial activity.

The ability of the Indians to find paying occupations in the new territorial enterprises is truly remarkable. They worked as lumbermen clearing lands for the white farmers who had taken up homesteads in the forests. The agent at Puyallup in 1878 estimated that two thirds of the land cleared for farms west of the Cascades had been cleared by Indian workers, indicating that work was plentiful for the Indian men in the timber camps. This occupation seems to have been open to Indians for many years. John O'Keane, the agent at Tulalip in 1890, reported that most of the young men on the reservation still worked in the lumber camps. Apparently some Indians must have gone into the lumber business themselves, because the Indians at Tulalip made 100,000 shingles that year, produced 130,000 feet of lumber at their sawmill, and sold 725 cords of wood to the steamboats that cruised up and down the inland waters. Such a massive undertaking was a feat in itself for people who had lived exclusively by fishing only several decades before.

Farming was another occupation that attracted Indians, but it attracted them in a peculiar way. When allotments were handed out, many Indians leased their lands to whites and then worked for the whites who came to farm them. It may have seemed a peculiar way to go about farming, but it left the Indian family free to do what they wanted for most of the year. Harvest time was a particularly favorite season for those people who worked as farmhands. During the harvest, a great many workers were needed for a short period of time, and many Indian families worked as migrant laborers in order to see friends and relatives from other reservations who would also work the harvest.

When the farmers began planting hops, used in the manufacture of beer and other drinks, Indians nearly monopolized the hop-picking jobs in both Washington Territory and British Columbia. Sometimes nearly the whole tribe would go hop-picking, a job that quickly became a traditional activity in the fall. Large picnics were held during the hop season, and dances, generally forbidden on the reservations by the agents, were held while the people were off working. Hop-picking seemed to replace the trading fairs that had been held earlier in the century, while the area was under British control. This pleasant ability to transform work they really enjoyed into a social event that was not really work seemed to characterize the Indian approach to life in those years.

The coastal tribes were able to maintain their fishing activities long after the tribes on the sound were forced into farming. These were the Makahs, the Hohs, and the Queets, traditionally whalers and sealers who ventured into the open seas in search of the large sea mammals. Their lands were rocky and almost impossible to farm, a fact recognized by their agents, who sought ways to help them develop their fishing as an industry.

Michael Simmons, who had been one of Stevens's assistants in the treaty negotiations, became one of the early agents at Makah; in 1860, he recommended that the government fulfill its treaty obligations and help the Makahs develop a fishing industry. "Halibut are taken in great quantities by this tribe," he noted, "and I would recommend that, in addition to the farming operations that should be commenced on their reservation, houses for salting and drying these fish should be erected, and that they should be taught to cure them after the fashion of the whites. These fish command a good price and ready sale, and I think a lucrative trade in them can be established."

Simmons left Makah, and Henry Webster, his successor, tried for three years to get the Makahs to farm. He finally came to the same conclusion as had Simmons, and he also wrote to the commissioner of Indian affairs about the tribe. "I am of the opinion that much benefit would be derived by encouraging them in their fisheries," he wrote, "and teaching them the proper method of preparing their fish for sale. By having a cooperage connected with the reservation, and supplying them with nets and salt, they could annually take greater quantities of fish, which could be sold for their benefit." The only thing wrong with the Makah fishery, apparently, was that the Indians prepared their halibut in a manner that was quite foreign to other people's tastes.

At any rate, the coastal tribes continued their fishing in the ocean waters for many years after the treaty. In 1881, the Indians of the Hoh tribe and the Queets village on the Quinault reservation sold twelve hundred dollars' worth of seal skins during the season. The Makahs continued to supply a great quantity of oil for the logging camps and machinery oil for the expanding industry of the new territory. When means were found to preserve oysters for sale in commercial markets in Oregon, the Indians of Shoalwater Bay, the little reservation that had existed on its own most of the time, engaged in a substantial oyster trade.

Perhaps the best way to understand the period from the end of the Indian war to the turn of the century is to remember that times were hard for both Indians and whites in the territory. New machines and, later, railroads continued to change the people and the land very rapidly, and while the new lands were considered to be filled with opportunities for the industrious, the old ways of living held a certain fascination for both the Indians and the longtime settlers. The Indians worked into the new economy and the new society with relative ease wherever they were allowed to be themselves. But many problems arose in this adjustment to new ways of living, and we shall see that life was still fairly unsettled for the Indians of the Pacific Northwest.

CHAPTER SEVEN

▲ ▲ ▲ ▲ ▲ ▲ ▲ ▲

While we have seen the relative ease with which the tribes of the Pacific Northwest adapted to the new economy of the territory in the half century following the signing of their treaties, we have not understood some of the difficulties that stood in the way of making a total adjustment to the new life. A number of, problems seemed to plague them consistently during this time, the continued hostility of the whites, in particular.

A distinction should be made between the old settlers and the new settlers and their relationships with the different Indian tribes. In general, the longer a person had lived in the territory the better he got along with the Indians and the more he loved the lands and peoples of the territory. The new arrival, on the other hand, saw only the possibility of making a quick fortune, thus causing most of the ill will between the races. The Indian agent at Tulalip, writing in 1864, remarked on the hostility of the new settlers to the Indians:

> This class of our population, as a general thing, do all they can to prevent the Indians from living on their reservations. There is a strong prejudice against the Indians by all classes, without, in my opinion, a sufficient reason. These Indians are very peaceably disposed and if there is ever any serious difficulty it will grow out of the abuse heaped upon them by unprincipled white men.

The agent concluded his analysis by remarking, "The military posts on the sound should be occupied at as early a day as possible in order that the Indians may receive such protection as they can afford." The situation thus had a potential for violence that would have meant using the army to protect the Indians!

This hostility seemed to abound in every area in which the new settlers saw Indians as competitors for either land or resources, whether simple farming or timberlands, fishing rights, or the use of shellfish beds. We will see later how this hostility ripened into discriminatory laws and actions when the territory became a state, but a good rule of thumb would be that whenever the whites saw that the Indians had something they wanted, hostilities grew and pressures developed until the government allowed the whites to take what they wished from the Indians.

The agents of the Bureau of Indian Affairs often fostered this hostility between Indians and white settlers as a means of gaining favors from the whites of the neighborhood. The agent for the Puyallups, for example, began very early to agitate for the elimination of some of the reservations established by the Medicine Creek treaty so that new settlers could have the choicest lands of these tribes. "Some of these reservations contain bodies of as good agricultural land as can be found in the Territory," he wrote in his annual report for 1864, "and white settlers here and coming into the Territory justly complain that such large bodies of rich, unoccupied lands are withheld from them, and not used by the Indians." The agent was rather blunt in his recommendations:

> There were four reservations set apart for the Indians of the Medicine Creek treaty, to wit, the Puyallup, Nisqually, Squaxin, and Muckleshoot. I respectfully recommend that the three latter be abolished or discontinued as reservations, and that the Indians belonging to said three reservations be removed to and settled on the Puyallup reservation.

This attitude, that the lands belonging to the Indians and guaranteed by treaty could simply be disposed of at the whim of the government, characterized the employees of the Bureau of Indian Affairs throughout this period and continues in large part today. The result of this attitude was that the Indians were never certain when the government was going to take their lands and homes away from them, and if any single factor hampered the progress of the tribes of the Pacific Northwest in adjusting to their new life with the whites it was the realization that the agents were not protecting them.

Throughout the decades following the treaties, the Indians tried to bring the agents around to their manner of thinking about the status of their reservations. The agent at Tulalip was rather alarmed at their arguments, and he commented on the Indian view in his report of 1877. He tried to consolidate the tribes of his agency, which included the Lummi, Swinomish, Port Madison, and Tulalip into one reservation, but the Indians refused to move. "The Indians interpret the treaty differently," he wrote "They say that the reservations were reserved by themselves as the permanent homes of themselves and children, and that the cession was of their lands other than the reservations. They therefore claim that the reservation lands belong to them absolutely, and it need not be added that the proposition to consolidate them with other tribes at another agency does not meet with their approbation."

The attitude of the Bureau of Indian Affairs was at best puzzling in view of the efforts of some of the agents to include every band of Indians in their agency jurisdictions in the available federal services. On the one hand, therefore, the policy that was advocated by some agents was to reduce the number of reservations to as few as possible, because the whites wanted the farming lands. On the other hand, agents continually sought out those tribes that had refused to go to the reservations, and when they could not get them to live on the large reservations they sought to establish new reservations for them.

Thus the agent of the Puyallup agency in 1879 made up a list of the bands and groups of Indians in his area that did not have a reservation, and he sought assistance for them. It is interesting to see this list in view of the fact that many people in the present state of Washington claim an Indian ancestry and often remember that their grandfather or grandmother lived in an area where there was no reservation. Perhaps some people claiming to have Indian blood really do have Indian ancestors! The agent found groups of Indians outside the established reservations at the following locations:

Grays Harbor Band—164 Indians
Gig Harbor Band—46 Indians on Puget Sound 35 miles north of Olympia
Mud Bay Band—41 Indians living 8 miles northwest of Olympia
South Bay Band—30 Indians living 6 miles northeast of Olympia
Cowlitz Band—66 Indians living near the mouth of the Cowlitz River 65 miles south of Olympia
Olympia Band—43 Indians living around Olympia
Cowlitz Klickitat Band—105 Indians living on the Upper Cowlitz river 40 miles southeast of Olympia
Lewis River Band—104 Indians living on the Lewis River 90 miles southeast of Olympia

When we remember that the traditional Indian village of this area consisted of some sixty to eighty people and that many small villages were found scattered on every riverbank, we can see that for many years following the treaties some Indian groups continued to follow their old traditions.

Over the years, then, many new reservations were established as the agents were successful in getting new groups of Indians settled permanently in one place. Many of these reservations are still in existence today. But the agents were also occupied with the sale of Indian lands and the reduction of treaty reservations, and many of the very smallest reservations today were once fairly large tracts of land, most of which were forced out of Indian hands and into the hands of whites at one time or another during those years. It is exceedingly strange that these totally opposed policies could have been pursued by the same group of people, but they were.

Adjusting to the government schools was a major problem for many of the reservation people. Almost every treaty contained provisions for education, usually in the form of promising a teacher for the children of the tribes. Few people understood what this educational service would be when the treaties were negotiated, and when they did find out what the government had in mind many Indians resisted the program. In the first place there was never any great amount of money available for schooling, and so on several of the reservations various churches operated mission schools with the approval of the government and some financial assistance from the Bureau of Indian Affairs. The mixture of church and state was regarded as proper for those frontier conditions, but it resulted quite often in the banishment of Indian religious ceremonies as part of the educational program. This practice only increased the antagonism of the older Indian people toward the white man's religion and education.

Because they faced this attitude of hostility toward their traditional ways, the Indians figured out a way to get around the government regulations and practices that forbade them to perform their religious ceremonies. They realized that the white men celebrated certain holidays and that these occasions were marked by a relaxation of the rules by the agent. On one such occasion at the Tulalip reservation, the Indians asked permission of the agent to perform some of their old dances and ceremonies as a means of remembering that they had now become citizens of the United States.

The agent was, of course, delighted that the Indians under his care were so serious about becoming citizens that they wished to perform dances and sing songs in honor of their new status. So he allowed them to hold a special celebration on the Fourth of July. When the ceremony began, it was obvious to one and all concerned that the traditionalists were using the occasion to perform some of their most important religious ceremonies. At first the agent objected, but cooler heads among the whites who had come to the reservation to enjoy the celebration calmed him down and the ceremonies went on with no interference. From that time there was an informal agreement, never spoken, that on national holidays the Indians would be able to perform even the most forbidden ceremonies without punishment.

George W. Bell, the agent at the Chehalis reservation, in 1882 evaluated the tribe's adjustment to the ways of the white man; it is very instructive to read his comments on their progress, because they illustrate the attitude of the Indian agents of the past century toward the reservation Indians:

> To be convinced that these Chehalis tribe of Indians, with some exceptions, are as really and highly civilized as the peasantry of European lands, and not a few citizens of this "land of the free" you have only to visit their homes, look at their little farms and farming utensils, wagons, horses, cattle, plows, harness & c, see them laboring honestly in their own fields or in the service of white neighbors, meet with them in Christian worship, and hear their songs and prayers and talks on the Lord's holy day.

In spite of their progress, Bell warned the commissioner about the Chehalis reservation: "I do not wish to represent this reservation as a perfect paradise. The serpent is here; and these people are lineal descendants of Father Adam and Mother Eve."

Other than the problem of separating religious teachings from the rest of their education, the Indians were suspicious of the life of the government schools. A typical school would have about a hundred children from ages six to sixteen enrolled. For the most part, these children would be members of the reservation families, although sometimes they would be from neighboring reservations. They received a basic education in reading, writing, and arithmetic for half a day and worked on the farm conducted by the school during the afternoon. While the boys were doing chores and helping to keep the place in repair, the girls were learning how to make clothes, how to keep house in the style of the white man, and other domestic skills. With this available and free workforce, the government schools were operated on a very low budget. After a while it became a question of whether the children were in school to learn or to keep the agency from running a budget deficit.

However, there were some good practices in the schools. In the government school at the Nisqually reservation, the agent established a special position for the older Indian students so that they could participate in the administration of the school. Five older scholars were selected to assist the teacher, receiving a salary of five dollars a month, a munificent sum in those days, for taking charge of the younger students during some of the activities. This program enabled the agent and the teacher to spend more time in actual teaching and planning of the programs, and many of the older students expressed an interest in remaining at the school after their graduation to work as regular staff.

Outside activities were encouraged by the teachers on some of the reservations, and the students often took an interest in things outside their immediate locality. At the Puyallup school, a chapter of the Good Templars organization was created in 1890. This organization was one of the early popular fraternal groups of the Washington Territory and had a very large membership across the Pacific Northwest. Indian students seemed to like the group, since they quickly became delegates to the district and grand lodge sessions of the organization and traveled to several conferences while still students.

The government schools unintentionally served as the scene of a great tragedy in 1888. The Indians of the region had no natural immunity from the strange diseases of the white men, and in the early winter of 1888 an epidemic of whooping cough swept through the government schools in the lower Puget Sound area, hitting particularly hard at Puyallup and on the Olympic Peninsula. No sooner did the whooping cough subside than the schools were wracked by a violent epidemic of measles. Indians of all ages perished in these epidemics, but particularly the children in the government schools suffered because they were concentrated in one place, where they could easily catch both diseases.

The winter saw a dreadful reduction in the number of Indians in the territory as they tried to apply their old medicines to the strange new diseases. Since some of the old treatments involved the use of steam baths and washing in cold streams, the treatments were nearly as bad as the sicknesses themselves. The agent at Puyallup described the effects of the two epidemics:

> In many cases children of the same family have had both complaints at the same time, or one closely following the other. Their systems are generally weak any way, and a great deal of mortality has been the result.

Even those students that did not die immediately of the whooping cough or measles found themselves weakened by the sicknesses so that they died of other causes. "In some instances whole families of children have been carried away," the agent sadly wrote. "I have in mind three families, each having four children, every one of whom has died."

In spite of these problems, which often discouraged the people, conditions remained fairly stable on the reservations during the latter half of the nineteenth century. The Indians everywhere made every effort to adapt their old ways to the strange and often contradictory ways of the Bureau of Indian Affairs. Agencies were continually shifted around, so that a reservation might become the center of activity for an area for a couple of years and then be abandoned when the policy was changed. Often the solemn promises of the treaty went unfulfilled and the tribal leaders were disheartened when they considered how much they had given up to secure services from the federal government.

The Indian agent for the Puyallups visited the Squaxin Island reservation some years after the Bureau of Indian Affairs discontinued its services to the Squaxins; and his report described a scene of desolation that might have softened the heart of any policymaker:

> After the removal of the agency from Squaxin, all improvements ceased and slow decay commenced there and still

continues. Most of the buildings erected there by the government have either rotted down or are in ruins. Most of the cleared land is covered with bushes, except a few acres of good meadow, which has been kept fenced and is mowed yearly for hay. A few of the old-time fruit trees are still standing and produce some fruit amid the wild bushes that have grown up around them.

If the government could build hope, its departure could trigger a sense of despair as well.

With all these adjustments to their old traditions, it may have seemed to many of the Indians that times had changed permanently, but we must understand this change as they did— not as an abrupt disruption of customs but a general and gradual shifting to new ways of living. Perhaps the best indication of this gradual change can be seen in the way that the various reservations came to govern themselves. Under the old traditions, the villages would be governed by the leading heads of families, who would meet in an informal session to determine village policy.

With the establishment of reservations and the necessity of several tribes' having to live on the same tract of land, the idea of chiefs became more formal as the leading men of each village gathered to represent the interests of their people in a general reservation council. When the Indian agents recognized the natural formation of informal councils of the different groups, they wisely made the council a regular feature of reservation life. Thus it was possible for the various reservations to evolve their own form of government, and this consolidation of many groups into a larger and more efficient governing body most probably would have developed in time anyway.

The Indian agent at Puyallup, writing his annual report in 1879, remarked on the establishment of the reservation council; taking advantage of the Indians' desire to govern themselves, he gave them the power to police the reservations. "I appointed a council of three chiefs," the agent reported, "with two sheriffs, to keep order, to try and punish for minor offenses, with right to special appeal to me. Such is the case with all the reservations under my charge except Puyallup, where they have a chief of police and six policemen." By the mid-1880s, nearly every reservation had its own reservation council, its police force, and a system of tribal courts in which the tribal judges heard cases and levied sentences subject to an appeal to the Indian agent in cases of severe punishment or unjust sentence.

The councils were expanded or reduced in number as the population demanded. The pay for policemen was taken from the income of the tribal courts, according to the following scale: five dollars a month for privates (gradually raised to ten dollars); twelve dollars for sergeants, and fifteen dollars for captains in the larger reservations.

What is so remarkable about the Indians of the Pacific Northwest is that during the latter half of the nineteenth century they made such remarkable strides in adjusting to their new situation. They did not really abandon old ways, for they continued fishing whenever and wherever they could. But they also recognized the increasing importance of the new goods and materials that the white man had brought to their lands. To get these new goods they had to have an income, and, as we have seen, the people found many ways of earning an income and preserving their old ways as well.

Again, they had made an important transition from the old life as suppliers of trading posts to small reservation communities able to bring together many different skills to serve the common welfare. On the whole, life was good and except for the sporadic epidemics against which they had no immunities, which took a dreadful toll of their children, it could be said that the Indians of the Pacific Northwest had created for themselves a new life with new customs and a very capable form of self-government. Such major adjustments have been rare in human history.

CHAPTER EIGHT

▲ ▲ ▲ ▲ ▲ ▲ ▲ ▲

In the closing decades of the nineteenth century, Americans felt they were fulfilling their manifest destiny in settling the western territories. Transcontinental railroads, which had been started during the Civil War, brought thousands of settlers to the western territories, and towns grew up alongside the great railroads. Towns and cities competed vigorously for the right to become railway terminals, and the northern route, which had been a chief goal of Isaac Stevens, naturally led to the Puget Sound area. Tacoma was chosen as the terminus of the Northern Pacific Railroad in 1873, and its chief citizens spent a great deal of effort publicizing their city as the metropolis of the great Pacific Northwest.

Statehood did not naturally follow the increase of population, as one would have expected. Before the Civil War, the northern and southern states engaged in vigorous competition to open new territories and admit new states to the Union. But following the Civil War, the trend was reversed, and the various territories were not easily admitted to the Union as new states. Washington remained in territorial status from 1853 to 1889, a period of thirty-six years, in which the population grew tremendously. Conflict between Democrats and Republicans helped to keep the northwestern states from being admitted. Neither party was able to decide which way the new states might vote politically, and accusations from both parties made admission of new states a hazardous venture for the leadership of Congress.

Finally a compromise was worked out, in the closing months of 1889, and Washington, Montana, North Dakota, and

South Dakota were admitted as states. The impact of statehood on the Indians of the Pacific Northwest was to be immense, but few realized it at the time. It is important, therefore, that we understand how much change was really brought about by the admission of Washington to the Union.

While Washington was a territory, everyone, Indians and white men alike, were under federal laws. The governor and the judges were both appointed by the president, and while they were often people of good reputation in the territory, there were cases in which the appointments were purely a matter of political patronage. But regardless of who was appointed, all officials had to carry out the federal laws of the United States, and among these laws were the treaties signed by Isaac Stevens with the tribes of western Washington. There was no intervening government to pass contradictory laws affecting treaty rights, and in this sense the territorial status of Washington served to protect the Indians in their hunting and fishing rights.

Washington was required to place in its state constitution a provision stating that it would never attempt to confiscate the lands or rights of the Indians without the express permission of the Congress of the United States. But this phrase in the constitution did not seem to the new officials of the state to be important, because most of the reservations had been divided into small farms by the Congress, and in the law allowing this division of Indian lands Congress had provided that a state could remove any restrictions that had been placed on the Indian lands once the period of federal trust had expired. Thus it seemed that on the one hand Indians were given a favored status in the new state and on the other hand the new state appeared to have some control over the Indians.

If the country had remained sparsely settled, perhaps the question of Indian rights, particularly fishing rights, might never have become important. But with the waves of new settlers brought into the Puget Sound area by the Northern Pacific Railroad, the problem of Indian rights began to bother the officials of the new state. Many of the settlers brought into the

Puget Sound area in the 1880s were of Scandinavian descent, and a substantial proportion of these people were only one generation removed from their homes in Europe. They had arrived in the Midwest only thirty years before and were enticed westward by extravagant descriptions of the opportunities of the Pacific Northwest, fostered by the civic booster groups of Tacoma and Seattle.

The Scandinavians had a great fishing tradition, like the Indians, and the technology of canning fish had been developed to a very sophisticated science by the late 1880s. So conflict between the Indians, who had always fished but in a haphazard and noncommercial manner, and the new settlers, who fished in an efficient and commercial manner, developed. The Indians' first response to the expanding fisheries of the area was simply to fish and sell their catch to the new canneries, which were springing up everywhere. For a while this compromise seemed to work, but as more and more canneries were built, the fish runs declined seriously, and soon the Indians and the whites were competing for fish on grounds that had traditionally been reserved by treaty for the Indians.

There were other developments that were just as important in the way that people began to look at Indian rights. Timber was a very important resource, and as logging camps expanded into the wilderness, hunting was reduced to a few places as yet untouched by civilization. As settlements increased, game declined tremendously. Pressure to open the unallotted reservations for lumbering began to grow, and again the question arose concerning the rights of the state government over the lands of the Indians. Did the new state have the right to open lands to settlement? Could the new state enforce its laws on the reservations if it did not interfere with the services provided to the Indians by the federal government? These were new questions, and no one seemed to know the answers.

The first inclination of the whites in the new state was to take some of these questions to the courts to get an official interpretation of the treaties by the judges. At this point a controversy developed that has not been satisfactorily settled to this day. Which court, state or federal, was capable of correctly interpreting the Indian treaties? During territorial days, the courts run by the federal government generally interpreted the treaties in favor of the Indians. Now, with the creation of state courts, which were naturally inclined to support the rights of the state against the federal government, decisions seemed to indicate that state courts would favor the elimination of Indian rights in favor of the new state government.

Even the federal courts seemed to change with statehood. Some of the territorial officials had been appointed to federal court positions when the territory became a state, while others had become elected officials of the new state. The older judges and federal attorneys, in trying to emphasize the continuity between territorial and federal law, relied heavily on territorial precedents in deciding their cases. But the situation had changed a great deal in that judicial appointments were now subject to the political approval of the new state senators and congressmen, who were dependent upon the voters for their continued stay in office.

In territorial days, political decisions were often based upon the simple proposition that what was good for a continuing growth of settlement while keeping faith with the Indians was a proper decision. Now, with statehood, mixed political motives entered the picture for the first time. Even the most dedicated federal official always had to remember that he could be removed for politically unpopular decisions and that if he made decisions that were popular he could easily move from a status of appointed official to senator, congressman, or governor in a future election. Thus decisions deeply affecting Indians many times reflected the desires of the federal appointee to launch a political career sometime in the future.

We can see that many of these considerations worked to create a situation in which Indian rights became a minor consideration in a larger political arena involving a great many factors not present during territorial days. Enforcement of laws and popularity of decisions became the most important aspects of the Indian relationship with the new state. It was not long after statehood that this complex situation generated its first series of conflicts.

In February 1890, in one of the first acts of the new state, a commissioner of fisheries was created, and the following year a Department of Fisheries was established with powers to supervise fishing within the state. No mention was made in the early reports of the state fishing commissioner of any problems with Indian fishing, but that was probably because the problem made its first appearance in three cases, heard in the new federal court, that vitally affected the interpretation of Indian fishing rights, a problem still relegated to the federal government.

The treaty of Neah Bay preserved, as we have seen, the rights of the Makahs to go whaling and sealing in the ocean off the Northwest Coast. Over the years, this industry had expanded quite substantially, and by the late 1880s the Makahs owned several large whaling vessels and were engaged in extensive whaling activities. In the spring of 1889, Chestoqua Peterson, a Makah, purchased a whaling vessel and named her the *James G. Swan* after a longtime, highly regarded Indian agent at Neah Bay. The *James G. Swan*, with a full crew of Makahs, went sealing in Alaskan waters under the provisions of the Neah Bay treaty. The ship was captured by a US Navy ship and impounded for violating an act that prohibited the killing of fur seals within the waters ceded to the United States by Russia in 1867.

The case came before Judge Hanford, who was the federal judge of the Northern District of Washington in March of 1892. He used the case to emphasize the continuity of the new federal court with the old territorial courts and then came to an astounding conclusion about the treaty rights of the Makahs. After reviewing the treaty of Neah Bay, Judge Hanford remarked: "It is obvious, however, from the language above quoted, that the treaty secures to the Indians only an equality of rights and privileges in the matter of fishing, whaling, and sealing. The guaranty is of rights in common with all citizens of the United States, and certainly such treaty stipulations give no support to a claim for peculiar or superior rights or privileges denied to citizens of the country in general."

This interpretation was incredible in its implications. The judge appeared to be saying that the treaty promised only that when fishing laws were finally created, Indians would not be automatically banned from fishing, that they had the rights of any citizen. The decision flew in the face of the territorial laws and reversed the manner in which the Stevens treaties had traditionally been interpreted for nearly forty years. At this point the story becomes somewhat fantastic. Four years later, a US attorney brought a suit against a man named Winans and several others who were preventing the Yakima Indians from fishing in the Columbia River in eastern Washington. The case was heard in the federal court for the Southern District, and the judge turned out to be Judge Hanford, who promptly ruled against the Yakimas, using the same arguments he had used against the Makahs four years earlier.

William Brinker, then US attorney for Washington, refused to believe that the treaties had done nothing more than guarantee equal treatment of Indians and whites, and so, the next year, on receiving complaints from the Lummis, in northern Washington, he filed suit on their behalf against the Alaska Packers' Association, which had practically confiscated the traditional fishing grounds of the Lummis at Point Roberts. The case was filed in the Northern District, where, it was felt, the decision would be more favorable. But who should appear as judge? None other than Judge Hanford, who ruled against the Indians for the third time in five years, using almost identical language.

Testimony given by witnesses in the *Alaska Packers' Association* case was strangely contradictory. In general, the white witnesses testified that they had never seen any Indians fishing at Point Roberts, at least any Lummis, and the Indian witnesses swore that the place was a traditional fishing site of the tribe. To give some idea of the extent of the fishing controversy, one of the whites, a Mr. Adams, testified that in 1893 he had purchased 62,799 salmon from the Indians at Point Roberts and had paid $5,180.74 for them. This averages about eight cents a fish, and the fish, sockeye salmon, usually ran about fifteen pounds each. If the Alaska Packers had not outrightly taken the Indians' fishing rights, they had certainly underpaid the Indians to such an extent that these rights became virtually worthless.

Hanford's decision affected not only the Makahs, Lummis, and Yakimas, but all the fishing tribes of the Northwest, who now witnessed the virtual abrogation of their treaties by the newly established state government.

We are not privileged to know what happened behind the scenes in the federal government, but suddenly the decision was made to appeal the Yakima case to the Supreme Court and allow the Makah and Lummi cases to stand as final decisions. The *Winans* case was appealed by the US attorney and was finally decided by the US Supreme Court in 1905, nearly a decade after it was first decided by Judge Hanford.

The Supreme Court, of course, had no political considerations involving Washington State whatsoever, and it gave a very strong decision favoring the Indians, which has become the definitive precedent in the history of Indian fishing-rights law. "The treaty was not," the Supreme Court said, "a grant of rights to the Indians, but a grant of rights from them—a reservation of those not granted." The Court thus agreed, as we have seen, with the arguments used by the Indians at Tulalip against consolidation of their lands. The subsequent history of the Indian fishing-rights struggle has seen this strange alignment many times. The Supreme Court and the reservation people seem to hold the same theory of how a treaty is to be interpreted, and the white population and the state and lower federal courts often hold the oppositive and incorrect view.

At any rate, the fact that the Supreme Court had interpreted the Stevens treaty phrases in line with the record of negotiations of the treaty and in line with former decisions made when Washington was a territory left little impression on state officials or the general non-Indian populace. From 1905 on, Indians would be in court almost continuously trying to defend their fishing rights against the intrusions of the white fishermen. For all practical purposes, the Lummis and Makahs had lost their fishing rights until another day, when they could get a review of their disastrous decisions. Their struggle was made much more difficult in that, though Judge Hanford's interpretations were wrong, their cases, for some strange reason, were not appealed.

While keeping in mind the endless conflict over fishing rights that began in the 1890s and continue until the present time, we must now turn our attention to the fate of individual tribes who had to fight another continuing struggle. The region was still being settled, and the drive for additional lands was ever present. In the succeeding chapters we shall see how a number of tribes lost a great portion of their lands when they were unable to get the federal government to protect them, thus falling victim to the drive for total settlement of the area. We shall examine the struggles of the Lummis, the Nisquallies, and the Puyallups against the land speculators and the Bureau of Indian Affairs, who sought to take their lands.

Before we look at the fate of individual tribes, however, we must recognize that for the Indians the admission of Washington to the union as a state meant the end of an important era of peace and friendship with both their white neighbors and with the federal government. Thereafter the treatment of the various tribes would bring about a great sense of resentment over the generations and create in the Indians of the Pacific Northwest a fear and mistrust of white society and political institutions. Many of the problems of today come from the injustices suffered by these people in the first decades of statehood, and it is difficult, even today, for Indians to forget what happened in those early years.

CHAPTER NINE

▲ ▲ ▲ ▲ ▲ ▲ ▲ ▲

The Puyallups were one of the major villages that signed the treaty of Medicine Creek. Under this treaty they were given a reservation that consisted of 18,050 acres going from the eastern shore of Commencement Bay eastward toward Mount Rainier. Since the reservation covered almost the same area as did their aboriginal villages, the Puyallups experienced few disruptions in their lives as a result of the treaty. In the years following the treaty, they provided fresh salmon to the new settlements around Puget Sound and began farming and raising cattle.

As is evident from the Indian agent's reports, the farming ventures of the Puyallups were fairly successful over the years and they had one of the first and largest of the reservation police forces in the western area. The Presbyterian Church established one of the first missions to the Indians among the Puyallups, and over the years a very strong church congregation grew up on the reservation. Even today, the majority of the people are nominally Presbyterian.

Since the policy of the government was to teach the Indians farming, the Puyallups tended to settle on the eastern portion of their reservation, where the lands were rolling and capable of being cultivated. They still maintained a large fishery on the shores of the bay but allowed the lands on the bay to remain uncultivated because they were hilly and because the natural materials for building smokehouses and preserving fish grew in abundance on the slopes of the shores of the bay. When the reservation was divided into small tracts of land under the allotment program initiated under presidential order in January of 1886, the people were given forty-acre tracts of farm land on the eastern border of the reservation and eighty acres of wilds or wooded lands on the western portion of the reservation as their share in the tribal lands. An agency tract of 585 acres was reserved for school purposes.

The Puyallups were generally regarded as one of the most progressive and stable Indian communities in the Pacific Coast region. They did not wait for the government to provide things for them but often took the initiative in getting things done. For years they were connected with the town of Puyallup by a ferry that took their wagons across the Puyallup River, and they petitioned the government to build a bridge for several years. When the bridge was not built, they decided to build it for the government, although under the treaty it normally was the responsibility of the United States to provide such things as roads and bridges.

The tribal leaders met with a delegation of local white settlers and officials of the county and worked out a suitable compromise. The tribe agreed to provide one thousand dollars, the local farmers who also needed the bridge gave five hundred dollars, and the county gave fifteen hundred dollars. In 1887, the bridge was built, enabling both the Indians and the local white farmers to get their farm produce to market in Puyallup. The Indian community participated in other local activities and made many contributions to the social life of the county. They had a very good brass band with military uniforms that took part in county and sometimes state celebrations and was generally regarded as one of the best bands in the state.

By all reasonable measures of adjustment the Puyallups had become useful and friendly citizens of their local community. But fate played a very ironic part in the lives of the Puyallups. The towns of Puyallup and Tacoma had originally been chosen as sites for small trading communities due to their proximity to the Puyallups, who provided a significant amount of trade for the newly arrived white settlers. Over the years both Tacoma and Puyallup had grown immensely, and by the 1890s real estate agents were enviously eying the plush Puyallup lands.

In 1886, when the government divided the Puyallup lands into small allotments, the Indians were restricted from selling their lands until such time as Congress removed the restrictions on sale. But in the same act that gave the president authority to divide the Indian lands was a clause giving the state legislatures the right to remove the restrictions on the sales of Indian lands with the permission of the Congress. In other words, if the officials in Washington could be convinced that the Indians were capable of selling their lands and making good use of the proceeds, the states could simply merge the Indians into the general population.

A combination of real estate agents in Tacoma realized the bonanza that would result if they could get the Indian lands on the local real estate market, and they began to plan how they could accomplish this end. Recruiting two Puyallups as their representatives, the real estate combine began to secure leases on the various Puyallup farms. The plan was very tricky and very illegal and depended as much upon the willingness of the two Puyallups to lie to their own people as on the dishonesty of the whites to misrepresent the situation to federal and state officials. In this story there were no heroes, only unfortunate victims of man's greed.

Under the allotment act that divided the Indian lands there were provisions allowing Indians to lease their individual holdings for a period of no longer than two years. The real estate contracts provided that the Indians would lease certain of their lands for a period of two years with the right of the person holding the lease to renew it for as many succeeding two-year periods as he wanted. But the leases also had the provision that if any of the lands were taken out of restricted, federal status the leases would become deeds of sale and the lands would become the property of the leaseholder. In this way the real estate combine hoped to get around both the federal laws and the treaty of Medicine Creek, which made such sales illegal.

As soon as the leases had been made, the real estate people began pressuring the state legislature to pass a law removing the restrictions against sale from the Puyallup lands. The idea was that if the state acted swiftly and decisively, the officials in Washington would feel that they had no choice but to agree to what had been done. And the choicest of the Puyallup lands would fall into the hands of the speculators. The people in Tacoma were especially anxious to get their hands on the Indian lands. The Puyallups owned almost half of the shoreline of Commencement Bay, and the natural growth of the city of Tacoma would be to expand completely around the bay because of the city's large shipping interests.

The Northern Pacific wanted the Puyallup lands to establish a better route into Tacoma, and they especially wanted the school lands of the agency in order to build additional switching and terminal facilities. As the pressure grew for the sale of the Puyallup lands, lawyers for the railroad dug up a questionable agreement made between General Milroy, who had been agent for the Puyallups in 1876, and the Northern Pacific representative, by a strange coincidence a General Sprague.

What had apparently happened during the first years of the territory is that Milroy and Sprague had signed an agreement whereby the Northern Pacific could use the Indian lands for a railway to the Puyallup coalfields some miles east of the reservation. The two men had signed the agreement in violation of federal law but had gotten a council of the Puyallups to agree to the terms. The only promises made in the agreement by the railroad were that it would pay any damages it caused and

> that during the construction of said branch line preference will be given in the employment of Indian laborers, over white and Chinese laborers, when the Indian laborers will perform the work required to be done as well and as cheaply as it would be done by white or Chinese laborers.

Needless to say, few Indians were hired by the railroad, because the company was always able to get the Chinese laborers to work better and more cheaply than either the whites or the Indians.

But the railroad had never had the nerve to try to get the agreement ratified by the Congress, because it apparently did not want the deed to receive any more publicity than it already had. In 1885, Agent Eells of the Puyallup reservation wrote to the commissioner of Indian affairs about the alleged "agreement" and implied that the agreement had not been fulfilled. Commissioner Atkins, in his reply, seemed to indicate that the whole matter should be left alone. But this shady history of the alleged agreement with the Puyallups made the railroad even more eager than the real estate combine to get the matter settled as quickly as possible.

The result of all this agitation was that a special commission was appointed to go to the Puyallup reservation to investigate the conditions of the Indians and make a report recommending how the matter should be resolved. A commission of three men was appointed; they arrived in Washington State in January 1891 and went directly to the reservation, where they contacted Indian Agent Eells and began their inquiry. The Indians, and even people in the Bureau of Indian Affairs, hoped that the commission would get to the bottom of all the excitement among the Puyallups.

But the commission had other ideas. It is not possible to trace whether or not the real estate agents or the railroad or both influenced the commission, but their actions on the reservation made it highly likely that they had already decided to slant everything in favor of immediate sale of the reservation lands to the real estate combine. They discovered that there were already 146 contracts signed on some 9,200 acres of Indian lands, but they did not regard the contracts as illegal. The total amount of money paid to the Indians at that point was some $30,000, and the commission itself estimated that the eventual payments under the contract would be some $700,000. They reported to the commissioner of Indian affairs that they regarded the contracts as valid.

The commissioner was very angry at their report, and he wrote an angry letter to the secretary of the interior denouncing the commission and its report. "On reading the report of the Commission," commissioner of Indian affairs Thomas J. Morgan wrote, "my first and deepest impression was that of profound disappointment at the results. I feel constrained to say that the work done by the Commission is not at all satisfactory."

When one examines the report handed in by the commission members, the anger of the commissioner seems entirely justified. They deliberately changed their instructions to investigate the conditions on the reservation by adopting their own interpretation of the law under which they were appointed. The commission members gathered the frightened Indians at one meeting and asked if any of them were dissatisfied with their land contracts. "In reply to the sixth question, whether any allottees who have made such contracts are dissatisfied with the contracts and wish them set aside," the report noted, "we have not been able to get definite answers from all or any considerable number of them. A few say they are dissatisfied. Quite a number say they are satisfied; but most of them appear to be afraid to say."

Because the Indians were afraid to complain against the conditions on the reservation, the commission members used their fear as the excuse they needed to fail to investigate the conditions under which the contracts had been made, noting, "if the Indians were afraid, or even disinclined, to say among themselves whether they were dissatisfied with their contracts, they would hardly have been communicative to us in regard to the circumstances under which they made them." One would have thought that the duty of the commissioners would have been to question the real estate agents about the contracts if the Indians refused to talk.

But the commission moved with a perfect excuse about why they had refused to talk with the real estate agents. "To get at the real truth in that regard," the commission report stated, "both parties to the contracts should have been examined. The examination of either alone would have furnished one-sided statements, which would probably be misleading if not untrue. As we did not interrogate the Indians, we saw no reason for interrogating the white men with whom they had made contracts." The commissioners therefore filed a report on the Puyallup lands without talking seriously to either the

Indians, who were apparently selling the lands, or the real estate agents, who were apparently purchasing the lands. When the local newspapers started to inquire exactly who the commission was talking with, the commissioners refused to discuss any of their business, thus keeping the whole investigation from the eyes and ears of the general public also.

The commission based its recommendation that the lands be taken out of restriction on very suspicious reasoning. They had been sent out to determine if the Puyallups were being cheated or not, and their reply was a classic example of double talk. "We cannot see any good reason why, for a community of only 600 Indians," the report announced, "there should be held a great body of land that stays the growth of a city of 40,000 people, if a way can be devised, without injustice to the Indians, to open it to the acquisition and occupancy of all who may be able and willing to pay a fair price for it, particularly when the Indians are very desirous to sell."

Commissioner Morgan had a ready answer to the commission's contention that the Indians were ready to sell. In his letter to the secretary of the interior, Morgan commented: "That the Indians are happy in this trade is no more valid as an argument for its consummation than is the happiness of the child who is led to barter a diamond ring, of whose value it is ignorant, for a stick of candy that appeals to its appetite." Commissioner Morgan had understated the Indians' knowledge of the true value of their lands by quite a bit. The Bureau of Indian Affairs evaluated the reservation lands at $273.50 per acre on the average, and the commission was willing to allow the lands to go for the $700,000 price, or $75 an acre.

But there was an additional fraud involved in the proposed land sales. The commission classified the western reservation lands, those on the shoreline of Commencement Bay, as "wild and unoccupied" lands and therefore of little value. Commissioner Morgan pointed out that in the very instructions given by the secretary of the interior to the members of the commission prior to their departure for the Puyallup reservation it was stated, "Some of the lands are said to be worth as high as $6,000 an acre, while the water front alone has been estimated to be worth millions of dollars." Morgan expressed profound skepticism that the commission could overlook its own instructions and appraise the lands so low.

It seemed as if the Puyallups were doomed from the start, however, because when all the confusion was finished, it turned out that everyone had been against them from the very beginning. The two Indians who were working with the real estate agents collected their fees and attended the final meeting of the commission members with the tribal community. Even Agent Eells was openly siding with the commission in their effort to cover up the real truth. As the final meeting ended, Agent Eells, in what is a remarkably preserved aside taken down by the secretary to the commission, whispered to the commissioners, "It would be a good plan to let them shake hands with you as they pass out."

In spite of the best efforts of commissioner Thomas Morgan, who tried to stop the exploitation of the Puyallups two years later, the US Congress, using the inaccurate report as its justification, passed a law that required the sale of almost all of the Puyallup reservation. The Northern Pacific Railroad Company got its mysterious and illegal agreement ratified, and only the lands not used for the cemetery, some of the school grounds, and the homes of the Indians were not sold to the real estate people in Tacoma. The law further provided that those Indian lands held by the people on the eastern side of the reservation could be sold after ten years.

The one thing the law did not do was to extinguish the boundaries of the Puyallup reservation, and we shall see later that this omission made a very interesting legal point a couple of years ago. But the loss of so much land caused the Bureau of Indian Affairs to neglect the Puyallups after that, because they argued that their real task was to preserve the lands of the Indians and the Puyallups had no lands left. Following the final sales of the Puyallup lands, the state fish and game wardens began arresting the Indian fishermen in spite of the provisions of the Medicine Creek treaty, arguing that the Puyallups had

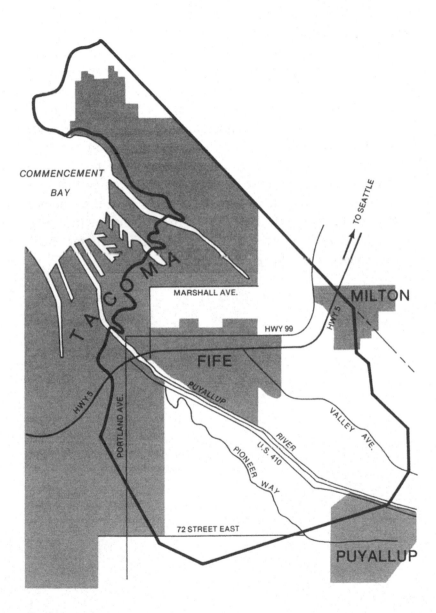

The original Puyallup reservation superimposed over a map of modern Tacoma, Washington.

only the right to fish on their reservation and that they had no reservation left. Thus the tribe that once ruled the waters of Commencement Bay and the Puyallup River was reduced to a small group of Indians huddled in poor housing on the banks of the river, on scattered tracts of land not worth selling.

Today, only about thirty-five acres of land remains in the hands of the Puyallups, and it is a cemetery; some of the allottees still have small tracts covering about three hundred acres, but these lands belong to families and not to the Puyallup tribe itself. Tacoma, of course, has greatly expanded, and the real estate agents made a great deal of money from the helpless Indians. The tragedy of the Puyallups is not so much that they lost their lands but that members of their own tribe helped others to get their lands and that the protection promised them by the United States at the signing of the Medicine Creek treaty turned out to be nothing at all.

CHAPTER TEN

▲ ▲ ▲ ▲ ▲ ▲ ▲ ▲

The tribes of the Medicine Creek treaty seemed doomed. Of the three major groups signing the treaty—the Puyallups, the Nisquallies, and the Squaxins—only the Squaxins were to keep their reservation intact. The Nisquallies and the Puyallups had their ancestral lands torn from them by the government. Like the Puyallups, the Nisquallies had long been friends to the white settlers. Their traditional lands were situated on what became known as the Nisqually prairie.

The prairie was a lush and rolling meadow and proved so fertile that the Hudson's Bay Company chose the site for its agricultural ventures when the fur trade began to ebb. The Puget Sound Agricultural Company was established in 1838 by Dr. John McLoughlin as part of the diversification of the activities of the Hudson's Bay Company. Fort Nisqually, built in 1833 for the fur trade, proved to be the community center around which the British settlers gathered. After the area was ceded to the United States following the agreement on the Oregon Territory, the claims of the British to the lands of the Nisqually prairie continued and were finally settled in the 1870s, long after the old settlers had passed on.

By the time of the American treaties, the Nisquallies were well acquainted with the agricultural exploits of the settlers. They had themselves begun to raise crops, and many of the Nisquallies had large herds of horses and cattle. Fort Nisqually became Fort Steilacoom in 1849, when the Americans began to rush into the lower Puget Sound region; it was generally regarded as the most important military post in Washington Territory west of the Cascades, because of its long history as a trading post and gathering place.

While the Nisquallies had a long history of friendship with the British, they were not very fond of the Americans. Holding the major part of the rich prairie lands and owning fishing rights along the Nisqually River, which emptied into the southernmost part of Puget Sound, the Nisquallies felt the intrusions of the American settlers much more than did the other tribes of the region. Everyone who came to Washington Territory seemed to pass through the lands of the Nisquallies.

In 1854, when Isaac Stevens called the tribes together to sign the Medicine Creek treaty, the influence of the Nisquallies was such that the Indians gathered at little Medicine Creek, in the heart of the Nisqually lands. Stevens asked each chief to make a map of his country so that he could put the maps together and determine where he would place the reservations. Leschi, then chief of the Nisquallies, immediately suspected Stevens's motives and refused to finish his map. Had it not been for the tact of George Gibbs, Stevens's assistant, who was very friendly to the Indians, a war might have broken out then and there between the Nisquallies and the Americans.

When Stevens designated the land that was to be the Nisqually reservation, emotions grew even more tense. He had chosen a rough, rocky plain far away from the Indians' traditional fishing sites and even some distance from their prairies. The new reservation was unfit for anything, and the Nisquallies immediately protested. Stevens departed for the other treaty meetings without offering any compromise to the Nisquallies, and the rumor quickly spread that Stevens was determined to confine the Indians in a reservation of eternal gloom, aptly called by the Nisquallies Polakly Illahe. Conflict was building even while Stevens was sending optimistic reports back to Washington, DC, about his success in negotiating with the Indians west of the Cascades.

As the Indians became more terrified of Stevens's real plans, word came from the eastern part of the territory that the Yakimas had begun to fight the Americans. On January 26, 1855, Leschi gathered a force of Nisquallies and Klickitats and, as we have seen, attacked the little settlement of Seattle, ultimately with little success. Due to the treachery of fellow Indians and to the superiority of American naval strength, Leschi's attempt to repel the settlers failed. Nevertheless, Indian pressure was brought to bear at the conference of August 1856 at Fox Island, where Stevens finally relented and set aside a good reservation for the Nisquallies.

But things had gone too far for Leschi. He was captured in the fall of 1856, shortly after the Fox Island conference, and was placed on trial by the settlers for murder. His old friends from the Hudson's Bay Company worked hard to save him, because they felt that the Nisquallies had had ample provocation for war in the manner in which Stevens had disregarded their complaints. Even the military officers who had fought against Leschi appealed for his life, contending that he had been captured during a period of war and was therefore a prisoner of war and should not be tried by a civil court for acts committed during military hostilities.

Leschi's old rival Chief Seattle entered an eloquent plea for Leschi, mustering the most simple logic one could imagine:

> Leschi rebelled against bad treaty. White man gives Leschi's people new treaty. White man must know, in his heart, that first treaty was unfair. Or why give new treaty?

The old Duwamish chief felt that if Stevens had admitted his error at Fox Island and drawn up a new and better reservation for the Nisquallies, then Leschi's reason for starting the war against the whites was fully justified. But the settlers saw in Leschi a spirit of independence and rebellion that they did not wish to encourage among the Indians, who still outnumbered them.

On February 19, 1858, after several trials and many appeals by both whites and Indians had been turned down, the settlers hanged Leschi for his part in the war of 1855–56. The greatest Indian patriot of the Puget Sound region went to his death secure in the knowledge that in his rebellion and fight against overwhelming odds he had secured a suitable reservation for his people. It was, perhaps, little enough satisfaction, since in later years many of those who had been so determined to convict Leschi for murder admitted that he probably had not even committed any killings.

The original Nisqually reservation had contained a mere 1,280 acres about two miles west of the mouth of the Nisqually River in an area of steep cliffs covered with a dense underbrush. During the Fox Island negotiations, this reservation was changed and the Nisquallies received a new reservation, on the grassy meadow along the Nisqually River east of the old reservation, containing some 4,717 acres. The new area was part of the lands the Nisquallies had traditionally used for their horse herds, and so it was much more acceptable to the people.

Life on the Nisqually reservation was about the same as life in other small communities during the latter half of the nineteenth century. The Indians had long since learned about farming and ranching, and they engaged in those activities as a supplement to their fishing. Their horse herds grew and their farms blossomed, and of all the Indian villages west of the Cascades the Nisquallies were perhaps the most successful in adjusting to the new ways of the white man.

As we have seen earlier, the Nisqually school was so advanced that students were hired as assistants to the teachers, receiving as a salary a sum equal to that received by the Indian police, five dollars a month. The problems that occurred with some frequency at other reservations never seemed to plague the peaceful Nisquallies. In 1884, the Bureau of Indian Affairs began to survey the Nisqually reservation so that it could be divided into allotments for trial members in accordance with then-existing government policy. The idea behind this division of tribal lands, as we have seen, was to use the magical powers of ownership of private property to further civilize the Indians, and the Nisquallies were among the first to come under the new policy.

An indication of how cohesive the Nisquallies were as a community may be their reaction to the allotment of their lands. After the government agent had marked off the individual allotments and informed each tribe member where his lands were and what the Bureau of Indian Affairs expected of him, the Nisquallies held a community meeting. They had never been faced with individual ownership of lands before, and the idea was very foreign to their customs and to their religion. Land, like water and air, could not be divided, according to their understanding, because the Great Spirit had created it, not man, and He had not wanted it divided among men as if it were a thing. It was a living being, the mother of mankind, and had to be treated as such.

The problem the community faced, therefore, was to avoid antagonizing the Indian agent and at the same time avoid violating their deepest convictions. So they fenced off the entire reservation with rail fences and used the whole 4,717 acres as a common pasture for the community. Inside the rail fence, individual families fenced off their garden plots and homesteads so that the cattle and horses would not destroy their gardens. The agent, of course, was baffled at the Nisquallies' solution to the problem and wisely decided to let well enough alone. For more than forty years, the Nisquallies maintained a common pasture; their fence marked off their little community and way of life from the rest of the territory with its hustle and bustle.

Unlike their neighbors the Puyallups, the Nisquallies were not close to the expanding centers of population such as Tacoma and Seattle, and there was no reason to suppose that they would ever fall victim to the land speculators who were quite prominently at work in the Puget Sound area. But such was not the case. By mid-1916, war fever was in the air and everyone expected the United States to become involved in the European war. Speculators were well aware that a dollar was to be made in land during the war.

In December of 1916, Jesse O. Thomas Jr. and Stephen Appleby of Tacoma went to the nation's capital and had a quiet meeting with the secretary of war. They promised to secure seventy thousand acres of land for the army in Pierce County, Washington, in return for the secretary's promise to build a fort and maintain a division of men in the county. Land prices

would boom, of course, and the profits to Tacoma businessmen in supplying the fort would be enormous. All they had to
do was build the patriotic fever to a hysterical pitch and then
present their plan.

As war approached, patriotism escalated in Tacoma and
soon it was an accepted conclusion that the only proper way
to win the war in Europe would be to have a division of men
stationed near Tacoma. The county authorities began a program of condemnation of lands to be given to the army for the
fort, and those landowners who understood what was happening seemed to receive generous appraisals of their lands while
those who showed some hesitancy at the program seemed to
receive somewhat lower valuations. The program went very
smoothly until it reached the boundaries of the Nisqually
reservation.

Indian land was, of course, land held by the United States
for the Indians, and it could not be taken over by county
authorities without the permission of Congress. So a careful
program had to be devised to seize the lands under the guise
of patriotism with the thought that in the general frenzy of
war fever certain legal niceties could be overlooked. The first
move against the Nisquallies was a tour of the reservation by
General Burr of the army and the Nisquallies' agent from the
Bureau of Indian Affairs. The general strutted about the riverbank solemnly explaining the situation to the Indian agent
and remarking that he was concerned primarily for the safety
of the Indians should the fort be established.

A panicked agent wrote to the commissioner of Indian
affairs in December 1917 about his tour with the general:

> An investigation of the grounds in company with Gen-
> eral Burr showed that the safety of the Indians during
> the hours of target practice would require the removal of
> the Indians from both the upland and the river bottom,
> to avoid ricocheting shells; that is, the entire reservation
> would have to be abandoned during those hours.

The agent rather innocently informed the general that it would be a good idea to try to lease the lands from the Nisquallies for the duration of the war, because the provisions of the Medicine Creek treaty and the price in lives that the Nisquallies had already paid for their lands was more than the army or Pierce County could afford. The agent might have simply stated that under no conditions would the Indians have parted with their lands but, since the war fever was intense in Tacoma, he dared not say anything that might be interpreted as hostile to the war effort.

The general reported on the tour to his superiors, and a series of letters began to pass back and forth between the Departments of War and the Interior concerning the necessity of giving up the Nisqually lands for Fort Lewis. The Interior Department was in favor of leasing the lands to the War Department, while the army and the businessmen in Tacoma were intent on securing clear title to the thirty-three hundred acres as agreed upon in December 1916. While these formal letters were traveling back and forth in bureaucratic circles, the army acted.

Indians were ordered to leave their homes and not return until they were given permission to do so. Some families left but many stayed, and they were simply loaded on wagons with some of their household goods and transported away from the area. A number of Indian families were given just a few hours' notice before the army arrived to move them, and some of the people spent the remaining months of the winter in makeshift shacks along the Nisqually River wondering why the Bureau of Indian Affairs could not stop the confiscation of their homes and lands. But with the high state of excitement then prevailing in Tacoma, the Indians were afraid that they would be accused of disloyalty if they complained, and so many of them simply left the reservation without saying anything.

Early in 1918, without the knowledge of the Bureau of Indian Affairs, the authorities of Pierce County began condemnation proceedings against the Nisqually lands on the north of the river, which were the best part of the reservation. When the Interior Department discovered what was happening, officials lodged a protest, albeit not a very strong one, and the army agreed to purchase the lands from the Indians. The War Department appointed an appraiser and urged the Bureau of Indian Affairs to do the same. The bureau appointed the head of the Cushman School, an educator, as their representative, and very shortly the two appraisals were forwarded to officials in each department in the nation's capital. The War Department representative valued the lands at $57,920.60, while the Bureau of Indian Affairs representative figured the lands were worth $93,760.

In April 1918, a compromise figure was worked out that totaled $75,840, and a decree was entered by the local court vesting title in the lands to Pierce County. The legality of the transaction was not questioned, because of the hysterical fear that raising such questions might be regarded as treason in view of the war. The army in effect purchased the Nisqually land long after it had removed the Indian owners by allowing a local court to transfer the land titles to Pierce County, which in turn was bound by agreement to cede the army seventy thousand acres in return for the construction of a fort near Tacoma. At best, it was a shadowy transaction, unworthy of the US government, but, under the circumstances, not unlikely.

The Indian agent soothed his conscience by the thought that if the transaction was illegal, Congress would find some way to compensate the Nisquallies after the war. The agent was partly correct, because the controversy over the confiscation of the Nisqually reservation refused to die, and in the 1919 Indian Appropriations Act a section was inserted requiring the secretaries of war and the interior to report to Congress on the advisability of reacquiring the lands of the Nisquallies from Pierce County. Apparently Congress did not believe the official War Department version of how the lands for Fort Lewis were acquired and wanted some joint statement from the two government departments on what had transpired.

So a special investigating commission was sent out to Tacoma to learn what had happened two years before, in the hysteria of war fever. In the spring of 1920, the report was finally filed with the House of Representatives Committee on Indian Affairs. Even the official version did not do credit to the United States. The report was purged of accounts of Indian families dispossessed of their homes in midwinter, but it still contained enough material to shame the two departments for their roles in the confiscation of the Indian lands.

The two department representatives first advised against restoring the lands to the Nisquallies under the theory that they were now comfortable in their new homes. Where they received such information is questionable, since the report does not indicate that they talked with very many of the Indians who had been forced to move. The second outstanding feature of the report is the acknowledgment by the two representatives that the Indians did not receive fair value for their lands regardless of how they were appraised. One white man owned land adjoining the reservation—land not nearly as good as the Nisquallies'. He received more than $32,000 for 1,350 acres that had no river bottom lands or running water to make the land valuable.

Most puzzling was the response of the county attorneys when asked about the transaction. The investigators asked Mr. J. T. S. Lyle, one of the attorneys for Pierce County, for a copy of the army's deed to the lands. The attorney refused to give a copy of the deed to the investigators, and when they inquired at the county offices they were informed that the deed had never been filed! The county assessor did inform the commission that had he been allowed to value these lands for tax purposes he would have appraised them at $66,650, and the commission noted that county assessors are notoriously generous when appraising lands for tax purposes.

Perhaps the best indication of how badly the Nisquallies were cheated is the condition in which they found themselves when they tried to purchase lands for new homes on the river after they had been paid for their old allotments. Willie Frank, for example, had an allotment of 205 acres on the northern side of the river that was taken for the army post. With the money he received for the lands, he was able to purchase only six and a half acres on the south bank of the river! Other

Indians found themselves in similar circumstances, and many simply moved away to live on other reservations where they had relatives.

The investigators finally recommended that Congress appropriate another $85,000 to be paid to the Nisquallies as additional compensation for their lands. The legality of the whole transaction, dubious at best, was never mentioned. The only comment made in the report to Congress regarding the justice of the proceedings noted

> that owing to war-time conditions and influences the county attorneys at the time of the condemnation proceedings took the fullest advantage of the situation, with the result that the Indians received considerably less than their lands were worth, and have not been provided with lands of like character and location and of equal advantage and acreage.

Although the investigation clearly showed that the Nisquallies did not lose their fishing rights in the condemnation proceedings, the state began harassing the Nisqually fishermen following the confiscation of their reservation on the theory that they had lost everything when the county received the lands. The Nisquallies and the state fish and game departments began an undeclared war over fishing rights that has lasted until the present time, with the Indians continually complaining that if the state officials really knew the history of their tribe they would see the justice of the Indian cause.

We shall return to the fishing-rights controversy and the Nisquallies later, because their story, far from ending, is continuing today in more heroic terms than ever before. We need only note that the suspicions of Leschi, the great Nisqually chief, about the intentions of the white settlers were unfortunately fulfilled nearly two generations after his valiant effort to achieve justice for his people, and it is tragic to note that the lands he secured with his life were taken from his people under the guise of patriotism in a wholly unnecessary act.

CHAPTER ELEVEN

▲ ▲ ▲ ▲ ▲ ▲ ▲ ▲

Not all the Indian stories in the Pacific Northwest have been as grim as those of the Puyallups and Nisquallies. Some of the tribes, such as the Makahs and the Quinaults of the coastal region of the Olympic Peninsula, lived in relative isolation from the growing cities of Puget Sound and had very few intrusions by non-Indians. Other tribes, such as the Lummis and the Swinomish of the Georgia Straits region, seemed destined to survive as communities even though they had a difficult time of it.

The Lummis, who traditionally lived around Bellingham Bay and the San Juan Islands, in the northern portion of the inland waters, have a unique history and one that is, in a very important way, representative of many Indian tribes. We have met them briefly already at the negotiations during the treaty of Point Elliott and in the *Alaska Packers' Association* lawsuit in which they lost their fishing rights through no fault of their own. But let us go back for a moment to see how they fared after the treaty of Point Elliott.

Of all the villages that attended the treaty at Mucklteoh, or Point Elliott, no villages were better represented than the Lummi villages of the Bellingham area. At least a dozen chiefs and headmen attended the proceedings and signed the treaty. It was perhaps due to the size of their delegation that the Lummis secured a reservation in the heart of their ancestral lands on the island of Chah-choo-sen, where the Nooksack River splits and sends two branches into the inland waters—at Lummi Bay and at Bellingham Bay. The Lummi homelands remained relatively unknown during the fur-trading period, because the largest trading center was at Fort Langley, on Vancouver Island, and the avenues of trade bypassed the Lummis. In 1852, a couple of years before the treaty with Isaac Stevens, two white men had arrived in the area and set up a sawmill on Whatcom Creek, several miles from the largest Lummi village. The area, while attractive, was no better or worse than other places closer to the larger settlements, and the prospect of development remained remote in the years following the treaty.

But in 1858, gold was discovered in British Columbia, and in a sudden rush thousands of miners passed through the Bellingham area in search of the goldfields of Canada. The little settlement of Whatcom became a leading center for outfitting the miners, and the Lummis shared in the prosperity of the gold rush. Unfortunately they had no more foresight than did the whites at Whatcom and in the summer of 1858 they sold all their canoes at high prices to the miners wishing to canoe up the Nooksack to British Columbia. By the end of the rush, the white settlement at Whatcom had grown tremendously and the Lummis were back building canoes for the coming season's fishing, richer, somewhat wiser, and certainly swearing never again to sell every canoe, no matter what the prices.

Even though coal was discovered in paying quantities in the Bellingham area, settlement did not grow as fast as in other parts of the territory, and the Lummis and their white neighbors settled down to a life of comparative ease. The Bureau of Indian Affairs supervised the Lummis and provided schooling for them through a contract with Father Chirouse, a Catholic missionary who established a school on the nearby Tulalip reservation; for a period of twenty-one years, this school was the only one available to the children of the Lummi tribe.

Finally a day school was established at Lummi, and they received a resident farmer to help them with their farming activities. Like many other government employees, the two people assigned to the Lummis were determined to carry out their program of civilization even though the circumstances at Lummi made the feasibility of any profound transformation impossible. The reservation was covered with a thick growth of cedar, and when the agent surveyed it into allotments and began his farming program, problems began to pile up rapidly. The men were recruited to cut and burn the trees, some of them the finest cedar in the country, so that the land would be clear for farming. But since the land was really an island, clearing the trees resulted in the creation of many swamps and pools of almost perpetual duration. While the agents gave an optimistic report on farming at Lummi every year, listing, as we have seen on other reservations, bushels of wheat, corn, and other crops, it was apparent from the first that farming was not an occupation that would be very profitable on the reservation.

The Lummis had to seek other work from the very beginning, because their farming ventures simply proved impossible, and very shortly they were working in lumber camps, serving as day laborers, fishing commercially, mining coal, and working on the steamboats that traveled up and down Puget Sound. It was the Lummis who first discovered hop-picking and made it into an annual tribal event by taking friends and relatives north to British Columbia to work in the hop fields. Early newspapers recount the astonishment of the people of the area at the sight of the whole tribe embarking on a six weeks' trip to the hop fields, taking small children, old people, and invited guests with them.

The fishing activities were severely hampered, as we have seen, in the 1890s, when the US attorney failed to take the *Alaska Packers' Association* case to the Supreme Court, where the Lummis would almost certainly have had their rights upheld. But while they were restricted in their fishing at Point Roberts and other sites some distance from the reservation, they maintained fishing sites in the neighborhood and continued to fish as they always had. In a classic understatement of the situation at Lummi, the commissioner of Indian affairs reported in 1895:

> The Indians, as a rule, are not systematic farmers. Farming is with them the incident and not the business of everyday life. Some of them, the more thrifty and industrious, have well-cultivated farms and comfortable houses, and are

anxious to have their children educated. They generally
live like white people. Those, however, are the exception.
A large majority spend most of their time in their canoes,
fishing, especially during the salmon season.

The commissioner might have admitted to himself, and
warned future commissioners, that the program to turn the
Lummis into farmers was probably not going to work. Following the *Alaska Packers' Association* case, state officials seemed
to concentrate their efforts to enforce the state fish laws on the
Lummis rather than any other tribe, and incidents began to
multiply involving the Lummis and the state fish wardens. The
Bureau of Indian Affairs, while it dodged controversial incidents, generally tried to support the Lummi efforts to maintain fishing sites. But their efforts generally backfired because
of the weak-hearted support they gave the Lummi fishermen.

In 1913, for example, the agent at the Lummi reservation
and the state fish commissioner made an agreement to have a test
of the Lummi treaty fishing rights, and Harry Price, a Lummi,
agreed to be arrested by the state fish commissioner so that the
state supreme court or federal district court could make a definite pronouncement whether or not the Lummis had a right
to fish free of state regulation. Price was arrested and the case
began to travel through the courts, with the state fish commissioner confident that he would be vindicated in his contention
that the state had the right to regulate the Lummi fishermen.

The Lummis won the case, and the infuriated fish commissioner refused to abide by the decision, announcing that
he would continue to arrest Lummi fishermen, thus inciting a
massive protest by the tribes of upper Puget Sound, who had
followed the case with great interest. The large-scale Indian
protest scared the federal officials, who promptly made themselves scarce, feeling that it would be unpopular to carry out
their duties to protect the Indians as required by the treaties.
Whatcom County, where the Lummi reservation was situated,
was in an uproar, and the situation grew tense. No one knew
what the Indians would do next.

But the Lummis were supremely confident, now that their federal protectors had fled the scene, and they instructed their lawyer to seek a permanent injunction against the state fish commissioner, forbidding him from arresting any Lummi fishermen. The Bellingham *Herald*, the county's most vocal newspaper, was disgusted at the whole affair, a little astounded that the Indians knew enough about the white man's law to use it effectively, and announced:

> At least it will force Commissioner Darwin to come into court and file informations to which demurrers can be taken, something which, the petition recites, he has heretofore refused to do.

Instead of proving that the Indians were violating the law, Commissioner Darwin had been arresting the Lummis and failing to show that they were violating any law, but in the process of arresting them he was confiscating their canoes and fishing gear, thus preventing them from fishing.

Darwin escaped the injunction through the cooperation of the federal officials and continued his harassment of the Lummis. But his determination to prevent the Lummis from fishing led to a very serious, and in some respects humorous, situation two years later. Some Austrian fishermen arrived in Lummi waters in 1915 on a fishing trip. (Actually they were simply fishermen on a ship flying the Austrian flag, making them, in a technical legal sense Austrian citizens, even though Austria is landlocked and has no fishing fleet.)

The Lummis, seeing this strange ship in their waters, refused to allow them to fish, and Darwin and other state officials supported the Austrians. The US attorney, who was supposed to defend the Lummis, also took the side of the Austrians, and the situation looked very suspicious indeed. Both state and federal officials argued that the Lummi fishing rights extended only to the high tide and that other people were allowed to fish in the waters that bordered the reservation.

When the Indians became convinced that they would not

receive any assistance from either state or federal officials, they promptly got into their canoes and paddled out to the Austrian ship and arrested the Austrians and took them back to the reservation as prisoners. With their newly acquired prisoners hidden in one of the Indian homes, the Lummis sat back to watch the proceedings.

Telephone lines hummed between Washington, DC, Seattle, and Bellingham, and before the day was over officials in a very high position in the nation's capital were trying to explain to the president and other assorted officials why a boatload of Austrian fishermen were being held captive by the Lummi Indians. With the First World War just beginning in Europe, it was the last kind of incident that the United States wanted to happen. Dr. Charles Buchanan, the Indian agent at the Tulalip reservation, was sent on a delicate mission to negotiate with the Lummis, while other federal officials received a blistering reprimand for letting things get out of hand. Buchanan secured the release of the Austrians after hearing the Lummi side of the story, and when the full story became public the state fish commissioner decided to stop his harassment of the Lummis. Very promptly.

Events took a strange turn for the Lummis after they won their battle with the state fish commissioner, and they found themselves confronted with a prolonged attack on their lands. In 1873, the president had set aside their reservation with carefully described boundaries, and the reservation as defined in the order signed by the president gave them slightly more land than the treaty had provided.

The lands had been allotted to individual tribe members in 1885, and over the years some of the lands had been sold, leaving a pattern of Indian landholdings that resembled a checkerboard, with Indians owning some tracts of lands and non-Indians owning others. Prominent businessmen in Bellingham had purchased some of the allotments that bordered the tidelands, and in 1919, led by a man named Romaine, they claimed ownership of the tidelands, and the resulting clamor led to a lawsuit by the United States to clarify who owned the tidelands. It seemed to be a ridiculous controversy at the time, because the tidelands are that part of the shore covered by the motion of high and low tides—in other words, simply a stretch of beach that we see when the tide is out. In that stretch of beach, however, are the clams and other shellfish, which are very tasty and very valuable.

The court ruled that the Lummi reservation covered not only the lands allotted to the tribe but also the shoreline down to the low-tide line. The businessmen of Bellingham were disappointed, of course, because the Lummi beaches were beautiful and ideal spots for summer cottages, and there had been a lot of discussion of getting control of the shore properties and developing recreation areas on the reservation.

The beach issue did not remain quiet for very long. Eleven years later, when even more Indian lands had been sold, a man named Stotts purchased an Indian allotment on the shore and claimed that his property went into the water and included the beach and waterfront. The case again went to court, and the question was whether the shoreline belonged to the tribe or to the individual property owners. The Lummis claimed that the presidential order establishing the reservation gave the shoreline to the tribe and not to individuals who later received allotments.

Again the court ruled that the Lummi tribe and not individual property owners held the title to the shoreline. It would have seemed that there were no more questions to be determined regarding the Lummi beach, but the following year one of the owners, a man named Boynton, claimed that the shifting of the shoreline in the time since the reservation was established had given him a section of beach because the water had intruded into his property lines. So the Lummis were back in court to protect their beach, and once again the court found in their favor. Even though the beach line may vary from time to time according to the height of water, the court ruled, the ownership of beach follows the water, and property lines have to give way to the general ownership of the beach.

Perhaps the most spectacular aspect of the *Boynton* case was the testimony of an old Lummi who had worked on the original survey of the reservation boundary in 1873. The old gentleman came into court hardly able to speak English and recalled almost precisely how the original federal surveyor, fifty-eight years earlier, had walked over the wilds of the reservation setting survey stakes and determining where the reservation boundaries were. When he was able to go to precisely the same locations nearly six decades later and point out the markers and places designated on the reservation map, it was no contest, and the judge ruled in favor of the tribe.

The Lummis were far from preserving their reservation lands, however, because the reservation had been divided up into little farming tracts of forty acres, and over the years much of the land was sold by individual Indians. As each piece of land left Indian hands, the reservation grew smaller and the people received less attention from the Bureau of Indian Affairs, who argued that their job was only to protect the Indian lands, not to provide services to the people who lived on the lands. Although this attitude was in direct conflict with the treaty at Point Elliott, the Lummis were helpless to prevent the government from withdrawing its services from them.

After 1931, when the *Boynton* case was decided in their favor, until 1968, when the tribe began to get aggressive about protecting its lands, the Lummis suffered a general decline in their fortunes. The government day school was closed, and the children were sent to local white schools off the reservation, where they were not welcomed. Land speculators continued to pressure the Bureau of Indian Affairs to sell the Lummi lands to them, because the lands were becoming increasingly valuable as recreation properties. Finally, by 1968, there was only one tract of land in the whole reservation that bordered the shore, and it was owned by a prominent Lummi family. All the other shoreland had been sold over the years. While the tribe still owned the beach and the people still dug clams, there was profound gloom among the Lummis that with the sale of this final piece of land they would no longer have any way to get to the beach.

In 1967, the Lummis suddenly discovered that plans were under way to locate a magnesium-oxide reduction plant on

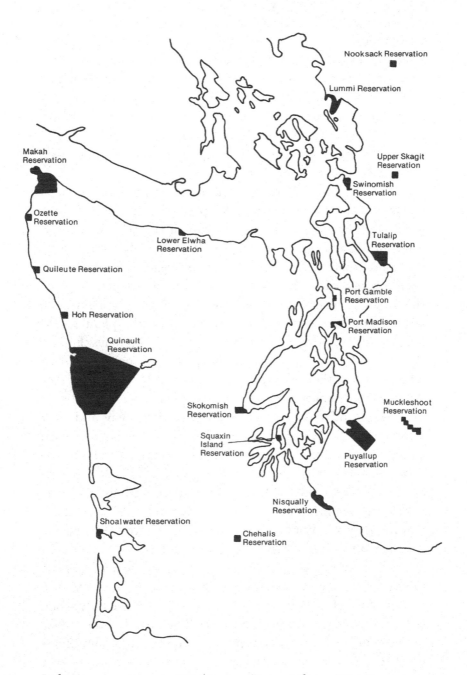

Indian reservations in Washington State at the present time.

Lummi Bay. The plans were to bring the raw ore into the bay by ship and use the fresh water of Lummi Bay in the reduction process. The raw ore was a deep green, olivine color and, once processed, would produce tremendous heaps of waste that would permanently destroy all marine life in the bay. The people were terrified at the thought of destroying the bay, but they seemed to have no choice. The large corporate and banking interests were eager to have the new industry, and even many of the white people in the county saw the new plant as a means of developing the county.

About a week before they had to make the final decision whether to accept the ore-reduction plant, the Lummis encountered Dr. Wallace Heath, a marine biologist who was interested in aquaculture, the scientific farming of seafood such as salmon, clams, and oysters. When Heath discovered that the tribe was just about to approve the ore-reduction plant, he became concerned, being an ecologist, that the plant would destroy surrounding fish life in the neighboring bays, and he agreed to visit Lummi Bay and give a professional opinion on whether or not the new plant would hurt the fisheries that provided the only continuing source of income to the Lummis.

Heath and the Lummi leaders toured the bay and took samples of the water in various parts of the area. Heath announced that the bay showed great potential for the development of an aquaculture, even though the idea was very new and few people had tried to build a successful aquaculture. When the Lummi discovered what was required for an aquaculture, they surely must have smiled at the irony of history. An aquaculture needs that stretch of beach between high and low tide and depends, in a freshwater bay, on the action of the tides to provide movement and fresh water every day. And the stretch of beach between high and low tide was the only thing left in the original reservation that still belonged to the tribe!

We will discuss the Lummi aquaculture in a later chapter, because it is one of the most unique experiments ever undertaken by a tribe of Indians. But it is comforting to learn that while many of the other tribes in the Pacific Northwest lost their beloved homelands in strange and unjust ways, the Lummis somehow were able to save precisely that part of their ancestral lands that was most valuable. There may be a force in history that sometimes compensates for the tragic experiences of people.

CHAPTER TWELVE

▲ ▲ ▲ ▲ ▲ ▲ ▲ ▲ ▲

The twentieth century brought many changes in the lives of the Indians of the Pacific Northwest, but perhaps the most profound change was the gradual settlement of the region and the erosion of concern shown by the federal government for the various reservations. While the state was unsettled and large stretches of territory had few residents, there seemed to be a great need for special government schools and services for Indians. But gradually more and more towns and cities grew up, some at the expense of the tribes, as we have seen in the case of Tacoma, which took the lands of the Puyallups and Nisquallies in two separate incidents.

With the increased settlement in Washington State there was a decrease in the number of services provided by the federal government to the tribes. Perhaps the first tangible indication of the change was the closing of the different reservation day schools. These reservations had each received government school and a teacher, and for nearly a generation they had enjoyed the benefits of an elementary education at their homes. As local educational programs expanded, government officials began to question the great expense of the reservation day schools. They argued, and quite persuasively, that since the Indians and the whites worked and played together, there was no reason why they should not be educated together.

So, over a twenty-year period beginning about 1900, the day schools on the reservations were closed. The various reservation governments reacted in various ways. Some of the people wished to have their children in the local school systems, because they felt that the children would receive a better education than they were getting in the government schools. But other Indians felt that the government had intended to provide special schooling for their children under the treaties made by Isaac Stevens, and so they saw the closing of the schools as another indication of the government's going back on its word.

With the closing of the schools came a general reduction in the number of government employees on each reservation. No longer did the government provide a boss farmer to supervise the farming activities of the Indians, and the Indian police, who had been so effective in helping to govern the reservations and protect the people from intruders, were also eliminated, leaving many reservations without any police protection at all.

But it was becoming more difficult for the federal government to provide services to the various reservations because of the very technical problems that began to arise regarding their lands. When the reservations were established, it was clear that all the lands were held by the federal government in a trust for the tribes who lived on the reservations and that federal laws would be applied to those who committed illegal acts on the Indian lands. As the individual allotments were sold by Indians and purchased by non-Indians, the lands themselves became taxable, because they were no longer held by the federal government. And state officials began to argue that if they were taxing the lands inside the reservations they should have the power to enforce state laws inside the reservations also.

This very complicated problem became known as jurisdiction. Who had the authority to enforce the rules of law on the reservations? Whenever it was convenient for the state to claim the authority, state officials would assert themselves, and whenever it was convenient for federal officials to claim their privileges, they would do so. We have already seen that when neither the state nor the federal officials exerted themselves, the Indians claimed their own authority, as the Lummis did in the arrest of the Austrian fishermen.

The jurisdiction problem was only one of the problems that arose with the withdrawal of local Bureau of Indian

Affairs agents from the reservations. The state fish and game departments were unusually energetic about enforcing the laws against the Indians, and without a local representative of the Bureau of Indian Affairs to speak up for them, many Indians were arrested for fishing under the provisions of the treaties. Practically all the tribes continued their traditional fishing activities, and the loss of land and confusion over jurisdiction created great hardships for them.

When the commission was sent out to investigate the situation of the Nisquallies, the first thing they learned was that the confiscation of the riverbank lands had led to great hardships, because the Nisquallies could no longer fish for their food and had so small an income from their other activities that they could not feed themselves. Father DeDecker, the local Catholic missionary to the Nisquallies, told the commission, "This fishing privilege was the most valuable right they lost by being dispossessed of their lands." "Their main dependence for meat was fish," Father DeDecker related, "secured by them from the Nisqually River where it passes through the reservation where they fished unmolested and dried large quantities of salmon for winter use."

The Nisquallies were similar to many tribes in their daily diet during these years. Their meals generally consisted of bread, potatoes, and salmon, which they either boiled, barbecued, or baked. Quite often, the poorer Indian families lacked money for potatoes and bread after they lost their lands, and salmon was the only dish served. "Most of the Nisqually Indians ate fish daily," Father DeDecker told the investigating commission; "in fact, if deprived of fish some of them would have nearly starved." It was the same with the other tribes.

It might not have been so hard on the Indians to have their fishing regulated had it not been for the dreadful conservation practices of the white farmers in the area. They saw only a land of plenty and apparently thought that the salmon were inexhaustible, for they took no care to see that the fish were used wisely. An old settler in the Puyallup Valley who spent his whole life near the Puyallup reservation described the common practice of the new farmers to use the salmon for fertilizer in their fields:

> At the headwaters of a short creek emptying into the Puyallup River, which in turn in a few miles poured its accumulated water into the tide water of Puget Sound, I have seen the salmon so numerous on the shoal water of the channel as to literally touch each other. It was utterly impossible to wade across without touching the fish. At certain seasons I have sent my team, accompanied by two armed men with pitchforks, to load up from the riffle for fertilizing the hop fields.

If we remember the very careful ceremony of the first salmon, which the tribes held with the first run of the fish to ensure the continual return of the salmon to the river, we can understand the heartbreak and resentment felt by the Indians who were being arrested for fishing while the white farmers were carelessly wasting the fish by using them for fertilizer.

Seeing these great injustices, the Indians organized to fight back, and over the years a number of organizations were created to bring the tribes together in a common fight against the fish and game departments. The result of these frequent clashes was that the state departments would often relax their efforts to arrest the Indian fishermen until a court case could be initiated that, everyone hoped, would settle the question once and for all. The state attorneys almost always attacked the treaty clause that gave the Indians the right to fish "in common" with the other citizens, claiming that the treaty only gave the Indians the same rights as everyone else. While the state might win the first hearing of the case in a state court, which viewed the arguments sympathetically, the state would lose when the case was appealed to the federal court, which normally followed the Indian understanding of the treaty.

But the Indians were not always successful in the federal courts. One of the most important movements in the 1920s saw all the tribes of the Point Elliott treaty area band together in a large claims suit against the government for failure to fulfill the treaty requirements. In those days, the idea of Indians suing the United States for failure to fulfill treaty obligations was a very new thing, and the tribes had to secure a special law from Congress in order to file their suit. The story of the tribes of the Pacific Northwest was well known in Congress, and it was hoped that the suit would settle all the questions concerning the treaty.

The case was finally decided in 1936, and the Indians did not receive any money for the loss of their lands. If the case did anything, it illustrated how differently the Indian and the white man had always looked at lands and ways of living. The court felt that the treaty was really just a contract to sell a tract of land and interpreted the document accordingly, insisting on the literal interpretation of the various words and phrases. The Indians understood the oral tradition their fathers and grand-fathers had passed down by word of mouth, and this tradition consisted of the promises Isaac Stevens had made that were by and large not recorded on paper at the time he spoke. The case was one of the first in which a group of Indians had gotten an opportunity to present their arguments. As a result, there was great confusion among the experts for both the Indians and the government about what documents and testimony really were essential to determine the meaning of the treaty. It was a mistake that the Indians would remember a generation later.

A happier note on treaties was recorded early in the twen-tieth century, when the descendants of the Chinooks on the Pacific Coast were able to get a congressional committee to review the old treaties signed by their grandfathers and Anson Dart. In 1906, the secretary of the interior was authorized to send an investigating committee to Oregon and Washington in order to interview the remaining Chinooks and determine how many people still lived in their old homelands. A consid-erable number were found, and the Congress made a special appropriation to compensate them for the failure of the United States to ratify their treaties.

Shortly after the Lower Chinooks received their payments on the 1851 treaties, their northern cousins who lived along the beaches of Washington were given allotments on the Quinault reservation in that state. The original reservation had been very small, because the Chinooks and the Cowlitz and other small villages had refused to sign a treaty with Isaac Stevens, and so there was no need to give the Quinaults and Quileutes, who had signed a treaty, a large reservation. But about thirty years after Stevens signed the treaty, at a time when the Bureau of Indian Affairs was busy establishing reservations and failing to notify its local agents, the Quinault reservation was greatly expanded, and Indian agents were ordered to encourage other tribes to settle at Taholah, the headquarters of the Quinault reservation. It was not until the 1920s that any serious movement rose to take up lands on the reservation, and many of the people from the scattered bands simply accepted allotments at Quinault and continued to live in the small beach communities where they had traditionally lived.

When the Great Depression swept across the country, the Indians of the Pacific Northwest reservations fared much better than their white neighbors. They had been used to living under the simplest of conditions, and fish had always been the mainstay of their diet. It was no hardship on them to live in the isolated reservation communities and continue to fish and dig clams. In fact, the government programs that were created as part of the New Deal effort to provide employment for the millions of Americans who were out of work proved quite compatible to the Indians of the Pacific Northwest. The most popular program was the Civilian Conservation Corps (CCC), and camps were set up on some of the reservations. Since the government could not refuse local Indians a chance to participate in the program, many Indians joined the CCC, and for the first time in reservation history, a steady employment program was made available to reservation residents.

Of much more importance during the depression years was the startling reversal of federal Indian policy. Ever since the reservations were established, the official policy had been to teach the Indians agriculture and ensure their eventual assimilation into local society. As we have seen, the constant intrusions of settlers on the reservations led to the creation of reservation councils and Indian police forces and eventually to the appointment of local Indian judges to govern the Indian communities. Thus, while the official policy was to stifle Indian self-government, in practice the Indian agent had no alternative but to help the Indians develop their own governments.

After the turn of the century the reduction of government employees meant a decline in the fortunes of reservation governments also. While the tribes had a local Indian agent, it was fairly easy to get his daily opinion on how things should operate, and people showed a great interest in developing their communities. But with the reservations lacking agents and decisions being made in remote places under the various consolidations that were taking place in the Bureau of Indian Affairs, people lost interest in reservation affairs and drifted away.

In 1934, President Roosevelt and Indian commissioner John Collier formulated a new Indian policy, which allowed the tribes to organize their reservations as federal corporations and govern the communities themselves. The law that made this policy possible was called the Indian Reorganization Act, or, more popularly, the Wheeler-Howard Act, after Senator Wheeler of Montana and Representative Howard, who sponsored the legislation.

A number of the smaller reservations accepted the Indian Reorganization Act and organized tribal governments under its provisions. The best part of the act was the provision that the secretary of the interior could purchase lands and give them to the tribes that had lost out during the previous decades, when it was federal policy to sell Indian lands. Although many of the smaller groups saw this provision as the best argument for accepting the act, they were to be disappointed. The intent of Congress had been to purchase lands for Indians in those parts of the country where lands were selling very cheaply and to restore those lands. When the policy was applied in the state of Washington, people quickly noted that the lands that could be purchased to add to the reservation holdings were very expensive, in some cases the acquisition of waterfront properties and other badly needed tracts of land costing more than the Bureau of Indian Affairs was able or willing to spend. In addition, local whites who were being forced to sell their lands because of difficult financial problems did not take kindly to having the government purchase their lands and give them to the Indians.

The Indians of the Pacific Northwest did not really benefit from the provisions of the Indian Reorganization Act as other tribes in the nation did. In fact, the act probably confused their legal status even more. The tribes who developed constitutions under the act were supposed to receive the same powers of self-government as the larger tribes in other states. But when the government refused to provide them with land over which they could govern, it created a difficult situation in which the tribal councils had all the powers of a state of the union but very tiny parcels of land over which to exercise these powers.

In spite of the difficulties in developing new governments, many of the reservations made great strides in the years before the Second World War. Local industries were started, and fishing activities increased tremendously, with some tribes starting small tribal fish markets where the Indian fishermen could sell their fish at a better price than they would have received from the local fish buyers. Different types of activities were started to raise funds for the tribal governments. Some tribes sold tribal fishing and hunting permits to outsiders to raise funds. When tribal courts were established, the income from fines levied in these courts were made available to the tribal governments. And probably most important, the developing community spirit of the reservations led to the establishment of fairs and powwows, which were used to raise money.

The Indian Reorganization Act allowed freedom of religion on the reservations for the first time since they were established. The first Indian agents had banned most of the old ceremonies, and the Indians had had to hold their most sacred ceremonies in secret or, as we have seen, under the pretense of celebrating the Fourth of July or other holidays celebrated by the whites.

Perhaps the biggest change before the Second World War was in education. People in the Bureau of Indian Affairs had always believed that Indians were good at working with their hands but that they could not be educated to perform administrative tasks that required a formal knowledge of American institutions. The Indian Reorganization Act gave Indians preference in employment in the Bureau of Indian Affairs, and it allowed tribes to give loans to their members for educational purposes. With this official encouragement, many Indians of the Pacific Northwest began to attend college. Others sought employment in the Bureau of Indian Affairs and began to work their way up in the civil service. For the first time in history the horizons of the people were raised above the local level, and they began to understand how the rest of the world lived and worked.

The Second World War practically devastated the Indian programs all across the nation. There were few government funds available to be spent on Indians, because of the war effort, and since many of the people moved to the cities to do war work and most of the young men joined the armed forces, the reservations appeared to be practically deserted. The only thing that the Bureau of Indian Affairs could do was to encourage Indians to participate in the war effort and keep a skeleton force working to sell lands and arrange timber leases. Victory gardens were encouraged, and Indian fishermen were not bothered, because they were busy providing food for the people as they had been for nearly a century and a half. The victory garden project was so successful that bureau employees tried to continue it after the war.

Following the war, when the Indian veterans returned to the reservations, they started many changes. One of the first things they did was to enter into community life and try to get the tribal governments back on the road to development that they had begun before the war. Almost every reservation had its local post of the American Legion or the Veterans of Foreign Wars, and these Indian posts took an active part in community development, sponsoring scout troops, youth programs, community fundraising projects, and beautification programs. Many of the Indian veterans had seen foreign countries and believed that they could build the reservations up the way other peoples were now building up their communities.

Eligibility for veterans' benefits enabled many of the Indian vets to start small businesses; fishing was the most popular. Before the war, few Indians had done more than fish in their traditional manner with a canoe or nets. Now they began to purchase deepwater boats that could compete with non-Indian fishermen in large catches. By the end of the 1940s, dozens of Indians were in commercial fishing, thanks to loans from their veterans benefits, and long voyages along the seacoast to Alaska and California to catch salmon and tuna were not uncommon.

By the 1950s, most Indians lived in the same manner as did the whites of the area. Most of them had moved away from their reservations and now held industrial jobs in the cities or in small towns, particularly in airplane manufacturing, a major industry in Washington State. The few people living on the reservations mostly fished or ran small farms and remained very traditional in their attitudes toward life. They continued many of the customs of their ancestors and looked with some suspicion at the Indians who had moved away from the reservations.

The people who lived in the large cities, while they did have jobs and were determined to make a success of their new lives as city dwellers, developed a great nostalgia for the reservation. They missed the community gatherings and the slower and friendlier way of living on the reservations. In the cities it was difficult for relatives to visit them, and with jobs they often had to miss the old celebrations they had enjoyed at home. To cure their loneliness, they traveled home as often as possible and often visited other reservations for celebrations in order to enjoy the few hours of Indian life they provided. The result of such extensive visiting was that the Indians got to know each other again, and the isolation that the different reservations had often felt in the old days gradually faded as they were able to travel. In many ways, the Indians went back to their pre-white days, when people spent a great deal of time traveling back and forth visiting.

In the 1950s, the salmon catches began to decline rapidly. There was little realistic control over the fishing industry, and the new techniques for catching fish meant that there were fewer and fewer fish returning to the spawning grounds each year. Like a ghost out of the past, the old controversy over fishing rights began to heat up again. By the midfifties the Indian commercial fishermen could no longer compete in the deep waters because of the cost of fishing boats. A good fishing boat cost about $125,000, and even with a series of good seasons behind him an Indian fisherman simply did not have the income to purchase the better equipment, so most of the Indians returned to their canoes and nets along the rivers.

With an increasing number of Indians now fishing in their traditional river sites, the state fish and game wardens became determined to gain jurisdiction over Indian fishing. They claimed that the Indians were ruining their conservation programs by fishing on the traditional fishing grounds without supervision. In 1947, the state legislature had designated the steelhead trout as a game fish, and this meant that it could not be sold commercially, like salmon. There was little controversy at first over the designation, but as more and more white sportsmen began fishing for steelhead and more Indians were forced to return to the rivers, serious conflicts broke out.

The states of Washington, Idaho, and Oregon made a concentrated effort to force Indians to purchase state fishing licenses, and arrests were made of Indians for fishing without state licenses. When these cases began to be decided by the higher state and federal courts, the old arguments over the phrase "fishing in common with other citizens" became the most hotly debated words since "Fifty-four forty or Fight." By the beginning of the 1960s, the Indians were determined to fight to the death for fishing rights, and since they were so scattered around the Puget Sound area and shared so many things in common, fishing became the great issue on which all Indians agreed.

Sentiment gathered rapidly in the late 1950s as the Indi-ans watched the civil rights movement make impressive gains in the South. Younger Indians began to speak out at Indian meetings urging the older people to engage in similar protest movements to clarify the treaty rights once and for all. Since everything was moving toward a general Indian protest in the Pacific Northwest, the actions of the game wardens only fueled the fires of resentment that were burning among the Indians. In the next chapter, we shall see how the fish-in came about and what that accomplished. It is enough here to note that the idea of self-government, which had been planted in the depression years and had always been alive among the people since before the coming of the Americans, was now a mature idea in the minds of the Indians of the Puget Sound area.

CHAPTER THIRTEEN

▲ ▲ ▲ ▲ ▲ ▲ ▲ ▲

As we have seen previously, there seemed to be continuous conflict between state officials in the fish and game department and the Indians of the various reservations over fishing rights. It was almost a standard rule that Indians would lose in the state courts but would win when they appealed their case to higher, federal courts. Thus it was that state officers devised a special strategy for dealing with the Indian fishermen. They would arrest the fishermen and confiscate their nets, knowing that if the Indian fishermen were without their nets or boats during the short time of the salmon run on their river, the effect would be to stop Indian fishing altogether.

As the decade of the 1960s opened, more and more Indians were appealing their cases and the state had to devise a different strategy to prevent them from fishing. At first the technique was to refuse to return the confiscated fishing gear under the theory that it was forfeited to the state simply because the Indian was arrested. Since the fishing gear often cost several hundred dollars, one arrest in a fishing season would put the Indian fisherman out of business until he could find a job and save the money needed to purchase new equipment. As the Indian determination to fish grew stronger, the favorite technique was to use such brutality in making the arrest that the Indian could be charged with resisting arrest, and the charge of fishing, which the state was sure to lose, would not even have to be filed.

Tensions grew rapidly on the rivers of lower Puget Sound as more and more Indians resented the unfair tactics of the state fish and game officers; and as Indian resistance grew, the state also grew more oppressive. In October of 1963, the state obtained an injunction against the Indians to prevent them from fishing in the Green River, and in January 1964, Pierce County Superior Court issued an injunction against the Nisquallies, closing that river below the Nisqually reservation, where most of the Indians had moved following the confiscation of their reservation during the First World War.

Where other tribes might have flinched at the opponents, the Nisquallies, who had fought one war against the United States to preserve their fishing, promptly organized a group called the Survival of American Indians, dedicated to fighting any encroachments on their off-reservation fishing rights. Modeling their tactics somewhat after the civil rights movement in the South, the Indians had a fish-in early in 1964 to protest the actions of the state. They felt that with publicity, their story could be told to the public and the state would be forced to back down and stop its attempts to get Indian fishing banned on the two rivers.

The fish-in did attract attention, and in March actor Marlon Brando, who had been active in civil rights marches in the South, arrived in Washington State to participate in a demonstration in Olympia, the state capital. Brando and a Nisqually paddled out into the river in plain sight of the state game officials and lowered a net into the river. They were promptly arrested for illegal fishing, but, as the Indians figured, this arrest created problems for the state. Every day that Brando would spend in jail would mean national publicity for the fish-in and the possibility of more people coming to help the Indians. So a legal technicality was created and the state dropped the case against Brando in an effort to escape the publicity he was bringing to the fishing-rights issue.

The organizer of the fish-in was a very talented Indian teenager, Hank Adams, an Assiniboin Indian who had grown up on the Quinault reservation on the Pacific coast of Washington. Hank moved into a leadership role in Survival of American Indians several years later and was to prove more than a match for both state and federal lawyers. In 1964, however, Hank was so young that most experienced Indians in the fishing-rights struggle did not know him; nor did they see, as he did, the need for developing contacts with policymakers in Washington, DC, in order to get the fishing-rights problem taken seriously by federal officials. Hank went to Washington, DC, and began visiting the offices of senators and congressmen, asking them to introduce legislation to preserve fishing rights.

Senator Warren Magnuson of Washington introduced two resolutions in the US Senate designed to solve the fishing-rights problem. Senate Joint Resolution 170 would have recognized the Indian treaty rights, but it provided that the state could regulate the off-reservation fishing, while Senate Joint Resolution 171 would have made the United States purchase all off-reservation fishing rights for a cash settlement. Magnuson held hearings in Washington in August 1964, and members of most of the tribes of the Pacific Northwest appeared at the hearings, as did the fish and game departments of Washington, Idaho, and Oregon. The states, of course, were content with the idea of the federal government's purchasing the Indian fishing rights, but the Indians protested so vigorously that both resolutions were allowed to die in committee.

While the tribes of Washington, Oregon, and Idaho all had treaty fishing rights, the struggle quickly resolved itself to one between the State of Washington and the Puyallup, Nisqually, and Muckleshoot tribes over the steelhead run on the Puyallup, Nisqually, and Green rivers in February and March of each year. Other tribes in other states might get an occasional arrest by state officers, but the struggle centered in the Tacoma-Olympia area with the smallest tribes in the area. The state departments carefully avoided any confrontations with the larger tribes, such as the Yakimas, who lived east of the Cascades and kept a very capable lawyer on call to handle their problems. The Nisquallies and Puyallups had no lawyers and no funds for lawyers, and so they were natural victims.

In February 1965, a group of Nisquallies and Puyallups sent a Petition for Action to the US attorney general asking for his assistance in a case then being conducted. They called his attention to a federal statute that reads: "In all states and territories where there are reservations or allotted Indians the United States attorney shall represent them in all suits of law and in equity." But the Justice Department refused to assist the Indians, with the excuse that it had not helped them in the past in this area, even though many previous cases, including the *Winans* case, clearly indicated the opposite.

The Indians went to the state capitol at Olympia again that February, but the demonstration attracted fewer people and it appeared as if some of the Indians were getting tired of the struggle. October 1965 saw the most violent confrontation of the conflict. The Indians at Frank's Landing were fishing in the river across from Fort Lewis when a boat of game wardens attacked them and spilled them from their boat into the water. Fights broke out, and several nights later the state game officers attempted a night raid on Frank's Landing, which was federal trust property, a clear violation of federal statutes.

On October 13, the Indians announced that they would fish under their treaty, and the resulting publicity drew an unusual number of well-wishers and state officials to the landing. When the Indians put a canoe into the water, the state officers charged and a desperate battle ensued. The Indians used paddles, sticks, and stones while the state officers, outnumbering the Indians nearly five to one, had large clubs. Women and children were beaten, and the men, aware that the game wardens probably had snipers hidden in the bushes, put up a token fight, afraid of being assassinated from ambush. The Indians were arrested, and on the October 26 the Survival of American Indians Association marched in protest at the federal courthouse in Seattle.

The following spring, Dick Gregory, the black entertainer deeply committed to human rights, arrived to assist the Survival people. He was arrested while participating in the fish-ins, convicted of illegal fishing, and jailed. Gregory served his sentence in the Thurston County jail, where he conducted a hunger strike. This incident gave the Indians a much needed boost in morale, for despite the fact that he was needed so

badly by his own people in the South, Gregory had nonetheless come up to Washington to help the Nisquallies.

By mid-1966, the Indians, under the leadership of Hank
Adams, had learned a great many things about fighting the
state and federal officials. They carefully researched the status
of Frank's Landing and were able to show that it was in fact a
legally constituted part of the reservation under the act confiscating the Nisqually lands. They pointed out that there were
about 4,500 non-Indian commercial fishermen taking about
80 percent of the salmon in the sound and offshore before the
Indians even got a chance to fish and that there were 187,525
steelhead cards issued to non-Indians and 140,375 fishermen actually out fishing. When the public saw these figures
and realized that fewer than a thousand Indians fished in the
whole state and not more than a couple of hundred fished the
three controversial rivers, public opinion began to shift.

In March 1966, the Muckleshoot tribal council approved
a fish-in designed to establish a test case. Four Muckleshoots
gill-netted salmon in the Green River near Neeley's Bridge, a
traditional fishing site. They were arrested and convicted in
court and appealed the case. The Indians were granted a retrial
in January 1968, and the United States, which was halfheart-
edly trying to appear as the defender of Indian rights, hired
Ms. Barbara Lane of Victoria, British Columbia, as an expert
witness in anthropology to testify on the treaty rights of the
Muckleshoots.

The Indians had never enjoyed the services of a scholar
to help them prove their case, while the government thinking
was that an anthropologist would make it seem as if the United
States was fulfilling its treaty responsibilities. Federal officials,
not really expecting Barbara Lane to discover anything new,
were content that the Indians' accusation that they had failed
to do their duty would be easily squashed.

But it turned out that Barbara Lane was a first-class scholar,
who could spend endless hours in obscure research just to
check a source of information. When she got on the stand in
the retrial in King County Superior Court, a revolutionary

change occurred in the fishing-rights struggle. Citing sources of impeccable origin, she calmly reviewed the history of the treaty and informed the court that the Muckleshoots were indeed treaty Indians and that the intent of the treaty was to preserve all traditional fishing sites for the Indians. The rest has become Indian history. Barbara Lane has been recognized as the leading authority on the Pacific Northwest Indians and has testified in numerous cases, always finding additional materials to make the Indian case even stronger.

The Indian case was hardly won, however, because the two major cases, those involving the Puyallups and the Nisquallies, had by this time reached the Supreme Court of the United States, and in June the Court announced its decision. The Court was unanimous in finding that the state had jurisdiction over off-reservation fishing. Justice Douglas's opinion, comparing the prosecution of Indians for off-reservation fishing to the prosecution of Indians for crime committed outside the reservation, was so confusing that even state officials complained that they did not know how to enforce the ruling. In essence, the Court ruled that Indians had off-reservation rights and that the state could regulate them but not in a discriminatory manner.

The first action by the state officials was to return to Frank's Landing in an effort to test the Supreme Court decision or at least to obtain a situation in which they could get another court to expand that ruling. But the Nisquallies maintained that Frank's Landing was protected by a federal trust and that the state therefore had no right to arrest anyone there. State officers patrolled the river around Frank's Landing, and it was apparent that a confrontation was imminent. In a well-publicized Citizen's Letter to His Governor, Hank Adams informed the governor that the Nisquallies were armed and would resist the game wardens. "The Armed Guards are under specific instructions to use weapons ONLY to prevent the specific actions by State enforcement officers to (1) trespass upon this property for the purpose of making an arrest or serving a state-issued warrant of arrest; and (2) trespassing for the purpose of confiscating the fishing net emplaced in the river off Frank's Landing and affixed to it," Adams wrote.

"If State enforcement officers attempt to proceed upon the Property of Frank's Landing after being warned against trespass," the letter continued, ". . . the weapon will be used against the trespassers. Likewise, if the net is emplaced in the water off Frank's Landing, the weapon will be used against any State officer placing a hand upon that net." "The weapon" was the one gun the Nisquallies proposed to use against the state officers. They preferred to restrict their use of arms to one identifiable weapon in order to prevent the state officers from maintaining that all the Indians were using guns and giving them an excuse to shoot up the landing. A bloody confrontation was avoided when the state knew the Indians were serious.

By the fall of 1969, the state had eased off quite a bit from its former hardline stand against the Indians. The Department of Fisheries allowed an off-reservation Nisqually fishery to exist near the reservation but carefully excluded the people at Frank's Landing in partial punishment for their resistance. But the people at Frank's Landing carried guns and fished anyway.

The big confrontation occurred the following year at a fishing camp near Tacoma on the old Puyallup reservation. A large number of Indians were fishing near a railroad bridge when they were surrounded and brutally beaten and arrested. Their cars and personal property were confiscated, and many cars were destroyed by vandalism while in police hands. The brutality against the Indians was incredible; nearly six hundred state officers participated in the "great Tacoma bust." A Chicano girl, Dolores Varela, took pictures of the police brutality and carefully hid the film when she was searched, thus providing evidence that the police had simply brutalized the Indians.

I happened to be in New York City the week after the "bust" and had an opportunity to be a guest on the *Dick Cavett Show*. Dick very graciously allowed me a full half hour to show pictures of the incident. The public outcry was immediate and proved a great embarrassment to the Nixon administration. Federal officials promptly announced that they had filed a major lawsuit against the state of Washington to protect the Indian treaty fishing rights but that the publicity from the Tacoma "bust" had not influenced them at all! They were planning to do so anyway, White House spokesmen asserted, and the timing was just a coincidence.

At any rate, the suit *United States v. Washington* was filed in federal district court in Washington. The state used its best lawyers, and the federal government had a fairly competent set of attorneys for the first time. But the Indians also had Barbara Lane as their expert witness, and by this time she knew more about the treaty than any of the lawyers on either side. The case took about three years to hear. Judge George Boldt, who heard the case, began the hearings on a note of ridicule, implying that the Indians' ability to present any rational basis for their interpretation of the treaty was remote at best. But the judge changed his mind as more evidence was presented, and in the end he found that the Indians did indeed have treaty rights to fish and suggested that an allocation of one half of the fish to the Indians might be a fair division of the resource.

While the Boldt decision, as it is called, is very unpopular in the Pacific Northwest, it is a faithful rendering of the law based upon the best evidence made available to the court. It is doubtful if any future case on fishing rights will see such a mass of evidence put forward in support of a legal question. Under the decision, the tribal governments have the duty of policing their traditional fishing sites and of drawing up a tribal fishing code that would indicate an ability to cope with the very complex problems involved.

Perhaps the only sour note on this greatest of all Indian legal victories has been the response of the Interior Department, the people committed by federal law to act as the protector of the Indians. After the Tacoma bust, Hank Adams discovered that the Bureau of Indian Affairs people had told the Tacoma police they had the right to arrest the Indian fishermen and, in fact, encouraged them to do whatever was necessary to prevent the Indians from fishing. The bureau hastily backtracked when the publicity of the bust proved so embarrassing to the government.

Following the Boldt decision, the tribes asked for federal funds to assist them in developing tribal codes and ordinances for carrying out their responsibilities under the decision. Although nearly $600,000 was allocated by Congress to assist the Indians in fulfilling their responsibilities as outlined by Judge Boldt, the money was very slow in coming, and Hank Adams tried to find out why the Interior Department was not carrying out its task of helping the Indians get organized. Adams discovered that the Interior officials had planned to see that the money went to Washington State agencies rather than to the tribes!

The fishing-rights struggle continues today, and headlines in the State of Washington are filled with the angry protests of sportsmen and commercial fishermen who feel that the Boldt decision is robbing them of income and recreation. The Indians are angry because they sincerely want to carry out a regional program of conservation and supervised fishing rights under the new responsibilities they have been given. But the Bureau of Indian Affairs, which has responsibility to help the Indians, continues to do everything in its power to prevent the tribes from acting and to foment conflict between the Indians and the sportsmen.

River net fishing has not been the only struggle of Indians in the Pacific Northwest in recent years. As part of their program to raise funds for court costs, the people at Frank's Landing began a program of selling cigarettes on their allotment. Under the Medicine Creek treaty provisions, the Indians agreed to cease their trade with Vancouver Island, and Hank Adams interpreted this phrase to mean that aside from trading with the British there were no other controls imposed on Indian commerce by the treaty. So the Nisquallies purchased cigarettes in Oregon and transported them to Washington, free of Washington State tax, for resale to anyone who would drive to the landing.

The state tax officials responded in the same manner as had the game wardens. Trucks carrying the cigarettes into the state were confiscated and sold, while the people were harassed frequently by tax officials. The irony of the situation was that there were several military reservations in the state (including the infamous Fort Lewis) where people could purchase tax-free cigarettes, and therefore when the state argued that it should have taxing power over federal reservations, it was not simply attacking the Indians but was attempting to tax the military posts also. The military personnel found themselves being used against the Indians in the fishing-rights struggle and in the same boat with the Indians when it came to purchasing items free of state tax.

The Indians solved the problem in a very clever manner by using the giant federal bureaucracy against itself. Realizing that it was also federal law that no one could confiscate the US mail, the people at Frank's Landing simply mailed large cartons of cigarettes to themselves to be delivered at Frank's Landing. The cigarettes were insured, of course, and the moment they were delivered at Frank's Landing they were leaving the hands of federal employees and being unloaded on federal trust property. The state had no chance to intervene in what was really an all-federal operation, and so today the Nisquallies at Frank's Landing have a nice cigarette store where they make a comfortable income with which to pay for new nets, lawyers, and other luxuries they have never had.

No one knows how long the struggle between the State of Washington and the tribes of Puget Sound will last, but it certainly seems as if the state has finally met its match in this generation of Indians. The contest was unequal for so long, with merely a handful of Indians at Frank's Landing resisting the combined powers of both the State of Washington and the US government, that hardly anyone gave the Indians much of a chance to win. But they had a great determination that would have pleased old Chief Leschi no end, and when the smoke finally cleared they stood tall as the winners, with both state and federal people protesting that they had *always* been in favor of Indian rights.

CHAPTER FOURTEEN

▲ ▲ ▲ ▲ ▲ ▲ ▲ ▲

Not all the fishing activities of the Indians of the Pacific Northwest have involved the violence and legal complications that
the Nisquallies, Puyallups, and Muckleshoots have suffered.
The Lummis have used their treaty rights, preserved even in
the face of severe pressure by fish commissioner Darwin earlier
in the century, and created one of the most unique experiments
in the United States: an aquaculture, the scientific farming of
seafood such as oysters, salmon, and trout.

You will recall that by the 1960s, about all the Lummis
had left of their original reservation established under the
Point Elliott treaty was the land that was exposed between
high and low tide. The rest had been sold by the Bureau of
Indian Affairs over the years to non-Indians, and only one
tract of land that bordered the bay remained in Indian hands
by 1968. You will recall that in late 1967, the Lummis were
approached by representatives of a corporation that wanted to
build a magnesium-oxide plant on Lummi Bay.

When news of the proposed plant was heard in Bellingham, Washington, people began to get concerned that the pol-
lution from the process of reducing the ore to metal would
ruin the fishing and recreation areas in Whatcom County. As
this concern spread, a fortunate meeting occurred between Dr.
Wallace Heath and some of the Lummis who were searching
for an alternative use for the bay. Heath is a most remarkable
person. Trained in desert ecology at the University of Arizona,
he was at that time teaching at Western Washington State College in Bellingham and was very involved in developing natural and ecologically sound uses for lands and waters.

Heath worked as a volunteer in his spare time for one of Whatcom County's ecological groups in planning a countywide program for the preservation of lands and waters. He visited the reservation and inquired why the Lummis were thinking of bringing the industry to their lands. The older and more traditional Lummis told him that they had been told there was no other use for such a freshwater bay. Heath knew a great deal about the old aquacultures of Hawaii, which the Natives had built in those islands centuries before the coming of the white man, and he suggested that the Lummis think about developing an aquaculture.

The idea of systematically raising salmon, oysters, clams, and trout appealed tremendously to the traditional Lummis. They had always been fishermen, and they wished to continue their traditions if at all possible. The next tribal meeting was flooded with the older people, who demanded that the idea of an aquaculture be given a chance. "After all," one of the elders said, "if it doesn't work we can always go ahead with the industry, but if the industry fails it will have ruined the waters forever and we can't do anything then." The tribe approved the idea of looking into the possibility of creating an aquaculture on Lummi Bay. They asked Dr. Heath to do some preliminary surveys on the bay to determine whether it would be feasible.

The State Oceanographic Commission gave the Lummis a grant of one thousand dollars to survey the aquatic life of the bay, and in the summer of 1968 Wally Heath and four Lummi teenagers donned their diving suits and charted out the contours and marine life of Lummi Bay. By fall they had determined that the bay was an ideal place to build an aquaculture. The tidelands could be converted into a large pool with just the right depth to allow a number of fish to grow, and it appeared that oysters could flourish in the large pond that would be created. The tides could be channeled into the pond every day by a gate regulating the flow of water, so the Lummis would not even have to pump water back and forth to create circulation.

The Lummis had learned over the years to be extremely careful in revealing their plans to the Bureau of Indian Affairs or the local whites, and so they first sought a clarification of their legal rights to the bay. Fortunately the previous summer Congresswoman Julia Butler Hansen of Washington had asked the regional solicitor of the Bureau of Indian Affairs to clarify the rights of Indians to control the waters of their reservations, and he had stated that they owned the waters and could control them. The opinion had originally been written to clarify the status of the lands and waters of the Quinault reservation on the coast, but it applied to all the tribes of the Puget Sound area.

Since this legal opinion had already been widely circulated in the state, there was no way that the Bureau of Indian Affairs could deny that the Lummis owned the tidelands, and so they were free to go ahead with their plans. Dr. Heath had many acquaintances in the field of aquaculture, and they began to visit the reservation at his urging. Dr. Victor Loosanoof, professor of marine biology at the University of the Pacific and one of the world's foremost shellfish experts, came to the reservation and gave suggestions. Charles Black, a San Francisco businessman and husband of Shirley Temple, had developed a project at Pescadero Bay in California to grow oysters. His advice also aided the Lummis.

Through the Oceanic Foundation and Drs. Tim Joyner and Anthony Novotny, fisheries biologists of the Bureau of Commercial Fisheries were brought to meet the Lummis, and Taylor Pryor, president of the foundation, did everything he could to assist the Lummis in recruiting the best minds possible. The experts were quite impressed when they saw what Dr. Heath and the young Lummis had done: they already had a 1,000-foot-square grid chart laid out on the bay, and by using this chart they could determine the exact acreage and water level of every part of the bay. Having received encouragement from the experts to proceed, they packed their bags and headed to Washington, DC, to see if they could get a grant from one of the federal agencies to build the project.

In February 1969, the Economic Development Administration gave the Lummis a grant of $143,220 to begin research and training on the aquaculture, and in June of that year the

Indian Desk of the Office of Economic Opportunity gave the tribe a grant of $300,000 to begin construction of a small oyster-, trout-, and salmon-raising pond of 4.4 acres. Hopes for success ran high. The problem was that none of the Lummis had ever done anything of this magnitude before, and experts in pond construction had predicted that they would have all kinds of difficulties in getting the pond finished.

But no one had reckoned with the determination of the Lummis to build their pond. Experts said that the Lummis should plan to get fifty feet of dike built every day, and if they succeeded in meeting that rigorous schedule they could feel proud of themselves. But the Lummis were risking everything on this project, and so they all turned out to work on the pond. They did everything from operating the heavy equipment to grabbing shovels and moving the dirt by hand when necessary. Before anyone knew it, the Lummis were building one hundred feet of dike a day—an incredible rate, considering their tools.

The pond was dedicated with a galaxy of movie stars, senators, and congressmen in attendance and was followed by a salmon bake and plenty of other seafood. The people began immediately to raise oysters and trout and salmon in their new pool. By this time most of the teenagers had fallen in love with the project, and they began making new plans for their careers. Many went back to schools they had left in disgust several years earlier and started studying harder than they had ever studied to learn about shellfish in order to work in the project when it was finished. The tribe had a special aquaculture class, which taught all about the fish and oysters, and many older Indians who had dropped out of school years before enrolled in the classes. Everyone wanted to learn. I visited several of the classes, and some older Indians who knew little English could catch a fish and dissect it and name every part of the fish in Latin!

The original plans of the Lummis were to proceed very cautiously and build a 220-acre pond after they had shown that the 4.4-acre pond could successfully be used to raise fish.

But the first results of the small pond were so outstanding that they decided to go ahead with a giant, 750-acre pond, which would put them into the commercial oyster and salmon market immediately. The 750-acre pond was a real challenge. It was one thing to close off less than five acres and raise several thousand salmon and oysters, but in a 750-acre pond they would be thinking in terms of hundreds of millions of salmon and oysters, and one change in temperature or sudden shift in the acidity of the water might destroy everything.

Another gigantic problem was simply building the pond. It was fairly easy to build a square pond of earth and rock dikes in the large bay, but building a 750-acre pond required closing most of the bay off. The tides were not bad on Lummi Bay, but as the dike was extended across the mouth of the bay, the area where the water could flow became narrower and narrower, and so the water rushed through this opening faster and faster. The dike would reach a point, after construction was nearly finished, when the tides would be so fast that they would carry away all the dirt that the people could place there in an eight-hour shift. At that point the Lummis would have to use the traditional method of closing a dike worked out centuries ago by the Dutch.

Even with all these problems apparent to them, the Lummis decided to go ahead with the larger pond, and in July 1970 the Economic Development Administration, impressed with what the tribe had accomplished already, granted them $1.5 million to build the large pond. The tribe began work immediately, very carefully using the grant to create additional jobs on the reservation. Since they needed gravel for the dike, they purchased a gravel-rich tract of 140 acres formerly belonging to the reservation, thereby cutting cost of materials. Nineteen Lummi men purchased gravel trucks of varying age and carried the gravel to the dike, avoiding the need for contracting the hauling job to a more expensive company.

In every way imaginable, the Lummis scrimped and saved because they realized that the cost of closing the dike would be so enormous that they would need every cent they had.

To save money, many of the Lummis would come out to the dike in their odd hours and volunteer their time, after having worked a full day on their other jobs. Even grandmothers and grandfathers found ways to contribute to the job, if only by bringing sandwiches and hot coffee to the people working on the night shift. Sometimes they simply came out to the dike to encourage the workers and look with pride on the great dike that was slowly creeping its way across the mouth of the bay.

The dike, about three miles long, extended from Sandy Point around the major part of the bay to a point on the shore where the small pond had been built. By late fall 1970, the Lummis were averaging more than two hundred feet of dike per day. This construction involved hauling tons and tons of rock for a base to the dike and thousands of tons of sand and gravel to fill in between the rocks and finally thousands of tons of dirt for the top of the dike. The width of the dike was approximately sixteen feet at the top and ninety feet at the base, while its height was about sixteen feet. Building the large pond was unquestionably a tremendous undertaking.

The Lummis worked all through the winter, and when spring came, the rains, which fall almost continuously in the Pacific Northwest, increased and hampered the work to a great extent. Yet whether it was rain or shine, the determined Lummis kept working.

By late May they were ready to discuss closing the dike, and they called on a Dutch expert to advise them on how to do it. He flew over from Holland, carefully surveyed the dike, and suggested that the Lummis use the traditional method in view of the tides, which, since they were now confined to a small area, became very harsh and powerful. The traditional method of closing a dike was to build a large breakwater in front of the opening and allow the tides to crash on the breakwater while the people quickly filled in behind it. He told the tribe that it would cost about $300,000 to close the dike—an amount the Lummis did not have.

Dave Hudson, one of the engineers who was helping to direct the project, came up with a novel idea that saved the day.

He had Lummi aqualung divers pin a sheet of polyvinyl filter cloth over the bottom of the entrance to the bay. He figured that when the tide came rushing in, it would hit the plastic sheet and press it down on the floor of the bay instead of acting as a big scoop and digging the sand out. The sheet, when it was finally attached, covered an area of nine acres! Of course there were many smaller pieces, about the size of half a football field, fastened together to form this bigger sheet, but placing this much plastic flat in a rushing tide, forty feet below the surface of the water, was quite an accomplishment, especially when one considers that some of the Lummi aqualung divers were only teenagers.

June 4, 1971, was chosen as the day to close the dike, and for weeks before the big event the Lummis worked night and day on the dike. They piled up gigantic piles of rock, sand, and gravel about a hundred yards from the edge so that on the day of closing they could simply move these monstrous piles with bulldozers into the opening. Every day, they saw the piles get larger and larger, but they realized that they had to close an opening some eight hundred feet wide in the deepest part of the bay without interruption.

Finally the great day came. Almost every member of the tribe turned out to work, from the smallest baby to the oldest grandparents. Twenty-seven dump trucks were brought to the dike, ready to charge to the gravel pit or to the place where they got their dirt. With ten giant earthmovers on the dike and several smaller bulldozers, the work was commenced. Working for thirty hours without stopping, the Lummis moved fifteen thousand cubic feet of rock, gravel, and earth into the opening in a frantic move to close the dike before it rained.

They finished, dead tired, seven hours before experts had predicted they would. The television stations had all been alerted to be at the dike at noon to film the closing of the dike. I was living in Bellingham at the time, and the Lummi leaders told me to be at the dike at noon to see the celebration. When we all got to the dike that morning, we were told that the Lummis had finished the closing at five and that everyone was at the picnic grounds celebrating. Not only had the Lummis finished the closing of the dike, but when I got out there at noon, one could not tell where they had filled in, because they had not merely closed the gap but had finished the task completely, including grading the sides.

With the large pond now finished, the Lummis had to build a number of breeding ponds to raise the fingerlings in. The tribe built a large trout-breeding pond at the foot of the Cascades near their old friend Mount Baker, where they could raise the trout to a respectable size before taking them in trucks down to the large pool. In the process of developing the trout hatchery and breeding pond, the Lummis discovered how to transform the trout from a freshwater fish to a saltwater fish. Using Donaldson trout as their test species, the Lummis showed that it is possible to get the trout accustomed to living in saltwater in a matter of three weeks. When the Economic Development Administration learned that they had made such a discovery, it encouraged them to keep the process a trade secret of the tribe, and it remains so today.

In August 1972, the Lummis completed a large oyster hatchery built in the style of a traditional cedar longhouse. The hatchery is completely modern and is designed to produce 100 million seed oysters a year, making it the largest producer (in relation to the money invested) in the world. When the fish hatchery is placed together with the oyster operations, the Lummis are capable of producing 10 million fingerlings and 100 million oysters every year—a tremendous amount of seafood by anyone's standards.

Everything did not go as smoothly as one would imagine in the development of the aquaculture, however, and the dissension was in part due to the Bureau of Indian Affairs. They had tried a great many development schemes at Lummi, and in 1967, the very year the Lummis began thinking about the aquaculture program, the Bureau of Indian Affairs let it be known that they had given up on the Lummis and would no longer try to help them with development. The bureau had strongly supported the industrial development behind the scenes and was further angered by the refusal of the Lummis to approve the project.

As the aquaculture program expanded, the tribe needed to make various changes in its constitution and bylaws. A dissident group of Lummis, a handful of people who had supported the magnesium-oxide plant, wanted a provision written into the tribal constitution enabling them to launch recall petitions against individual tribal councilmen until they gained control of the council. The bureau saw this constitutional change as a way to get control of the tribe once again and insisted that the tribal rolls be brought up to date before a vote on the constitution could be held.

It had been traditional in the Pacific Northwest for the off-reservation people to oppose reservation developments on the theory that tribal funds should be divided on an individual basis, and the bureau thought that by making every Lummi eligible for membership in the tribe, eligible to vote on the constitution, it could best support the group that was against the aquaculture. So bureau employees scurried around locating Lummis who had moved away from the reservation years before, and a campaign against the aquaculture began. But the tribal leaders were much more aware of Lummi opinion than the Bureau of Indian Affairs, and they took care to inform the off-reservation members of the opportunities that were being developed for all tribe members.

The off-reservation people were very impressed with the new aquaculture program, and many of them looked forward to the day when they could quit their jobs in the cities and return home to the reservation to work. When the vote on the constitution was finally held, the proaquaculture group swamped their opposition, the amendments to the tribal constitution were defeated, and the Bureau of Indian Affairs was left with a very embarrassed expression on its face. They had only succeeded in arousing a lot of interest, publicity, and support from off-reservation tribe members for the aquaculture project.

A much more dangerous group that fought the Lummis was the Lummi Bay Beach Association. It was made up of white property owners who owned lands along the beach. They had a great influence in the city of Bellingham and went to great lengths to criticize the aquaculture as a waste of money and a dangerous precedent in allowing uneducated Indians to run things. Their first major attack was issued prior to a hearing held by the US Army Corps of Engineers on the issuing of a license to the tribe to build the experimental pond.

Four petitions were sent to the army listing various reasons why the project should not be built. The problem was that about fifty-nine people had signed the four petitions over and over again, averaging nearly four signatures apiece. On one petition, five people signed three times each. They all accused the Lummis of trying to create a 2,200-acre pond that would harm wildlife and boating, although none could understand or explain how a pond designed to grow salmon, trout, and oysters scientifically could harm the wildlife.

Then a letter-writing campaign began that was truly incredible. Letters came from as far as Texas complaining about the aquaculture (although it was certain that the aquaculture would not affect property values in Texas). One letter writer accused the Lummis of deliberately placing oysters on the beach to cut the feet of trespassers, while others said that the project was a plot to cut off the wind. The chief accusation was that the fish would create a deadly smell that would stifle breathing.

When the hearing was actually held, the Lummi leaders took each and every complaint and patiently explained how the aquaculture would help improve rather than harm conditions. It was, of course, no contest, and the opposition made such fools of themselves that the army had no choice but to approve the permit. One of the most vocal opponents of the project was a graduate student at the college who wrote many letters against both the project and the Lummi leaders. After the large pool was authorized and the tribe had a large training grant from the Office of Economic Opportunity, he demanded a job from the Lummis as a counselor!

One of the best things that happened to the Lummis was their meeting with Christopher Blake, a playwright and noted gourmet cook. The Lummis were in Washington, DC, trying to get a grant, and they visited the National Press Club for lunch. They carried with them large posters illustrating the nature of their project, and since they had no place to put the posters while they ate, they simply propped them up in the lobby of the Press Club.

While visiting the club, Blake noticed the posters and asked where the Lummis were. They met over lunch, during which the Indians explained their project and their need for publicity in marketing their fish and oysters. Impressed, Blake returned home to New Orleans with a promise that the Lummis would send him samples of their products. Using these, he created several special new dishes and demonstrated them in the National Press Club and in an exclusive San Francisco restaurant.

With this very good publicity, the Lummis set about creating their own brand, which features a smiling Lummi on the label. They now ship and sell salmon and oysters all over the country. They have recently begun talks with Japanese businessmen about shipping seafoods to Japan under a special arrangement. Other tribes have copied the Lummis, and now several aquacultures are being planned by tribes of the area, and some inland tribes such as the Paiutes of Pyramid Lake, Nevada, are planning a freshwater-lake aquaculture.

Everyone is pleased that things have worked so well. And many people see a special providence in the aquaculture. When a tribe is reduced to owning only that land which is uncovered between high and low tides and still manages to turn that land into something very productive, it seems as though somebody up there is watching out for them.

CHAPTER FIFTEEN

▲ ▲ ▲ ▲ ▲ ▲ ▲ ▲

The Pacific Northwest today is a scene of great activity. Not only are tribes beginning to recapture old cultural values and traditions, but the conflict between the Indians and the whites is at a fever pitch because of the struggle over fishing rights. In the past ten years, through the persistent efforts of such people as Hank Adams, the Indians have been able to present a fully documented story of their deprivation in the courts, and as judges have heard the amazing stories of federal and state oppression of Indians, court decisions have turned around to favor the tribes.

In 1970, as we have seen, the federal government was finally forced to sue the state of Washington because of the massive bad publicity coming out of the arrests at Tacoma. The case, known as *United States v. Washington*, dragged out for more than three years and was finally decided favorably for the Indians. The evidence was so overwhelming that even the judge, who began the case with an anti-Indian attitude, concluded that the Indians, under treaty, were entitled to half of the fish harvested in the waters of the state each year.

While the United States seemed to be supporting the tribes, it turned out that once again the Indians were being deprived of their rights by their federal trustees. Primarily through the hard work of Indian lobbyists, a sum of $600,000 was appropriated by the Congress to assist the tribes in developing their own tribal rules and regulations for controlling fishing by Indians. But after the money had been appropriated, the tribes waited months for the Interior Department to consult with them about how the funds were to be allocated.

They discovered that the Department of the Interior was stalling while trying to figure out a way to give the money to the Washington fish and game departments. Thus, once again, the victory of the tribes in the courts and Congress was being taken away from them by behind-the-scenes manipulations of the Interior Department.

It was not the first time in recent years that the Interior Department had blatantly violated federal laws. In the late 1940s, the Bureau of Indian Affairs signed timber-cutting contracts on two gigantic tracts on the Quinault reservation. The Quinaults have the last good stand of western red cedar left on the coast, and with the lumber market in good condition and the quality of Quinault cedar so high, the larger trees are *each* worth between $10,000 and $15,000.

Over the years, the Bureau of Indian Affairs has refused to police the manner in which the timber companies are cutting the timber. They have assigned one person to supervise the timber cutting; he arrives on the reservation in the middle of the morning and spends a leisurely day, returning to his office in time to go home at 4:30 PM. Cutting of the timber begins at seven o'clock in the morning and often continues until dark. There is no accounting of the amount of timber cut in the hours when the bureau employee is not present or of what happens to the logs once they are cut. There is presently a lawsuit filed against the United States contending that the manner in which the bureau supervises the harvesting of Quinault timber leads to many practices that deprive Indians of a significant amount of income.

In 1970, the tribe began a new fish-hatchery program and was using the freshwater streams on the reservation as spawning places for the salmon. But the logging companies in their harvesting of timber destroyed a great many of the gravel beds necessary as spawning places. They had made it a practice to cut almost everything on the different tracts of forest land and were clear-cutting the Quinault lands, in direct violation of a federal law prohibiting clear-cutting of timber on an Indian reservation.

By the fall of 1971, things were clearly out of hand. The forest was being totally destroyed, and no replanting was being done even though the Bureau of Indian Affairs was collecting 10 percent of the income from the timber for a reforestation program. And the salmon spawning beds were being rapidly destroyed by the giant machines used in cutting the timber. So the Quinaults blockaded the logging roads leading off the reservation, demanding that something be done about the situation. Two old cars were dragged across the narrow bridge connecting the timberlands and the state highway, and when the county police officials tried to serve a summons on the Quinaults, the vice-chairman of the tribe, Joe Delacruz, took an ax and chopped the summons in two.

The Interior Department, worried that things were becoming troublesome, promised to send out a special task force to discuss the problem. A selected group of bureaucrats arrived at the reservation and talked with Indians and lumber company people alike. When the Quinaults pointed out the damage to their fishing program and the federal prohibition against clear-cutting their forest, they were told that the federal government only had a *moral* duty to preserve the forest, not a *legal* duty, even though it was clearly written in the Code of Federal Regulations that it was illegal to clear-cut Indian timber. In spite of the obvious liability that present practices seem to be creating, the Bureau of Indian Affairs has still not stopped the bad cutting practices, and the fish program remains in jeopardy because of the destruction of the spawning grounds. It seems as if only an act of God will be able to prevent the Bureau of Indian Affairs from supervising the final destruction of the Quinault reservation.

Activism seems so romantic: people visualize a heroic young Indian fighting the forces of destruction against almost impossible odds, always overcoming because his cause is right. But the Indians of the Pacific Northwest learned long ago that there is a great deal of danger and very little romance in their struggle. In January of 1971, Hank Adams and another Indian were checking the Nisqually fishing nets early one morning along the Nisqually River. While the other Indian walked along the riverbank, Hank fell asleep in the back of his car. Suddenly the door was opened, and as Hank raised his head sleepily a voice shouted, "This will teach you damn Indians."

A rifle barrel came into view, and as Hank tried to clear his head the rifle was fired point-blank at him. The bullet passed completely through his body and through the car door on the other side. Some white sportsmen had ambushed him! Hank was rushed to the hospital and, after emergency surgery, recovered. When he complained to the police about his near-fatal visitation from the two ambushers, the police called him a liar and demanded that he take a lie-detector test. They accused him of shooting himself in order to get publicity!

Hank refused to take a lie-detector test unless he was allowed to have an outside witness present who could testify to the results of the test. He figured that the police would simply change the results of the test and tell the newspapers, most of which were writing anti-Indian stories, that Hank had shot himself. When the police learned that they would have to have an outside witness observe the test, they refused to give it.

As far as can be determined, Hank Adams is the only Indian who has been ambushed by sportsmen because of the fishing-rights struggle. But there have been other incidents nearly as disturbing. In 1973, the Washington National Guard, while on summer maneuvers at Fort Lewis, used the Nisquallies as their theoretical enemy, and war games were played that involved an invasion and extermination of the Nisqually tribe. When the Indians discovered that they were the subjects of the summer frolic, they protested to state officials, who gave a very lame excuse about Indians being too sensitive. Later the Nisquallies discovered that the Department of Game was keeping files on their personal lives to determine how they could best control the Nisquallies.

The fishing-rights struggle will probably continue for the rest of the century or as long as the Indians have the strength to continue it. Considering that most of the tribes have been fishing for centuries in the same places they are fishing today, it seems unlikely that they will abandon their traditional life within the foreseeable future. The pity is that the odds are so heavily against the Indians. Whites, particularly sportsmen, blame the decline of fish on the Indians and completely overlook the effects of the great power-generating dams and the many heavy industries that pollute the river. Even the public doesn't seem to realize that there are so few Indians who actually do fish that even if they were to fish day and night all year long, they would not make much impact on the total number of fish.

In 1974, under the new decision of Judge Boldt, which allowed the Indians to catch their share of the fish, state officials went out of their way to juggle the figures of fish catches in an effort to show that Indian fishing was destroying the catch. The catch of fish seemed to be greatly declining as a result of Indian fishing, and Governor Dan Evans asked President Ford to declare the salmon industry a major disaster area, apparently in an effort to gain a favorable political image among sportsmen. Everyone was busy accusing the Indians of ruining the fishing industry until Mike Moyer, the director of planning for the Swinomish tribe, began to recite hard facts and figures about the 1974 catch.

The total Indian catch in 1974 was up 5 percent from the previous year, but the total was still only 12 percent of the total number of fish caught in the state. The reason why there had been such bad fishing was that the number of days allowed to fishermen had been reduced. But in spite of the reduction in the number of days on which whites were allowed to fish, 1974 was the second-greatest year on record for the salmon industry. State departments in charge of selling fishing licenses had deliberately oversold the number of licenses so that each fisherman would feel that he was being deprived of his livelihood because of the lower number of fishing days allowed.

In 1974 the purse-seine licenses increased from 330 to 437, a 32 percent increase. Gill-net licenses increased from 1,303 to 1,988, a 53 percent increase. Moyer pointed out that in the Skagit River alone fifteen thousand coho salmon were allowed to escape capture and return up the river to spawn instead of the usual five thousand. So from every angle except superficial statistics, 1974 was a good year for fishing, particularly for the salmon industry, and there were a record number of fish allowed to return to their spawning grounds.

By bringing out statistics, the Indians were able to show that, far from ruining the salmon industry, they were hardly catching many more than they had always caught but that the state officials had ensured that many more fishermen than usual would fish fewer days than usual and would return home from their fishing discontented and mad at the Indians. The fishing-rights struggle seems to be one in which Indians continuously have to fight not only state and federal officials who are violating federal laws but the people who figure statistics, to prevent them from creating an artificial situation in which no one is ever sure what the facts are.

Since about 1967, the smaller tribes in the Puget Sound area have organized a group called Small Tribes of Western Washington, or STOWW, to present their case before the government and the public. The founding president, Roy George, a Nooksack, built a strong, politically active organization that exerted great influence among the Indian tribes of the country, and his successor, Leo LeClair, a Muckleshoot, has concentrated on the development of good programs that are designed to serve the many small Indian communities in the area. While STOWW has concentrated so far on political organization and program development, there is every indication that economic development programs built on the fishing rights of the different tribes will eventually bring all the tribes together.

From a widely scattered grouping of villages to the modern organizations of today, the Indians of the Pacific Northwest have made great political strides in learning how to come together for a common purpose. While some parts of their old culture have vanished, they have discovered new things to replace them, and with the Lummis and the Quinaults taking the lead in the development of aquacultures, the future shows a much greater promise than the past has delivered.

As the other tribes finally develop their fishing resources, there are plans to create a regional Indian label for sale of canned fish products, and one day you may be in the neighborhood supermarket and see a smiling Indian on the label of a can of salmon. You will know from his smile that things are still pretty exciting in the Pacific Northwest.

AFTERWORD

▲ ▲ ▲ ▲ ▲ ▲ ▲ ▲

STEVE PAVLIK

Vine Deloria Jr.'s *Indians of the Pacific Northwest* was originally published in 1977 and remains the classic and authoritative one-volume Native history of this region. This book focuses mostly on the tribes of western Washington's Puget Sound—the body of water now officially known as the Salish Sea. Since that time, much has happened with the tribes in this region, enough so that an entire book can and should be dedicated to this topic. For the purpose of this afterword, however, I will focus on only a few areas that have been of most importance to tribal people: the successful struggle to finally secure inherent fishing rights, the ongoing campaign to restore the salmon, the emergence and rapid growth of Indian gaming and economic development, educational self-determination and general school improvement, and the revitalization of tribal culture.

Vine concluded his discussion of fishing rights with *United States v. Washington*—the famous Boldt decision, which in 1974 reaffirmed the inherent right of the tribes to fish at the "usual and accustomed" places but, more controversially for most Washingtonians at the time, allotted 50 percent of the annual amount of harvestable salmon to tribes. As Deloria predicted, this federal district court decision handed down by the conservative judge George H. Boldt—one of the most thoroughly researched and comprehensive decisions in the history of American jurisprudence—did not end the fishing controversy. The State of Washington, led by their fiery state attorney general

Slade Gorton, openly defied the court's ruling on the grounds that it was so radical it would most certainly be overturned by a higher court. Gorton was wrong. The Ninth Circuit Court of Appeals upheld the Boldt decision, and soon afterward the US Supreme Court refused to review the case. The state responded by simply refusing to enforce the decision. At this point, Judge Bolt lost his patience with the State of Washington and declared that the federal government would take over control of fishing law enforcement. The legality of this drastic action was also upheld by an appellate court. The state continued to encourage its commercial and sport fishing groups to file lawsuits, and the resulting chaos eventually forced the US Supreme Court to once again take up—for the seventh time—the issue of Northwest Indian fishing rights. On July 2, 1979, in *Washington State Commercial Passenger Fishing Vessel Association v. Washington*, the highest court in the land upheld the entirety of the Boldt decision in a 6–3 decision. After three-quarters of a century of litigation, the State of Washington was finally forced to acknowledge tribal fishing rights. The Boldt decision served to usher in the era of scientific fish management. No longer could the state make unsubstantiated claims that tribal fishing was depleting the resource. It also brought tribes to the table as comanagers of fish and other natural resources. In 1974, the Northwest Indian Fisheries Commission was formed to allow treaty tribes to collectively organize and implement their own fish management efforts. Billy Frank Jr.—the iconic symbol of the Northwest Indian fishing rights movement—has served as the director of this organization since 1975. Although the treaty tribes found it necessary to return to the courts and to the Boldt decision once more, in 1999, to win their inherent right to harvest shellfish, relations between the tribes and the state have greatly improved, and today the two entities engage, if often times uneasily, in cooperative fish management.

While the fishing wars had come to a close, the campaign to save the salmon has just begun. More than a century of commercial overfishing and the degradation of habitat have combined to drastically reduce natural salmon runs to only a small fraction of their historical abundance. In recent years it has become difficult, if not impossible, for tribal members to make a living as full-time fishermen. The Northwest Indian Fisheries Commission and its twenty member tribes have led the way in attempting to preserve the few remaining runs of wild salmon while intelligently reintroducing hatchery-raised fish into the ecosystem. Washington State tribes now operate more than forty fish hatcheries and other facilities that produce and release back into the wild more than 35 million salmon each year. But despite the best efforts of tribes and others, salmon populations continue to decline. The key to salmon conservation is habitat restoration. Salmon are anadromous fish, meaning their life cycle includes a time period spent at sea before they return to freshwater rivers to spawn. Urban expansion, river-choking dams, unsound logging practices, poisonous runoff from industries and farms that pollute both rivers and oceans, the effects of climate change, and a multitude of other factors have all combined to destroy salmon habitat. In 2007, tribes again successfully invoked the Boldt decision to force the state to begin removing the hundreds of culverts that had impeded the return of salmon to their spawning grounds for decades. Tribes have also lobbied successfully for the removal of outdated hydroelectric and recreational dams that have produced sediment and debris detrimental to the production of salmon. In 2011, the Elwha River Dam was the first to be removed—largely through the lobbying efforts of the Lower Elwha tribe—and allowed that river to flow free for the first time in one hundred years. Other dams have been targeted for removal, and it is believed that this trend will hopefully contribute to salmon restoration on impacted rivers.

Fishing rights and the restoration of salmon are issues that are synonymous with tribal sovereignty. For tribes in the Pacific Northwest, treaty rights mean little if there are no fish to catch. In 2011, the treaty tribes of western Washington came together to produce a major report entitled *Treaty Rights at Risk: Ongoing Habitat Loss, the Decline of the Salmon Resource, and Recommendations for Change*. In this paper, the tribes have called for greater federal leadership, intervention, and direct action to protect and restore salmon habitat and, consequently, for the government to uphold tribal treaty rights.

In general, Northwest coast tribes continue to rely heavily on natural resources. With the decline of salmon populations, it has become extremely difficult. In addition to fishing, a number of tribes, particularly those on the Olympic Peninsula, possess considerable timber resources. For these tribes, the Intertribal Timber Council, a national organization founded in 1974, effectively plays the same role as the Northwest Indian Fisheries Commission does for fishing tribes. Currently, the Quinault, Tulalip, and Makah Nations are the three largest tribal timber producers in the region.

In 1987, the Supreme Court decision *California v. Cabazon Band of Mission Indians* acknowledged gaming to be an inherent right of tribal sovereignty and thus opened the door to casinos springing up throughout Indian Country. Nowhere was this emerging wave of Indian gaming facilities more apparent than in the Pacific Northwest. In Washington State there are now twenty-two tribes operating twenty-seven casinos, generating $1.6 billion in 2010. The vast majority of these casinos are located in western Washington and especially along the Interstate 5 corridor connecting Portland, Oregon, with Vancouver, British Columbia. Many of these casinos have evolved into resort facilities and vacation destinations for people living in the larger Northwest urban areas. In addition to gaming, many offer first-class entertainment and several have even expanded to include golf courses. Revenues from casinos have dramatically changed the economic reality for many tribes. Tribes have used casino monies to benefit their people in numerous ways, mostly in improving the quality of health and education. From immunization to diabetes prevention, from school retention programs to college scholarships, casino revenues have greatly enhanced the standard of living for thousands of tribal people in the Northwest. Casino monies have also been used to enhance housing, police and fire protection, and numerous other programs. In addition, the State of Washington has also benefited greatly from Indian gaming by having .5 percent of all machine revenues given to various statewide charitable organizations. In recent years, this has amounted to about $5 million annually. In addition, casino monies have also given tribes and tribal people more disposable income—much of which also benefits the state businesses and tax revenue. A 2010 study by the Harvard Program on Economics reported that tribes were growing "economic engines" that conservatively contributed almost $3.5 billion to the Washington State economy. Most of this money was casino generated.

Another benefit of casino revenue is that it has allowed tribes to become important political players in both state and federal politics for the first time. The Washington State Indian Gaming Commission and a number of individual tribes, for example, have been able to support candidates at both the state and federal levels who share tribal views on issues like social welfare, human rights, and especially the environment. In addition, a number of tribes are now able to afford full-time lobbyists in Olympia and Washington, DC.

Other than the casino industry, economic development that benefits individual tribal members on the reservation continues to be insufficient, and unemployment levels remain high. Some tribes are beginning to invest casino revenues into economic development and creating small business opportunities, but much more needs to be done. Tax-free tobacco and fireworks sales bring in some money, but this income is rather marginal or seasonal at best.

Educational achievement levels among Native Americans in Washington State remain dismally below the national average compared to non-Native students. But definite improvement has been recorded in terms of reducing the high-school dropout rate and increasing graduation numbers. In addition, the establishment of a number of tribally run schools is also a promising development. The number of Northwest Native students attending and graduating from mainstream colleges and universities, although still relatively low, has also shown steady improvement. Undoubtedly the most important development in

Indian education over the past several decades has been growth
of the tribal college system. The Lummi Indian School of Aquaculture was founded in 1973 and then was chartered in 1983
as Lummi Indian College—a two-year school granting associate degrees. In 1988, the institution recognized a broader man-
date to serve all Northwest tribes and was renamed Northwest
Indian College. Today, Northwest Indian College, in addition to
offering numerous associate degrees, offers two fully accredited
bachelor's degrees—one in Native American studies, the other
in Native environmental science. In all, the college provides
academic courses to more than twelve hundred students from
more than one hundred tribes at its main campus in Lummi
and its seven satellite campuses.

Since the 1970s, a cultural revitalization movement has
also swept the Northwest. This movement has manifested
itself in a number of ways. Not surprisingly, most Northwest
tribes have sought to renew their ancestral ties to the salmon.
Many tribes, for example, have brought back First Salmon ceremonies, which honor the return of this fish to tribal waters.
Traditional tribal arts such as wood carving, the weaving
of cedar into hats and other items, have also experienced a
renaissance. The Coast Salish Institute at Northwest Indian
College and a number of tribally run schools have dedicated
themselves to preserving and teaching their languages and the
cultural values that have long sustained their people. The most
spectacular cultural effort can be seen in the annual canoe
journeys that take place each summer. This event began in
1989, when nine traditional cedar dugout canoes—eight from
Washington and one from Bella Bella, British Columbia, Canada—participated in the Paddle to Seattle, making the journey
from to their tribal communities to the Port of Seattle to participate, somewhat ironically, in the one hundredth anniversary of Washington statehood. In the years since, this event
has grown to nearly a hundred traditional oceangoing canoes
from indigenous nations, from as far north as Alaska and the
Queen Charlotte Islands and as far south as Oregon, paddling
to a common destination, most often a host nation among the

Coast Salish people. The journey itself may last two or three weeks for some tribes traveling from some of the more northern points of origin.

One of the more controversial issues in terms of cultural restoration has been the efforts of the Makah Nation to bring back whaling—a practice that has literally defined the Makah people since time immemorial. The 1855 Makah Treaty very specifically acknowledged the right of this tribe to hunt whales. As in the case of salmon, commercial non-Native whaling drove most whale species to the brink of extinction by the 1920s, and the Makah voluntarily ceased hunting the gray whales, which had traditionally sustained the tribe. Strict conservation efforts brought back whale populations, and in 1994 the gray whale was removed from the endangered species list. When the Makah sought to renew their whale hunting tradition on a very limited basis—with support from the federal government and the International Whaling Commission—they met with fierce opposition from some Washington State officials and various environmental groups. The issue has twice reached the Ninth Circuit Court, in *Metcalf v. Daley* (2000) and *Anderson v. Evans* (2002). Although both cases acknowledged the right of the Makah to hunt whales, they delayed any such hunts until such time the Makah submit satisfactory environmental assessments—a condition widely viewed by the tribe as a simple delay tactic used by whaling opponents. It remains unclear at this time what the ultimate outcome of this issue will be.

For tribes, the restoration of culture as manifested in language, ceremony, arts, and, in the case of the Makah, the right to whale is not simply a matter of window dressing but rather a matter of survival. When a culture disappears, a people disappears with it. Most reservations in the Northwest face serious social problems, especially among their most precious resource, the youth. There seems little doubt that problems such as gang membership and the rapidly increasing use of illegal drugs among Native youth is a direct result of alienation from their cultural heritage. Saving the youth begins with saving the culture. Saving the culture begins with saving the environment.

One final issue to be considered is the status and place of urban Indians. As with Indian Country in general, the majority—more than 60 percent—of tribal people in the Pacific Northwest live in cities. In Washington State, there are more than thirty thousand Native people living in the Seattle-Olympia area alone. Many of these Native people are from Northwest tribal communities. Some can trace their urban existence back to the devastating termination policy and relocation program of the 1950s and 1960s. Others moved to cities later simply because of the lack of economic opportunity back on their home reservations. How to deal with these displaced relatives—what rights and privileges should be afforded them—promises to be one of the most important issues that must be addressed in the future.

For the Indian tribes of the Pacific Northwest it has always been—and will always be—about survival. Since the first moment of contact, they have been forced to endure efforts to dispossess them of their land and deny them their inherent sovereign rights as a people. They have withstood assaults against their language, spiritual beliefs, and identity. And in recent years, they have been forced to fight for the very land and especially the salmon that has always given them life. Throughout it all, they have survived. They have always been here and will always remain the original and true inhabitants of the Salish Sea region.

INDEX

▲ ▲ ▲ ▲ ▲ ▲ ▲ ▲

ABOUT THE AUTHOR

▲ ▲ ▲ ▲ ▲ ▲ ▲ ▲

Vine Deloria Jr. was named by *Time* magazine as one of the greatest religious thinkers of the twentieth century. He was a leading Native American scholar whose research, writings, and teachings on history, law, religion, and political science have not only changed the face of Indian Country but stand to influence future generations of Native and non-Native Americans alike. He authored many acclaimed books, including *God Is Red.*

SP

Praise for Liza Cody

"Add Liza Cody's name to that remarkably long list of British women who have a special flair for turning out stylish, literate mysteries."   —*Washington Post*

"Electric with suspense, fast and funny ..."   —*Publisher's Weekly*

"A tour de force."   —*Los Angeles Times*

"Cody's writing is so lively that one can only throw in the towel and revel in her sure-footed blend of realism and comic fantasy."
                    —*Times Literary Supplement*

"One of the best conceived and beautifully drawn characters in modern crime fiction."   —*Mystery News*

"... one of those characters, like Salinger's Holden Caulfield or Morrison's Sethe, whose voices are so rich they create a whole world out of a few sentences."
                    —*Maureen Corrigan, National Public Radio*

"Ferocious stuff ... Exceedingly funny ... Truthful too."
                    —*Literary Review*

"It's like a rock-and-roll version of *Pilgrim's Progress*."
                    —*Philadelphia Inquirer*

Gimme More
LIZA CODY

BLOODY BRITS PRESS
Ann Arbor and Alnmouth
2009

Bloody Brits Press
PO Box 3671
Ann Arbor MI 48106-3671

BLOODY BRITS PRESS FIRST EDITION
First Printing October 2009

First published in Great Britain in 2000 by Bloomsbury Publishing plc

Printed in the United States of Amerrica on acid-free paper

Cover designer: Bonnie Liss (Phoenix Graphics)

Bloody Brits Press is an imprint of Bywater Books

ISBN 978-1-932859-65-2

Mixed Sources

Product group from well-managed
forests and other controlled sources
www.fsc.org Cert no. SW-COC-002283
© 1996 Forest Stewardship Council

FSC

Bitchcraft

"She's a kindhearted woman,
she studies evil all the time."

Robert Johnson

I am the bitch who puts her bags on the empty seat beside her. If you want to sit next to me, you have to ask my permission. Even when I'm traveling scuzz-class. Especially when I'm traveling scuzz-class.

The train was hot and crowded. Coats were rolled like loft insulation in the luggage racks. Frayed and fractious children squawked. Weary travelers tried to blank them out. I had the scuzz-class blues.

We waited. It would be a few minutes before the doors closed and after the initial scramble, anxious lethargy blanketed the train.

"Um, 'scuse me."

I looked up into a pale twitchy face.

"I'm in a jam," he said. "Can you help me out?"

I pulled off my headphones. "Depends," I said.

" 'Cos me an' my wife we're really in a jam," he said. "We've got to get to London and I ain't got any money. See, my social security check didn't turn up and we got on the train without a ticket."

He was talking very fast, looking over his shoulder and sweating.

"And the ticket inspector's coming and we'll be chucked off and fined. And we've got to get to London to see our little kiddy who's in hospital. At the children's hospital. She's very sick."

I tried to look down the carriage to see where the inspector was, but the man was blocking my view and I couldn't even see his wife.

"It's only ten quid," he said. "Each. Twenty quid. I wouldn't ask, but I'm really desperate. You'll get it back. My social worker's meeting us at Paddington. So you'll get it back in fifteen minutes. Twenty quid for fifteen minutes. What d'you say? I'm really sorry I got to ask, but the inspector's on his way and we're so desperate."

He wasn't giving me time to think. I smiled at him slowly.

3

"Please," he said, sweating, twitching. "Can you help me?"

"OK," I said.

"Jesus, thank you," he said, holding his hand out. "Only twenty quid."

"Calm down," I said. "Why don't you and your wife take a seat?"

"The money," he said, hand still outstretched, fingers shaking.

"I'll take care of the inspector when he comes. He'll take a credit card."

"Will he?" he said. "Oh, right. I'll fetch the wife."

And off he went, so quickly that he didn't catch my most helpful sympathetic smile. What a waste.

I craned my head round the back of my seat and saw him approach another woman farther down the carriage. He was still talking very fast, sweating, twitching, nervous. Not his wife, then.

It's none of my business how a man makes a living, but this woman was trying to keep two small children under control, and there aren't many who make the effort. She already had her hand in her handbag and I thought: effort should be rewarded, not punished. Maybe the man's effort should be rewarded too, but not by a woman with two small children who still has kindness to spare for a stranger.

I got up and walked toward them, still wearing my most helpful, sympathetic smile. I tapped the man on the shoulder.

"How're you doing?" I asked.

"Shit," he said. "Why don't you fuck off and mind your own business?"

I didn't say anything. I just smiled at him.

"Fuck!" he said. He ran down the carriage and jumped out onto the platform.

The shuttle lurched and started off slowly.

"What was all that about?" the mother asked.

We passed the twitchy man, still standing on the platform. He saw us watching and gave us his middle finger. Three times. Hard.

"Was he conning me?"

"Yes."

"How do you know?"

"I offered to pay for him by plastic," I said. "He doesn't want a ticket. He wants cash."

"Oh," she said, blushing.

I went back to my seat, thinking about the blush. The mother was

4

embarrassed because a man had marked her out, seen her weakness and exploited it. Probably everyone she knew exploited her kindness—her husband, her children, her friends as well as strangers.

As for the twitchy man—well, he wasn't a very good hustler. He had some things right. Speed, not giving your mark time to think, social embarrassment, they're all good strategies. But the sick kiddy was crude. He should have worked harder on a less plausible story because a less plausible story is more likely to be believed. You have to be imaginative and articulate if you want to be a successful hustler. Or pretty and charming. You have to be able to reward your victim one way or another.

They don't call them *confidence* tricks for nothing. A good scam is based on a relationship, even if it only lasts for thirty seconds. Your mark has to *want* to give you something. And to be a good scammer you should want to give them something back.

I used to have long legs, long hair, long eyelashes, and dewy youth. I was willing to share them with strangers, even for the price of a train ticket. I looked fabulous and I didn't have to pay for anything. Why? Because people wanted to be seen with me, if only for thirty seconds. I looked like a reward for a rock star. If you top the chart with your latest album, you deserve someone looking like me to swish into clubs with. It's expected. I'm part of the package.

I mean I *was* part of the package. Not any more. Dewy youth, nowadays, is not what I have to offer. And when did you last see a superstar of my generation swishing into a hot club with a woman his own age on his arm?

The shuttle rolled into Paddington. The mother collected coats, bags, children, the pushchair, and unloaded them. No one stopped to help her. Not even me. I'd saved her twenty quid—that was my good deed for the day.

But as I overtook her she said, "I should have thanked you, but I was too confused."

"That's OK," I said, moving on, not wanting to be caught.

"No, really," she said. "I'd have forked out twenty pounds like a lamb and it's more than I can afford."

"I know," I said, backing away, suddenly distressed.

5

"So thank you."

Her toddler son gave me a blindingly sweet smile and silently offered his packet of crisps.

I took one. If a man wants to give you something, take it. Even if it's a potato crisp and he's only three years old. It's what he's got to give.

That is a scammer's skill. It's a judgment you make almost instantly. What will your mark part with happily? Set the right price and you're halfway home.

Mr. Twitch set my price at twenty quid; the same price he set for a harassed mother. That was the cause of my distress. It was comforting to remember that he was a very crude scammer and presumably incapable of fine judgment, but it was, all the same, a bad jolt to my confidence.

Twenty pounds, Mr. Twitch? That's your price, not mine. Not for this girl. Not even now. I don't live on a fixed income and I don't spend my days with only two rowdy toddlers for company. Although, sometimes, when I meet one with a blindingly sweet smile, I do wonder what I missed.

But that's just sentimentality. Blindingly sweet smiles come two-a-penny. I had one myself, and I used it mercilessly.

A smile is a mask. Mr. Twitch used a different mask. His was a furrowed brow, anxiety. But he was too nervous. He couldn't control the sweat, and that's because he didn't believe. You have to believe in your mask to control it—like I believe in smiles and tears and the power of a song.

Once, when I was very young, I was scammed myself by a song, a smile, and a tear. A legendary bluesman called Dude Dexxy convinced me that he wrote "Honey Crawl" on the spot when I walked into Crawdaddies one summer night. I'd blagged my way past the doorman—I was underage—and I was standing, uncertain, not knowing where to hide, when this deep, dark voice from the stage said, "Hey, little girl. You. Yeah, you. Come close. This one's for you." Me. He noticed me. I went to the stage and literallly sat at his feet while he played "Honey Crawl" and the crowd went crazy. I was too green and ignorant to know that he wrote it ten years previously and it was his groove number for pulling dumb little chicks. I just sat there with bass and drums vibrating through my body, with Dexxy's voice seeping through my ears to my heart until I felt I'd burst.

I didn't know he'd done time in a Louisiana jail for screwing and stealing from underage girls. A lot of them. Nobody told me his European tour was as much to escape the Feds as it was to feed London's hunger for legendary bluesmen.

He told me he'd been in jail, but when he told me, later that night, I believed it was something to do with racial persecution. And so it was—in a way. A good scammer manipulates truth with a light touch; the same way Dexxy manipulated me.

The odd thing is that I still feel proud that he picked me out as his mark, that he noticed *my* weakness. Even when he'd gone, taking my heart and a fat wad of my dad's money with him, when I understood I'd fallen for a sleazy line, when I knew "Honey Crawl" was an old song, I still felt a thrill. Because it's a great song and, one time, a legendary bluesman sang it to pull me. He set me on a path of my own, because by the time he left I was part of the legend: underage, leggy, wild child who had been touched by a god and burned. There were so many musicians, who wanted to be gods themselves, who wanted to touch the girl who'd been burned by a genuine, gold-card, legendary bluesman.

Dexxy burned me, but he showed me my métier. There was no doubt that I'd sat at the feet of a master. I was his mark and I was marked by it. He showed me that anyone can be made to believe anything, and that I too *want* to believe. Nobody is immune—and that includes you, babe.

Somewhere, in my inexperienced little brain, something clicked and I asked myself—Do you want to be a mark all your life? Or do you want to wear the mask and make 'em pay? Because youth and beauty is a ready-made mask. If you are young and beautiful, everyone wants a piece of you anyway. So why not make them pay? Why give away for free what time will erase? You only have it for a short while, so use it.

CR CR CR

7

But that was then. This is now. What is my mask now that youth and beauty are no longer mine to use?

Let me show you. But you must attend because I'm only going to do this once and I'm going to do it fast.

Right in front of Paddington station is the Great Western Hotel. Climb a few stairs, push through glass doors, cross the lounge, slide into the ladies' room. Check the cubicles. All empty. Remove coat. Check mirror. I am wearing a simple long-sleeved, navy blue dress, low-heeled shoes, dark stockings, light makeup. I look like a respectable working woman.

I hide my coat and bag under the counter. Carrying only a magazine, I leave the ladies' room and walk purposefully through the hotel lounge. I put the magazine down on one of the coffee tables, turn right again, and go into the dining room.

It's lunch time and very crowded. I am looking for someone who is already there. I make that obvious, and none of the restaurant staff stops me.

I take in the whole room. I look right, left. Someone is waiting. I don't know who she is, but she's here, and she must show herself quickly because I haven't got long.

There she is—wearing the smart business suit of middle management. She's with two younger women, she's tapping her credit card on the tablecloth, looking round for a server, still talking to her companions who are finishing their coffee.

I'm looking for her, I'm joining her. I smile at a waiter as I make my way over to her table. He can see I'm meeting someone. He can see I have a purpose. He doesn't stop me.

I arrive at the woman's table. I stand at her left-hand side, exactly where she expects to see me.

I say, "Can I bring you anything else, ma'am?"

"Just the bill," she says, hardly looking up.

"Are you in a hurry?" I say. "Shall I take your card?"

She offers me her credit card. I remove it smoothly from her fingers and walk away—out of the dining room, through the hotel lounge, into the ladies' room. I put on my coat. I take a bright Liberty's scarf from my bag and wind it casually round my throat.

I throw my bag over my shoulder. I leave the hotel. I snag a taxi.

This incident took longer to relate than it did to execute.

What sort of mask was that? In fact, there were three. When I was in the lounge, carrying a magazine, I was a hotel resident. When I went into the dining room, I was one diner looking for another. When I spoke to the woman, I was a waitress. The trick is that waitresses do not carry handbags but hotel residents do. The magazine stood in for a handbag. On an unconscious level, people recognize what your function is by what you wear, how you act, what you are or are not carrying. The mask, therefore, is whatever your mark expects to see. It doesn't matter if it is glossy hair and a beautiful face or a business-like, polite demeanor—the same rules apply.

I changed my shoes in the taxi. I changed my scarf, my hairstyle, my lipstick, and my polite demeanor. Little things—all of which tell you that the simple navy blue dress may be understated but it is extremely expensive. It would keep a mother and two kids in chicken nuggets for years. Or it would have done when I first took possession of it. But that was a few years ago.

I needed something hot and new for my next appointment and I don't believe in buying my own clothes—not when a bank or a credit company can buy them for me. In other words, I don't believe in using my own credit card. Spending my own money on clothes is a sign of failure. Besides, nowadays, I need to spend a lot of money to look like someone worth spending money on.

My next appointment was with a man called Barry, who has a lot of money to spend. I hadn't seen him for years, and in those days he wanted me so much he dribbled.

But those were the days when I did not have mature reflection to bring to a situation. I have maturity in spades now, and reflection tells me that I should not have taken his drool personally. My mark, Barry, is an Englishman and, as such, he was far more interested in my lover than he was in me. He wanted me because he admired to the point of obsession the man who had me. Barry was a rich hanger-on. A sucker for talent and glamour, he was our satellite, always creeping close, like a lizard drawn to a hot rock. He needed heat but couldn't generate any for himself.

Yes, my mark is a reptile and I am the heat. He wants what he always wanted—which is to be at the center of a charmed circle; though the charm wore out a long time ago, the magic turned against itself, and a third of the magicians are now gone. Including my lover, my playmate, golden Jack.

Jack is the one everyone remembers. Jack is the one who defines me. He gives me an identity, even now. Oh yes, I owe everything to Jack. I am Jack's survivor—his rock-widow.

So I need a rock-widow's frock: something dark, mysterious, and tragic. Plus shoes to show off the legs, because legs last longer than faces and should attract the attention they deserve. Unbelievable fuck-off shoes, with a hint of S-M. I want to clothe myself in mystery from head to hem, in decadence from hem to heel. A good mask, like a good hustler, should touch the truth lightly and pass on by. A good hustler should use a stolen credit card quickly and throw it away. Card, discard, and move on.

Shopping done, I checked in at the Savoy, where the receptionist delivered a hand-written note. The note read,

> Dear Birdie, I do hope you'll be comfortable here. Old memories, eh? Please, <u>ring me as soon as you get in.</u> Can't wait to see you— Barry.

I said, "If a Mr. Barry Stears rings, would you tell him that I'll meet him here at eight? I don't want to be disturbed till then."

"I'll make a note of it," the receptionist said.

I went upstairs. I ran a bath. I remembered Barry and his character-istic anxiety. "Ring me as soon as you get in." Underlined. Fat chance. I remembered Barry who had to eat his last meal of the day by 7:30 or his ulcer grumbled. I smiled. Both of us, so far, were running true to form.

I bathed. I lay down. I rested. At seven, I ordered a fresh crab salad from room service. I began to dress. The salad came and I ate it. I did not want to be hungry or look hungry.

At eight, the phone rang. I ignored it. It rang again at quarter past, at half past, and at a quarter to nine.

At nine, I went down. Heads turned. Did you think they wouldn't? Why? It is too easy to assume when you've passed the celebrity-girlfriend stage that you're invisible. But invisibility is only a different sort of mask. If it isn't a convenience, bag it and bin it. Be Someone. Don't just enter—sweep in.

I swept. Heads turned.

Here is Barry, a plump chump in a Savile Row suit. He thinks designer spectacles will make him look hipper.

He says, "Birdie! My God ..." He has been expecting me to apologize for making him wait. I can see that on his face. His face changes as his expectations change. He is off-balance already.

"Hi, Barry," I say, as if I last saw him yesterday. "Where are you taking me?"

"I thought we'd eat here." He has obviously been keeping the *maître d'* sweet for the last hour.

"Don't you know the *good* places any more?"

He rises to the challenge and we go to the Café D'Arte.

So far, so good. I can still make him want to impress me.

You have to be a bitch to force a man to impress you. Being nice does not get you a room at the Savoy or the wherewithal to look utterly cool at the Café D'Arte. It never did and it never will.

Whatever Barry was expecting, it was not a nice woman. A nice woman does not take the piss out of you to your face or even behind your back. A nice woman does not kick you in the balls when, after a couple of lines for courage, you pluck up enough spunk to dribble into her *bustier*. She does not say to her starry boyfriend, "Hey Jack, queer Stears just tried to hit on me."

"Kick him in the balls," said Jack.

"Again?" I said.

"Whatever turns you on," said Jack. He laughed, but the next day he chartered a plane and we went to Antigua. "Fuckin' rich groupies," said Jack. "They think they own you."

He didn't like it. He thought I had a thing about rich men, and I let him. It kept him on his toes, kept him hungry.

As I swept into Café D'Arte, David Bowie was sweeping out. He came to a dead halt and his satellites piled up behind him.

11

"Birdie Walker! Jesus—I thought you were dead."

"Dead to the world," I said, "exclusive, reclusive, elusive. There's a difference, you know."

"I *do* know," he said. "Call me."

I sweep on by. What a piece of luck! Barry is weeing himself—he's with a woman who knows David Bowie. That's Barry in a nutshell.

We sit. We order. Barry would like to ask for a glass of milk for his ulcer. I watch the struggle between common sense and narcissism. Narcissism wins—as it always did—and he orders wine. It is an important indicator.

I am very casual. I scope the room. Barry tries to gain my attention by pointing out the hot new writers, a sculptor, a singer, assorted socialites, a couple of MPs and bankers.

"You've been out of touch for so long," he says.

"Being here reminds me why," I say.

"It's changed."

"Three times, at least."

"Yes," he says, "but it's all coming back. You wouldn't believe the interest the present generation's showing in the old music. *Our* music."

I look at him. He has enough grace to blush, but he goes on quickly, "I told you in my letter, I've done a book, and a couple of series for the BBC and Channel 4."

He waits for me to approve. I raise one eyebrow. Old groupies don'tdie. They turn into music nerds.

"They went down very well," he says hurriedly, "rave reviews, et cetera. People can't get enough."

Food comes: soup for him, a decorative arrangement based on an artichoke for me. He begins to gobble his soup. Good. I can spin out an artichoke forever. I can make him ravenous.

He says, "Of course, Jack and several others of the people you—er—knew were central to my programs. You were in there too—that old footage of the Dock Concert, Live at the Hall, other stuff. And the pictures Bailey took. Birdie, you were the quintessential rock chick."

"Was I *really*?" I say. Does he honestly think that being called a rock chick will appeal to my vanity? Yes, he does. He has made a career out of his own sideline association with musos, so he must think we are made of the same stuff.

He has finished his soup. I suck delicately on the end of an artichoke leaf. He goes on. "I'm a bit of a celebrity myself, now; a pundit, whatever." He watches me eat.

"Why didn't you get in touch, Birdie?" he says. "You knew I was looking for you two years ago. I talked to your sister and all I got was the big block."

Always the wrong question. You shouldn't be asking why I haven't been in touch for two years, Barry, you should be asking why I'm in touch now.

"Where have you been, Birdie?"

"Fishing."

"Fishing?" says Barry, astonished.

I nod and select another artichoke leaf.

"I thought you'd be married to a millionaire by now."

"Why?"

"Why?" He's astonished again. He has never questioned his judgment of me. He says simply, "Because you loved spending money."

Now this is true, but if that were all there was to it, Barry, why was I fucking Jack and not you? At the beginning, certainly, you could have bought and sold Jack and the whole band twenty times over.

"You're right," I say. "I still love spending money. I'm very good at it."

"And have you got enough now?" This, to Barry, is the central element of his pitch. Because, if you haven't figured it out already, Barry is pitching to me. It is why a man I once kicked in the balls is paying for me to stay at the Savoy instead of dropping me down the deepest hole he can find.

"If I remember correctly," he says, "enough for you is a *lot*."

"Absolutely correct, Barry," I say, and I take my time choosing an artichoke leaf. It's painful for him to watch. His stomach hurts and he wants his second course. It's driving him crazy, watching me picking fastidiously at an intricate vegetable. Good. He will come to the point more quickly because he will believe that if he does, he will be controlling the situation. Hunger and impatience are my friends but his enemies.

13

"So, how *are* you doing these days, Birdie?"

"What you see is what you get," I say, secure behind my obscenely expensive frock and fuck-off shoes: the frock and shoes he hadn't expected to see on someone who has been off the scene for so long.

"Shine like silver, ring like gold," I say.

"What?"

But I shrug and don'texplain. It's a song: "Take This Hammer." Taj Mahal used to sing it and one night I told Jack, "Your hammer 'sure 'nuff shine like silver, ring like solid gold.'" He liked that. He picked out the chords till he could play it for me. I lived for those moments. God, he was good, and when he wasn't off his face, he surely did shine like silver, ring like gold. Alone, for once, and quiet, listening to old recordings by legendary bluesmen, picking out chords, riffs and fills, putting a new spin on them, making them his own. That's how the great songs pass from old to young hands, from old to young ears. Old love to new love, nothing starts from scratch. But you, Barry, you can sit and watch me eat artichoke till the angels weep and I won'ttell you anything important. Because you won'tunderstand the important things. A great song isn't safe in *your* hands.

Barry says, "You're an expensive woman, Birdie. You cost Jack a fortune."

"Yes," I say. "And worth every penny."

"Well, Jack seemed to think so."

Oh yes, indeed he did, Barry, and you'll never understand why.

"What I'm getting at, Birdie, is that maybe, these days, you don't have quite what you were used to."

"That's true," I say, scraping the flesh off another petal. "However much there is, it's never enough."

"I'm in a position to help you," Barry says, smugly. "I can put you back on the map, Birdie."

"Where I've always longed to be," I say. "Another fifteen minutes of fame."

"Don't tell me you didn't love it," Barry says. "You lapped up all the attention. There was a time when you couldn't open a paper or magazine without seeing your own face. Don't tell me you wouldn't want that again."

14

"Even the bad bits?" I say. "Besides, that was a different face. Who'd want to see it now?"

"You'd be surprised," he says. "I'm telling you, everyone's fascinated by the old rock aristocracy. Roots, genealogy—they can't get enough."

He pauses. He's pitching, but he doesn't know how to hook me. I wait, eating tiny particles of food, making his stomach rumble.

"The episode about Jack's era was a huge success. I got Teddy and Goff—they had some terrific stories. But I wish you'd responded when I tried to find you because there was something missing. In those years—those truly great years—you and Jack were joined at the hip. You were there in all the footage and all the stills. But not in person, not in the where-are-they-now section. The guys were great but . . ."

"Music's a very blokish business," I say. "All you need is a couple of guys."

"Wouldn't you like to redress the balance?"

"There isn't a balance."

He looks at me, he looks at the artichoke. It isn't even half eaten.

"There's money in it, Birdie," he says. "Money for old rope. I'm making a compilation program for the anniversary. It's devoted exclusively to Jack. Maximum budget. I can get you top whack."

"Not interested," I say.

"A memorial," he says. "Aren't you interested in keeping Jack's memory alive?"

"His memory's very much alive without me making an exhibition of myself for your benefit."

"You wouldn't be making an exhibition of yourself," Barry says. "And it'd be for Jack's benefit."

"The dead don't need benefits."

He glares at the artichoke. It's his personal enemy, and so am I. A waiter comes and asks if we're ready for the next course.

"Yes," says Barry.

"No," I say, because every time I say no, my price goes up, and Barry is becoming twitchy. Two Mr. Twitches in one day—how lucky can a girl get?

"OK, Birdie," he says, "final offer: if appearance money won't do, I can negotiate production fees."

"Oh yeah?" I say. "What would I have to do for that?"

"Nothing. Really. You get a credit, more money. No work, no hassle. Just show up. Supply some of the material—for which you'll be paid handsomely—we do the interview . . ."

"Material," I say.

He drags his eyes away from my plate and forces himself to meet my gaze. My eyes should be bland and blue. His aren't. I smile my sweetest smile. His cheek flickers.

"I told you I talked to Teddy and Goff," he says. "They say the Antigua Movie exists."

"Do they now?"

"Everyone said the Antigua Movie was the biggest myth in rock history. But Teddy and Goff say it's no myth. They say Jack had a crew with 16 mil cameras and they filmed and taped all the sessions. Teddy told me you might have it."

This, of course, is why I'll sleep at the Savoy tonight. This is why the man who hates me is courting me. It's why he dribbled on me years ago. It isn't me he wants, it's Jack. Creep closer to Jack. Seduce his sidemen. Maybe they'll deliver him into your frigid grasp. Buy him. Own him. Warm your chilly bones. And when you can't do that, Barry, court his chick, his bitch, his widow.

"Mmm," I say. "Who knows? Jack left me *so* much."

"Bitter?" For just a second, his cold dislike shows, but he looks quickly at my neglected plate. I push it away. I don't need it any more. Barry's cards are on the table. All I needed to make him show his hand so soon was an artichoke.

Now he's relieved. He signals the waiter who removes the artichoke and brings us the second course. With a full plate in front of him, Barry is in control again. Rich as cream, smooth as butter.

He says, "OK, Birdie, tell me about it. You two suddenly, for no apparent reason, upped and split to Antigua. After a couple of months, Goff, Teddy, and some of the others join you. You've hired some tin-pot Caribbean studio and you put down all the songs and ideas that turned into *Hard Candy* and *Hard Time.* Right?"

"That's right," I say. "You know all about it. So why bother me? *Hard Candy* exists. *Hard Time* exists. No one's taking them away from you."

"They were the end product. Amazing, classic, seminal stuff. Jack's definitive statement. His finest work. But it seems to come out of nowhere."

"The magic of rock'n'roll."

"The albums aren't the whole story."

No, Barry, not to you they aren't, not when you're a groupie, the monarch of music nerds—when what *you* want are the out-takes, the between-takes dialogue, the fights, the *gossip*—when you ached so badly to know what it was *really* like to be Jack you tried to fuck his chick and, for one brief spasm, be where he had been.

He says, "Jack took the studio tapes to the record company, mainly acoustic stuff, I'm told—like a notebook full of bits and pieces. When the album was finished, there was no further use for them. I've been to the record company, I've spent days in their vaults. The guys there say they were lost, cleared out, I don't know. That's what happened in those days. No one had the least idea of the value of what they were throwing away."

"They had *no* value," I say. "As you say—a notebook—not Jack's 'definitive statement.' "

"How can you say that, Birdie?"

"Because I'm not like you, Barry. What the artist wants to give is good enough for me. I don't want what he had to do to make the gift possible. The rough cuts were not what Jack wanted anyone to hear."

"Easy for you to say. You were there all the time. You know. You heard. What I'm hoping is that the film of those sessions in Antigua will help fill in the gaps. It would, in any case, be a valuable social document."

"Why?" I ask innocently. "The music's important, but a film of *ad hoc* sessions, work in progress, has no value at all."

He steadies himself with forkfuls of steak and potatoes and says, "Excuse me, Birdie, but are you the best judge of what is valuable? I've studied the work and researched it, and written articles on it for years. If I may say so, I'm the one who's, almost single-handedly, kept it alive while tastes changed again and again."

"You've done a good job."

He checks my eyes for sarcasm, but all he sees is bland and blue.

17

"Yes," he says. "I have." He rewards himself with food. "OK, Birdie, straight question. Were the sessions filmed? Yes or no?"

"Yes, you know that already. Goff or Teddy told you."

"Then what happened? Where is the film? Was it made?"

"Sort of," I say. "No, not really."

"What do you mean?"

"Look, Barry, it was just a bunch of Berkeley film students we met on a beach. It was just a couple of guys with Eclairs and another guy with a Nagra. We were all bumming around, having a good time."

"But they were there, damn it, with film in their cameras, at the Antigua sessions. What happened to the film?"

"They took it back to the States to be developed and edited."

"Who were they, Birdie?"

"I can't remember the names. It was years ago. We spent a load of time stoned, with people drifting in and out. What did Goff and Teddy say?"

"They didn't even remember Berkeley. I suppose that's something at least."

"Why?"

"To help me track it down."

"What?"

"Jesus, Birdie, haven't you been listening? The film, the film, the film."

I pause for a moment before my precision bombing raid. I say, "But Barry, there was no film. All that happened was that these guys stung Jack for a heavy slice of bread for materials and time and what they produced was crap. He'd lost interest by that time, anyway. People were always trying to rip him off."

I sit back and watch the explosion in Barry's head.

"Produced?" he says. Sweat pops out of his face like bubbles from a baby's mouth. "You say they actually produced something. You've seen it? Jack saw it?"

"Of course. Jack paid for it, didn't he?"

"What did you see, what did Jack get for his money?"

"Three hours of this and that in three big film cans."

"Three *hours*?" Barry is dribbling again. It makes me quite nostalgic.

18

"And all the raw stuff they didn't use. Half a roomful of cans and boxes. I'd no idea it'd take up so much space. We tiptoed around it for days before Jack took it all out to the garden and burned it."

Barry's face collapses. "Jack burned it?" he whispers.

"Of course," I say. "It wasn't just that he'd paid for it. He wanted it so that he could destroy it. By that time, people were already taking things, souvenirs, whatever, just to say they had something of Jack's."

Barry's collapsed face stains red and I wonder what *he* took. I say, "It was freaking him out. He had dreams about little pieces of himself being cut off and bleeding away. He wanted to see a shrink, but he couldn't trust anyone. So he sort of destroyed the evidence. It was, like, if he had nothing, no one could steal it."

"So *he* destroyed the film?"

Didn't I tell you? It's no use explaining anything to Barry—he has no understanding whatsoever. I sigh and get on with my job.

"He burned all the stuff that wasn't used."

Hope flares like a distress beacon. "And the three hours?" he croaks.

"Oh, he kept that under the bed," I say airily. "He wasn't *completely* paranoid till a few months later."

I love messing with Barry's head. It renders him so powerless that he can't ask the next question. He has even forgotten to chew.

I say, "Look, Barry, I don't know what you want me to say. When Jack died, the vultures descended. Nearly everything that wasn't burned was stolen, even his music rights. I rescued what I could, but it wasn't much."

"The film?" he croaks.

"Maybe," I say.

"Maybe?"

"I never looked," I say. "There's stuff I haven't looked at for years. Life goes on."

Yours did, he wants to say. You went off with the next brightest star as if Jack never existed. He wants to say that as far as he's concerned, I am one of the vultures. Oh, he really wants to say it. Poor puppy. I smile at him. He's coming to loathe my sweet smile.

He controls himself. "So you might have it somewhere?"

19

"Don't know. Possible."

"Where?"

"Oh, there's stuff all over the place."

"Can I look?" he says.

"Certainly not," I say. "Anyway, it's probably not in England."

"Not . . .?"

"No. Look, Barry, I'm tired—I've been traveling all day. And as I'm only spending one night in London, I want to get up early tomorrow. There are people I want to see before I leave."

"But you can't leave," he says. "Nothing's settled."

"That's your problem. You've been badgering me to come and talk to you. I came and talked. Now I want to go home."

"I don't even know where you live. How can I get in touch?" He is almost wailing. "You haven't finished dinner yet. You haven't heard my proposition."

"Yes I have—you said 'final offer' when you were talking about production fees. And the food's cold." I reach for my handbag. There's something emblematic about a woman reaching for her bag. It frightens Barry to death.

"Wait," he says. "I didn't mean *final* final offer. Birdie, sit down, will you, please?"

I sit down again, sideways on the edge of my chair, where he has an intimidating view of my legs and the fuck-off shoes. Long legs, S-M shoes, ready to walk, Barry, out of here or all over you. Your choice.

"When I said, 'final offer,' Birdie, I just meant the program budget. It's the *program* which has a limited budget, Birdie, *I* don't. If that film exists, the sky's the limit as far as I'm concerned."

"Lawd, lawd, lawdie," I say. "I had no idea . . ."

"You could buy a fair few frocks and take a couple of luxury cruises on what I have to offer—if the film exists."

"Tempting," I say. "But I'd have to take a few cruises to find the damn thing first. It could be anywhere. For instance, after Jack died, Mick Jagger lent me an island and I left stuff there. And then I was in LA and I left stuff there too. And, who was it?—I don't remember—but he had a big house on Paxos, or was it Naxos? I got around. You know that."

He knows that. Everyone knew about it. The paparazzi chased me all around the world—Birdie in full flight—and told everyone all about everything.

I say, "And I'm not going to re-run that trip just to suit you, Barry."

"Lent you an island?" Barry is appalled and impaled, as usual, on a superstar.

"Don't you believe me?" I say. "Well, darling, you know all the old faces. Ring him up and ask him to look for your film. Maybe he can afford the time and trouble. I can't."

There—message delivered, loud and clear. It reaches Barry and he sits staring at me with embarrassment, greed, and social intimidation leaking from his forehead and upper lip. He's wondering why, after all these years, he still can't afford me. He should have me over a barrel: I'm an aging broad and everyone knows they mean less than nothing. He's offered me biscuit and a little media attention, so I should be licking his hand and wagging my tail. Age should have softened me and made me malleable.

Instead, I walk, I stalk, I shimmy out of Café D'Arte and disappear into the night. Walker by name, walker by nature. I don't even need a lift.

Except that I did need a lift. My feet hurt. Pride and adrenaline don't last long these days. I was tired. I took a cab back to the Savoy, ditched the shoes, loosened the zips and straps, and lay down with Memphis Slim on my Walkman. Then I rolled a joint and went to bed, hustled out. Risks taken, pitches pitched, nothing to do but wait and see how much Barry wanted to redeem himself in his own eyes. A lot? A little? Not at all?

21

Part 1

INTRODUCTIONS

"When the music starts to play, she slides out on the floor,
Dancing without a partner . . ."   Keb' Mo'

I

First Impressions

When George first met Linnet Walker, she seemed to sail through his window like an exotic bird out of a clear blue sky. In fact, it was a gray day and she walked through the door like everyone else. She didn't perch on the edge of his desk and sing, or preen iridescent feathers— but afterward, George could never quite lose the impression that she did.

He was not an impressionable man. His partner, Tina Cole, was, if anything, even harder-nosed than he was.

"CV?" Tina asked. "Did she leave a CV?"

"She didn't even apply for the job," George said, still bemused. He blinked as if adjusting his eyes back from bright to dim light. "I think she just came to look us over."

"She wants a job but she thinks we might not be suitable employers?" Tina said. "Bleeding nerve!"

"She isn't exactly a school leaver spraying applications all around the neighborhood," George explained. "She's a ..."

"She's a what?"

But George didn't answer that one. He polished his glasses and said, "How many have we interviewed, Tina? And how many of those can write a simple letter? Spell even halfway correctly? Read a spreadsheet? Fill in a client form? Operate this labyrinth of a computer? Is there a single one of them you'd want answering the phone?"

"This isn't a straightforward job. We might have to do some in-house training."

"What management manual did you find that euphemism in?" George looked at his colleague with a mixture of affection and exasperation. "Do me a favor and explain if by 'in-house training' you mean we'll have to teach some adolescent how to spit out her gum and hide the cigarettes before telling a client to 'park his arse.'"

Tina snorted with laughter. "Oh, George," she said, "we have interviewed some lulus."

"And we haven't found one we'd even trust as a receptionist—never mind give access to confidential files. We're in the security business, for God's sake. We're supposed to be secure. And confidential. And tactful. And don't say, 'It's early days.' It's been five weeks, and we're still hanging on by our fingernails without any office help."

It was nearly eight in the evening. Outside, the traffic was quiet and sleepy. All the other businesses in the street had packed up and gone home except for the Chinese takeaway and the pub, where trade was picking up. The street was in its nighttime mode. But Cole-Adler Security still had a lot of catching up to do.

Tina sighed and said, "Go home, love. You look shattered, and Fay will have my guts for garters. We'll sort it out in the morning, you'll see."

For once, it was Tina who cast herself in the parental role. Usually George was the one who soothed, sorted, and sustained. But methodical, calm George was tired. His comfortable flesh looked almost too heavy for him to carry.

"Go home," Tina said again.

"You too," George said. "We've both reached the point of diminishing returns."

He was right. They were both tired of running on the spot, of never getting anything done because of the time wasted answering phones, chasing invoices, buying stamps. Cole-Adler Security needed help. Cole-Adler needed a competent office manager.

On his way home, riding the rickety blindworm called the Misery Line by those who knew it best, George thought about Linnet Walker. She was not the sort of woman you'd want to meet when you'd just dropped your cheese and pickle sandwich into the laser printer. He knew what a man of his age and weight looked like from behind, and he knew that the sight was not improved by bending over to scoop mature cheddar out of sensitive electronic equipment while

26

swearing softly and repetitively. But, he reflected sadly, that was exactly what Linnet saw when she walked through the door.

He was expecting to interview a job applicant. He was also expecting a woman who wanted a burglar alarm. He was expecting, too, the accountant for the annual audit. In fact, he had triple-booked himself by mistake and it was too late to put it right. Then he'd made matters worse by trying to print out the sheets of incomings and outgoings which the accountant would need.

George was no whizz-kid. Gadgetry mystified him, and it was many, many years since he qualified as a kid. Pen and ink was his technology. Left in charge of the electronic memo system, he remembered nothing, triple-booked himself, and fed his lunch to the laser printer.

He heard Linnet come in and, without straightening or turning, he said, "Just a minute. Sorry. Bugger. Are you the job, the alarm, or the money?"

A soft amused voice answered, "Which would you like me to be?"

"A brain surgeon," George said. "I think I'm performing a frontal lobotomy on this printer, but I don't know where to find the front."

"Front is my specialty. Let me look at that. My hands are smaller."

At which point, George's reading glasses slid down his nose and joined the cheese and pickle sandwich. He stood up in despair and allowed an angel to redeem him.

Later, at home, when he tried to describe the incident to Fay, he could only say, "God, I hope she takes the job. She's like an answer to a prayer."

"I hope so too," Fay said. She was patting moisturizer onto her face, getting ready for bed. "You're exhausted. You shouldn't be working like this. Not now. What's she like?"

But George, justly renowned for his careful, police-trained accuracy, couldn't seem to remember.

"She's good with gizmos," he said. "She cleaned the printer and she figured out the bloody computer."

"Well, that's worth a week's wages," Fay said. "The way you talk about that machine, anyone'd think it was a landmine. What's she like with people?"

"Even better." George was remembering that when the accountant arrived he had still been flustered and afraid he'd miss the client.

"I'll wait for the client," Linnet said. "Don't worry." And ten minutes later, with the accountant settled in his office, George returned to find that not only was the client happily leafing through brochures but the information the accountant needed was printed up and ready to take through. He felt suddenly that the placidity which was his normal response to life might one day come back to visit him.

"Maybe she won't come back," George said, climbing wearily into bed. "Maybe she took one look at the mess I made of the printer and decided she'd rather scrub toilets."

But two days later, Linnet did come back for a meeting with Tina.

"Bloody hell," Tina said afterward, "I only just stopped myself chaining her to the desk to prevent her leaving. Has she got a black belt in charm, or what?"

"See what I mean?" George said, happy to find out that hard-nosed Tina could be as susceptible to charm in a woman as he was.

"No CV, though," Tina said. "And only two references. Although I suppose that's what you'd expect from someone who's been looking after her mother for the last ten years."

"I'll check the references," George said.

"You won't," Tina said. "I will. I don't trust any man as desperate as you."

When she rang the first of the referees, she found herself talking to a French restaurateur.

"Linnet?" he said. "Oh you mean Chouette. I always call her Chouette. She is my darling of darlings."

"Er, yes," Tina said, "but can you tell me what capacity she was employed in, and how reliable she was?"

"She saved my life," the extravagant voice told her. "Without Chouette, I would be peeling potatoes stilll. I would be bankrupt. My friends would be weeping at my graveside ..."

When she put the phone down and sorted fact from hyperbole, Tina decided that Linnet had been employed as a general business manager. She must have walked into a restaurant with absolutely nothing to recommend it but a talented, flamboyant, and hopelessly disorganized chef. She set up a system which allowed it to flourish, and had a pudding called the Bombe Chouette named in her honor.

"So I asked why she left," Tina told George, who was grinning from ear to ear. "And he said, I quote, 'Oh but what more could she do? Ze seestem is fulepruf. She merst fly away.'"

In the end, it was George's grin which made up Tina's mind. She realized she hadn't seen it for months, and she felt responsible.

He said, "For God's sake, Tina, let's get Linnet in here and see if she can set up a 'fulepruf seestem' for us. I'm tired of being worried to death."

"And just hope she doesn't fly away wiz ze petty cash?" Tina said. "I'll call this other referee first, if you don't mind."

She called and reached a freelance photographer, who was equally fulsome in his praise of Linnet.

"She put him on the map," Tina reported back to George. "It seems she was exceptionally good at getting him work. Oh, and did you know that she's 'remarkably photogenic'?"

"And did she fly away with the petty cash?"

"No," Tina admitted. "OK, OK, she's a saint and a genius. But I can't think of one good reason why a saint and a genius would want to work for us."

"Can you think of a good reason why we shouldn't ask her to?" George said.

"I don't want to pay anyone who's more photogenic than I am," Tina said. "Oh, go on, George, give her a tug. I know you're dying to."

So Linnet Walker came to work for Cole-Adler Security, and George regained his good humor. He went back to being the kindly, placid, methodical George Tina relied on. He even looked younger. If that were the only change she noticed, Tina would have been happy to pay Linnet's wages. But the change to George came about because of changes in the office.

First, Linnet cajoled the computer into a simpler, more humane attitude toward its owners. She also kept a handwritten diary on the desk to log appointments and calls. This was specifically for George, but Tina found herself preferring it too.

Then she arranged their days for them so that they always had time to talk to each other. She made good use of their time, and she seemed to know by instinct which partner would suit which client and vice versa. The clients responded miraculously by paying up at the first time of asking and practically thanking her for the privilege.

Conversely, the suppliers seemed suddenly to become very lenient about their payments. Cole-Adler no longer had to pay for their hardware up-front or cash-on-delivery. Bills came in a leisurely fashion and, at last, a balance was struck in the war between income and expenses.

"I don't understand it," Tina said. "Last month, these bastards were practically dunning us. Now they're sending us free samples and purring."

"Don't understand," George said. "Enjoy and shut up."

"It's her confidence," Tina said. "Have you heard her on the phone? You'd think she was sweet-talking an industrial giant—but you *know* it's only the warehouse foreman so he'll send us a gross of window locks tomorrow instead of next week. And she seems to know how to talk to *everyone*, from ponce to pauper. As if she's at home in any bloody situation at all. I wonder how old she is."

"Didn't it say on her CV?"

"No CV. Remember? Oh well, maybe I'll ask her."

But, in the end, Tina didn't ask and Linnet's age remained a mystery. She was clearly a mature woman, but she moved quickly and gracefully like a girl. Clothes, however cheap and simple, looked exotic on her. Her vocabulary was racy and up-to-date, but the letters she wrote were models of restrained, educated phrasing.

It's all contradictory, Tina thought, but she was busy, so she didn't think about it for long. After the first week, she began to relax and think that Linnet could cope with anything and everything. There was no need to watch her or check up on her, so Tina took George's advice: she shut up and enjoyed.

II

The Sister

My sister was up in the loft, making something from diamonds of colored silk. Robin is always making something. She always leaves the back door open too. The crazy lady trusts people. No matter how many times she's been ripped off, she believes in the perfectibility of mankind, the essential goodness of her neighbors. Either that, or she has a memory like a lace condom. She even trusts me.

"Hey, Robin," I said. "Leaving the door unlocked is one thing, but leaving your handbag on the kitchen table as well, that's just asking for it."

"Lin!" She turned, scissors in one hand, swatch of cloth in the other. She dropped everything and came around her worktable to give me a big hug.

"You never said you were coming. You look fantastic. Are you staying? How are you?"

I put my arms around her, feeling the softness of her shoulders, the silky graying hair on my cheek. Life must be so much easier when you give up on your looks.

The warm welcome took us down to the kitchen, where she made coffee and offered me homemade chocolate chip cookies. When her kids were small, she used to make chocolate chap cookies for Jimmy and chocolate chick cookies for Grace. She was that sort of mother.

The house is Victorian and it's the only one in this street which hasn't been broken up into flats and bedsits. It's much too big for Robin since her dumb husband left her and the kids went to college. But she won't move out. Jack bought this house for Mother when Dad died, and Robin would never sell anything which has the slightest connection with Jack.

Robin adored Jack. I mean truly. It made me laugh, because usually

31

she was utterly resistant to my friends and my way of life. Usually, when she met one of my men, you could see her thinking, Oh yeah—another flashy talent, another narcissist, all mouth and image but no substance. Robin was into substance. She was always looking for someone I could settle down with. She never accepted that settling down was her thing, not mine.

So when she met Jack, who was as flashy a talent as ever lived, it amused the hell out of me to watch her succumb. She could have curled up like a little mouse and existed, completely happy, in his pocket. And she wouldn't have minded if he failed to notice her, or forgot she was there. Which was just as well, because Jack, true to form, hardly noticed her at all.

There are Marys and there are Marthas. Some men go for one, some for the other. Jack was a Mary-man if ever there was one. He didn't even see Marthas.

And if you are looking for male equivalents to Mary and Martha you might find Icarus and Sisyphus. Robin was looking for Sisyphus. She respected constancy and consistency. Substance. But she was enchanted by Icarus—the high flier with unreliable wings who got burned.

She married a Sisyphus and he left her, ten years later, for a younger Martha. He left her with two small kids and a barmy mother. So much for substance. That's what happens when you give yourself up to love and family.

I never give myself up for anything. But it's very useful to have a sister who does.

I didn't eat her chocolate chip cookies. Once you start on Robin's baking, you can't stop—and I don't want to look like her. She isn't fat, exactly, but she's soft and mumsy. No one would stop and wonder who the hell *she* was at the Café D'Arte.

"What're you doing in town?" she asked.

"Bit of this, bit of that," I said. "Remember that creep Barry?"

"You're not seeing *him,* are you? Oh, Lin, he's a thief."

"Well, yes, sort of. He's still after memorabilia. And, Robin, I need the money."

"No!" she said. "You can't let him have *anything.*"

"I won't if I can possibly help it. But it made me think."

"What?" she said. "You can't stop protecting Jack."

"Jack's past protection."

"No! He isn't. That bastard wants to turn him into Elvis."

Poor Robin. She cares so deeply about someone who's long, long gone.

I say, "But what am I going to do? It's a mean old world out there. Am I supposed to guard the flame for the rest of my life? You can't eat flames."

"Lin, Lin, ssh," she says. "Here, drink your coffee. What's happened? Tell me."

She's so soft. This won't take long.

"Nothing," I say. "Nothing new. Just people hassling me. I'm supposed to be writing, but they're messing with my head."

I allow her to comfort me because that's how she comforts herself. Then I say, "I wish I had something solid: a job to go to; someone to tell me what to do." This is precisely what she wants to hear because it's what she thinks herself.

She says, "Stay here, Lin. I'll keep everyone off your back while you sort yourself out."

"But people know you're my sister. They'll call here."

"They do anyway," she says. "There's a pile of mail for you in the hall cupboard. I'll just keep on saying what I always say: I haven't heard from you, I don't know where you are."

I say, "Robin, you're too sweet. I can't ask you to do that. These are real hassles—I've maxxed out on my credit card and I've run up some debts. I'll have to get a job—it may take some time to sort myself out."

"Stay as long as you like," she says. She looks anxious. Debt gives her the shakes. It reminds her too much of the past.

"You'll straighten yourself out," she says bravely. "You have before, you will again."

"I'll help," says poor deluded Robin. "What sort of debts?"

Now this is an interesting one. Again, I must get the price right. But this time I have to find an amount which is outside her range, or she will be tempted to help me out. It must be beyond her ability to bankroll me, but it must be possible for me—with hard work and application—to pay off in stages.

"Shit a coalpit," she says, when I tell her. She falls silent and chews the knuckle of her ring finger—a sure sign of high anxiety.

I'm such a bitch, and it's time to pull back a bit.

I say, "I'm owed money too. That's what caused the problem. Dog Records owes me for work I did with one of their new signings. And they've asked me to look at some raw talent in Oxford next week. They pay slowly, but they do pay in the end. The trouble is, it's all a bit hand-to-mouth. I'll have to figure something out while I wait."

She says, "You can stay here. It'll hardly cost you anything. If you *could* find some sort of job . . ." Her voice dies under a justifiable weight of uncertainty. It is not simply rich living I am renowned for, it is also a contempt for sustained effort. I get bored and bolt. In short, I am flighty.

"Oh, Lin," she says, "you could make a success of anything if only you . . ."

"Put my mind to it? Hung in?" I smile. Because it's funny how sisters define themselves in comparison to each other rather than by an objective standard. Thus, hanging in is Robin's thing. Bolting is Lin's. There are times, of course, when Robin bolts and Lin hangs in, but those, according to family lore, are exceptions. Robin is the peat fire, Lin is the firecracker—that's how we are stereotyped. And very useful it is too.

We decide that I will stay with Robin, however reluctant I am to take advantage, and that she will filter all calls and act as my early warning system. While I take on the terrible task of "sorting myself out."

Perfect. Job done.

It was hardly worth the effort. I could have just turned up with my bags—she would have taken me in anyway. But I wanted her invitation. I want her to feel she is actively protecting her little sister.

I could have told her that I'd already lucked into a job, but I want her to feel that she has a stake in putting me on the right track. If you want someone to do a good job for you, you should build in job satisfaction, build in a degree of achievable success. Make her a shareholder.

She sat at the kitchen table, nibbling a cookie, her eyes vacant. She looked thick. She isn't thick, but she dreams her way through problems. She doesn't analyze—she tries on scenarios, like clothes, until she finds one she's comfortable with. Just then, she was dreaming her way through what she imagined was my problem. And if what she imagined was true, eventually she would solve it for me. Unfortunately, I misled her.

I said, "Robin, sweetie, let me put a rinse on your hair."

"A rinse? Why?"

"Gray hair is so aging. It makes you look ten years older than you really are."

She laughed, distracted from my problem, and dismissed the subject without a second's thought.

"Remember Auntie May?" she said.

I laughed too. Auntie May was our mother's sister. She lived in Weston-super-Mare and worked as a waitress-cum-chamber maid at a hotel there. She had preposterously red hair and when we were kids she convinced us that it was natural. She said that redheads never went gray. Redheads, she made us believe, had the secret of eternal youth. We were far too young to be interested in eternal youth and, in any case, we wondered why she bothered to be vain about her hair when her face was so old.

Robin said, "Funny. Auntie May was younger then than we are now. And weren't we little snots? We mistook panic for vanity."

"Weston-super-*Merde!*" I said.

"Snob," said Robin.

Something happened at home the summer Robin was twelve and I was ten. We never found out what. We were packed off one morning in August and Auntie May picked us up at the coach station at the other end. No explanation. All Auntie May ever said was, "Your dad's gone and Done Something."

"What?" Robin asked, chewing her knuckle.

"Never you mind," said Auntie May. But Robin did mind, and when she wasn't chewing her knuckle, she chewed the ends of her hair. I was excited: my dad had Done Something worthy of high secrecy, a hushed voice, and a pursed mouth. As far as I knew, neither my mother nor father Did anything. But the Something he did was big enough to send Robin and me away alone for the first time in our lives; and to bring our girlish hopes and fears face-to-face with a grown woman's delusions and disappointments.

May was never married. She had no children. In another age, she would have been the spinster doomed to live with one married relative after another. She might have been happier for that. Because although spinsterhood was by then an archaic concept, singularity was not yet accepted as it is now. The single woman was neither an economic force nor was she a political entity. She was still considered an unfulfilled creature. She had an impoverished independence but no dignity or respect.

Yes indeed, poor Auntie May. She had a string of what she called gentlemen friends. These gentlemen friends bewildered the shit out of Robin and me. Clearly they were too old and seedy and unattractive to be boyfriends. Clearly Auntie May was too old to have boyfriends. But they could reduce Auntie May to tears by being half an hour late for a walk along the sea front.

Watching her get ready for a date was a revelation. Off came the plain black dress with the white Peter Pan collar. Off with the white nylon slip, the Marks and Spencer cotton underwear, the thick stockings and flat shoes. On went Mum Rollette and a squirt of Diorissima. And the running commentary began: "Always apply perfume to the pulse points. See these veins in the crook of my arms. Well, my skin's very thin there. I'm famous for my thin skin. Never call it scent, dear, it's perfume. My skin is so delicate some of the perfume seeps into my blood. It even finds its way into my hair."

On went the lacy underwear. "White is for purity, black is for sin. Red is too crude for words, children. If you want my advice—stick to coffee color or ashes of roses. No, it isn't pink, Lin dear, it's ashes of roses. No, that isn't pink either, it's cyclamen. It enhances the color of my skin—makes it pearly. Redheads have very pearly skin."

There I was in my ten-year-old skin, watching, horrified, and wondering if the seriously demented lace contraptions May wore were an obligatory part of becoming a woman. I could not imagine what process would give me a body which would need such preparation, such lifting and separating, tucking and tweaking. I thought of it happening all at once, like in the horror movies. I could see myself walking into a mad scientist's transformation capsule. He would flick a switch, laser lights would flash, I would writhe in pain as, before my eyes, flesh bulged and wobbled, coarse hair sprouted, breasts extruded like sausages from a sausage machine. Then I would walk out of the capsule slowly on feet which hurt because my toes were bent and bunioned. I was a woman and it only took two minutes.

Now, of course, I know that the mad scientist is Father Time. But then aging and womanhood looked like a dirty trick played on an innocent victim to turn her into a disappointed idiot. Demented underwear, it seemed, was the badge worn by a grown-up woman to set her apart from the rest of the human race.

Oh, it was a formative experience, all right. Only five years later, sitting at the feet of a legendary blues man, in torn jeans and a skinny sweater, I remember the sudden pang of acute doubt about my cotton briefs and no bra. I should not be in adult company—not because of my age and the licensing laws, but because I was wearing the wrong underwear. Or, more specifically, hardly any at all. Would Dexxy be singing *Honey Crawl* for me if he knew? Answer: yes, of course he would—extreme youth and inexperience were part of the attraction. If not the *only* attraction. I thought it was me, but it wasn't. It was only young skin. One is never too old or too young to be deluded.

"You can come with me as far as the beach," said Auntie May, "but I'm not introducing you to my gentleman friend. He thinks I'm too young to be an auntie."

Robin and I were too young to understand what she really meant. What we puzzled over was how she could be too young to be an aunt when she was three years older than our mother.

"Your Auntie May has a heart of gold," Dad said when we got home, "but she's a very silly woman." And we accepted his judgment. We had, as Robin said, mistaken blind panic for vanity.

III

The Band

InnerVersions is a clever-dick band from Oxford. Sapper, lead vocals and rhythm guitar, spent a year at Exeter College before dropping out. He likes to give the impression that he barely made it to the tech. He doesn't want to be thought of as an elitist bastard. Dram, lead guitar and backup vocals, studied art at St Martin's. He's less shy about his education and talent. Corky, bass, actually did go to Oxford Tech and he has a qualification in psychology. He never mentions it. Flambo, drums, did two years Eng Lit at St Katherine's. InnerVersions is Flambo's brainchild. He can't sing, he can't write songs, but he knows, absolutely knows, what the band ought to sound like. Karen, keyboards and backup vocals, went to the Guildhall School of Music. She doesn't know how the band should sound, but she shags Flambo, so she agrees with him.

Each member of InnerVersions has learned something about the craft of music-making. Each has a little talent. All are hugely ambitious. All would deny it. Together, they are constantly at war. Separate they are nothing. They are intelligent enough to know this, but they are dumb enough to hide their intelligence.

They want to look like an inner-city warehouse band, but they want to sound like Cream if Cream were playing today. They want to be more famous than the Beatles. They want to be richer than the Stones. Cream, the Beatles, and the Stones were making their names before the members of InnerVersions were born. But Sapper, Dram, Corky, Flambo, and Karen know the legends. The legends serve to feed them and keep them hungry.

After a couple of years playing the pub, club, college circuit on a mixed repertoire of original songs and covers, InnerVersions were taken up in a lukewarm way by a record company called Dog. It wasn't what the band had been dreaming of, but shit, you've got to start somewhere.

The trouble is that they know, know, *know* that they're more talented and prettier than bands who are doing a lot better than they are.

They need a little bit of luck—a little bit of magic. That's all. And when it is offered to them, they need the wit to recognize it for what it is.

Karen recognizes it almost from the beginning. The others are skeptical. Flambo is dismissive. He says, "You *are* shitting us, aren't you? The deal is, we sign, you pay, we get studio time. That's the deal. We do not get a makeover from an old tart everyone's forgotten. That *ain't* the deal."

"Well . . ." says the A&R man.

"Come on," says Flambo.

"I'm bringing her to the Cellar Club tonight," says the A&R man, who may look like a limp rhubarb stalk but who has an implacable side to his nature. "Talk to her afterward."

"Fuck off," Flambo says. "We're staying the way we are. If you don't like us, why sign us?"

"We haven't yet," says the A&R man.

"Like, listen to the man," Sapper says.

"Who else has she worked with?" Karen asks.

"Recently?" the A&R man says. "Dream Therapy. You know 'On Your Toes'? Six weeks in the charts. That was one of her co-writes."

"Six weeks in the charts." Sapper repeats the phrase like a mantra.

"I didn't know that," says Karen.

"Industrial secret," says the A&R man. "Bands want to do their own songs, but sometimes they need help with writing and arranging. People who spin-doctor songs and don't get credited are usually called producers. But there are a few who do it just for the money."

"Fuck off," says Flambo.

"Six weeks in the charts," says Sapper.

"In your dreams," says Corky.

"Suck it and see," says Dram.

"Birdie Walker," says Karen, who has read some of the books and seen photos of Birdie in a coffee-table volume called *Chelsea Chicks—Faces in Film and Fashion (1965-85)*.

"I thought she was just a rock'n'roll mattress," Corky says.

"You mind your fucking manners," says the A&R man. Up to now, he's sounded like a public school type. InnerVersions stare at him in surprise: there's more than a touch of Rottweiler in this limp rhubarb stalk.

A typical InnerVersions gig goes like this: there is a smallish venue, like the Cellar Club. There are two bands. One band is trying out: it's new, maybe a college band. It opens while people are coming in, buying drinks, horsing around. No one dances. Then InnerVersions come on for their first set. They have better equipment, a better sound. They are known to the audience because they've been doing the local circuit for two years. Some of their numbers are danceable and, if enough beer or pills have been swallowed, people will dance. InnerVersions call these people their Following.

They know what it's like to be the opening band. They know how depressing it is to perform for people who aren't there for them, who aren't listening, aren't responding. They know how crucial it is to have a bunch of people, even a small one, who will show up because InnerVersions are on. Their Following is very important.

Between sets, the band goes to the bar. They mix with their Following. Drinks are bought, pills popped. And why not? The band and the Following are contemporary. There is no distance between them.

It's a democratic, friendly scene which InnerVersions would sell their souls to escape. Given half a chance, they would be behind crowd-control barriers, in limos, holed up in luxury hotels, recording in LA studios. Friendly, democratic scenes are what you leave behind when you succeed big-time. They are what you return to when you fail. If, that is, you don't self-destruct first and never return at all. Heroic failure is also a romantic option. There are mythical burnouts.

Tonight, Karen is thinking about one mythical burnout. She knows Birdie Walker will be somewhere in the audience, watching and listening, so she is thinking about Jack and the nature of heat. There's the heat of animal magnetism. Jack had buckets of that. Talent's hot too. Jack had loads of that as well. Luck? Timing? Yes. Yes. Shake them all together and you get a chain reaction. Magnetism and talent rubbing together, igniting a spark, a series of small explosions, which generate publicity, which flows along invisible wires, which in the end light the big fire called fame. Jack's fame eventually became too hot even for Jack to handle. It burned him to death— fame and flame.

To Karen, it seems emblematic. Life and death were in cahoots, producing something dangerous and symbolic. Almost like art, Karen thinks, because she is romantic about art.

She is in no danger, herself. She's stuck behind her keyboards, way behind the three guitarists. There's supposed to be a baby spotlight on her, but it isn't working, so she's doing her thing, supporting the guys, almost invisible. Which, she thinks, is just as well. She's getting some annoying feedback and between numbers she's fiddling with the amps. If InnerVersions were a name band, there'd be engineers and roadies to do it for her. If they were a name band, she wouldn't be using knackered amps. She'd have state-of-the-art hardware and someone to carry and maintain it for her.

She looks across at Flambo. He's the only one who's noticed her difficulty. The others aren't listening. Flambo's arms are shiny wet blurs. He's whacking out a complicated pattern, but he turns his head toward her and frowns. She gives him a despairing shrug. They are playing a number called "More and More." It's eight minutes and forty-five seconds long. Karen wishes it was three minutes long and called "Less and Less." Then the set would be over and she could get help with her amps. But "More and More" is one of their groove numbers and the Following are on their feet. She switches from the Roland to the Korg because the Korg feeds through a different amp. It's the wrong voice and some of the extra sounds are missing, but at least she can play without her ears being blitzed.

Flambo scowls ferociously. She tries to ignore him. In a minute, there'll be a thirty-two-bar drum break, which will cheer him up and give him something else to think about. She doesn't usually look forward to drum breaks, but now she can hardly wait. Dram's lower E string has gone flat and that's annoying her too.

For a moment, she wishes she were at home, eating chocolate and watching TV. With her qualifications, she could teach music at a school, never have to get up in front of a live audience. Chocolate and TV. Chocolate to rot the teeth, TV to rot the mind. No hard-edged, glittering ambition, no knife-edged teeter between success and failure. At the moment, she would give up anything for the chance to sit at home in the dark and not be judged in public. At the moment, she thinks "More And More" is trite and repetitive. She doesn't want to play it here, with everyone listening and watching. It doesn't represent her. It's just a long, loud, pointless wank.

To make matters worse, out there, somewhere behind the lights, behind the Following, is Birdie Walker. To Karen, Birdie Walker is a woman who *knows*. What does she know? Karen can't say, but it has something to do with how to *be* a woman—something alien and dangerous, to do with glamour, collective desire, spells. She has been somewhere Karen has never been and isn't sure she wants to go. She has been the woman every man wanted and every woman wanted to be. She has had the men every woman wanted and every man wanted to be. She was close to the music everyone wanted to make. She was close to unbelievable success and tragedy.

No unbelievable anything for me, Karen thinks dimly, standing there in a nothing club in Maidenhead, about to endure another one of Flambo's thirty-two-bar drum solos. She wants to switch off the Korg and go home. Switch off and fuck off.

Four bars into the drum break, without even thinking about it, Karen hits a button. The LCD screen on top of the keyboard flash-es "harpsi," and Karen begins to play a left-hand pattern which runs counter to the drum pattern. Down low, fast, staccato, the harpsi voice sounds like someone grunting—uh-uh-uhn-erh.

Flambo is so surprised he nearly falls out of his pattern. He throws Karen a look of pure hatred. He grits his teeth, steadies, and sticks with it.

The next twenty-eight bars are like a skirmish in a war. Flambo digs in behind his battery. Karen flashes in and out with guerrilla raids. She assaults his steady, heavy barrage with a light, sharp, almost Cuban cross-rhythm.

Sweat flies from Flambo's hair. Karen looks up and sees Corky grinning at her. Corky enjoys friction. She closes her eyes and concentrates.

Afterward, Flambo says, "What the fuck do you think you're playing at? Don't you *ever* do that again."

Karen says nothing. She walks offstage and threads her way through the Following at the bar. She's frightened and elated.

She feels as if she has blurted out the first thing to come into her head—it might be inane or obscene. She doesn't know. One thing is certain, though—there will be a very nasty row when Flambo gets her home. By the time it's over, she may not have a home. Or a band.

She sees the A&R man waiting, so she turns and ducks into the cloakroom. Elation shrivels. She slips into an empty cubicle and locks the door. There's wet tissue on the floor. Some sad woman has scrawled the words "He beats me" on the wall. Underneath, someone even sadder has written, "Do you like it?"

Karen grabs a fistful of bog paper and blows her nose. She doesn't want to cry, but there's a hot ache behind her eyes. Life is spent hiding your feelings in tiny, smelly places.

"Sick," Karen says out loud. She waits till she thinks there's no one around and then she leaves the cubicle to wash her hands.

There is a woman leaning casually against the door; gold blonde hair, black Levis, a man's jacket.

"Oh shit," says Karen, "you're Birdie." And instantly, she's positive the Cuban cross-rhythm was inane. Inane is all she's capable of tonight. Or ever.

She says, "Don't worry, I'm giving it all up. I don't want it. I can't do it."

Birdie says, "Wash your face. Don't let them see you cry."

Birdie says, "If you want to give up, by all means give up. But don't do it from a position of weakness."

Birdie says, "Don't run away. Flounce."

Birdie says, "Never flounce without lipstick." She adds, "Lipstick is a metaphor." And Karen starts to laugh.

43

She borrows Birdie's lipstick. Birdie backcombs her hair into an aggressive, tousled mass. Karen stares into the mirror and watches her own dim image morph into lioness.

"What're you thinking?" says Birdie.

"'He *beats* me,'" says Karen." "'Do you *like* it?'" "It's on the bog wall."

"I saw," says Birdie. She chants, "He beats me. Do you like it?" Call and response.

Karen: "Lipstick is a meta*phor.*"

Birdie: "I *saw* it on the *bath*room wall."

"Way to go," says Birdie. "Your first bog wall song."

"The guys won't do anything with lipstick in it. Except maybe 'Paint lipstick on your nipples.'"

"Banal," says Birdie.

"Yeah," says Karen, who has never painted lipstick on her nipples. She may be in a band, but suburban repression still has her chained to her parents' garden gate.

"OK?" says Birdie, and they leave the cloakroom and go to the bar.

"She fucking seduced you," Flambo says later. "I know her type: divide and conquer. You let her walk all over you."

"She can seduce me any day of the week," murmurs Sapper. "Is she gay?"

"Banal," says Karen.

"I dunno," says Dram. "I reckon she could swing whatever way suited her. There's something *fleurs-du-mal* there."

Karen does not go home with Flambo. For once, she takes the initiative and a taxi she can't really afford. She disappears without explanation.

"Watch it," Corky says to Flambo. "You could lose your grip. *And* your block vote."

Corky is excited. He sniffs change on the wind like a hound scents a fox. In the politics of the band, the block vote, Flambo and Karen together, gives Flambo more power than Corky thinks he should have. If Flambo lost his grip and Karen's vote was up for grabs, Corky might grab her.

He doesn't exactly want her, he's never seen her as anything but an extension of Flambo, but she has more music theory than the rest of them put together and he needs someone to shape his ideas. At the moment, it's Flambo's ideas she's shaping.

It doesn't occur to Corky that Karen might have ideas of her own. Rock'n'roll, after all, is a dick thing—a young dick thing—and Corky is a young dick. He has ideas but no imagination.

He says, "Hey guys, what d'you call a drummer who's just broken up with his girlfriend?"

"Homeless," says Dram.

"A wanker," says Sapper.

"Ha-fucking-ha," says Flambo. "Here's one for you—what do you call a sad fuck who hangs around with musicians?"

"What?"

"A bass player," says Flambo. "Thank you and good night." He wishes he could walk away like Karen, but at the moment he's driving the van with all the gear and the others squeezed in around him. It's another thing he plans to criticize Karen for—she walked off without helping to load the van.

But, of course, when he gets home, the flat is dark and silent. He sits. He waits. His grievances breed like rodents. Karen has fucked up. Karen *is* a fuck-up. She isn't even pretty. Where does she think she gets off—acting like a bleeding girl? She *always* helps hump the gear. Carry your own bags, Karen, open your own doors. If you want to play with the boys, don't expect any special treatment. That's the arrangement. And speaking of arrangements, what the fuck was that harpsi riff? Who told her she could do that? Arrangements are Flambo's thing. He's the one who knows what InnerVersions should sound like. He's the man who makes the decisions.

Flambo drinks from the neck of a cheap wine bottle. Clumsily, he rolls a joint. A guy's got to come down after a gig. Normally, Karen would roll the joint with her fast little fingers. Good with her hands, our Karen.

Flambo stirs restlessly. He has after-gig jitters and no one to soothe him with bacon and eggs. Restlessness segues into scratchy irritability, and from there it changes tempo and becomes randy anger. He watches the door and waits. He imagines Karen in a bath with Birdie; they are soaping each other. Later, they sprawl in his bed doing a sixty-niner. This is going to be good. But first he unzips his fly and pisses on them. They like that. Oh yes, they do.

But Flambo does not have fast little fingers and, unlike Karen, he isn't good with his hands. So, afterward, he feels almost as raw and empty as he did before. He sleeps in his chair, facing the door, head lolling.

Karen, at her parents' house, goes to sleep in her old bedroom, under her old Wonder Woman duvet, and here she dreams one of her fear-of-failure dreams. She dreams that she is on stage with a superstar, who might or might not be Sting. She is playing the Korg, but it is perched on top of an upright acoustic piano. She can't reach without stretching. As she plays, the Korg starts to heat up and melt. It drips and oozes down onto the acoustic piano until there is nothing left of it to play. The superstar who might or might not be Sting watches contemptuously. "Stir it with a wooden spoon," he says, "or stay out of my kitchen." Karen looks down at her hands and sees that she is trying to play a large pot of soup.

Sometimes, late at night, when she looks at the linear beauty of a piano keyboard, she thinks of the clean, logical progression of semitones which walk, step by step, ineluctably from low A in the bass across seven octaves to high C. Cool reason and symmetry. Each scale doing the same thing yet feeling so different to the fingers. The relationship of chords, inevitable, bound together in groups by a chain made of numbers. It's all too perfect. It excludes her. She can't imagine who invented this ultimate music machine. A mathematical genius? An acoustition? A nerd? She doesn't think it could possibly have been a musician.

She imagines the kind of musician she knows rolling a spliff one night and saying, "Yeah. I think what we need is a machine which will render the precise tonal relationship between eighty-eight notes at the touch of a finger. Yeah—but I can't get my head around it tonight, man."

Now, here she is, playing a computer which looks like a piano keyboard but which can sound like a horn, a violin, a clavichord, marimbas, percussion, or raindrops. It can remember sequences. It can split. It can do just about anything short of climb on a table and dance. In fact, it can do more than Karen can think of to tell it to do.

And here is InnerVersions in a scraggy little rehearsal room in Fulham. They are fooling around with a number called "Howl." Birdie Walker looks up from her notes and says, "Drop in a minor chord there."

Flambo says, "Fuck off, you can't because . . ."

Karen drops in the relative minor and it sounds right. It leaves more space for the lyrics, which were always too dense. And Karen wonders, "It's obvious. Why didn't I think of that?"

But she didn't. Birdie did.

Birdie takes Karen to a voice coach, which alarms the shit out of Sapper and Dram.

Birdie takes Karen to a terrifyingly cool hairdresser in Mayfair, which alarms the shit out of Flambo.

"What's she doing to you?" he says. "More to the point—*why*? Are you being groomed for fucking *stardom*? Is that your game? Because if it is, I'm telling you right now, this ain't a girl band. Never was, never will be."

Corky says, "We need a bit of color."

"Then Sapper can dress up like a drag queen for all I care. He's the singer."

Sapper doesn't say anything. In the last few weeks, he's noticed that Karen is singing a lot more harmonies than Dram. He's noticed that whereas Dram's harmonies are there or thereabouts, Karen's are accurate. It makes him think he should be more accurate with the melody line. It's an unnerving thought because he's already turned down the offer of a voice coach and cut himself off from a chance of immediate and quick improvement.

It seems as if two camps have formed, with Sapper and Dram supporting Flambo, while Karen and Corky support Birdie. Sapper is beginning to wonder if he chose the wrong camp.

To begin with, it was obvious: Flambo is a mate, Flambo likes Sapper's voice, and his ideas. Flambo is the drummer and he isn't in competition with Sapper. That threat always came from Dram. But Flambo said it was creative to have artistic tension between singer and lead guitarist—look at Aerosmith, look at Oasis. There were a million examples. And Sapper agreed.

Now, though, Sapper is confused. Yesterday he had a sudden insight, and he is often confused by his own insight.

They were working on one of his songs—a song that neither he, Flambo, nor Dram thought needed work. It just needed recording. But Birdie said it could do with a change of perspective.

Why? It's a song called, "Won't Go Home With You," and it's about a rude waitress. It's based on a real-life encounter Sapper had with a woman in an Italian restaurant. In it, he notices the smear of her lipstick and a scar on her hand. She puts him down but takes his money.

"OK," Birdie says, "but the verse is too long and wordy. Cut to the chorus more quickly. Give the chorus a different voice."

Sapper doesn't want to, but Birdie keeps coming back to it. She fixates on the scarred hand.

"It's only a detail," Sapper says in exasperation. "It doesn't matter."

"It does to her," says Birdie.

Whose song is this? Sapper wants to say. Is it mine or yours? But he says, "Is it mine or the waitress's?"

"Both—if you want it to be interesting," she says. "Yours if you want it boring."

So, reluctantly Sapper starts to work with Birdie and the chorus becomes the waitress telling the singer about the scar on her hand. She says, "Thirty-nine stitches, those sons of bitches, God how it hurt. They made me eat dirt. Don't you ever tell Mama, Don't cry."

When Sapper sings it, Birdie gets him to growl in a mocking way. She puts the harmony a fifth above to give it a harsher sound. Karen isn't around, so Birdie sings it herself. What emerges is a tired, hurt woman who won't take any crap from an attractive young man.

Sapper would never have written a song like that by himself. But when he listens to the playback he realizes that the chorus now defines the song and that the song is dark and much stronger.

The A&R man drops in and hears some of it. "Better," he says. "Way more punch. Could be a single."

And Sapper feels proud.

"I don't think you guys understand what proper A&R is," the

A&R man adds. "A&R is whatever it takes. And sometimes what it takes is a song doctor."

And Sapper feels humiliated.

Proud. Humiliated. Confused.

The A&R man takes Birdie aside and Sapper watches their private conversation through an open door. He can't hear what they're saying, but he's sure they are talking about him and his song. He hopes Birdie isn't reporting that he gave her a hard time, that he thought the song was perfect and didn't want to work on it. His dim little insight is that there might be people around who know more about stuff than he does. Well, anyway, different stuff.

In fact, the A&R man is worried about his job. Dog Records has a new boss and the company is cutting some of his bands. Others have been in preproduction far too long. Is Dog edging him out? He thinks Birdie has friends in high places and perhaps she'll put in a word for him.

Sapper, watching through the open door, sees Birdie pull her sweater down over her fingers as if her hands are cold. He can't see her face, but her pose is defensive. She looks like something out of an old French movie—the faulty strip lighting in the corridor is stammering and her hair flares in staccato bursts. The A&R man has more to say. Then he stoops and kisses her on both cheeks. He turns and walks away. Birdie, starring in an old French movie, remains. She doesn't watch him go. She stands, head lowered, thinking.

When she returns to the rehearsal room, Sapper feels her absence more than her presence. During her talk with the A&R man, she has become detached from Sapper and he misses the warmth.

IV

Dancing for Daddy

Before he met me, Jack was managed by a man called Sasson Freel. Sasson and Jack went to the same school and Sasson got Jack's first band its first ever gig at his sister's birthday party. Sometimes it happens like that—a bunch of fifteen-year-old kids banging away in their dads' garages or school music rooms become hot property. And the first kid to pass his driving test and acquire wheels can find himself with hot property on his hands.

But not for long. As they say, rock'n'roll is here to pay, and where big money is involved amateur management is about as much use as shoes are to a mermaid.

People say I came between Jack and Sasson. They say I was the greedy bitch who intercepted Jack on his way to stardom; that I attached myself to him, rendered him fuck-struck, and pushed him toward fame and the highlife. They say that I was so impatient for Jack to become a gourmet meal ticket that I separated him from his old friends, corrupted him, and introduced him to the professional sharks of the music biz. Oh, what power I had.

It simply isn't true. Well, true and simple aren't words which sit comfortably side by side, but apart from that—it didn't happen that way.

Nonetheless, some things get said so often that even the participants in a story come to believe them. You wouldn't think that either Jack or Sasson would accept alien versions of their own story, would you? But it was convenient to both of them for Jack to forget about his ambition and for Sasson to forget his incompetence. If they wanted to forget those critical facts, they had to replace them with fiction. And why go to all the bother of inventing a fiction when fans and critics had already done the job for them?

Well, who cares how it happened? The important thing was that I hadn't spoken to Sasson in years. And now I am going to meet him for lunch at that Hyde Park Corner hotel which used to be a hospital. Not my choice of venue.

As a matter of policy, I am always late for an important meeting, but judging just how late to be is a fine art. It's easy with people like Barry because what you are demonstrating is indifference and contempt. With others, it's a question of reminding them that you're worth waiting for. Sometimes you do it to demonstrate how important and busy you are.

What I wanted to show Sasson was not indifference for him, but indifference for time itself. I wanted to show him my arty side. He knows it exists because, at several steps removed, he pays me for it. He has recently become Managing Director of Dog Records. And, whatever he thinks of me personally, he also thinks that I'm capable of giving some of his baby bands, and their baby songs, a bit of spin and polish.

To give him credit, when he was frozen out of Jack's charmed circle, Sasson must've admitted to his own shortcoming. Because after wasting a few months ranting about ingratitude and betrayal he got a job with Wild Management and later became part of a consortium which set up an independent label. In other words, he learned the business and understood that there was more to it than the blind luck of being at school with a major talent.

He came to understand that the music business is business, not music. True, he made quite a nice chunk of change for a few musicians, but he made a fortune for himself. He became a serious player in a dirty game. How serious and how dirty? I'm beginning to find out, thanks to a small South London security firm with a good computer and an extensive network of contacts.

Now that I can research Sasson Freel, I've come to admire and despise him in equal measure. What I've found out makes me a little afraid of him.

Working for a security firm would be a truly unprofitable use of

51

my time if I didn't have an agenda of my own. But I always do have an agenda of my own, and I don't work for peanuts unless my employers can supply me with the facilities I need to make a bigger score. Cole-Adler provides me with research facilities. The score is information.

There is a problem, though: if you want, successfully, to pose as a good employee, a reliable office manager, a loyal wage-slave, you have to think like one. And after a while you begin to feel like one. Feeling like a good employee is death to the entrepreneurial soul. The fox, posing as a rabbit, feels like a rabbit. And, believe me, it's dangerous to go to lunch with another fox if you happen to be feeling like a rabbit.

I caught myself walking up Sloane Street, looking at expensive shop windows like an obedient office worker who has asked for and been granted time off. Obviously I wasn't ready for Sasson.

I turned into the Connaught Hotel to steady myself and adjust my mask. I was angry with myself. I used to be able to switch characters at the speed of light. It isn't just your skin which loses elasticity as you get older.

I followed two well-heeled American women into the cloakroom. There's something reassuring about cloakrooms in big hotels: they're designed to make you feel worth pampering. Even the tint and tilt of the mirrors give you a rosy view of yourself and your place in the world. You're valued.

I checked my reflection for weakness, spiritual flab, and lumpy mascara. I found a hint of doubt in my eyes. Bad, very bad. I thought, I've been in this cold, cramped, soggy, snobby little country too long. I'm beginning to look as if I know my place.

Behind me, the American women smoothed their non-iron garments and blotted their lipstick. I gathered that they were off to tour the public wing of Buckingham Palace, to trot through royal halls fast enough so that they could hit the stores afterward and still manage tea at Brown's. They wore energy and confidence like I wore *L'Air du Temps*.

In the mirror, my eyes seemed to flinch. I envied the Americans their certainty and I knew I couldn't meet Sasson with docile eyes. I turned my back on myself.

"Buckingham Palace?" I say. "How lovely. Have you any connections there, or are you just doing the *public* tour?"

The mark I pick is the taller of the two. She has honey beige hair to match her foundation. She stands securely on tennis player's legs.

"Excuse me?"

"Oh, I'm sorry," I say. Very English. "I shouldn't have butted in. But I was there only a few weeks ago—sublime, of course. I just wondered if you ... But I shouldn't have mentioned ..." I am playing with my own trepidation.

"No, go on," the beige mark says. "I didn't know there was anything but the public tour."

"Well, you have to make a special appointment," I say. "And it is quite expensive."

The other woman says, "I'm surprised my travel agent didn't put me down for it. This is supposed to be a deluxe vacation." She is wearing sage green silk, a lot of gold, and an avid expression. Whatever's happening, *this* one won't want to miss out.

"Well, never mind," I say. "Perhaps another time. It's a shame, though—it's nice, occasionally, to be able to do something not everyone gets to do."

"What should we ask for?" the sage-and-gold woman says. "I mean, we're going there anyway. We could get an upgrade."

"It doesn't work like that," I say regretfully. "You see, your guide would be a Royal Equerry."

"A Royal Equerry," breathes sage-and-gold, a sturdy, gleaming fish nibbling my bait.

"So, you'll understand that it isn't simply a question of renegotiating at the box office." I return to the mirror and take a small gold powder compact from my bag. Delicately, I touch my face with the tiny puff. It is exact mimicry of what these American women were doing five minutes ago. I'm just like them except that I am English and, therefore, infinitely foreign.

"In fact," I say, smiling through the mirror at my beige mark, "the box office doesn't come into it at all." I give the words "box office" a little extra flick so that the bait will fly out into deeper water. I'm wondering why I've picked the beige one as my mark. I did it

53

instinctively. She is the taller, slimmer one, but it isn't always true that physical characteristics are a clue to social status. However, we are all animals and animal judgments can prove to be useful.

I smile at her again, humorous, rueful. "Oh, it's all so boringly British. You can't get a thing done in this country without introductions and connections."

She smiles back at me. She is making an inventory of her own. My accent, naturally, is impeccable and intimidating—it whispers "culture." The venue, an expensive hotel cloakroom, is reassuring. She cannot place my clothes. But my hair has a shining insouciance which, she probably estimates, cost the earth. But am I sound? Would I pass muster at her club? She isn't stupid, but she is in a foreign country, which can have the same effect.

She comes to a decision. She extends a beautifully maintained hand and says, "Sylvie Glick."

Yes! I was right, beige is the social leader.

"Diana Beresford," I reply, noting an unexpected pang at my impromptu choice of *nom de guerre*. Mr. John Beresford was a name Jack used when he wanted to make anonymous travel plans or reservations.

Margaret, the sage-and-gold one, comes directly to the point. "So," she says, "what do you get to see that other people don't?"

"It's a suite of quite small rooms," I say. "I believe they were used most particularly by Edward VII for his more private assignations. The, er, family still occasionally employs them for the same purpose. But the art and antiques are exquisite."

"What do we have to do to get in?" Margaret says. She is quite transparent: the tour of Buckingham Palace is already ruined for her. Behind the tapestries and security guards is another world that Joe Public does not have access to, and of course it's more wonderful than what she's been offered. This is the story of her life—what she already has, by its very nature, is not special. What she has is always spoiled by what she doesn't have.

"Well," she says, defending herself from Sylvie's scolding glance, "she, I mean, Diana, she's been there. She must know somebody." She turns her disappointed gaze on me and goes on, "Tomorrow we're flying up to Scotland. The guys are crazy to play at St. Andrews. A coupla days in

London is all we're getting. I might've guessed we'd be fobbed off, even though we paid top dollar."

"What a shame," I sympathize.

"So we really wanted these two days to be something to remember," Margaret goes on. A disappointed, middle-aged child.

"We-ell," I say. I raise an eyebrow in the direction of the social leader. Her decision. Her responsibility.

"We can't ask you to put yourself out," she says, "but if you have a number we can call?"

"I do have a number," I say. "It's a personal contact. I could just enquire, if you like. But I should warn you, it's expensive."

"How much?" says Sylvie.

"I'm not sure," I say. "I'll enquire about that too. It's unlikely to be less than a hundred pounds a head. If that's too steep for you, please tell me now because I don't want to waste my friend's time."

"What's that in dollars?" asks Margaret.

"I don't know." I'm cool. No pressure. These women are hooked. I don't have to go any farther. I can meet Sasson feeling like a fox. This one, you see, was for laughs, for ego, a practice hit. It wasn't for money.

But sometimes, as in the past, my detachment acts as a come-on. And now I had two very hot-to-trot American women on my hands.

We left the cloakroom and went to consult the husbands. Sylvie's was a man who knew beyond any question that he was an Alpha male. Sylvie might be the queen of the women's cloakroom, but he was king of everything else.

The women make their pitch. I sit, nonchalant, on a fake regency sofa, uninvolved. I look at my watch. Time is passing. Sasson is ten minutes' walk away. If I leave now, I will be five minutes late. I watch Sylvie's husband, and without warning I find myself imagining lying in bed with him, playing the whore for him in a way that Sylvie, with her tennis player's legs, would find impossible. I can imagine his prudent passion, his puritan pornography. A few years ago, I would have bet on myself to make him part with a Central Park apartment within a week. I stop the thought dead and look at my watch again.

Sylvie's husband is The Banker. All decisions depend on his indulgence. His. Money, time, all his to dole out or deny.

55

Suddenly, I hate the prick. I get to my feet. I say, "Sorry, I should be on my way."

"Oh, Diana," Sylvie says, "I didn't realize ... But my husband says ..."

"Don't worry," I say, looking at my watch again. "No harm done. It was a pleasure to make your acquaintance, but now I really must go. I hate to be late." I nail her husband with a smile of pure charm and regret.

"Wait," says The Banker. "Can't I persuade you to stay for a few minutes longer? Sylvie was just explaining the deal."

"There's no deal," I say, taking offense. "You've misunderstood."

"I used the wrong word," he says smoothly. He detaches himself from his wife and isolates me a few steps away. A practiced power move. "The girls are very keen on this palace tour thing and I hear that you know a Royal Equerry."

"Let me explain," I say. "It was just friendly chit-chat, and all I was offering was an exploratory phone call. Your wife is a very charming woman."

"It takes one to know one," he says, eyes warm and focused. "Would you like to use my phone?"

"I'll use my own," I say. And then, to punish him for the warm focused eyes, which probably worked on his secretary but which he should never have used on me within two paces of Sylvie, I add, "If I do get through, and if my friend is willing, would you be interested in the *Private* Portfolio?" Always dress a punishment in a reward's clothing. "Just the *men*," I say softly, and my smile is full of dare, amusement, and complicity. I know you're flirting, my smile says, but how far will you go?

The words may not have registered, but the smile certainly has. "My god!" he says. "They keep that sort of thing at the palace?"

"What sort of thing?" I say, with just the hint of a dimple.

He laughs. Naughty boy.

"It's amazing." I let my lashes tremble. "Raphael, Leonardo, Rubens, Michelangelo. Well, Michelangelo you might expect, but *Fra Angelico?*"

"Good grief," he says.

"And hardly anyone has ever seen them. Only the cognoscenti even know they exist. It'll cost a little extra, of course."

56

"Make the call," he says.

I move off a few paces. I produce my phone book. I look up a number. I punch buttons. Reception is poor. I go to the hotel door. I have a two-minute conversation with my sister. The Banker hovers.

"Well?" he says, as I snap the phone back in my bag.

"Well, you're in luck," I say. "But can we solve the money problem? You can't hand traveler's checks to a Royal Equerry. You can't be seen paying him at all. It's etiquette or protocol or something."

The Banker is good at solving money problems. And so am I. He can lay his hands on a lot of cash and I can relieve him of it. We both do what we're good at. Dance for Daddy, little girl, and make him pay.

My reflection in the window of Harvey Nick's didn't flinch at all, so I dropped in and bought an extraordinary velvet jacket. A prize. The velvet was dark, dark green, crushed, and antiqued. The soft fabric caught the light and glowed. It draped and floated. The design was so clever that you couldn't tell whether it was brand-new or a rare art-deco hand-me-down. Exactly right for Sasson, and the best part of all—it was a present from The Banker. I saw it, I wanted it, The Banker bought it instantly. And now I was half an hour late for lunch, which, in the circumstances, seemed exactly right too.

The walk into the hotel was a walk into parallel time. Walking beside me was baby Birdie, bleeding from a wound in my shoulder when one of Jack's fans stabbed me with a pair of hairdresser's scissors. Another Birdie was carried in—miscarried, actually, after Jack, wired beyond sanity, beat me up. Yes, Saint Jack could be hard to handle after a concert and so could his fans.

It looked like a hotel, it smelled and sounded like a hotel, but it will always be St. George's hospital to me. I even met Sasson here once, when Jack OD'd on goofballs and Southern Comfort. Happy days!

The Sasson I knew then and the Sasson I met today were also as different as hospital and hotel. Yesterday's Sasson wore jeans and a sloppy sweater. He did the I Ching, bet on no-hopers in the Grand National, watched Grand Prix motor racing on TV with a tab of acid under his tongue, and was always in love with some pretty girl or boy who had problems but never, ever wanted to go to bed with him. Yesterday's

Sasson was permanently eager and always disappointed. His hair was Spanish black, his eyebrows met in the middle, and he would've died rather than wear a collar and tie. No suits for yesterday's Sasson.

Today's Sasson *was* a suit. His tailor had constructed him. His eyebrows were plucked and the Spanish black hair was steel gray. Poor, rumpled, dark Sasson was gone.

I said, "Remember visiting Jack here?"

"Here?" he said. "Birdie, you're late. Whatever are you talking about?" Even his voice had grown richer. His accent was now patrician.

"EMI were sniffing around, waving a contract, and I was totally panicked and rang you. You came running and we schemed all night about a food-poisoning story and how to get Jack up for the London Uni gig so that they'd never know. And then, after we'd spent all night in a state of advanced paranoia, Jack woke up, bright as a newborn chick, and we all went next door to the Pizza Express for American Hots."

"Good God," Sasson said. "I haven't thought about that for years. Was that here? I remember the EMI deal fizzled out—which was probably just as well, in the long run."

"Well, well, well," I sighed. "You remember the paper; I remember the pizza. No wonder you're so prosperous and I'm so broke."

He scopes the jacket and smiles. "Word games, Birdie," he said. "You always were good at those." But his smile was smug. He's up. I'm down. As far as he's concerned, the seesaw has come to rest in its proper position.

"Let's go through to the restaurant," he said. "They've been keeping our table too long." He led the way.

"Why did you pick this place?" I asked. I know the answer, but I don't want him to know I know.

"I live just around the corner," he said. Belgrave Square, to be exact—as up-market a slice of property as a sloppy young London lad could ever have hoped for.

"Mmm," I say with a barely concealed little shiver.

"What?" he says, poised in the entrance to the restaurant. The *maître d'* is on his way over. I touch his arm with two fingers. I want to know how much room I have to maneuver in.

"Memories," I say. I remove my light fingers and clasp my own arms, feeling the silky velvet. Hesitant, reluctant posture. I wince ever so slightly at a convenient clash of cutlery.

"Did you know?" I say, so softly that he has to bend toward me to hear.

"What?"

"I lost a baby here."

"No," he says. But he did know. He treated me with embarrassed care for weeks afterward. Jack told him, even though he promised he'd never tell a soul. That was Jack's way: when he was ashamed, he always tried to spread the load and redistribute the blame. And Sasson would have been scared. It was A Woman Thing. We were all so young. None of us knew anything about miscarriages. Hell, I hadn't even known I was pregnant till the doctor told me I'd lost it. As for the post-gig violence—well, Sasson would have seen that from Jack's point of view. It was just speeding, out of control. It was just Jack, strung to snapping point. Understandable. Boys identify with boys. Consequences come as a nasty shock.

"What do you want to do, Birdie?" Sasson says. He shows no annoyance whatsoever, just the same embarrassed concern he'd shown years ago. He remembers.

I turn my head away. "It's all right," I whisper. "But I'd be much more comfortable next door."

"Let's do that, then," Sasson says and takes charge.

I stood back and watched him explain and apologize to the *maitre'd*. He was firm, quick, and polite. No fuss. I wondered what he thought about violence against girlfriends nowadays. Had he understood the reality or was this patrician *noblesse oblige*?

We went outside and I felt the wind blow the velvet against my body. My hair flowed like water across my face.

"Just like that *Rolling Stone* cover picture," Sasson said suddenly.

"Hah!" I said. "Never kid a kidder, but thank you."

"You look well," he said, returning to formality.

Inside the Pizza Express, neither he nor I ordered an American Hot. Instead we ate salads and he began by asking after Robin. I was surprised he remembered her name, but maybe he'd prepared for this meeting too.

Then he asked about InnerVersions.

"What do you think?" he said. "The A&R report was equivocal."

"Hmm," I said. "Could be something in the mid-list if current trends persist for a year or two. Could be not. Depends what Dog has in mind."

Sasson didn't take the bait, so I went on, "The frontman's quite pretty. He has a goodish voice, which could come up with polishing, but he has a lot to learn. There's a girl with a lot of musical talent but very little in the pretty department. The others are betwixt and between."

"Meaning?"

"Meaning, unless Dog wants to invest more development money, at the moment there isn't enough shaggability to compensate for naïve musical ideas."

"Brutal," he said, "but succinct."

"But they're improving rapidly and would improve even more if the label is willing to commit time and money. You could have a nice little earner if you're at all interested in your mid-list."

"We put you with them."

"Peanuts, Sasson, and you know it. Dog always puts me with bands that aren't ready for a big commitment."

"We trust your judgment, Birdie."

I smiled sweetly.

"Damn it, Birdie," Sasson said, "I know that smile. It means you think I'm talking through my underpants."

"It means, what's your interest, all of a sudden? The Managing Director doesn't usually ask me for an interim report. In fact, I've worked with several Dog acts in the last few years and this is the first time I've met a top exec. And how long has it been since we met?"

"Too long," he admitted. "I just wanted to know how you were doing."

"Fine," I said. "Fine and sweet as sugar candy."

"Good."

My bland blue stare met his bland brown one across the table. We both smiled.

"So is it true?" I say.

"Is what true?"

"That you are Dog's new hit man."

"Is that what they're saying?"

"They're saying that you're cutting the dead wood, redefining Dog in order to make it attractive for a big buyout. Or it's going belly up."

"Amazing," says Sasson. "Where *do* these stories come from?"

"Paranoia in the record industry—amazing indeed," I say.

"Are *you* paranoid, Birdie?" Neat little sidestep there, Sasson. I laugh.

"Have some wine," Sasson says, "and don't worry." He fills my glass. "I believe," he goes on, "that every now and then, there is a minor clear-out on the ground floor. You needn't take it as anything more dramatic than prudent housekeeping."

Needn't I, Sasson? Well, that's nice to know.

I sip the wine. It's simple and tasty.

He says, "Really, Birdie, you mustn't worry. Your instinct for trends will always be useful, whatever happens."

The sum of all my experience, experiences, and experiments—the net weight of my talents is reduced to an "instinct for trends."

I put my glass down and closed my eyes. Lunch with Sasson was beginning to feel like an unsuccessful fishing trip. I could feel a boat rocking under my feet, wind in my face. The dark red ball of a setting sun tells me it's time to gun the motor and go home, but I flick my wrist and send the hook and line sailing out into a pool of still water between the writhing mangrove roots. One more time, just one more time. There's slim silver snook in there.

What's fascinating about fishing is the uncertainty. If you *knew* you could always catch a fish, it'd be called catching. But you don't know, so it's called fishing.

"Birdie?" Sasson said. "You aren't listening."

"What did you say?"

"I was wondering if you'd like to have coffee at my place. I have a wonderful new espresso machine and I can make it much better than they can here."

One more time? "Why not?" I said. But I picked up my wine glass again. The Pizza Express was safe and cheerful. Conversation clattered around us, echoing off the marble surfaces. I was in no hurry to move. Maybe getting in here would be my only victory. Such a small thing—to make Sasson change the venue of a meal—in other ways his well-kept exterior remained impregnable. He was regarding me with amused dark eyes, not giving anything away.

Yesterday's Sasson had been such a transparent, eager fish. And yet power and money suited him. The extra weight seemed like substance rather than fat. Old, sloppy Sasson dithered whereas this strange familiar man lurked with quiet confidence.

He emptied the wine bottle into my glass and said, "What're you thinking, Birdie?"

"Not thinking—listening to the reverb in this restaurant," I said promptly. Because when a man says he wants to know what you're thinking, the odds are fifteen to one he's lying. I went on, "Remember 'Going Down in the Diner'? The diner reverb we dubbed on to the coda?"

"Good lord, Birdie," he said, sitting back in his chair and looking at me with narrowed eyes as if trying to read someone else's paper from a distance. "You *do* have an eidetic memory, don't you? It's odd. You never struck me as someone who lived in the past."

"I didn't have much past to live in years ago."

"I remember some things," Sasson said, "but they're just facts, like old newspaper articles. They don't *live*."

"How gray," I said. "As a matter of interest, Sasson, doesn't the word 'eidetic' refer to visual memory? I was talking about a sound. What's the word for that? Ear-detic as opposed to eye-detic?"

"Aural," Sasson said flatly.

"Boring," I said.

He shook his head. "What is it with you, Birdie? Games, games, games. You haven't changed at all."

"Why should I?"

"Age," he said. "Real life. No money. Aren't they humbling experiences?"

A slap in the face, no less.

"Humbling to whom?" I said sweetly. "Are you humbled by your age or your real life?"

"But I'm not you," he said. "I never had it all and lost it. No peaks to tumble from."

"And you were never a woman. So youth and beauty don't matter. You aren't 'humbled' by gray hair and a paunch. You never made anything except money, so your work will never go out of style. You were never stylish. You were never judged for the way you looked or your shaggability or your 'instinct for trends.' You just sell what stylish shaggable people produce."

"Birdie, I ..." He was flustered and dithering now. I was relieved to see it because letting myself go has no place in my scheme. It's indistinguishable from letting myself down.

"Games!" I said in disgust. "You think of games as winning and losing. Why can't games be merely playful?"

"Because yours, yours and Jack's, were always designed for the bright and beautiful. You never gave the rest of us a chance."

Aha, I thought. An old wound. It went some way to explaining his surprising outburst.

I said, "Now who's tripped over memory? I make a bad pun and young Sasson cries 'foul.' Were you 'humbled' by your youth, Sasson, the way I'm supposed to be 'humbled' by my age?"

"Yes," he said, vehemently. "That was the wrong word. I apologize for it. But yes. I could never keep up."

"With what?"

"With Jack. And you, when you came along. You made matters infinitely worse. At least, before you turned up, I was part of the team. At least I was useful. You changed the game. The team became you and Jack. Everyone else excluded. Everyone else made to feel dull and plodding."

I said, "Couples are like that. All couples exclude."

"Yes," he said, "but ..." It seemed as if he was going to go on, but he restrained himself. I'm sure he would've said, "But Jack was different. Jack was special. Every piece of Jack you took was a piece I couldn't keep for myself."

Picture. A young guy with Spanish black hair picks up the phone.

63

An agent is offering his talent a soon-to-be-very-famous photographer for his new album cover. When he puts down the receiver, he rushes to tell his talented friend. Without knocking, he opens a door and sees the golden body of his talented friend asleep naked on indigo satin sheets. A golden girl sprawls like an exhausted kitten across his belly. The talent opens a sleepy, sensual eye and says, "Fuck off, Sasson."

Picture. A young guy with eyebrows that meet in the middle knocks at a door he would have previously walked through without thought. There is no reply, but he can hear a piano being played, so he thinks it's all right. He opens the door and sees his golden friend sharing a piano stool with the golden girl. He has his left arm around her shoulders. She has her right arm round his waist. He is playing chords with his right hand. She is playing a skipping bass line with her left. He is singing nonsense words. She is harmonizing with a shoo-wa line. They are both trying not to giggle. The young guy with the single eyebrow says, "Sorry, Jack, but ..." The music stops. The giggling voices shut up. Two heads turn simultaneously. Two pairs of Siamese cats' eyes blink. Jack says, "Fuck off, Sasson."

Sorry, Sasson, but it was a romance. You wouldn't expect to break in on Jack and Jill's honeymoon, would you? So why were you so hurt by Jack and Birdie's? Why was *everyone* so furious when they were excluded? Answer that one honestly, Sasson, and see what it tells you. It won't tell you anything about love that you don't already know. But it might tell you a little something about your attitude to a star.

Now, that's a sorry nest of snakes to uncover in the Pizza Express at Hyde Park Corner. It wasn't my intention. It wasn't Sasson's, either. But, whatever he says about memory, he's as much a victim of it as I am. I intended to use it but, instead, it used me. He wanted to keep memory and me at arm's length. But it seems we both jumped out and bit him.

Lunch is a bust.

It was time to fold my hand and pass.

I put the wine glass down and say, "Thank you so much for lunch." Good little girl. I say, "And thanks so much for your offer of coffee, but I'm afraid I have to blow."

"Please don't go," he says, without meeting my eyes.

This was unexpected. I thought he would be relieved. No one likes a witness to a lapse of control. And, if I'd read him right, his control was something he prized.

I watched while he composed himself. Which is to say, I watched him put the table straight. He folded his paper napkin, tidied the cutlery, rearranged the salt, the pepper, the flowers, as if they were on an office desk. When he was satisfied, he turned in his chair and beckoned a waiter. The waiter came immediately and, calmed by obedience, Sasson's rich patrician manner returned. He asked for the bill.

Only then did he make eye contact. "That was stupid," he said. "You must be right about memory. But I didn't come to pick at old scars and I certainly didn't mean to be insulting. I don't know what happened. But I do hope you'll come to my flat for coffee. I promised an old friend we'd meet him there."

An executive apology: the apology of a man or woman who would not apologize if it weren't tactically necessary.

I raised one brow and gave him my blue Siamese stare.

"Barry Stears," he said smoothly. "I believe you had dinner with him a few weeks ago."

So that was what lunch was about. Not a meeting between old friends. Not my baby band. Bloody Barry. I put my elbow on the table and rest my chin on the heel of my hand. It's a pose which does wonders for your jaw line. You can also hide any expression of distaste which might twist your perfect lipstick.

Oh yeah, summon the tricky little lady, soothe her with lunch and small talk. Keep filling her glass and then lure her to your apartment with promises of a slick new espresso machine. She'll fall for that, won't she? Then you can spring Fat Barry. And the big bad wolf will eat her all up.

"Look," Sasson says, "I know you don't take Barry seriously, but he's become a media heavyweight and you'd be wise to listen to him."

"Forgive a crude question," I say, "but what's it to you?"

"Well, you don't answer his letters or his e-mail. You don't return his calls. Your sister won't let him in the house. Why? He's harmless enough."

The waiter interrupts by placing the bill in front of him. He snaps his platinum card down and waves it away without looking. Careful, Sasson, that might have been me.

I say, "Sorry, but I don't want to meet Barry."

"Why?"

"Because he's a grave robber, a body snatcher."

"Come now, Birdie," says Barry's ambassador, "there's no need to get emotional about it. He isn't as bad as all that."

"You *know* he's as bad as all that," I say. "And I repeat, what's it to you? When did you become Barry's messenger boy?"

He looks at me. "There's mutual interest here. Dog owns the rights to *Hard Candy* and *Hard Time*. What Barry has in mind—the definitive appraisal of Jack, the life and work—will stimulate sales. Mo'Zee has all the previous product. They're enthusiastic. In fact, they're putting up preproduction money. They'll publish the book too. It's a neat little package, Birdie, and it's all ready to go."

"So go," I say.

"It won't be definitive without you."

"Then it won't be definitive."

"In which case, both the BBC and VH1 will pull out."

"Good," I say. "I'm tired of myths and legends."

"No one else is," Sasson said. "Barry tells me you have the Antigua Movie. And I know there was a whole raft of stuff in Jack's collection—photos, audiotape."

"Barry's probably got most of that already. He was thieving from us even before Jack died."

"Oh Birdie," Sasson says, "I'm sure you exaggerate."

"Do I?" I say. "Everyone was at it. They'd say it didn't matter—like nicking towels or ashtrays from a hotel—just a little souvenir. Jack won't notice—he's got plenty. He won't miss a little photo, he won't mind if private letters disappear or personal conversations are taped secretly."

"Yes, I know," he says. "It can be very trying. But Barry was a friend."

"Barry was a groupie. He still is."

"Nevertheless, he's a groupie with a big fat checkbook who can

66

pay a big fat fee. In fact," he adds, as if he's only just thought of it, "I can arrange things so that you don't have to deal with Barry at all."

"You can?" I say, with a cute little flutter of surprise.

"Why not? Dog has an interest. I know things have been tough for you lately. But we can turn that around."

I sigh, pure longing and nostalgia.

"Of course you're right about Barry," Sasson says sympathetically, "but he does talk a good game. Maybe he hasn't changed, though."

Yeah, Sasson, maybe he hasn't. But you have. You seem to be making a bid which could cut Barry out of the deal. I can still get to you, babe.

I gather my purloined velvet around me as if I'm cold, and say, "I'm so tired, Sasson. This thing follows me everywhere I go like a long shadow. I used to have some protection … I really miss that."

"Are you on your own now?" He leans forward, interested. He really, truly doesn't know a thing about me. Dog's accounts department and a few commissioning producers know more than he does. And all they have are my sister's address and one of my e-mails.

I shrug my shoulders and say wistfully, "Nothing lasts." Poor Birdie—she's had the best and now nothing less can ever match up. She's softened by nostalgia.

Sasson leans across the table and takes my hand. He says, "We have a history, don't we? Not an easy one, admittedly. But wasn't I always pretty straight with you?"

Yeah, you were, Sasson. You resented me in a pretty straight way. It's true, I always knew where I was with young Sasson.

"Yes," I agree. "You were pretty straight. But Dog wasn't."

"That's contractual, Birdie. That's to do with accounting periods and lawyers. Besides, back then, it wasn't even Dog."

"Copyrights and title," I say. "I was cut out every which way." I don't withdraw my hand and nor does Sasson. It's a warm clasp. Forgiving. He will forgive me for being a greedy bitch if I'll play nicely now.

"Maybe it's time we looked at all that again," he says. He strokes my knuckles with his thumb. It's a nice hand, warm and smooth. Yes, he has a good hand. All the cards, where contracts, royalties, and deductions are concerned, are in his hand. All the lawyers are in the palm of that hand too.

I say, "I'm tired of fighting. I just want to know that, if I supply any new materials to you, they belong to me. I want to be accepted as the owner of my own image for a change. I want to be paid for my own work."

"If there are any new materials, we'll sort it out," Sasson says, dismissing the crux of the matter with a reassuring squeeze. Does he have any idea how many reassuring squeezes this old hand of mine's endured? How quickly the reassuring squeeze turns into a stranglehold?

He goes on, "It all depends on what you have. What's on the film, Birdie?"

"Music and memories," I say. "A lot of beach stuff, as far as I can recall. But the bit Barry wants is the recording work. I don't know—it was a long time ago."

Sasson has his reactions well in hand now. He shows no particular interest. He says, "We'll have to show it to the lawyers. But I promise you that if you give it to Dog you'll be fairly compensated."

Now's the time to withdraw my hand.

I say, "It's not just the film. It's the music rights, the publishing, copyrights, authorship … That whole can of worms."

"We'll look at all that again," Sasson says. "Just show us what you've got."

"Oh Sasson," I sigh. "Give me a break, man. I don't even know where next month's rent's coming from. If you cut my baby band, I'll be out of work again."

"Your baby what?"

"InnerVersions. The band I'm working with."

"Never mind that," says Dog's Managing Director. "We've got much more important things to think about. What we're talking about is nothing short of a multimedia event."

"I know," I say. "But I don't want to rake up the past. What concerns me is making a living in the here and now. Making music, working with a young band which needs a commitment from you."

"But compared with Jack, they're nothing," he says, looking puzzled. "What was it you said? Not good enough musically to make up for … what was it … shaggability?"

"They need help," I admit. "I was trying to find out how committed Dog was to its could-do-a-lot-better-with-a-little-help bands. And you wouldn't answer. I did not say they were 'nothing.' It's not up to me to dismiss them or sign them. That's up to you. And you'll probably never hear them."

"I'll come and listen to them if you like." He lets a little of his irritation show. He nearly had me, and now, for some whimsical reason, I've changed the subject.

"They aren't ready," I say. "If you want to show some interest, give them a few months' more development—enough to polish up a tight set list. Let them record it. And then send them out to open for one of your name bands. Let the punters choose. That's the fair way. That gives them a chance to make something slowly and test it against a live audience."

"That seems fair." Sasson pretends to think about it. "But I don't know what the bean counters'll say."

"Just give them something to sell—could be two or three numbers on a single. Count units sold at live performances. Also, and this is important, ask a producer to persuade the frontman into voice coaching. He's okay, nice natural voice, but imprecise. And there's a nasty gap between his head and chest voices which exercises could fill in fine."

Sasson stares at me. He says, "You never used to be this analytical, Birdie."

Did I not, Sasson, babe? I used to wear a T-shirt which said, "Speak slowly, I'm a blonde." Nobody but me saw the joke. I used to be very young, very pretty, and very fanciable. Everyone looked. My God, how they looked. But no one listened.

Sasson says, "This front man—this singer—is there something going on that I should know about?" He's smiling, intimate, sharing what he thinks is a pleasantry.

Abruptly, I rise to my feet. I walk.

Head high, long easy strides, velvet swinging, I walk out on Sasson Freel—every inch of me a wounded queen. An immaculate exit. Eye-catching too. Several heads turn to watch my passing.

Outside, moving as fast as I can without actually sprinting, I turn east and disappear down the underpass. Not bad for an old broad.

Sasson would try to make a dignified departure from the Pizza Express. He would reason that when he got outside I would be somewhere in sight. He would think that I wanted to be caught, mollified, petted, and stroked because, otherwise, why did I walk? Women want to be caught. Women want to kiss and make up, be reassured. Women always give you a second chance, don't they, Sasson?

Not this one. And anyway, it was time to go. Time to let him think or stew a little. He just gave me a good excuse.

I walked along Piccadilly, mingling with the tourists, thinking, yes, it *is* time to go. I was tired of juggling two jobs and sorting out other people's lives for them. I'd been reliable for weeks, and being reliable is boring and exhausting.

I stopped at a public phone and called the office. The sweet old man answered the phone. I tell him that my niece has been involved in a motor accident in Paris.

"Of course you must go," he says. "How very worrying."

I say, "I'm the only one in the family who speaks halfway decent French."

"Don't bother about us," says Mr. Adler. "Just tell us if there's anything we can do."

"You're very kind," I say. And it's true. The lie was especially chosen for a kind man.

"I shouldn't be gone for more than a week," I say, anxious and regretful.

I took a taxi to Maida Vale and an address nobody knows. After that, with a sizable slice of fuck-you money, I went back to Robin's house.

The next morning I was on a plane to the States. I even wangled myself an upgrade. Birdie flew away. Club Class.

Stretched out, ankles crossed, sipping complimentary wine, I breathed out slowly. Yes! It was time to bask in the sun, to go fishing for real fish, to let the mud I'd stirred up in that cold English pool settle. I get restless and claustrophobic in England. It's all too tight for me, and reliability just isn't my thing. When I got back, one way or another, things would be clearer. Sometimes success depends on knowing when to take yourself out of the game.

I wanted to empty my mind, to feel loose, but images of Sasson leaked in. In the old days, I wouldn't have given him a second thought. But somewhere, in the intervening years, he had muscled up. He now had power, status, and money. I'm almost Darwinian about that. A man or woman with power and status is far more useful to me than one without.

But along with the benefits comes the danger. A man or woman with power and status should be manipulated with caution. They are strong, often at the expense of people like me.

V

Victim of Comfort

When Junior Moline's career stalled, there was no one to blame but Junior, and he was too laidback even to do that. On his business card, if he could find one, it said: "Producer/Engineer," and it's true that he'd had his moments. Years ago, he'd worked with some very big names. Years ago, he'd been going places. He'd traveled all over the world, on tour with bands, in studios with bands. And then, one day, he found himself in New Orleans.

What he always said was, "They don't call New Orleans the Big Easy for nothing. Well, I'm big and easy myself, where else should I go? My feet got stuck in the Mississippi mud."

It could be said too that his mouth got stuck to the business end of a chillum, and his arse got stuck to the cane chair on his lady's balcony, and his ears and heart got stuck to the throb of Delta blues.

It wasn't that he didn't work. He did work. Regularly. Seven days a year. On the last weekend of April and the first weekend of May, during the Jazz Festival, anyone could find him out at the Fairground, wearing a sweat-stained Stage Krewe T-shirt decked with backstage passes. Happy as Larry, balancing instruments, monitors, and microphones.

"One-one, two-two. One-one, tsu-tsu. One-one, chu-chu. Little more off the top there ... One-one, tsu-tsu. Yeah, got it." Seven acts a day with only thirty minutes between them to break down one set and then sound-check for the next lot.

Yes, he worked hard then, his big feet slapping across the boards in open-toed sandals, and as the day wore on, his outsize jeans slipped lower and lower and his T-shirt slid higher until everyone in the crowd below could see what he called his double bass.

Sometimes, friends and acquaintances, partying out there on the other side of the crush barrier, would call up rude remarks about his increasing girth. And he would call back, "Do you mind? I'm proud of this—I built it myself. Brick by brick."

Then, laughing, a friend might lob a can of Miller Lite over, and later, backstage, Junior Moline would sit back, replacing fluid lost in the thirty-minute scramble. He would feel the beer vibrating in the can to the beat of bass and drums. He'd know that everyone in front of the giant stacks of speakers would be feeling something close to cardiac massage from the sound he'd helped to produce. Sound waves, punching through the hot, humid air, rattling your ribs, nudging your lungs, and hammering on your heart. Exactly how live music ought to be felt out there in the sun.

Junior Moline loved the Festival. Once a year, all the talent spawned and nurtured around the Delta crawled out into the sunshine and made sweet music for New Orleans to dance to. Jazz, blues, cajun, zydeco, R&B, rock, latin, reggae, country, with a dash of hip-hop, African, and Native American for seasoning. There was a gig for everyone. No matter what you played, there was always someone to dance. No matter how badly you danced, there was always someone to play for you. And there would always be people like Junior EQing the sound.

In the beginning, it was the Festival that brought him to New Orleans. He first came with an American band he'd been recording with in London—out of England's tight gray fist into the hot wet light. A climate he fell into, relaxed into, like a warm bath on a cold night.

The band was Thieves Like Us, long ago split and divorced. But the lead singer and guitarist was Cy Fuentes, whose solo career became the stuff of music fairy tales—or cautionary tales—depending on your point of view.

Sound engineering for Thieves Like Us had been, at that time, a significant step for Junior. It was one of those steps from which his own career might have taken off, had he not been seduced by the Big Easy. But, more significant in the long run, was his meeting with Birdie Walker. Sometimes, lounging on his lady's balcony, he remembered the first meeting. She was ushered into the sound booth, like so many celebrity girlfriends, with a mixture of indifference and curiosity—another pretty chick there to admire the talent on the studio floor. She was there, he thought, to be impressed and also because while she was there she couldn't be with anyone else and she couldn't be out spending the star's money. The usual thing.

The half-glance he gave her took in a jailbait adolescent body, long blonde hair, and coltish grace. Cy's new babe was a baby, and Junior might have felt sorry for her except that he was too busy, and in those days even baby chicks didn't merit any sympathy: they were part of the furniture.

As the night wore on, though, he noticed something else: unlike the other chicks he'd seen come and go, she didn't get bored or read magazines or whine. Nor did she run around, rolling joints and fetching refreshment for the band. She paid attention. She didn't chat or ask questions or in any way interrupt, but he became increasingly aware that she was watching every move he made. At one point, when a discussion between the band and the producer turned into a slanging match, she sat on the floor as if the dramatic interlude was too boring to witness. Junior's feelings were similar. He said, too quietly to be heard by anyone else in the booth, "If it was me, I'd put in some silly brass."

"What?" she asked, just as quietly.

"They're fighting about strings," he said. "Stupid idea. But they do need something, and if it was me ..."

"What do you mean 'silly brass'?"

"Well, like a bass tuba or a sousaphone—a bit of deep-down oompah for extra beat and texture."

She considered this for a moment, smiling dreamily. Nothing else was said.

But the next day, late in the evening, a bewildered, spotty young man with a bass tuba was shown into the studio. Cy's explanation to the producer even recycled Junior's description, silly brass. Junior, of course, got no credit, either for the idea or the description. Nor did Birdie. Cy took that. All Junior got was a long, slow wink from Birdie.

The real payoff came later when he was hired to produce Wild Jack's second album and found that he'd been hyped as a soundman with imagination. And who should turn up with Jack to the first meeting? She was a little taller perhaps and more polished, but the long blonde hair and the lazy wink were the same.

The wink, Junior thought, was absolutely something to write home about. Birdie turned her head so that no one but Junior could see the winking eye. Then, without moving any other facial muscle, she slowly dropped one eyelid. It was like an illusion: one half of her face went to sleep while the other remained sweetly attentive. Everyone else in the room saw only her perfect profile. It was the first hint Junior had that with Birdie what you saw was *not* what you got. What you saw, of course, was so beautiful that it was hard to respond to her as anything but a visual feast. "Blinded by beauty," Junior said, ruefully explaining why even he had been slow to take her seriously.

"If she'd been a guy or a bit uglier," Junior said, "who knows what she might have achieved."

He once heard Jack say to her, "Jesus, babe, you don't have to *do* anything. You just gotta *be*. Sit there with your mouth shut and you're perfect. I love you."

With half the world, as it seemed then, aching for Jack to love them too that sounded like a compliment. You're perfect. Jack loves you. Stay that way and shut up. What a trap, what an insult, Junior thought later. But only years later, and only after years of being looked after by a short string of independent women—the sort of women a lazy, easy-going man is attracted to. Because if a lazy, easy-going man wants the support of an independent woman, he learns to listen to her. If you don't pay the piper, you don't call the tune. But you really should listen to it sometimes, or you'll end up a lonely, lazy man.

What surprised Junior was the way his acquaintanceship with Birdie slowly turned into an on-again-off-again friendship. He was surprised that he still knew her, and even more surprised because it was she who kept in touch. At first, he thought that her interest in his job was because he was useful to her. If she studied his working practices and his vocabulary, he thought, she would look less like the gorgeous idiot everyone thought her to be, and she could stay one step ahead of the competition. But then he noticed that what she knew was of no importance whatsoever. Because no one listened to her. Even Jack, even when he was using her as a co-writer, backup singer, or piano player, behaved as if he was indulging a pretty child. Jack might come in with a rough track to show the band. It would be clear that the harmony voice was hers and that she was playing the electric piano pad which underpinned his guitar tiffs, and that half the lyrical ideas could only be hers. And even though that rough guide was what the whole studio used to build a polished song, the most Jack would say was, "Ah well, got to keep the girl amused—can't let the girl get bored."

Music was man stuff—unless you had a voice like Etta James or Aretha Franklin, in which case you would be allowed to sing.

Birdie did not have a big black voice. What she had was soft, white, and, worse, English. She could not even be a respectable harmony singer. Her growing feel for melody and harmony was not something she could use herself. She could only give it away to people who would make it sound right.

At one time, Junior thought she might want to use his expertise to give herself credibility. And it was true that she did. But even now, when he hadn't recorded with a Name for years, she still played him tapes of what her "baby bands" were doing and listened to his comments and suggestions. He knew that nowadays there were other, more useful, people to use as sounding boards. He was out of it. The big time had ticked away.

But still she kept in touch. Even when he was flat broke and couldn't offer her so much as a sofa to sleep on when she showed up and hung out. Then, it was her turn to offer him notions—money-making schemes to tide him over. Schemes which were actually scams: how to blag a free meal, how to con the bank into giving him more credit, how to fake references for a suspicious landlady. In other words, she taught him how to get by in an expensive place without a penny in his pocket.

"Swimming under water," she called it. "Survival techniques, so's you can hold out till the next breath."

Eventually it occurred to Junior that this was, quite simply, how Birdie lived: someone else paid the bills. What was more, people seemed to fall all over themselves for the privilege. He knew he should have despised her. He knew that he should despise himself, but he could never quite summon up the energy. Drifting, as he did, between boom and bust, what he felt was a kind of kinship.

Maybe she just fuckin' likes me, he thought, when he thought about it. Maybe it's because I never hit on her. Maybe with so many sweaty erks pawing her all the time she could relax with a lazy technician who considered her out of his league.

Birdie, he thought, used to be the most beautiful woman he'd ever seen. And both men and women couldn't seem to keep their hands off her.

He remembered once leaving a restaurant with Jack. What were they doing? Probably having a preproduction meeting about *Hard Candy*. After about two hours, Jack called his car. Jack would never leave anywhere until he knew his transport and security were in place. Even so, on this occasion, word got out and Jack, Birdie, and Junior had to wade through a boiling crowd of photographers and fans to get into the car.

Junior, in those few violent moments, had a confused nightmare impression of grabbing hands and flashing lights before he was bashed on the head and dragged into the car. The car lurched slowly away, covered in kids. Kids on the roof, kids clinging to the hood, kids spraying hearts in shaving cream or Miracle Whip on the windscreen. Kids writing "Screw me!", names, phone numbers, in lipstick on the windows.

Inside Jack was screaming furiously at the chauffeur and the security man. Birdie was trying to make herself decent. Her shirt had been yanked so violently that there were no buttons left and her skirt was torn to the waist. Even her lacy black underwear was in tatters.

Junior, who was feeling shocked and stupid, said, "Ain't stardom just peachy?"

Jack sat back, adjusting his own vandalized clothing, and said, "I reckon I must be one of the few men in the world who knows what it's like to be a beautiful woman. Junior, give the girl your jacket."

Junior struggled out of his jacket and Birdie put it on without a word. It was big enough, even in those days, to cover her to mid-

77

thigh. She wrapped it around her like a dressing gown and sat with her arms folded across her chest.

All legs and eyes, Junior thought, trying not to stare.

"Yeah," Jack said, reading his mind, "she'd look like a doll if she was wearing a brown paper bag. They try, but they can't seem to ruin her."

Birdie said nothing. Of the three, she appeared to be the calmest.

"You look like a rape victim," Jack said. "Battered and beautiful. Want a fuck?" His hands were shaking and his eyes were raw and angry.

"Do *you*?" asked Birdie.

"Yeah," said Jack.

"Then go fuck yourself," said Birdie, in her soft, white, English voice.

"I could throw you out there to the wolves," Jack said.

"You could," she agreed. She searched in the small bag she always carried and produced a gold powder compact. Inside were a few capsules wrapped in tinfoil. She gave two to Jack and offered one to Junior.

"What are they?" he asked.

"Peace," Jack replied, stuffing the capsules into his mouth. "Time out of war. Cessation of hostilities. Surrender."

"Jelly babies," said Birdie.

Junior shook his head. For the rest of the trip, he remained as shocked and stupid as he had been at the beginning.

What had Junior seen that day? He replayed the incident in his mind many times, especially after Jack's death. Because rumors surfaced in the press, persistent rumors which even now floated around on the Internet. They claimed that Birdie was Jack's murderess—that she had set the fatal fire, that she had drugged Jack so that he couldn't respond to the emergency, that she had supplied him with enough scag to kill six horses and then burned him and his house to destroy the evidence.

What had he seen? Two young people under great pressure? Jack's unexpected thuggish side? Birdie controlling Jack with drugs?

Surely not that. Junior knew, better than most, that the Name, unless he's desperate or a moron, never carries his own stash. That's the roadie's job, or the friend's, or the girlfriend's. At a pinch, it might even be the sound engineer's. No one wants the Name to be busted. So, while it might look as though Jack's girl was supplying, it was more probable that she was simply carrying. Even so, when Jack died and was sanctified—as is the custom with beautiful young rock stars—Birdie was demonized. And the underground rumble was so hostile to her, so full of conspiracy whisperings, that Junior himself wondered if a small percentage might be true. Lost in Louisiana, away from the action, he read stories about mythic strangers called Jack and Birdie the way a child might read stories about Snow White and the murderous wicked stepmother. The stories, he felt, had more to do with folklore than fact, but they were as infectious as germs and, like germs, they multiplied.

Every objection was countered: why would Birdie do away with her meal ticket? Well, said the anonymous accusing voices, Jack was already fed up with her. He was going to dump her. He was seeing someone else. She was about to be publicly humiliated.

No, said others. She wanted his money. She had secretly forced Jack to marry her. In Vegas. In Mexico. In Tahiti. In Cuba. He was furious with her for her extravagance. He was going to cut off her funds. He was going to divorce her.

Wrong. She was a member of a coven. The Sisterhood of Ishtar. An extreme right-wing/left-wing sect. She was a hypnotist. She involved him in satanism. When he woke up and wised up, she had to kill him.

That's stupid, said others. Why ignore the obvious? Birdie was seeing someone else. Jack caught them together. There was a fight. Jack was killed. Birdie torched the house to protect her reputation and her lover.

Who was her lover? Ah, now *there's* a loaded question. He had to be big. Someone worth protection. So let's begin with the British Royal family. The long list of possibilities began with Prince Charles and worked its way through sheikhs and kings. It included any of the fifty richest men in the world who were not gay. Industrialists. Politicians. Film stars.

And so on, and so on. It was enough to make a lazy man's head spin. And, being a lazy man, Junior simply turned his back on it, as he did with anything that caused him hassle. It was easier not to think about it. If he thought about it, he might have to do something about it.

He might have to leave New Orleans and find out for himself what the truth was. He might have to accuse Birdie himself. Or he might have to defend her.

It is best to know nothing if you plan to do nothing.

Besides, Birdie never defended herself. Perhaps that was her greatest crime. She spoke to no one. She gave no interviews. Even Jack's funeral was a secret affair—the cremation, wags said, had already taken place and no one could find a grave to desecrate. Birdie was never seen in mourning. If she wore black, it was because black was stylish and it suited her.

"Why don't you set the record straight?" Junior once asked her.

"Which record?" sighed Birdie. "To whom? People think what they want to think. They aren't interested in the truth. They only want a good story. With pictures. If I so much as open my mouth, I'll only be giving them weapons to use against me."

Ambiguous, Junior thought. And then remembered how experienced she was with journalists and photographers. Experienced enough to be forever on guard. He'd often wondered why the famous or notorious didn't simply keep their mouths shut more often, since they were made to look such idiots when they opened them. Damned if you do, damned if you don't, he mused. He himself would surely be damned for what he didn't do if there was any choice in the matter. So his feeling of kinship with Birdie strengthened.

He was glad she didn't want to talk about it because, deep down, he didn't want to know. That was heavy stuff. Heavy feelings. Hassle. Better to smoke a little herbal and chill. Don't let it get to you, man. Who needs it?

That's eventually what he said to Teddy when Teddy unexpectedly came knocking at his door. At first it was, "Hey, man! God! Shit—how long's it been?" Thinking, fuck, if he hadn't said his name, I'd never've recognized him. Bald, for fuck's sake. What happened to all the hair?

Teddy used to have authentic rocker's hair, which he waved like a banner for the cameras. In all the pictures of Jack on stage, somewhere behind or off to the side, you'd see Teddy with those streamers of rocker's hair. Or Teddy, the typical autistic axman, curled over his guitar, hiding behind his own tangled vines. That was one of his favorite poses—the recluse in the spotlight. Especially after a solo. Camera-shy, and modest with it. Wanker, Junior thought. Because nothing could have been farther from the truth—every scrap of tension between Jack and Teddy could be put down to the perpetual war waged between frontman and sideman.

"Those were the days," Teddy said, from the prison of Junior's woman's armchair. "Don't you miss it?"

"Dunno 'bout that," Junior said. "I don't miss the friction or the nerves. I was fuckin' getting ulcers back then. Everyone on your case all the time. No, I was glad I got out of it when things got *really* brutal."

"But not before Madison Square Garden." Teddy really did sigh then. Because Madison Square Garden was the venue of the famous ax'n'sax thrash, which Junior captured for all time on *Jack's Back Live in the USA*. It was one of those rare occasions when Jack was forced to step away and let Teddy take center stage—a time when they'd asked Al McQueen, sax maestro, to sit in, and Teddy's solo on "Packet of Ten" turned into an extraordinary exchange between guitar and sax. A battle in which neither was prepared to yield. Lunge, parry, riposte. Hit and run. Trading bar for bar, blow for blow, it was a passage of pure musical aggression fueled by pure adrenaline. It was a sponta-neous event which usually only works live. But Junior, going mental at the mixing desk, caught it and preserved it, as if he knew it would be special even before it happened.

Both Junior and Teddy were justifiably proud of what they did at Madison Square Garden all those years ago. The ephemeral made permanent.

"Man, you were the best," Teddy said.

"Oh yeah," Junior said, skeptical, remembering all the mixing wars. If for some reason you wanted to mix Goff or Wills up at Teddy's expense, you had a fight on your hands. It was all like that. Every band member wanting to be heard loud and clear. No one satisfied. No one wanting to be the texture behind. Every silly sod a soloist, Junior thought. All at the same time. Then Junior was the ignorant bastard who was paid exorbitant sums to wreck their careers.

"I was working with Wills in New York only last week," Teddy said. "Do you see any of the old faces these days?"

"People drift through," Junior said. "Like *everyone* comes around April, May."

"I mean us," Teddy said. "Jack's people."

"Anyone comes to N.O. and looks me up, I see 'em." Junior snapped open a couple of cans of Bud and passed one to Teddy. Outside, dusty afternoon sun fought its way through the hanging jungle on the balcony and began to creep into the room. Time to pull the blinds. Junior thought about it, but tipped a little beer down his throat instead. Having company was hard work when you didn't know what the company wanted after all this time.

"Goff told me you kept in touch with Birdie," Teddy said, looking round for a glass. There wasn't one.

Uh-oh, Junior thought, time for the blinds, and he heaved his bulk off the sofa. While he threaded his way through his woman's delicate knick-knacks, he said, "She's still in the business, you know."

"As much as she ever was," Teddy said. "I'm surprised anyone wants to know. How old is she now?"

"Never asked." Junior busied himself at the window. It was a precise operation. His woman liked the blinds closed enough so that direct sunlight was blocked from her paintings, carpet, and soft furnishings, but open enough to air the room. He didn't usually give it as much attention as he was giving it now.

"She's still a full-on bread-head," Teddy said. "You know she's always fighting the labels to give her half Jack's royalties?"

"Yeah?" said Junior, padding back to the sofa. "Well, that ain't nobody's business but hers."

"You might as well say I co-wrote," Teddy said. "Which I did. Or even you. Think of what *you* put in. Jack would've stayed a fucking pub player without us."

"Improbable." Junior lowered himself into the cushions. "Jack had the magic from very early on."

"Oh, he was the best frontman in the business, I'll grant you that. No one could sell a song better than him. But whose song was it? That's the question."

Junior looked at Teddy over the rim of his beer can. Confrontation, he thought. Hassle.

"Well?" Teddy asked, leaning forward.

"I don't think about it, man," Junior said. "I got well paid for what I did. So did you."

"That's open to question too. How much did you make when the albums were re-released on CD?"

Junior didn't answer. This was what he didn't need. This murky, dirty music-business talk—resentful victim-speak. It got you in a bean-counting mood and you ended up feeling you'd been shafted all your life. Everyone else was getting rich off your creative input. Only the stars could fight and win. Nobody else even fought. They just gathered in small rooms and bitched. About money. About recognition. About contracts, credits, and Christ knows what-all else.

What the fuck, Junior thought, everyone knew it was a dirty business, and everyone still wanted to be in it. So you signed an agreement and you were happy to get the gig. But when the gig turned out to be a money-maker and you weren't cut in … When there were big-time winners on the music lottery and you were never one of them … Bitch, bitch, bitch.

But it was justifiable bitching. You *were* shafted. The fat cats *were* blowing smoke up your arse. You thought about it. You started bitching. You got hassle. You got ulcers. And, if you were called Junior Moline, you got out. You sucked on your beer can, you sucked on your chillum and went back to loving the music. Forget about hating the business— that takes too much energy, man, that just fucks with your head. Listen to the sounds and kick back.

New Orleans was the place to do that. There was a pair of buskers under Junior's window right now, noodling on "A Place in the Sun" and doing it more than justice. This was a town where buskers could sound better than Eric Clapton. Junior tuned Teddy out and tuned the buskers in. Yes. One voice. Two acoustic guitars. Pickups, ampli-fier, two small speakers. He could imagine two old guys on folding chairs, guitar case open at their feet to catch a few thrown dollars. Crap equipment—all of it beat-up and warped by the wet heat. Ah, but that voice, man, those finger-licking riffs.

God bless their golden hearts, Junior thought. Better to have your gui-tar warped by the sun than to have your heart warped by a dirty business.

Teddy was saying, "C'mon, June, don't you want to claw some back? It won't cost you nothing, all you got to do is talk to Birdie."

"And tell her what, man?"

"Tell her to release the materials. All the Antigua stuff. I mean, you could help with the re-mix. We could all come away with another slice of the pie."

"Not me, man," Junior said, slowly. "I don't want any more of Jack's shit. Dead or alive, if it's anything to do with Jack, it's always a heavy scene. Everyone fussing and fighting. Bad karma, man."

"That's bullshit, June, and you know it. Don't hide behind that karma crap. This is a big deal. They're making a telly program. There's going to be a book. The full package. It's like our time came round again. All the old stuff's cool."

Unbelievable, Junior thought. Bald and still hungry. Still aching for the super-trooper and the big car. Whatever happened to counter-culture? Did it go under the counter when the bean counters took over the world?

"I don't know about you," Teddy said, "but I could do with the extra moolah. I got three kids and four mortgages to service. You never had any kids?"

"Not that anyone told me," Junior answered.

"Birdie didn't, either. Too busy looking after number one. But they say she's hit hard times now."

"We all have our ups and downs," Junior said.

"More downs than ups these days." Teddy eyed the sagging furniture. "What I'm saying is that Birdie's got access to stuff that could make us a lot of bread. If you don't want to be involved, well, cool. But I do. I think I'm owed, man. I was there on the film. I was playing in the studio. That stuff's as much mine as it is hers."

"Maybe," said Junior, who would say anything to avoid an argument, "but what am I supposed to do about it?"

"You don't have to do anything," Teddy said, to Junior's great relief "But didn't she, like, come to see you after Jack died? I mean, she did one of her disappearing tricks, so did she ever turn up here with stuff to store in your cellar?"

"There aren't any cellars in New Orleans," Junior said.

84

"The attic, then."

"Why would she do that? What stuff?"

"I don't know," Teddy said. "Who knows what women keep. They say she rescued everything of value after the fire. Pity she didn't rescue Jack, eh? They say she grabbed everything—stuff that wasn't hers—and took it out of the country. She'd have to store it somewhere."

"Not here, man," Junior said. "I've only lived here eighteen months myself. This is my woman's place."

"Oh well," Teddy said, losing interest.

"What're you looking for?"

"Nothing," Teddy said. "Her, actually. Thought I could persuade her to cooperate. Appeal to her better nature, if she's got one. I was Jack's best friend, after all."

You and whose army? Junior thought. It was amazing how many best friends Jack had after all these years. He said, "Can't help you there, man. I don't know where she's at."

"You must have an address."

"E-mail address," Junior said, vaguely slapping his pockets. "I only see her when she shows up. But I can give you the e."

"Got it. She isn't responding. C'mon, man, where do you send the Christmas card?"

"Christmas card?" Junior laughed. "Look, Ted, as far as I know she's been in L.A., Geneva, Kingston Jamaica, Kingston England, Kingston Ontario, Sydney, Berlin, and Tunis. All in the last couple of years. Oh, and Kuala Lumpur. She ain't what you'd call a home body."

"Shit," Teddy said. "When did you see her last?"

"Dunno. Oh, must've been May. Festival. She was scouting acts for a nightclub owner in Malaysia. That's how I remember Kuala Lumpur. He was even fatter than me and a damn sight richer, man. Best hotel in town. Three secretaries. If you want to know who's paying the bills, try Kuala Lumpur. Or better still, try her sister."

"Done that," Teddy said, standing up. "She was in London up to two weeks ago and then she took off. The sister doesn't know where to."

"Where are you staying?" Junior stood up too. "I might think of something."

85

"The Sheraton on Canal. Just the one night. Yeah, if you think of something, let me know."

"I'll look in my files," Junior promised. He padded barefoot to the door and watched Teddy go down the narrow staircase to the court-yard. Sharp shoes, he thought, but it's too damn hot for socks, even silk ones. Teddy slid a pair of celebrity shades onto his nose, raised a hand in farewell, and walked away into the dense, wet heat.

What, no limo? Junior thought and shut the door.

When he got back to the lounge, he saw, without surprise that Birdie was coiled in the deep armchair Teddy had just left.

"How the fuck did he find me?" Junior asked, flopping down on the sofa. "You could've struck a flint off me when he said who he was on the door phone."

"I thought you were superb," Birdie said. "Super cool."

"Yeah, well—I was having caniptions."

"Poor baby," Birdie said.

"You can laugh," Junior said, "but my shoulders hurt."

"How about some ice cream and a back rub?"

"Yes and yes."

"And then a game of cribbage," Birdie said, gliding away to the kitchen. "I've got to think fast."

"OK," Junior said, with less enthusiasm. He owed her four thou-sand, seven hundred, and twenty-nine dollars from cribbage games over the years. At a hundred dollars a win and a dollar a point, that represented a fair number of losses.

He remembered his own astonishment at seeing her play with Jack the first time he traveled with them. First-class on Concorde from London to New York, the compartment full of musicians and tour bigwigs. Ignoring them all, at the front of the plane sat Jack and Birdie with a deck of cards and a cribbage board, deadly serious. Rock stars don't play cribbage, he thought. But Jack did. When he was feeling unsociable, he played obsessively, game after game, dragging himself through the dead hours of travel.

Junior sat with his back to Birdie, digging Cherry Garcia out of a tub and licking it off a long spoon while she dug her thumbs into his shoulder muscles, loosening the kinks. Nothing was said until halfway through the first game of crib, when he was already trailing by seventeen points. Then she said, "Well, my guess is that Barry Stears sent Teddy to find you. It's the sort of thing he'd do. If it were Sasson ... I think Sasson would do something more sensible."

"What's going down?" Junior asked reluctantly.

"I don't think you want to know," she said. "But Teddy's right. There *is* a Jack-package on the burner and they're turning up the heat. You *could* make some money."

"Nah," Junior said. "Let it be."

"Why? Suppose they show up here with a film crew and want an interview. Suppose Barry asks a load of silly questions about the making of *Hard Candy*. You could ask for whatever you wanted."

"You wouldn't like that."

"Why not? They're going to do it anyway, and if they're interested in the production side you're The Man. At least you'd give them straight dope. I'd rather it was you than some ignorant ligger."

"What if they want personal stories?"

"That's not your scene," Birdie said, turning over the cards in the crib and displaying a nice double run for another eight points. She grinned and said, "Anyway, if it's stories they want, we could cook up a couple of dillies. I think you should ring Teddy and maybe take him out tonight. When's Sandrine coming home?"

"Sevenish. But I don't want to spend any more time with that son of a bitch."

"Who's in town? Anyone good playing at Tips or The House of Blues? You could take them both there. Sandrine likes a night out, doesn't she?"

"I'm broke," Junior said, feeling like a paper boat approaching Niagara Falls.

"My treat," said Birdie.

"Oh shit," said Junior. "What d'you want me to say?"

"I'll think of something. Don't worry. Just have a good time. Enjoy yourself. Sandrine didn't know I was coming, did she?"

"How could she?" Junior said ruefully. "I didn't know myself. And Teddy was quite a shock—he hasn't spoken two words to me in the last ten years."

"Yes, that was awkward, but you were terrific and I think we can turn it all round."

"We?" said Junior with foreboding.

Afterward, when Teddy rang the next day and complained that his hotel room had been broken into and that traveler's checks, personal stereo, laptop, and shaver had been stolen, Junior felt dismay but no surprise.

"Bummer, man," he said. "This town, eh?"

"All electrical goods," Teddy told him. "Good thing I didn't bring a guitar."

"While we were out dancing?" Sandrine said. "That's a shame." She was what Junior called a jolly dancer—plenty of bounce and footwork. It was the bounce that had caught his eye in the first place. Bounce and a D-cup. Junior liked Sandrine a lot. She had a good, steady job, and that was a turn-on too.

She said, "Tell him to give our number to the police in case they recover any of his stuff."

She was generous too, Junior thought as he relayed the message into the telephone.

"Fat chance of that," Teddy said. "Neither the police nor the hotel seem interested and I'm leaving in an hour."

"Where're you going, man?" Junior asked. "In case we hear anything."

"Thought I'd give LA a shot. Thanks for the tip."

The tip, of course, was Birdie's, so Teddy was about to take off on another fruitless journey.

"Well, good luck, man," Junior said, and hung up, thinking that Birdie was probably right: Teddy must be traveling at someone else's expense. If he was flying to the West Coast to look for a Chinese-American she-male who might or might not still have a house near Venice Beach, he was unlikely to pay for the ticket himself.

At dinner the previous night, when Junior, Sandrine, and Teddy were sitting round a courtyard table, Junior said, "If I was you, Ted, I'd look for Renée-Ronny Pang."

Teddy almost choked on his French onion soup. "That fuckin' pervert!" he said.

"Who's Renée-Ronny?" asked Sandrine, who was interested in the lives of the rich and famous.

"Never met her myself," Junior said. "But Birdie said she was a masseuse, an astrologer, and sometimes a sort of cabaret bandit. She was about as androgynous as you can get. One of those West Coast bands introduced her to Jack."

"He had a sore neck," Teddy said, "an old whiplash injury. The Thing treated it and then just stuck around. It was Birdie's friend, really. It was Birdie who was into all that freaky stuff. Not Jack. He was just trying to fuck with my mind. One gig, he even had her-him come on stage and try to smooch me. Shit!"

Now Teddy was flying off to see The Thing who made his skin crawl, exactly as Birdie predicted he would.

"Give them what they want," she'd said. "The trick is to know who wants what. Like the *National Enquirer* knows what its readers want. And Renée-Ronny certainly knew what the *National Enquirer* wanted."

"She really let you down," Junior said.

"Yes, those stories caused a lot of trouble."

"So why resurrect them?"

"They never died," Birdie said with a shrug. "You can't resurrect something which isn't dead. Anyway, the stories don't matter. All we want to do is remind Teddy and Barry that I stayed with Renée-Ronny after the fire. That I confided in her. Nudge Teddy in that direction."

Nudged, Teddy said, "Oh shit, yes—that crap: 'Jack Feared for His Life' and 'Beware the Blonde Bride—I saw it in the stars.'"

"Hey, I remember that," Sandrine cried. "I was just a kid, but my big brother had all of Jack's records. I remember seeing that headline at the checkout with my mom. There was a picture and the caption said, 'The smile of an angel, the heart of a demon,' and I thought it was so cool, you know, to be bad and beautiful, when I didn't even need a brassière or have a boyfriend yet."

"You're not saying all that tabloid stuff's true, are you?" Teddy said.

" 'Course not," Junior said, "it's garbage. But Birdie did tell me about going to see Renée-Ronny. Turned out she wasn't the friend Birdie thought she was."

"Surprise, surprise," Teddy said.

"She was looking for a port in a storm, only Renée-Ronny wanted to be Birdie's publicity agent—a real twenty-percenter, while Birdie just wanted a friend and as little publicity as possible."

"Poor Birdie," Sandrine said.

"They had a bust up," Junior said, "and when Birdie got up the next morning she found half the world's press camped out on Renée-Ronny's doorstep, and the other half in the living room. She told me she had to escape in just the clothes she was standing up in at the time, and she never went back for the rest of her stuff."

"What did she leave behind?" Teddy asked.

"Dunno, man," Junior said. "What she told me was, 'I hardly had time to grab my passport. I had to climb out the bathroom window and run across the garage roof.' I think she regretted it later."

"Regretted what?"

"Leaving things behind. She said once she wished she hadn't lost so much." Message delivered, Junior thought. The warm air trapped in the courtyard was making him sweat.

But Teddy wouldn't leave it alone. "I could've told her," he said, "but she wouldn't have listened. That pervert was toxic. But Birdie thought it was all *interesting* and *exotic*. She wanted Jack to be more androgynous. If you ask me, she had her eye on the gay market."

"You make her sound so cynical," Sandrine said. "She doesn't strike me that way at all."

"You've met her?" Teddy's eyes flicked from Sandrine to Junior and back again.

"Sure," said Sandrine. "She was here for the Festival. We had a party."

Junior laughed. The Festival *was* a party as far as she was concerned.

"I was really fascinated to meet her," Sandrine said, " 'cos you hear so many stories. She's like, a living legend, but there she was—she was working for some millionaire, but she still had time to hang out with us. She seemed, you know, just like one of us."

"She *is* one of us," said Junior, lying. She was never one of us, he thought. Fame, he thought, notoriety. It does something irreversible. No matter how old or how broke Birdie became, it would always surprise him to see her in Sandrine's kitchen, making a cup of coffee. She'll never be one of us, he thought. And it's not her fault. Because people like Sandrine were always amazed when she acted like regular folks, it was impossible for her to *be* regular folks.

And now it was a day later. Sandrine left the apartment to go shopping with friends and Junior was alone. Beneath his window a new set of buskers was doing a witty, raunchy version of "Frankie and Johnny." This lot were definitely into narrative songs. They'd already done "Stagger Lee" and the woman who sang gave it all the attitude it needed.

He looked around vaguely but couldn't place his chillum, so he sat and rolled a fat and ragged spliff. Then, with his lips tingling and his ears buzzing, he turned on his computer and, on a stoned whim, called up Birdie's name on the web. He wasn't focusing too well, because the first site to come his way was a porno page, and he tilted his head this way and that until he realized that he was staring at a picture of a very young Birdie being fucked from behind by a creature with the head of Bill Clinton and the body of a goat. He was invited to interact.

"I don't think so," he mumbled, out loud. "But now that you've reminded me, I did say I'd call."

He exhaled slowly, blowing sweet smoke at the computer. What time was it in London? Ahead or behind?

"Who cares?" he said to the abused image on his screen. "Now is now, wherever you are."

He dialed a London number. A soft voice said hello.

"Birdie?" he said.

"Birdie isn't here," said the voice.

"Oh," Junior said, stumped. "You sound like Birdie."

"Everyone says that."

"Do you look like her?" Junior was still staring at his computer, his head at an impossible angle. "Have you ever met President Clinton?"

"I beg your pardon?"

"Robin!" Junior shouted, a light bulb flashing on in his brain. "Don't hang up." He switched off the computer. Boy, was that a relief! "It's Junior Moline. We met years ago. Birdie asked me to call this number."

A moment later, Birdie was on the line.

"Mad axman flew to LA this afternoon." That was the message, wasn't it?

"Interesting," she said. "Thank you."

"Hostile," he said, "very hostile."

"Yep," she said breezily. "That's why I'm so grateful. I didn't want him on my tail."

Junior put the receiver down, wishing she'd chosen a different word. Then he thought about Robin. The serious one with the babies—that was her, wasn't it? No, not serious, he thought, just not blonde.

He found that he was sitting on his chillum, but by that time he didn't care any more. And he'd forgotten to tell Birdie about the break-in at Teddy's hotel room. Except, of course, he'd put money on the fact that she already knew—if he had any money, if he were a betting man.

"Birdie, Birdie, Birdie," he sighed, looking at the phone. "Better look out for that pretty tail of yours. Hassle comin' down."

Part 2

PAY THE MAN

"You're the man who squats behind the man who works the soft machine." Jagger, Richards

I

Big in Brazil

You want a rock'n'roll story? Well, here's one. It isn't about music, or drugs, or sex. It's about money and accounting. Still interested?

Early on, when I'd only just met Jack and he didn't have much more than a cult following, he wrote a song called "Dance for Daddy." It was supposed to be a slowish filler for the second album. A ballad—Jack didn't write many ballads. It was pretty but ordinary. And then, talking about it, we decided to give it a sort of bossa nova spin. We upped the tempo a bit and brought in congas and a bunch of South American stuff. Even so, it was an unremarkable track on an album which didn't get many plays in the UK. Jack was not on the Radio One play list at that time, so he didn't have a UK hit.

The album was released, sold slowly, and died. But a few months later, we got a call from a distributor who said, "Congratulations, you're number one in Brazil."

"Dance for Daddy" was a huge hit in South America, and the whole album went platinum in Brazil, gold in Argentina and Colombia.

Number one in Brazil, unknown in the UK.

Even so, Jack was thrilled. He'd never been number one anywhere. "It's coming, babe," he said. "It's on its way—I can feel it. Let's buy a house."

Because you'd think, wouldn't you, that a hit record anywhere in the world would make you some serious bread. Jack thought so. Me too. But that was before we found out about the now-you-see-it-now-you-don't nature of accounting for foreign earnings. Put it this way: we saw that Jack had earned a packet in South America, but we never saw a penny of it.

Here's how it went. At the time, Jack was recording for a little indie label called Cutz. Cutz did not have a foreign distribution arm, so for South America they sublicensed Jack's album to a record company whose head office was in Belize. There were other similar deals for the US, Southeast Asia, and Australia, but that's another story.

So, unknown to Jack, "Dance for Daddy" and the rest of the album was sublicensed to a company in Belize, which was collecting his earnings, taking a hefty cut, and presumably paying some tax.

Cutz might not have had a foreign distribution arm, but it did have an offshore account in the Cayman Islands. Eventually, money filtered out of Brazil, Argentina, and Colombia, to Belize, and from there it went to the Cayman Islands, where it was held in Cutz's account.

At first, when Jack told Cutz he wanted money to buy a house, he was informed that the company in Belize hadn't passed it on yet. They had a twelve-month accounting period and no money was expected until March. Cutz offered to loan him the money or set up the mortgage for him in the meantime. Alarm bells went off in my head. I told Jack to say no. Sasson Freel told Jack to say yes. Jack said yes and he bought a nice house on Camden Hill.

March came and went without Jack's bank balance growing noticeably fatter. I asked Sasson to find out what was going on. After all, he was Jack's manager and it was his job to find out. Sasson disappeared for three whole days and nights. He missed a gig in Plymouth. He never missed gigs. The boys in the band were furious, but Jack was worried.

Sasson came back unshaven, dirty, shaky, and with a dose of clap. He'd been in Brighton and he couldn't remember how he got there.

"I went to the meeting with Cutz," he said. "And then I had to get drunk. Jack, I'm so sorry."

So what happened to make Sasson go on a three-day bender? Poor young Sasson. Well, in the simplest possible terms, he discovered that he had helped Cutz to stitch Jack up. When signing agreements and consents on Jack's behalf, he only had his eyes on the US and UK sides of the deal. Like a lot of ingénues in the rock trade, he thought that everything began and ended with fame and fortune in the States or at home. You can't blame him exactly. Nearly everyone thinks the same. The rest of the world doesn't quite count. And no one expected Jack to be big in Brazil.

Cutz didn't expect it, either, but they did have the means to exploit it. What Sasson failed to notice, while signing agreements on Jack's behalf, was that there were two separate companies: Cutz UK and Cutz Cayman. Cutz UK dealt with the home market—which was pitiful. But Cutz Cayman dealt with the South American market, which turned out to be surprisingly lucrative.

"OK," says Sasson. "But it's still Cutz, so where's the money?"

Not so fast, young Sasson. Didn't you notice that you gave Cutz UK permission to sublicense Jack's work to subsidiaries?

"Yes, but …"

No buts, young man, it's right here in black and white. Cutz UK has your permission to sublicense. And so, *with your permission*, Cutz UK sublicensed to Cutz Cayman, who in turn sublicensed to a company with offices in Belize.

"OK," Sasson says. "But we're making money out there. Where is it?"

In the Cayman Islands, young Sasson, can't you read? Cutz Cayman is a holding company. It is holding Jack's money. You agreed to this, and here is your signature to prove it.

"So transfer the money to the UK."

You aren't listening, young man. We can't transfer any money. It's not ours to transfer. It's Cutz Cayman's. We aren't Cutz Cayman. We're Cutz UK. Separate companies. Don't you read what you sign?

"But," says Sasson, thinking fast, "surely Cutz Cayman has to account to Cutz UK?"

Of course it does, you pathetic excuse for a rock manager, but only at the end of the accounting period. And it isn't up for another nineteen years.

"*Nineteen years?*" Sasson shouts.

Keep your voice down, silly boy. You weren't shouting when you signed these contracts. You were only too willing to sign whatever we put in front of you. You practically tore our hands off to get to the pen …

No wonder poor young Sasson had to go on a three-day bender before he could pluck up enough courage to tell Jack—"Sorry, Jack, there's not going to be any money for nineteen years, and what's more, Cutz UK owns your new house. Because of my advice, Jack, you owe Cutz real money, but they don't owe you diddlysquat. Like it, Jack?"

Oh yes. Jack liked it enough to fire Sasson on the spot and to make his next album with a different label.

Isn't that a nice little rock'n'roll story? All about a silly little song called "Dance for Daddy."

Well, it taught me to dance all right. And I'm still dancing, because it didn't end there. What goes around in this business comes around. Sometimes more than once. And every time it comes around it gets better.

II

Hopelessly Devoted

There was a photograph of Jack in Robin's bedroom. It was the first image she saw in the morning and the last image she saw at night. He was sitting on a stone wall, wearing a loose white shirt open over his bare chest. The breeze swung through his sun-bleached hair, ruffling it into a halo around his head. He looked at her with a half smile, relaxed and amused. Behind him, the sky was blue, blue, blue as an angel's eyes. Blue as Jack's eyes.

When Robin took the picture, she was standing on the patio at Villa Verte and Jack was talking about how nice it was to be able to let his chest hair grow for a couple of weeks. No public appearances, no photographers. He didn't have to look like a hairless boy for the fanzines. So Robin pointed her camera at him and said, "So show us your tits."

There was very little chest hair anyway, and it didn't show in the picture even when she had it enlarged. He looked angelic, and you can't imagine an angel with chest hair.

He laughed at my joke, she thought with pride, even now. I could make him laugh. Everyone enjoys laughter. So I contributed something.

But it was a very small contribution and it didn't make up for the fact that Jack flew her and little Grace down to the South of France and that they were staying in a luxury villa with its own pool and games room. It didn't repay Jack for the car and chauffeur or the horribly expensive restaurants. Robin felt the debt keenly. Being the poor relation wasn't comfortable.

Robin cooked for him when she was allowed to. But even that wasn't necessary because of the chef. Her strengths were invisible, her weakness on display.

"Just relax, sweetie," Lin said. "Get a tan. You don't have to do anything." Lin had a tan like clover honey. Lin did not have a seventeen-month-old baby to look after. She could wear tiny sundresses and tinier swimsuits. Robin was already pregnant with Jimmy. She was heavy and clumsy.

"Doesn't matter," Lin said. "You're lovely pregnant. And you've had a hard year. Let it all go."

Robin didn't want to let anything go, and sometimes on a chilly English morning she'd look at the sun shining on Jack's angel face and try to remember every minute of one month in the South of France. One month under the same sun. Jack and Lin. Twins. Children playing. Irresponsible. Infectious. The only way Robin could match their lightness was to float in the pool, an extra-large T-shirt billowing in the water to cover her bulge. Mercifully weightless, but never irresponsible.

It was a floaty feeling she could only relive in the early morning, half awake, or at night, half asleep, before her weight caught up with her. The weight of years and loss.

Jack was dead. Mum and Dad were dead. She was a middle-aged woman. Her babies were not babies. Everything passes except for responsibility.

Sometimes she felt that age was simply a wrinkled mask you wore over a young face. Or an adult mask over a baby face. Jimmy and Grace, she felt, wore translucent masks, their baby features showing through like double exposures.

Robin collected masks. They hung in pairs, trios, or singly, from nails, over picture frames, hooks, mirrors, hat stands. They propped each other up on the mantelshelf, the desk, the piano. They came from every continent and every culture. Even paper or plastic faces which caught her eye at a fair or a market would be given a place, sometimes a name. Occasionally she thought that her masks had clearer identities than the people she knew. At least she knew they were masks. Whereas people ... How could you tell what people were hiding—with or without masks?

"A mask doesn't hide a face," Lin told her once. "A mask is a face. Everybody has more than one."

100

Robin had hundreds. Lin didn't have any. Or did Lin have hundreds and Robin only one? Were masks for protection, deception, or fun? All of the above? Or none of the above?

She dragged her gaze away from Jack's smiling face and got out of bed. Immediately, the phone started to ring. She didn't answer. The machine took the call. She pulled a flannel shirt on over her night-gown and padded barefoot down to the kitchen to make coffee.

She squeezed two sweet Florida oranges while coffee was brewing and drank the juice, staring out of the window into the garden. Persistent rain was making the pink and white mallows droop and drip.

Upstairs again, she showered and dressed. Two more calls came in. She ignored them. Before climbing up to the attic, she went to Grace's bedroom to check that there were clean sheets on her bed. Clean sheets, fresh towels. Grace was coming home today. Robin smiled and started work—fabric in her fingers, fabric feeding through under the punching needle. Real stuff she could cut and shape and sew. A garment which would turn out more or less as planned. A process she had some control over. Unlike life. Unlike people.

Two hours later, she raised her head and saw Lin standing in the doorway, watching her. She was so startled she nearly sewed through her finger.

"Hi, dreamer," Lin said.

"When did you get back?"

"Last night. The lights were out, so I didn't wake you."

Even the house told Robin nothing. She had slept, awakened, got up and worked, thinking she was alone. And all the time her house was sheltering another occupant, hiding Lin in silence.

She said, "You might have left a note."

"I was tired. I just crashed."

"And another thing," Robin said, unexpectedly cross, "when you lie to your boss, I wish you wouldn't use one of the children as an excuse. You told that nice man that Grace had an accident. It was almost like ill-wishing her."

"Oh, baby," Lin said, instantly contrite. "I'm sorry. It was the first thing to come into my head. I didn't think."

Robin could feel Lin eyeing her curiously. She ducked her head and switched off the sewing machine. She wasn't ready to be charmed or mollified. She said, "I don't understand. You seemed to like that job, but then you just split and lie, and all you leave me is a garbled message on the answering machine. So I can't do anything but pass on the lie, or stonewall."

"Oh sweetie, I'm so sorry ..."

"*And*," Robin plowed on, "*and* the phone's been going crazy. Day and night. I can't answer it any more. What if it was one of the children? An emergency?"

"I knew this wasn't fair," Lin said. "I knew it'd be too much for you. Look, love, I'll pack. I can be out of here in twenty minutes."

"I'm not asking you to go." Robin, all of a sudden, felt her attic was empty and hollow. Lin was her little sister, her third child.

"I've got to stand on my own two feet," Lin said. "I can get a room nearer my job. It'd be more convenient. And, for a while at least, no one'll know where I am. You'll see—it'll be all right."

"Lin, just shut up," Robin cried. "Why must you be so extreme? I don't want you to leave. It's just that when this began, you were going to get a job and pay your debts. You were doing so well. It was nice. We were a team. And then you just bugger off, and everything goes crazy."

"I didn't 'just bugger off,'" Lin said sadly. "It's the other way round. Things go crazy, and then I'm forced to bugger off. It's the same old story. Only this time it's worse because of the zeitgeist. Everyone's hunting me. Except it isn't really me they're hunting. It's Jack."

"Oh, Lin," Robin said, just as sadly. "What're we going to do?"

They went downstairs and Robin sat her little sister at the kitchen table while she made scrambled eggs, a green salad, and a big pot of tea.

She said, "I'm sorry I freaked. Don't take any notice." Lin looked so slight and alone. Why hadn't she put on more weight, Robin wondered. It was as if she'd been caught in a drop of amber by the trauma of her past life and condemned to be forever girlish, forever Birdie the Ultimate Chick.

Robin heaped the lion's share of scrambled egg onto Lin's plate with two slices of wholegrain toast, as if all her problems could be solved by a decent lunch. She thought, as she often thought, how sad

102

it was to be the golden girl when you were too young. Everything she'd envied Lin for when they were both young—her looks, her wit, her freedom, her lover—had all come back as nightmares to haunt her. All the blessings morphed into curses.

They ate in silence for a while and then Robin asked, "So where did you go? What did you do?"

"Devon," Lin said. "You know—Homer. It was fine. I wanted his advice about a song anyway. But I couldn't stay forever. Like you said, I've got a job now."

"Will they take you back?"

"I hope so."

Robin was about to give Lin some good advice about how to placate employers when the doorbell rang and they both jumped.

Outside in the light rain stood Grace, saying, "Why did you leave the chain on, Mum?" Behind her, a little off to one side, was a young man with a self-depreciating grin on his face.

Oh God, Robin thought, she's brought a boyfriend home. She didn't tell me about a boyfriend. She opened the door and the two young people came in, dragging backpacks and carrier bags.

Robin hugged her daughter, automatically gauging her height and weight. She seemed to have been looking after herself. Her cheek against Robin's lips was smooth and rosy. She smelled of shampoo and urban rain.

"This is Alec," Grace said. "Is there anything for lunch? I'm starving." She detached herself from Robin's embrace. She had her own priorities.

"Hi, Mrs. Emerson," Alec said, still wearing the lopsided love-me-do grin.

"Hi," said Robin, thinking, and who the hell are you? "We were eating scrambled eggs in the kitchen."

"We? Is Jimmy home?"

"No. It's Lin . . ."

"Lin!" Grace shouted. "Lin, Lin, Lin. Alec, come and meet my Auntie Lin."

Meeting Auntie Lin was an event. Meeting Mother Robin was not, Robin thought, moving a bag out of the way with one foot and following along to the kitchen, where she found Lin and Grace

103

doing a short Lindy-hop routine by way of greeting—a couple of spins, a couple of slides. It was something Lin had shown Grace when she was nine and recovering from chicken pox. Lin was fun, fun, fun. Lin Lindy-hopped. No one else's aunt did that.

"Wow!" said Alec. "You guys really move."

Robin slid past the dancers and took eggs, bacon, tomatoes, and mushrooms out of the fridge. There was a bowl of Grace's favorite king prawns marinating in ginger and garlic on the middle shelf, but she wouldn't cook those until she knew whether Alec was a fixture or a fitting. Temporary food till then.

She listened while Lin effortlessly asked all the right questions and provoked Grace into a stream of chatter about her new job, her friends, her shared house. Grace, within minutes, was feeling like the most fascinating creature in the world and showing off. Robin, quietly cooking, hung on every word. Why wasn't it a conversation a mother could have with her daughter? Stories, jokes. No defenses. Robin, the cook, was like a beggar at the feast, snacking on leftovers. And grateful. She didn't have to ask any direct questions and watch Grace clam up. She didn't have to feel intrusive and hear the dreadful, "Don't worry about it, Mum," which was supposed to be the all-inclusive answer to each and every question. Thank you, Lin, but why do I need you? I should be able to do this for myself.

She sighed and laid plates of food in front of the kids.

"Thanks, Mrs. Emerson," Alec said, dutifully, hardly daring to take his eyes off Lin and Grace, afraid of missing any sparkle.

And then, "Mum, can Alec stay in Jimmy's room for a couple of nights? When's he coming home? Next week? There's a party in Camden Town we want to go to."

All the questions she should ask, like, "Who the hell is Alec? Where's he from? Does he suffer from any communicable diseases?" All those sounded like clunkers and she didn't ask them.

She said, "I suppose so," and watched Grace slip from her chair and run out to show Alec his new quarters.

Lin said, "Who the hell is Alec?"

"I don't know."

"Boyfriend?"

"Don't know."

"Hasn't Grace mentioned him before?"

"Not that I remember. Why?"

"I don't know," Lin said. "Something's wrong. They don't seem to know each other at all."

"Do they have to?" Robin asked. "At that age …"

The sisters looked at each other. Two women of the same generation now, Robin thought. Two old broads fretting about the youngsters. She smiled. "We'll sort them out. He'll be no match for us."

"I should bloody well hope not." Lin smiled too. "Grace seems to be doing all right, doesn't she? You're not worried, are you?"

"Not really. She's settling in, getting used to real life."

"Well, then?"

"No worries."

"Mama's little baby?"

"Oh, I'll get over it," Robin said. "I just wish she'd tell me more."

"Don't be absurd," Lin said. "How much did *you* tell?"

"A damn sight more than you did."

"So will she—you'll see. Give her time. You're the best friend she'll ever have."

"Oh Lin," Robin wailed, "I feel so old and impotent."

"Well, you're not, kid. It's her. She's big and bouncy and feeling her oats. Making her mother feel like an old mare is part of the thrill."

"She must be thrilled to bits," said Robin.

"All the same, let's check Alec out, mmm?"

Robin got to her feet and said, "I'll go up and be the mother from hell, shall I? Embarrass the shit out of both of 'em."

"Whoa," Lin said, catching her hand. "I had something a little more oblique in mind. Let's just see if there's anything to embarrass them for."

"You're not going to …?"

"Leave it to me, Ms. Clean," Lin said, and wandered away to read her mail and go through the phone messages.

Robin, alone in the kitchen, cleared up, rinsing pans and stacking dishes in the washer. She made another pot of tea, but she didn't go back to the attic to drink it. She stayed at the kitchen table. She wanted to be at the hub of the house in case Grace decided to come down and talk. Fat chance, she thought, but you have to make yourself available.

Paralyzed at the hub of the house but on the rim of her own life, waiting, watching, listening. Like when the children were small. Or when her mother was going doolally. Always reactive, never active. I'm a counter-puncher. I'm the girl who can't get out on the floor and dance. I have to wait to be asked. Why?

This was the house Jack gave her mother when her father died. This was the house she moved into when her mother began to need care and her man left her. She wore it like a coat against the weather. It represented shelter and defeat—almost as if she'd come into the world unprepared and Jack had lent her his coat. She sat in it, perpetually wondering what would happen next.

At last, she heard footsteps on the stairs. But no one came to the kitchen. The front door opened and shut, and then there was silence. Grace? Grace and Alec? Lin?

Once, years ago, when the twin forces of her children and her mother were keeping her prisoner in the house, Lin came to stay. Out of the blue, she turned up with a single bag and camped out in the attic.

"Why?" Robin asked. "Where's Jack?"

"In the States," Lin said, answering the second question first, and the first one not at all.

For nearly a week, it was as if the doors and windows had been left open. Lin came and went. Sometimes she went alone. Sometimes she took one or both of the children. She even took their barmy mother to buy hats and handbags. She made Robin go to the movies or to visit friends. It could have been a holiday for Robin except that, for the whole time, she felt as if she were holding her breath. She was in suspense, tied by a skein of silk threads to the phone and the doorbell, waiting.

For what? For Jack to call? For Jack to come? Why? He wasn't going to call her. He wasn't going to visit her. It was as if she were waiting on Lin's behalf. Which was a complete waste of her emotional energy because Lin didn't seem to be waiting at all.

It was clear to Robin that something had gone badly wrong

between Lin and Jack. But Lin never said what it was. And Robin was afraid.

Lin wasn't waiting, she wasn't afraid. She stepped out and danced. She didn't seem to give a damn if Jack phoned or if he didn't. It was Robin who cared desperately that he didn't. And when at last he did, Lin was out and she didn't ring him back.

Then a long white car arrived at the door and the driver came in with a letter. Lin was out then too. Robin, aching with tension, gave the driver lunch. The letter sat on the table between them like an unexploded bomb.

Lin came home three hours later. She said, "Hi, Mr. Peters," to the driver, and took the letter up to the attic. She came down again a few minutes later and said, "Thanks, Mr. Peters. There's no reply. Would you like another cup of tea?"

Mr. Peters declined the tea, but used the phone and then left.

Robin said, "What's happening, Lin? I don't understand. Are you breaking up with Jack?"

"Maybe," Lin said.

"Maybe?" Robin asked pathetically. "Don't you know? Mr. Peters said he had instructions to take you with him."

"Instructions," Lin said. "My, my. Look, Robin, do you want me out of your hair? Are there too many people here? Is that the problem? Because I can easily find somewhere else. I can go if you want."

"No," Robin said. "It isn't that." But there she was, wanting Lin to go running to Jack as if her own life, freedom and happiness depended on it. Waiting, holding her breath for Lin to make the right move, or for Jack to say the right thing. Wanting to say, for Christ's sake Lin, resolve this so that *I* can breathe again. Lin, it seemed, was on the brink of throwing away something which was crucial to Robin. And Robin couldn't even begin to explain it. It wasn't her life—Jack wasn't her man.

"It's *my* life," Lin would have said, had she known. "Am I supposed to live it by your criteria?"

"Yes!" Robin would have howled. "Don't leave Jack. Be faithful, honest, and true. Put up with anything he does, but *keep* him." Because that's what Robin would've done if she'd been given the chance. Oh yes, she would. Without question. Then, maybe, things would have turned out differently.

Jack arrived in the dead of night when Robin was already in bed. He was tired, his eyes were ringed and sunken—not the angel boy in her photograph. He asked for Birdie, and Robin realized with horror that Lin had not come home from a date with someone almost as beautiful as Jack. Someone, Robin realized, she ought to have recognized from the glimpse she had of him through a Porsche windscreen.

She couldn't tell Jack that, so she asked him in and sat him in the living room, offering him tea, coffee, alcohol, whatever she could think of, chattering uncontrollably. Finally he asked for hot chocolate, more to shut her up, she thought, than because he wanted anything. And when she came back with it, she found him asleep on the sofa. So young, too young to be so weary. It nearly made her cry to see the drooping head and long eyelashes. She covered him with her patchwork quilt as if he were an orphan she'd taken in from the street. And yes, she would have kissed his eyelids if she hadn't been afraid to wake him. Because if she woke him she'd have to talk to him and she never knew what to say. She didn't know what interested him—or rather she didn't know what didn't bore him, and she suspected that she was boring.

So she crept out of the living room and went to sit at the bottom of the stairs, waiting to warn Lin. At first, she was angry with Lin. How could she go off with someone else? Then she was angry with Jack. Who did he think he was—turning up unannounced and putting her in this embarrassing situation? Last, she was angry with herself. Why was she getting in a state about her sister's boyfriend? That's all it was—her sister and her boyfriend had a row. It wasn't the end of the world. Lin going out with another guy wasn't high treason.

But it *was* the end of the world. It *was* high treason. Because it was Jack. That was the last unreasonable thought Robin had before she too nodded off.

Much later, something disturbed her, and she woke cold, stiff, and gummy-eyed. It was after five in the morning. She got up and peeped round the living room door. Jack was gone.

She tiptoed up to the attic. The attic was empty. Lin's bed was unslept in. Her bag was gone. Downstairs in the kitchen, she found a note on the draining board. It said, "Thanks for everything. Talk to you soon. Love, L."

Desolate, Robin went into the living room. The quilt was half on the sofa, half on the floor, like a sloughed snakeskin. The sofa was dented and rumpled. The mug of hot chocolate had been left where she put it, untouched, cold. She picked up the quilt, meaning to fold it, but it felt a little warm. A little heat was all that remained of Jack's visit. She wrapped herself in it and lay down where he had lain. She buried her face in the cushion on which he'd rested his head. And smelled her sister's perfume.

Sitting bolt upright, she said aloud, "You stupid, stupid cow." And then she went to bed. Something important had happened under her roof—under her nose—and she had missed it.

Always losing the thread, Robin thought, always missing the punch line. Enough. There was work to be done, so do it.

She went slowly upstairs and walked quietly past closed doors. She wouldn't intrude. Lin was in her mother's old room. Alec was in Jimmy's. Grace was in her own. Maybe. The only open bedroom door was Robin's. Was she really the only one in the house with nothing to hide or no one to hide from?

As she passed her room, she caught sight of an alien shape. She turned quickly and saw Alec in her bedroom.

"Hello," she said. "What're you doing in here?"

"Oh, sorry," he said. "I was looking for Grace." He smiled at her, apologetic, but not guilty. "Love your masks. Is that a picture of The Legend? His music's incredible. I only got into it recently, but I'm hooked."

"Yes, that's Jack," Robin said, warming to him. She sat on the edge of her bed. "Do you live in Bristol like Grace?" Alec might have been looking for Grace, but he'd found her, so he was going to have to put up with a few questions.

"Actually, no," Alec said. "And, before you ask, we met on the Net. We've been corresponding for months."

"No. Really?" she said, alarmed and fascinated. No sex yet, she thought. Is that good or bad?

"She signs on as g.ace, so it was a long time before I found out if she was male or female. We just hit it off, if you know what I mean. I suppose, in your day, it would've been a pen-pal thing."

In my day? Robin thought. Cheeky bugger. But Alec seemed to be too young to know he was insulting her.

She smiled and said, "So, this is the first time you've met? In person?"

"We decided that I'd meet her train and we'd let an element of chance take over. She'd described herself to me and I'd described myself to her. And we thought, if we recognized each other from the descriptions—like, if neither of us had been telling porkies—we'd be off to a good start."

He was laughing now, and blushing. Good, healthy teeth, Robin thought. Well, if they met on the Net, at least it means he can write.

He said, "I know it's a risk, Mrs. Emerson. People can say any old thing and you never know if it's true or not. But I recognized Grace straightaway, so I reckon she's the honest type."

"Oh, she is," Robin said. When she actually tells you anything.

"So I guess we both thought, like, OK. We can go to a party together and see how it goes from there. I don't know about you, Mrs. Emerson, but I like to get to know people slowly."

"We-ell," Robin said, pretending to think about it, "there's no point in rushing things, but you *are* in my bedroom and I don't even know your last name."

Alec looked mortified. He even squirmed. "Parry," he said. "Alec Parry. I'm such an idiot. Sorry."

He's a puppy, she thought, all wriggly and waggy. Odd how much more mature Grace seems. Perhaps she feels most comfortable with men she can control. Well, it's as good a way of finding out about men as any. Better than finding out about them from the ones who can control her.

She said, "Don't worry about it."

"But, in the same situation, my mother'd go potty. You're so cool, Mrs. Emerson. Your whole family's so cool."

"Wait till you meet Jimmy," Robin said, laughing. "Now, I must go and do some work. Grace's room is next to yours on the other side."

"Right," he said, "but I'm really glad I had the chance to talk to you."

"Me too," she said. A happy accident, she thought. It would've taken ages to learn as much from Grace. She hoped he liked garlic and ginger prawns.

She sat for a moment, after he left, staring absently at Jack's young smile. So, so long ago, Jack, what would you look like now? Would you be fat or thin? Would your hair be gray, like mine, or would you touch it up, like Lin? Would you have any hair? Would you be famous or forgotten? Would you have dumped Lin or would she have dumped you? Would I have ever really got to know you or would you still be an icon on my wall? If you were alive, Jack, would you still be a memory? After all, there are many more ways to lose people than by death.

Upstairs in the attic, she picked up the work Lin had interrupted. She was making an old-fashioned frock coat for a fat actor and she was taking pains over the detail because she knew he'd buy it from wardrobe when the production was over. He always did. But the cloth was heavy and dull, so after a while she put it aside and took up a riot of color—something she was making for a private client out of hundreds of pieces of off-cut silk. This was what she enjoyed most—making the fabric from which the garment would be shaped—holistic dressmaking. Very slow. Very expensive. Thank God for private clients.

And there, blinded by color, soothed by silk, Robin lost herself for a few hours.

"That's beautiful," Lin said, putting two glasses of white wine on her work table. "Who's it for?"

Robin blinked, slowly refocusing her eyes. She slid her reading glasses up on to her hair and said, "Rich old lady. It'd suit you better. Where've you been?"

"Out. Trying to mend bridges, but ..."

"Oh no."

"Sorry, darlin', I've been replaced—no more Cole-Adler pay packets. Don't look like that—it isn't the end of the world. I'll find something else. They're giving me a great reference."

"I suppose that's better than nothing." Robin stretched and then took a sip of chilled white wine. "Where are the kids?"

"Movies," Lin said.

"Well, I'm not worried about Alec any more. He's a puppy." And she told Lin the story of Grace and Alec meeting on the Net.

"Which site?" Lin asked immediately.

"Huh?"

"Never mind, sweetie. I'll find out."

"Does it matter?"

"It might," Lin said. "This is a guy who travels with a locked camera case hidden in a studenty backpack. For your information, he also has a big box of gossamer condoms and half a pint of lubrication gel, which he's carrying quite openly. And an ounce or two of very nice grass and some sweet little white tablets with doves stamped on them. He's not bothering to keep them hidden. Makes you wonder what he'd lock up, doesn't it?"

"Oh, *Lin,*" Robin said.

"Well, he's got the sex and drugs bit covered, hasn't he? So what's he doing for rock'n'roll?"

"Shit, shit, shit, Lin. I thought butter wouldn't melt."

"Well, they're going to a party." Lin shrugged. "Which bit upsets you most? You've got to assume Grace is doing all the usual stuff."

"Yes, but not under her own roof, my roof, with a stranger." With a sudden gut-lurch, Robin felt herself sliding into a knot of linear time. The thread of her life wove over and under itself in a pattern which had no end and no beginning. She was a responsible, experienced adult who felt like a mystified, frightened teenager. She was conversing with a responsible, experienced woman who was, at the same time, her little sister—the one who ran wild and took appalling risks, and yet always seemed to come up smelling of roses.

She, Robin, was the sister who stayed home, stayed in school, and studied hopelessly for the exams she only just scraped through. She had to keep trying. Because there must be one good sister, one good daughter, mustn't there? Above all, Robin hated conflict. Anger scared her. How many screaming rows could a kid endure?

Then, one day, it stopped. "I can't do this any more," said Lin, sitting on Robin's bed, skinny legs tucked under her. "Fighting's crap."

"So don't fight," Robin said. "You're never going to win. Parents hold all the cards. And I'm fed up with it."

"So'm I. But it's like being in prison. Parents control everything. Nothing's mine. Not even my time."

"We could go away to university. Somewhere like Edinburgh."

"That's years away. And that's the other thing—it'd be just like school. And school is as bad as parents. 'One fist of iron, the other of steel. If the right one don't get you, then the left one will.' Sing it, Robin."

They sat on the bed, two kids, singing "Sixteen Tons," Lin trying to harmonize a third above the melody and getting it wrong. Giggling miserably. Because Robin knew that realistically she didn't have a snowball's hope in hell of getting into university, and she didn't think Lin would even try. All she could see ahead of her were years of the same old, same old.

Now, she had a son and daughter and she was supposed to be the one fist of iron. She was supposed to be contemplating the control of her daughter—how to stop her doing what Lin so carelessly described as "the usual stuff."

The trouble was, she didn't have a clue. She was so busy avoiding confrontation that she rarely confronted Grace. So quite how much of the usual stuff there was in Grace's life was a mystery to her. Maybe Grace was simply getting away with it. Just like Lin did when, at the age of thirteen, she decided fighting was crap. Everyone was so relieved when Lin stopped needling and demanding that they failed to notice that she hadn't changed at all. She merely talked sweet, looked sweet, and appeared with clean hands at meal times. Precocious in the art of man-management.

Is Grace a good, sensible kid, she asked herself, or is she managing me? Am I skilled at avoiding rows, or am I a neglectful parent?

She said, "Lin, do you think Grace is like me? Or is she like you?"

"Grace is like Grace," Lin said, with her silly-question expression.

"Do you think she knows what she's doing?"

"Not for a moment," Lin said. "Who does? But she probably thinks she does."

"Then she's more like you," Robin decided. "I never even thought I knew what I was doing."

"Bollocks," said Lin. "You had it all mapped out."

"Did not."

"Did."

"It was a screwy old map, then," Robin sighed. "Nothing turns out the way you plan."

"Let's hope that's true for Alec as well. Some plans deserve a good trashing."

"Do I kick him out? Or keep an eye on him?"

"Oh, definitely keep him."

"But I really don't want drugs in the house."

"Mmm," said Lin. "We could probably sabotage those without being rumbled. If you want."

"The condoms are a symbol of social responsibility, don't you think?" Robin asked hopefully.

"We don't want to damage those."

"OK," Robin said, "let's do it." She was thrilled. Years of passivity and ignorance fell away.

In Jimmy's room, under the eyes of famous footballers and Nobel prize winners, Robin and Lin examined the guest's luggage.

He was very organized, Robin concluded. "He's got rich parents," she said. "Even the underwear's designer."

"Parents?" Lin said, raising one eyebrow. "Because he turned up with Grace? Because he acts like a puppy? I don't think he's as young as he's acting."

"No dirty laundry," Robin observed. "No. Categorically, positively, he isn't as immature as he seems. What're we going to do with his stash?"

"Turn it into something he'll throw away," Lin said. She slid her hand between two T-shirts and drew out a tobacco tin.

"Kitchen," she said. "Something noxious and smelly—like lighter fluid or turpentine."

They went down to the kitchen. Lin opened the tobacco tin. Tidy young Alec kept his pills in an airtight polythene sachet and his grass wrapped in tin foil.

"I want just enough turps to grind these pills into a semi paste.

114

They've got to stink so badly no one'd dream of putting any of it in his mouth. It's got to look like he was sold total shit and it degraded. Maybe a little green or yellow color to ram the message home."

"Are you sure?" Robin asked. "What if he gives some to Grace?"

"Well," Lin said, working with speed and delicacy, "I'm sorry to say this, but if Grace lets some strange guy put this stinking mess in her mouth she deserves to die."

"Lin!"

"Sorry, sweetie, but it's true. Oh, have a bit of faith in her. She's *your* daughter. *You* brought her up."

"Ok, but think what you took when you were her age."

"I never took anything that looked or smelled like this. Nor will she. And my bet is that Alec won't be offering it."

"What're you going to do with the grass?"

"Smoke some," Lin said, "while you go and piss on the rest. We want it so wet it won't light, and smelly enough to make their little eyes water."

"You're kidding?"

"You're a creative old broad," Lin said. "Think of something. Mother-love comes in strange shapes, I'm told."

"Amen," Robin said. The thread of her life looped and folded back on itself, intersecting at the point where two pre-adolescent girls took revenge on King Leer, the local dirty old man. King Leer was a retired major who lived on the route between school and home. He was in the Rotary Club, the Lions. A pillar of the community, their father said, making both girls collapse with stifled giggles.

For reasons neither of them understood, Lin was his number-one target. And for reasons Robin didn't understand even now, they never told their parents. Perhaps it was because all adults seemed to be malign, ranged like a cohesive army against children. Adult behavior was incomprehensible at the best of times. So a nasty old man waving his genitals at Lin, or squashing them against the glass of his front window whenever she walked by, might have been just another unpleasant manifestation of the power all grown-ups wielded against children.

Whatever. Lin, the rebel, rebelled. Scheming Lin planned. Thieving Lin stole a spray can of black enamel paint from their father's garage. Secretive Lin carried it hidden in her school bag for a week until the right opportunity came along. And, when the right opportunity presented itself, along with King Leer's exposed and swollen shaft, vengeful Lin sprayed him.

"Sorry?" she said, peaches and cream, "what is it you want me to look at?" She stepped forward, her right hand hidden in her school bag. And then she whipped out the spray can and pressed the nozzle. Fired straight at King Leer's naked crotch.

Horrified, Robin watched the mauve pink flesh turn shiny black. Up until then she never thought Lin would actually fire. She thought the plan was just another giggling, childish fantasy—what I'd do if I had a hundred pounds, where we'd go if we could fly. Not so. Quite deliberately, Lin sprayed the major's cock, his balls, his trousers, his shirtfront, and his horn-rim spectacles. Then she threw the can in his face.

"*Run!*" she screamed, and the girls tore away up the street, running, until they fell in an exhausted heap in the park. Horror and fright made them laugh till they choked.

They were laughing now, Robin dizzy from the grass and wine. Two grown women, two little kids, taking action against someone who offended them.

"I wonder what happened to King Leer," she said aloud.

"What on earth made you think of him?"

"Don't know," Robin said. "There were no repercussions, were there? And we were astonished. We thought Mum and Dad were going to come down on us like a ton of bricks. We thought that dirty old bastard would tell the police. We didn't realize that he couldn't. Unless he incriminated himself. I guess we're applying the same principle to Alec."

"Mmm," said Lin. "Good lesson, wasn't it?"

When the kids came home from the movies, they were horsing around as if they'd known each other all their lives. They made Robin wonder if she'd ever been capable of such instant, easy intimacy. Trust, she thought, based on the same taste in music, liking the same movie. How deceptive. What if one of you is lying? She was excluded. She had excluded herself by not trusting them. Betraying them again, she made lasagna and left the king prawns on the middle shelf of the fridge. Grace didn't notice.

Robin's secret was that she was keeping a secret. She was silenced by it, constrained, hiding her guilt behind pasta and salad. And Grace didn't notice. It was so simple. Robin felt a sick lurch of triumph.

Lin, more sinuous and supple, wove her way through the casual conversations and then went up with Grace to decide on party gear. Smooth Lin. Robin was still stoned but fighting it.

She sent Alec away to watch TV. She'd doctored his dope so she didn't want him helping her in the kitchen. She'd smoked some. She was light-headed, light-fingered, at his expense.

"What a rotten thing to do," she said out loud, wiping the counter in meticulous spirals long after it was perfectly clean. "Led astray— that's me. Lin, you're a bad influence—that's you."

But it wasn't true. Lin was helping her. Because she was anxious about Grace. And now she was helping Grace dress.

"I could help Grace," she said. "I'm good at clothes too. I am. Different, but just as good. Why didn't she ask me?"

" 'Cos I'm just a boring old mum," she answered herself. She nodded seriously at her reflection in the kitchen window and her boring old reflection nodded back.

Depressed, she turned away and went upstairs to her bedroom, past the row of closed doors. She threw herself on the bed and bounced a couple of times. Then suddenly, almost violently, she dropped like a stone off a cliff, crashing into sleep.

The piano woke her. She rolled over, dry-mouthed, and looked at the clock. The big hand was on the seven, the little hand was halfway between the two and the three. She was fully clothed and the light was on.

The same phrase was repeated over and over: Der-*lang* lang lang, ta-ta-ta *dum*, der-*lang* lang lang, ta-ta-ta *dum*. That was the bass line. It was accompanied by short bursts of trills and descending chords in the treble.

Twenty-five minutes to three. Morning or afternoon? Shit. She flopped off the bed and stumbled downstairs.

117

In the living room, Lin was coiled around the piano. She didn't look up. Der-lang lang lang …

Robin felt that if she didn't pour a cup of hot sweet tea down her throat straight away she'd die. She staggered to the kitchen.

She returned with the teapot and two mugs on a tray, feeling a lot better. Not bumping into furniture, she noted with relief.

"Tea, Lin?"

Der-lang lang lang …

Robin poured tea into the mugs and went over to the piano. She said, "What're you playing?"

Der-lang … " 'Eddie's Big Wheel' by Eddie Bo. Can't do it."

"Sounds all right to me."

"Well, it would," Lin said morosely. " 'Cos you don't know—he's one of those old piano players with a bit of God in every finger." Der-lang lang lang … She still wouldn't look at Robin.

"Are the kids back yet?"

"No."

"It's *three o'clock*, for Christ's sake."

"It's a *party*, for Christ's sake." Der *lang*.

"What's up, Lin?"

Ta-ta-ta *DUM*. Lin snapped the piano lid shut and leaned her elbows on it, still not meeting Robin's eyes. "Your daughter," she said, "and slick little Alec met on one of Jack's websites. Out there in cyberspace, with no one watching, everyone anonymous, everyone *communicating*, spilling their poxy guts out, thinking there'll be no comeback. It's OK, see, because they're all just a bunch of cyberspace cadets. You're *free*, like, you can be who you wannabe. You can be Jack and Birdie's niece, if you wannabe. Not Lin's, you notice. Birdie's."

"She told you this?" Robin asked with a cold, drafty prickle starting at her ankles. "But, Lin, you know she's so proud of you."

"Why? What's to be proud of?"

"Well, you're glamorous. You're fun."

"She didn't spill her little guts to Alec 'cos I'm fun. Grow *up*, Robin. And he didn't bring his state-of-the-art recording equipment into this house 'cos I'm good ol' Auntie Lin."

"Oh, Lin, *no*."

118

"Oh, Robin, yes. Plus a full set of burglary tools and a miniature spy camera. The only thing I didn't find was his press pass or PI license. Whatever he is."

"You unlocked his case thing? Oh Lin, I'm sure Grace doesn't know. She wouldn't let us down like that."

"I don't know what she knows. It was, 'Oh Lin, Alec thinks you're *fascinating*. Do talk to him. He's so sweet. You'll love him when you get to know him.' Did you tell her what I was up to? Who I'm working for? Where I go?'"

"I don't know." Robin felt queasy. "She asks about you. I wasn't keeping any secrets. It's *Grace*."

"Yes, it's Grace, all right. And I'm blown."

"Blown? Lin, we're talking about Grace. She knows well enough not to gossip. She's been told."

"And now she's doing the telling. g.ace. Start counting the spoons, Robin, and nail down anything you don't want stolen. Above all, don't open your mouth unless you want to see your tonsils in the tabloids."

III

Sold for a Song

If love is a bitch, young love is a bastard. You follow your heart, you follow your hormones, you follow a man. You don't lead. You trail around, helplessly doing and saying things that'd either bore you or make you blush if you were in your right mind. In other words, love is bloody inconvenient. I wish I could have back even half the time I've wasted on love.

Now Grace is in love. She was courted by computer, and within three hours of meeting the little worm she fell in love—at the movies, while he stroked the palm of her hand with his warm thumb. Someone was dying on the screen. Giant images of ragged, bleeding humanity failed to move her. But the touch of warm skin sent her heart tumbling all the way to Idiotsville. *C'est l'amour.*

Poor little g.ace @ *et cetera* slash *et cetera*: she's not to be trusted. Her young love is bloody inconvenient for me.

But what I have to ask myself is this: who sent the little worm, and what does he want? If I can answer those questions without him rumbling me, I'll be ahead of the game. Keep the enemy in view but don't let him know you're watching.

Sometimes, what you want simply falls into your hands. You walk into a small office to make an enquiry, for instance, and someone mistakes you for a secretary. By the end of the week, you have the keys to the safe, the use of the computer, a network of private detectives a phone call away, and a weekly wage. The wage, of course, is tragic, but the facilities are a goldmine. In effect, I can do my own research, and be paid for the privilege, with no one any the wiser.

No, I didn't lose this job. I lied. Bad Birdie—lying to her own sister.

120

But Robin talks to Grace, and Grace talks to Alec. And I do not yet know who Alec talks to. I'll find out eventually, but in the meantime, whoever he's talking to, he won't be telling the truth. I'll see to that.

I returned to a savior's welcome. Sweet old George brought me coffee and Tina, gruffly, put a jar of Japanese anemones on my desk. I noticed that a mere ten-day absence had put the strain back into their partnership. They were like a married couple who sorely missed their child's nanny. They should have built a third person into the structure from the beginning. I blame Tina: she takes independence and self-sufficiency way too seriously. But she is competent. It's lucky for me that she hasn't had time in the last ten days to become familiar with her own software.

I opened the mail and logged all the overnight phone calls. Then I sat in on their morning meeting to find out what I'd missed. There was nothing new—or rather there was more of the familiar. They asked me to make a new work schedule.

It's so easy. I'm like an air traffic controller deciding what can take off, what can land, and what should go into a holding pattern. They do the work. The clients pay. They order equipment and pay the bills. There's a direct relationship between service, goods, and money. You can see at a glance what's going on.

How very unlike the music business.

I should know—a few weeks ago, I thought I would need a private detective to follow the paper trail, the corporate maze, the legal knots which are my financial history. Who would imagine that a bunch of ideas worked out on a piano and guitar could cause so much trouble, heartache, and frustration.

We'd sit in a room, Jack and I, and just noodle with chords. Hmm, sounds nice, yeah, try the diminished seventh in there, oh yeah. Got a tune? Got any words to go with that? How about this for a beat?

No equipment to speak of—two heads, four ears, four hands, a piano, a guitar, a little tape recorder in case we were too stoned to remember, and a pad and pencil for the same reason. We made something out of nothing, golden Jack and I. Just ideas—those things in your head; things which simply wouldn't exist if you didn't give them a voice. How can anything so nebulous be the foundation of an industry so complicated, so twisted and vicious, that I needed a private detective to explain my small part in it?

I need an accountant and a lawyer too, but I don't trust them. Accountants and lawyers made me bankrupt for years and I still owe the taxman several hundred thousand.

Those nebulous, airy-fairy, arty-farty ideas took hundreds of people to produce, record, press, publish, promote, market, and sell them. They turned Jack into a god and a paper millionaire. They turned me into a bitch and a pauper. The god did not even own his own house. No wonder he burned it down.

If a guy thinks he must be very rich, and everyone treats him as if he's very rich, he spends a lot of money. It's natural. And, make no mistake, there was a lot of money. But it wasn't his. The millions weren't his earnings, as it turned out, they were only advances against earnings. Big difference. It means you don't know what you're actually worth, and worse, you don't know what you owe. That's what happens w' .. there's no straightforward relationship between services, goods, a... money. The difference between songs and security windows is a big one.

At midday, I logged in two new enquiries: a background search and a missing person. I thought my bosses would enjoy the change—their steadiest customers all want security advice and that's boring. Then I rang Ozzy Ireland on his mobile. It's no good ringing an A&R man before midday, and if he's any good you'll never catch him in the office.

"Hey, Oz," I said. "Word?"

"Hey, Miz Bird," he said, "when did you get back?" He sounded tired and I could hear a baby crying in the background. He'd never mentioned having a family. Not surprising: A&R doesn't mix comfortably with family life—certainly not for long.

"Did I wake you?" I asked nastily. "I could ring back."

"No, no," he said. "You're so hard to get hold of, now I've got you I'll hang on. I'm glad you called today. InnerVersions are trying out the new material at that club in Oxford tonight and some of the brass are coming."

"Who?"

"God, Birdie, I don't know what you said to Mr. Freel, but there's been some action around here."

"Yeah?"

"Someone from production came down and gave the guys a talking-to. The result of which is that Dapper Sapper's agreed to voice coaching—a quantum leap there, by the way—*and* they've got proper studio time booked. They're really putting some muscle into rehearsals now—not just hanging around beefing because we don't tell them they're geniuses every two minutes."

"Now I *know* they aren't musicians."

"Mee-*ow*," Ozzy said. "They're a nice little band, Birdie, and they come up lovely with a bit of polish."

"I told *you* that," I said. "But only if they gave Karen more of everything. Without her, you might as well call them Send In The Clones."

"The trouble with her is she just isn't …"

"Forceful enough?"

"Sexy."

"Silly me."

"No," Ozzy said, "I know what you mean. But to do her credit, she gave Flambo the push."

"Good girl."

"But that might mean we'll have to help them find another drummer. He still isn't happy, only now the others aren't happy with him, either. Pity, 'cos he's quite solid."

"Between the ears," I said.

"Anyway, the people on the top floor are paying some attention at last. So thanks."

"Don't mention it," I said. Although I was surprised; I'd been quite prepared to find out that my meeting with Sasson had gone the other way entirely.

"It's good to have someone like you in my camp," Ozzy went on. "To tell you the truth, I was beginning to think I was turning into yesterday's man. Glamour by association, that's what I needed. Still, I don't suppose you'll be working with the likes of me for much longer."

"Won't I?"

"Well not if what I'm guessing is true."

"And what're you guessing, Ozzy Ireland?"

"Well," he said, "the Jack stuff."

"What Jack stuff?"

"Fair enough. I know it's still under wraps, but I tapped into Dog's projected catalog the other day and I couldn't help noticing."

"Mmm?" I said cautiously.

"Well, I found a dummy promotion page. It presented ten new tracks and you were down for a production credit. I was really excited for you. Where did they find ten new Jack tracks?"

"Didn't you ask?"

"I don't think anyone's supposed to know. I only look at the future releases to see what's happening to my new acts. No one actually tells me anything."

"Is this item there for anyone to see?" I asked. "Or have you been steaming letters open—in a hi-tech sort of way?"

"Shit," he said. "You mean it's not a done deal?"

"You might say that."

"Me and my big mouth," he said, sounding pleasingly anxious.

"Oh, it's fine from my point of view," I told him. "I'm happy to know how they're thinking on the top floor. It'll give me more negotiating clout, but ..."

"Me and my very big flapping mouth. For God's sake, Birdie, don't tell them where the information came from."

I laughed. He was saying exactly what I was wanting to hear. He said, "Please, Birdie. I'm on a knife-edge as it is. Wrong accent, wrong era. Dog's dumping people right, left, and center. I'm fucked in the long run. I know that."

Oh yes, the music business is a greasy pole all right—hard to climb, terrifyingly easy to slide down.

"I think I'm only kept on the payroll because of this retro thing," Ozzy said.

"Why don't you get out?" I asked. I could ask myself the same question.

"It's what I know," he said.

Good safe answer, and I suppose I could say the same thing. "Or move sideways? Management? Work for yourself. Publishing?"

"Too much paper in publishing."

Amen, I said silently.

"I've thought about managing, though. I'm well placed to make a go of that. But I do need the old salary for a while yet."

"Well," I said, "InnerVersions needs a good manager. All they've got is a so-so drummer who thinks he's way more together than he is."

"It's a thought," he said.

"So think about it." But I could hear the baby crying again in the background and I wondered if he'd have the balls to jump before someone pushed him. And maybe he was too honest and too trusting. Look what he told me! He hasn't a clue how important that piece of information is.

I say, "Ozzy, I think maybe InnerVersions could be part of my negotiations with Dog. It looks like they're bending over backward to sweeten me up for that deal which you know nothing about and about which you kept your very big flapping mouth shut."

"You won't let on? Birdie, you're a princess." Some people are so easy to reassure.

I say, "But Ozzy, think about it. If Dog are trying to keep me sweet, and I want them to make a deal with InnerVersions, then chances are, InnerVersions could have a deal. How nice a deal depends on who's representing them. If it's Flambo, they'll be fucked-over twice before breakfast. However, if a guy with several years of experiences in the business and a good working knowledge of Dog took a hand in it …."

"See what you mean."

"Well, your first clients could be *paying* clients. Wouldn't that be a good start?"

"It needs thinking about," he says. Disappointing.

I say, "Hey, why don't I do it myself?"

"Hold on, Birdie, I said I was thinking about it." Better.

"I'm not management material," I say, as if I haven't heard him, "but I *know* I could cut a stronger deal than Flambo."

"I'd have to start my own business. It's expensive." Wimp.

"All I'd need is phone, fax, and p.c.. And lots of contacts," I say thoughtfully. "I could do it from home to begin with."

Jack and I had a company once. We set it up to protect his publishing rights and to buy back his old catalog. It was called Jackdaw Corps. There were four shares. He had three and I had one.

Ah, well, who cares? It became Jackdaw Corpse soon enough, and the liquidator sold it for a song to the very people from whom we'd bought back Jack's old list. Great idea, that one, *great* protection.

"Everyone needs protection," I say to Ozzy.

"I just had a thought," he says. "Maybe you're going to need representation too—with this thing I know nothing about."

In your dreams, Ozzy Ireland.

"That's a thought," I say. "Except obviously there's nothing to talk about."

"Obviously."

"On the other hand, if someone were representing me, perhaps I could get off wages and back on points for songs I write or co-write."

"Actually, I've never understood that about you, Birdie. Other people who deserve it less get way more credit than you do. Why?"

"Don't ask," I say. "You *know* what happens when you're in no position to bargain."

Like when all your earnings in the UK are already garnished because you owe an unimaginable sum to the taxman, and if you want to keep any at all you have to be paid in cash under the table.

"So you *might* need an agent or a manager?" Ozzy says. "Because it'd be a whole lot more attractive going into business for two clients than just for one."

"Are you hustling me?" I ask with a breathless, defenseless laugh.

"I'm offering to hustle *for* you," he says bravely. I listen carefully, but I can't hear the baby any more.

"Best offer I've had all day," I say. "Looks like we've both got a bit to think about."

"See you tonight?" he says.

Oh yes. Got to see if my baby band has learned to crawl while I was away. Has Karen acquired the balls to use her new voice in front of a crowd? Will Sapper support her on her songs the way she supports him on his? Has Dram brought a little more discipline and a little less arty-axman attitude to his technique? Might Corky have, just once,

126

played against a metronome and checked to see if his instinctive sense of time is quite as brilliant as he thinks it is? And Flambo? Will he ever come to the sad conclusion that he is not Mick Fleetwood or Keith Moon and stop being the playground bully?

Oh, yeah, the continuing saga of a baby band. Less a musical than a soap. Tune in this evening at a scruffy club near you for tonight's thrilling episode.

Meanwhile, I must cover my footprints and wipe away all traces of the private work I've been doing in this office—including the draft of an anonymous communication sent to Barry Stears about the existence of at least ten unreleased tracks by the great Jack. It was sent from LA and it told of how greedy, thieving Birdie Walker attached her sticky little fingers to materials that were rightfully the property of Square Hole Records and spirited them out of the country.

George and Tina marvel at my efficiency and the way I take care of every little detail, so that when they're out in the field, they never have to think about what's happening back at the shop. I make sure they never forget a piece of equipment or paper, and they never have to interrupt a job or a meeting.

I organize the shit out of them so that when they're gone they stay bloody gone and don't come back to find me trying to work out what happened to Cutz UK or where Cutz Cayman's considerable assets went. Or I might be following the path that Square Hole took after it was bought by XY, which was in turn subsumed by Mo'Zee, which may, in the near future, eat a Dog. It's a big project, because it's also useful to learn what happened to the personnel at each stage. Which MD turned up on which board? Who was paid off? Who died? Who's pulling all those tangled strings now?

It's a dog-eat-dog world out there in the music business. But the funny thing is that it isn't all music. Cutz Cayman, for instance, wasn't about music at all. It was about money. And the money from an odd little Latin number called "Dance for Daddy" didn't sit in a bank for twenty years gathering dust and interest. No, it was used to develop hotels and holiday villages all around the Caribbean. "Dance for Daddy" was a nice little earner. For someone.

Big dogs eat little dogs. Little dogs eat lesser dogs, and so on—down to the fleas on their backs. Poor fleas, hopping around, looking for a mouthful, writing their songs, hoping for a starring role in the flea circus—chomp-slurp, and you're history.

At the time, I never knew how small I was. I was courted and fêted, illuminated by flashbulbs. So was Jack. We were protected, transported, interviewed. Jack played to stadia. He was seen on TV by millions of people at a time. He was loved, sought after, waited for by heads of state. Nobody knew he was a flea. Except, at the end, maybe Jack guessed it himself.

We were at a celebrity charity auction once—the sort of glittering bun-fight where nobs and moguls are shamed by their wives into buying one of Lee Marvin's paintings or one of Barbra Streisand's fingernails or a denim jacket Marlon Brando wore once upon a time. Not our scene at all. In fact, so very not our scene that we ignored the invitation. But the organizer was a fan, and she needed yoof and live entertainment to jazz up her middle-aged freak show. And Jack was the happening thing. So she put the arm on the top banana of a TV station who owed her husband a favor. The top banana put the arm on the head honcho of Jack's US label. And the head honcho put the arm on Jack.

The deal was that Jack had to do a short acoustic set and then sell one song to the highest bidder and sing it especially for him or her. And me? I was the hottest chick in town, so what did I have to auction? Well, it was a kiss. Oh my! A true reflection of my talent.

It didn't matter that we were in a Bel Air studio at the time doing the overdubs for a record which was already over-schedule and over-budget. We were dusted off and wheeled out to be auctioned for charity.

"We're just meat on the hoof," Jack said, in the limo. "They might as well cut us up for the finger buffet and serve us with asparagus tips."

There was a sweet corollary to this incident, which I never told Jack: the plump and powerful pig who bought my kiss enjoyed it so much that he offered me five thousand dollars to spend the night with him. When it finally got through to him that I was insulted, he gave me a list of singers and film stars he'd bought for the same amount. Eventually he upped the offer to twenty thousand. At least when you play the whore you have a say in how much you're sold for. There's a very direct relationship between goods, services, and money in that business. I might have been a flea, but I was a flea who knew her price.

What I didn't know was that the pig videoed his night of passion. I found out years later when his son tried to sell the video back to me after the pig died of fatty heart disease. By that time, I had no money and no reputation anyway, so I just laughed. Who knows what happened to the video.

Today, a delivery man brought in a box of assorted stationery which needed to be signed for. While I was checking the contents against the invoice, he said, "What a way to spend your life, eh? Stuck in here, counting envelopes and paper clips. At least I'm out, driving around and meeting people."

He'd looked at me and thought I was someone who'd spent her whole life checking invoices. No twenty-thousand-dollar nights for a middle-aged office manager, apparently. No champagne adventures. I am what a delivery man expects to see. Perhaps I should start wearing lipstick to work.

That night, wearing lipstick, I took Grace and Alec to listen to InnerVersions. Oh, I'm so cool, I always know where the next band is coming from. What a rave! They know I'm working, but I include them. How kind. Party time.

The band was already playing when we walked in. They were playing what used to be an endless, shapeless number called "More and More." Now it's four minutes long and called "Gimme More." And it's tight. It's so tight that the dance floor is packed, and Grace heads straight for it, towing Alec by the hand.

I stood for a minute and watched the dancers. Clearly, they trusted the band. They got up and moved because it was easier to dance than to sit still and drink. The band carried them there and they knew they were in safe hands. It was a good sight to see—a visible sign of progress.

129

I was waiting particularly for the end of the break between two choruses, because if the band was going to lose its nerve and blow it, that's where they'd do it. There were two linking bars which could lose them all the trust they'd built. They had trouble with them because they were so spare and simple it made them nervous.

Here we go, hiatus time. The band stops playing. The solid mass of sound is suspended. Karen peels away with a lonely electric sound. She climbs into the sudden silence with an ascending run—a modified minor pentatonic scale, sixteen beats to the bar. Halfway up, she meets Corky coming down—a punched-out bass line, one and two, three, four, and ... wait for it now, hold your breath, we're coming home ... and *bang*, everyone hits the key chord together. And it's *loud*. Tension released. Whoosh. Oh yeah, let's *dance*!

Excellent. Well done, babes, mama's proud of you. Wasn't that worth a little work?

Karen is almost laughing, triumphant. Go for it, girl.

It was such a small thing—just two bars—but it depended on precision. The people from Dog probably wouldn't even notice.

They were sitting at a table in a central position, giving nothing away. I slid through the crowd and sat at the edge of the group, nodding hello to Sasson and Ozzy. Sasson was watching Sapper. I half closed my eyes and tried to see Sapper for the first time too, ignoring the fact that he was an arrogant little shit who still took his laundry home to his mother. Can he make me believe in him? Because, in this game, it doesn't matter a dry fart who does your laundry. It's the illusion that counts.

IV

Dance the Night Away

Helen and Petra stood side by side in front of the mirror, their slippery strappy dresses almost touching. They looked like sisters, but they were best friends.

Helen said, "Try it up."

Petra lifted her hair off her neck and turned slowly from left to right.

"You should wear it up," Helen said.

"It makes my face look too long," Petra said, staring at her own neck. A boyfriend once told her that she had a neck like a model. She loved her neck.

Helen, too, looked at Petra's slender neck. "You're right," she said. Petra had too many advantages already.

"No, be honest," Petra said.

"I was being."

"Oh, I don't know," Petra said. "I want him to notice us, that's all. Do you really think my face is too long?"

They were brimful of optimism and self-doubt. They knew which was the band's table. They knew exactly the spot on the dance floor they should occupy when the disco took over from the band. They had practiced cool moves and body-rolls in Helen's bedroom until they looked like a pair of sophisticated clubbers. Their dresses had caused rows with their parents. But was it enough to make Sapper look at them? And if he looked, what would he see?

"Oh God," said Helen. "I think I've started to bloat." She turned sideways in the mirror. "Do you think I'm looking bloated?"

"It doesn't notice," Petra said. She let her hair fall to her shoulders. A million magazines, a million pop videos, had shown her what the perfect face looked like. Surely hers was only a little too long.

"Oh God," they said in unison, and attacked their makeup again.

Sapper comes off stage, his skin vibrating, applause acting on him like a cocaine body-rub.

Someone presses a beer into his hand, says, "Good set, man. Wow."

Dram and Corky stumble toward him. What are they doing here? Surely he's alone. Two minutes ago, he'd owned the stage, the music. He'd been in sole command. The applause was his.

Dram says, "Fuck! We're shooting 'em dead tonight."

Stay cool. "It went okay," Sapper says.

"Get you!" Corky says. "Mr. Ice. You can't kid me. I saw you lapping it up."

Sapper tips his head back and lets a mouthful of beer slide down his throat. His throat feels like a polished, oiled tube, infinitely supple. Could be those vocal exercises mean something. Could be they're worth more than Flambo says.

He searches through the crowd, looking for Birdie. She's been so focused on his faults. Where is she when he's showing his strengths?

There she is, on the other side of the room at a table with the record company suits. She's languid, keeping her distance, making the hard club chair look comfortable. Before Sapper can decide to risk Corky's barbed comments about arse-licking and go over to talk to her, she rises and follows Karen to the women's room.

"Typical," Flambo mutters. "I always thought Karen was a closet dyke."

"She wasn't before she started shagging you," jeers Corky.

Karen began the set with shaking hands and her heart in her mouth. She ended it on an unaccustomed spasm of triumph. Is this what confidence is? she asked herself, this feeling that you have what you're doing under your own control.

The bit she never told the others in InnerVersions was that the weeks in the rehearsal room, the writing, arranging, and practicing were a pleasure to her. They bitched and complained. They said, "This is a farce and a waste of time: we should be out there, playing live."

132

She, on the other hand, felt for the first time that she was coming to grips with the material. In private.

Now they were testing the material and she still felt she'd kept a grip on it. Even in public.

The women's room is crowded. When she walked through, the other women turned to watch her and for once she didn't feel they would all start sniggering behind her back.

She takes several deep breaths to calm herself. Having tasted confidence, she is suddenly afraid of arrogance.

But Birdie hugs her and says, "Good stuff, kid. Mama's proud of you."

"You're just saying that," Karen replies automatically.

"There's only you between prod and proud," Birdie says. And Karen can't figure out what she means.

With the set finished, Helen and Petra have to jostle to keep their places in front of the mirror. They see Karen come in and go straight to one of the bogs.

"That's Karen," someone says.

Helen and Petra have seen her onstage, but they didn't know her name. She isn't Sapper, so she doesn't count.

"We could get to know her," Petra whispers. "It's a way to meet HIM."

The old woman who came in with Karen is washing her hands.

"Do you think that's Karen's mum?" Helen whispers.

A tall girl pushes through the swing door, all hair and energy. She rushes up to the old woman and says, "It's great, Lin. I wish I'd worn those other shoes."

She's the student type, jeans and not enough makeup. Helen and Petra automatically decide to hate her.

"Are you going to introduce us to the band?" the student type says.

"Sure," says the old woman.

Helen and Petra exchange an agonized glance in the mirror. They turn.

"Do you *know* them?" breathes Helen.

"Sure," says the old woman, smiling.

133

"Do you know Sapper?" says Petra, gasping a little at saying HIS name out loud. "Only, me and my friend think he's …" Helen jabs an elbow in her ribs.

"You know, the best way to meet a band is to ask for their autographs," the old woman says. "They'd like that."

"Really? I'd feel …"

"Yes," the old woman says. "If you say you really like their music and you think they're great—that's what they want to hear. How're they going to know unless you tell them?"

"I couldn't," Helen says.

"We'd die," Petra says.

"Could we?" Helen asks.

"Got any paper?" the old woman says. "And you'll need a pen."

Sapper suddenly finds himself surrounded by girls. At first, it was just two little honeys who hung back shyly and then plucked up enough courage to approach him.

"We think you're great," they said in a rush. "Can we have your autograph?"

"We really like the music," one of them said.

"Could you make it out to Helen?" said the other.

"And Petra."

Now he has a pen in his hand and he's modestly signing scraps of paper, beer mats, cocktail napkins, whatever they put in front of him.

He looks past the eager young bodies and sees Birdie watching.

Now she knows, he thinks. Now she'll see me for who I am.

He lifts his chin and turns his head, meeting her gaze from beneath lazy eyelids. It feels like a classic rock star expression. It feels good. He knows he's imitating something he's seen before, but he can't help it. He's starring in his own video. He sees himself from a distance, in a smoky club—somewhere blue-collar in the States. He is the tough outsider—the working boy genius—who catches the eye of the cool, unresponsive broad. In the next scene, he's onstage singing to her, backlit, lonely, but so irresistible. She begins to dance. In the next scene, he's dancing with her. Final scene: he walks away down a wet, lamplit street, carrying his guitar case. On the other side

134

of the road is a white limo with darkened glass windows. One of the rear windows rolls down and the cool but melting woman watches him walk away. There is just the beginning of a smile twitching at the corner of her mouth. She has plans for the tough, lonely genius. Oh yes, she does.

And it's all true. It's as if he's at last seen himself on MTV.

The thing that bewilders Ozzy Ireland the most about this gig is that he has recognized three scouts from other labels lurking in the crowd. Two come from little indie companies. But one is from MCA.

He points this out to Mr. Freel, who merely grunts in reply.

Later though, at the end of the first set, when the band is at the center of a surprising rush of female attention, he hears Mr. Freel ask the guy from production, "Just what have we signed this band for?"

The answer he hears is, "Interim contract. One of those suck-it-and-see things."

"How long?"

"I think three months."

Mr. Freel grunts again.

Ozzy catches Birdie's eye. She winks, long and slow.

He's beginning to feel he's associated with something which might not be an instant success but which is certainly not a failure either.

"Enthusiastic local fan-base," he says to Mr. Freel.

"Mmm," says Mr. Freel.

Whenever Lin introduced Grace to anyone, she never said, "This is my niece," or "Meet Grace, she's my niece." She always said, "This is Grace," as if Grace needed no explanation, no reason for being with Lin except as good company. It was one of the things Grace loved her for. She wasn't an add-on, or defined by her relationship. She could be an individual.

Tonight, she's meeting a lot of people: the band, the honchos from the record company. She's at the center of things. She's excited.

And she's lucky: she's with a guy who isn't afraid to dance. That makes him perfect. When she looks around the floor, she sees so many girls dancing on their own or in all-girl groups, while *she's* out there dancing with Alec. He isn't a particularly good dancer, but he's there. He doesn't show her up or drink too much or take the piss out of dancing like some guys do.

Grace doesn't know a lot of men who enjoy dancing. Check out any dance floor and you'll see what makes Alec special.

She's glad Lin likes him enough to invite him here tonight. And she's glad he likes Lin too. Somehow it makes Grace feel more attractive if one member of her family, at least, is warm, welcoming, and with it. Unlike her mother, whose suspicion is almost tactile.

Perhaps I shouldn't have brought him home unannounced, she thinks. But I thought Mum was flexible. She used to be nicer to my friends. Perhaps she doesn't want me to grow up. Perhaps she's getting too old.

Grace takes a drink out of Alec's glass and feels his arm around her shoulder. They're waiting for the band to go onstage again.

Lin comes over and says, "Can I leave the car keys with you, sweetie? You haven't been drinking too much, have you?"

"Aren't you staying to the end?" Grace says, disappointed.

"I've got to talk to some people. But if you've drunk too much to drive, call a cab."

"I'll drive," Alec says. "I've only had a couple of beers. I won't drink any more."

"Isn't he perfect?" Grace blurts out.

Lin laughs and says, "Whaddya think, sweetie? Shall we ask him to leave his name with the booking agent? Give him a call when we need a good roadie?"

"Why not?" Grace says, recovering.

Alec throws back his head and snorts with laughter. Grace feels she's been saved from her own obviousness.

The second set begins with "Thirty-nine Stitches." Sapper hits it with everything he's got. He *is* the guy in the restaurant and he's the waitress too. He's begun to describe the song to anyone who'll listen as a character song, and tonight, for the first time, he feels the characters inhabiting him.

Bathed in white light, speeding, he picks Birdie out of the shadows in front of him. This is partly her song too. They wrote it together. A song about a young man and an older woman. He's giving it back to her—exactly how she wants it—hot and hard.

There's a heaving mass of dancers between him and her—girls, like snakes, are just about wriggling out of their skins. But he can feel her eyes. She's watching.

Next on the set list is "Back in the Sweatshop." "Two nights with my baby—then back in the sweatshop again. Don't go, don't go, baby doncha leave me. Don't go, don't go, don't go."

He looks for her, but she's gone. Her shadowy chair is empty. She doesn't come back.

Well, fuck her—who needs her anyway? Plenty more where that came from. Look at 'em all! Booty by the ton. All hot for me. "But don't go, don't go, don't go. At least, my honey, stay with me until I've finished with you."

Right at the bitter end, in the alley behind the club, when his muscles are aching and his skin is chill with drying sweat, he tastes the sourness of partially metabolized adrenaline and amphetamine. He has gorged on live flesh, so how come he's still hungry?

Sated and wanting more, he sees two girls in strappy, slippery dresses hanging out near the van.

"Pudding?" Dram suggests. "Ours?"

"Aren't they a bit young?" says Karen.

"They're never too young to be up for it," Flambo says. "You go on home like a good girl. Unless you fancy some too."

"Which one is yours?" says Dram.

"Don't fuckin' care," says Sapper, edging forward. "The one with the neck. You two can fight about the other."

V

A Weird Little Man

The back of the Bentley was upholstered in blond suede. It was as big as a poor boy's double bed—not that I know a lot about poor boys' double beds. I leaned into the softness, closing my eyes. The ride was smooth enough to be sickening.

I wished I was alone. I wanted to empty my mind. But Sasson, who had been monosyllabic earlier, wasn't going to let that happen. The false intimacy in the back of a chauffeur-driven car was working on him.

"I hope you didn't think I was completely unresponsive back there," he said. "In fact, I think you're right—that's a nice little band you've got there. It's the commercial possibilities I have to consider."

I sat tight behind closed eyes and didn't answer.

He continued, "The singer seemed to be giving it a lot of topspin."

What did Sasson know about topspin? It was a silly metaphor. What everyone's looking for is a lead singer you can't drag your eyes away from, and that isn't something you can work on the way a tennis player works on a stroke. A singer's got it or he ain't—it's one of life's mysteries.

"What's the matter, Birdie? Nothing to say? I thought you'd be pitching for him."

"No. I've already told you what I think would be sensible and fair."

"You must have a personal opinion, though. I mean, think of the singers you've known. How does he stack against them?"

Sasson could answer that himself. He was goading me.

When I didn't reply, he said, "Well, he's no Jack. That's for sure."

Comparisons, comparisons. Poor Sapper.

I said, "If you only signed bands who stacked up against the stars, you'd only sign one every seven years and you'd be out of a job. You gotta have something new to sell. That's what you're in business for."

"True," he said. "There aren't many Jacks around. It's just that I don't have your knack for talent-spotting. I sometimes wonder, if I hadn't grown up with Jack, if I'd first come across him in a club like tonight, would I have spotted him for what he was?"

"Did you have a tin ear, Sasson?" I asked with mild curiosity. "Were you blind? Because you would've had to have been blind and deaf to fail to spot Jack."

"Yes." He sighed and mercifully shut up for a few more miles. We rolled on west at a steady eighty miles an hour, he in his corner, me in mine; he with his thoughts, me with mine.

We were going to Dorset—not Sasson's county. It wasn't his house we were driving to, and we weren't in his car. The man behind the wheel wasn't his driver. In short, the trip was not Sasson's idea.

It wasn't my idea, either—except that it is what I've been walking toward for years. So many little steps, one at a time, bring me to Nash Zalisky's doorstep.

Once, years ago, when he was still more or less a social creature, I met Nash Zalisky at a reception. Even then, he was a formidable character. His own independent label had just been bought out by Columbia and he had been transformed from a music industry maverick into a rich, rich maverick with a three-year exclusion clause in his contract.

I was being stealthily pursued by a man with a telephoto lens, and I escaped up a flight of stairs to a shadowy gallery overlooking the reception area. Nash was the only other person up there—watching the party from above as if it were his personal bullring.

He said, quietly, "Birdie, would you please go elsewhere. You attract too much attention."

"Where?" I asked, because I was looking for a private way out and couldn't find one. I looked down and saw Jack at the center of a crush of women.

He said, "You know, I always wanted Jack on my label, but I couldn't afford him. Now I can afford him, but I'm not allowed to work."

"Money has a price," I said.

He nodded seriously and we both watched the photographer look up and catch sight of us. With military precision, we took one pace back into the shadows.

He said, "I would like to go to the movies now. Would you allow me to take you to the movies?"

"If you know a discreet way out of here," I said, "I'll allow you to take me anywhere." At that moment, I was sick to death of being a peep show at a circus. I was sick of the hype and fuss and flattery, the grabbing and groping. If a quiet man wanted to take me to fantasyland and a darkened space, I wasn't going to stop him.

"Only I must warn you," he said, "I won't tolerate talking at the cinema. And afterward I do not want to discuss the film. Half-digested opinions drive me nuts. But I might want to hold your hand."

"Fair enough," I said. "My side of the contract stipulates no groping and you pay for the tickets. Deal?" I thought he was joking.

"Deal," he said. He wasn't joking.

We went to a Marx Brothers double bill at the Curzon, and we didn't exchange another word from the time we left the reception until he put me in a cab at the end of the second film. Then he kissed the hand he'd held all through *Horse Feathers* and said, "Thank you for your company. It was surprisingly restful."

I never saw him again from that day to this. But it wasn't the last time I heard of him. Quite apart from becoming a card-carrying eccentric and something of a recluse, when his exclusion clause ran out he came back onto the scene as a major player. Only this time he didn't let any of the big sharks buy him out. He was the shark.

Which, if my research tells me no lies, is why he can send a car for Dog's most important suit well after midnight, and Sasson will meekly hop in and drive away to Dorset when he'd much rather be home in bed. Better yet, he can send me a perfect gold and green orchid, packed in ice, and a handwritten invitation to a late supper. Oh my! Further, he can make Sasson very nervous indeed.

"I've never been invited to Badlands before," Sasson confessed, shifting uneasily.

"Invited or summoned?" I said. I was uneasy myself. The flower was exquisite, and I wondered if that meant Nash might think I was still exquisite too. Being a recluse sometimes means that a man doesn't keep a grip on time.

"So, you haven't seen him recently," I said.

"Who has? Well, he does come to town once in a blue moon—he hasn't completely cut himself off."

"What does he do with himself?"

"Well, I suppose you might say he's become the *éminence grise* behind all sorts of ventures."

"Which ventures?" I asked. "Dog, for instance?"

"One thing I know for certain," Sasson said, glancing nervously at the back of the driver's head, "is that almost everything you hear is wildly exaggerated."

"So there's no truth in the rumor that he heads a multimedia consortium which has its own cable company?"

"Where did you hear that one, Birdie?"

"Just gossip," I said, grinning in the dark.

"Nash doesn't like gossip."

"Tough," I said. "Non-disclosure invites speculation."

"You should know," Sasson said bitchily.

"Indeed I do. Is he your boss, Sasson? Are you obeying orders? Who are you dancing for?"

"Actually, Birdie, I don't have a boss as such."

"Right," I said, "and that's why you're dogging around in the wee small hours with a bitch you've resented for years."

"I don't resent you, Birdie," Sasson said in a voice you could pour from a cream jug. "I just wish I could get a line on you—you're so wayward."

I laughed and retreated. For the time being, fishing was a waste of energy.

We approached the house through iron gates set in a high wall. After about half a mile on gravel, the drive became stone-paved, and at exactly that point the chauffeur switched the engine off and allowed the Bentley to coast silently around the last bend. We had just enough momentum to bring us to the base of a flight of stone steps. The house was enormous.

141

I said, "Who's the king of the castle?"

"Shut up," Sasson said, sounding distinctly uncomfortable. "Birdie, please don't ..."

"What?"

But I didn't find out. We were ushered out of the car and pointed up the steps to a pair of colossal doors. The doors opened without any prompting from us and we entered a sort of baronial hall. The floor should have been tiled with marble, but instead it was covered in deep-pile green carpet—acres of it.

"Aha," I said. "The rule of silence persists."

"You remember," said Nash, appearing from behind a thick oak door like a leprechaun popping out from between the pages of a book.

"I didn't know you knew each other," Sasson said.

"Nobody meets for the first time," Nash told him seriously, "they only think they do. In fact, everyone has met everyone. It's just that they don't *know* anyone."

"I see," said Sasson.

"No, you don't," said Nash. "Would you like some supper? I'm cooking *carciofi ripieni di mortadella*."

"Er, wonderful," said Sasson, looking blank.

"Well, I know Birdie loves globe artichokes," Nash said. "Come along."

Miles of silent corridor led to a kitchen. The billionaire, it seemed, was doing his own cooking. Sasson and I sat at the kitchen table, drinking Cuvée Dom Perignon while we watched Nash carefully brown his artichokes. It was a sight to see: he was dressed in black except for a white collarless shirt, which looked like a priest's dog collar under his black sweater—a billionaire vicar cooking supper. He was still very slight and boyish and his buck teeth gave him the appearance of class nerd—the boy who would be surrounded and kicked to shit in the playground. But, up close, his skin was as dry and lined as a man of seventy's and his hair had been dyed an improbable chestnut color. A cookbook was open on the counter beside him and he studied it at every stage of the operation.

Nothing was said until the artichokes had been placed in a heavy metal casserole. He put damp kitchen paper between the lid and the pan—I didn't know if that was to muffle the sound of metal on metal or because it was what the cookbook told him to do.

This man, I thought, has been responsible for some of the loudest recordings in the history of rock music. I grinned and remembered how he'd sat through the Marx Brothers double bill with an earnest, anxious expression on his face, without once cracking a smile.

Nash sat down with us and poured himself a glass of champagne. He said, "Forgive me if I seem blunt, but I abhor small talk. I've heard that you are in possession of a quantity of Jack's recordings and a film which no one else has had sight of."

"I expect you've heard about all sorts of things, including artichokes."

Sasson said, "Birdie, please, no games."

"What a shame," I said. "I'm feeling playful."

Sasson looked at Nash and spread his hands in a helpless gesture. Nash looked at his watch and ignored us both.

Sasson said, "Do the materials exist? A simple yes or no. Is that so hard?"

I smiled at him.

"Look," Sasson said, "I know you want to be the center of attention and to be courted and all that, but I must point out to you that under the terms of Jack's contract at the time he died, all the outstanding materials ..."

"Just a minute," Nash said. He got up, opened the casserole, poked the artichokes with a fork, and then came back to the table.

"Where was I?" Sasson asked, thrown off his stride.

I said, "You were about to explain to the egocentric airhead that, whatever she may or may not have, she has no legal claim to it."

"Yes," agreed Nash, "and I was trying to divert you from that course. It isn't profitable."

"Not to me," I said. "But Sasson's right. Never mind the contract— Jack's estate was bankrupt and I went down with it. All his assets, *all* of them, Sasson, were sold to Square Hole Records to pay off the debts. And that included publishing rights in which I had an interest."

"Debatable," Sasson said.

143

"Then debate it with Inland Revenue. I am still liable for tax on earnings which, according to you, are not rightfully mine."

"You see," said Nash to Sasson, "I think Birdie's ahead of you. And if I may say so, it's contradictory to tell her that she doesn't own that which you are attempting to purchase."

"To take it a step farther," I added, "*all* of Jack's existing assets were declared for estate reasons, bankruptcy reasons, and tax reasons. Any new material, therefore, cannot exist. Which is a pity."

"Are you saying that new materials do exist, but you can't admit to them?" Sasson asked.

"Ding-dong," said Nash, without a trace of humor.

I said, "I'm not saying anything. Especially while this conversation is being recorded."

There was a moment of electric silence and then Nash said, "Sasson, I think you'd better leave. It's most discourteous of you to record a conversation between friends."

"But ..."

"I must insist. And please give Birdie the tape."

Sasson's face was dark with embarrassment and rage. He fumbled in his inside pocket and drew out a little dictaphone.

"I wasn't recording you, Birdie," he said. "I was recording the band earlier."

"Good explanation," I said, "when you already have access to the demo tapes."

"You're so tricky and paranoid, Birdie."

"Is that an apology?" Nash asked mildly.

"No," said Sasson. "Look, Nash, if I've overstepped I apologize."

"You'll find the car about a quarter of a mile down the drive." The speed with which Nash dismissed Sasson left me open-mouthed. Metaphorically, of course—a hanging jaw is not an attractive sight. I rested my chin in my hand and watched with a sleepy expression that masked my shock. For one thing, it was such an abrupt change of pace. For another, it only happened because I'd been trying it on. I didn't actually know Sasson was recording the conversation. It was always a possibility—given the way he was trying to pin me down, and given the way Dog was already floating the notion of an album with ten previously unreleased numbers on it. In those circumstances, Sasson was simply doing his job. Of course, I was doing mine too by refusing to be pinned down and creating diversions when the talk got too tight.

Another interpretation might be that I engineered Sasson's departure in order to get my hands on an extra artichoke. That alone would have been worth doing: supper was delicious. Some say, seize the moment. I say, savor every bite. Especially when you don't know what's going to happen next and you're in the company of a man who, for the last thirty years, has always been on the winning team.

True to form, Nash didn't speak while eating, and afterward he simply beckoned. I followed him along the padded corridor, through the hall, and into a room furnished sparsely with sofas and books. He sat, leaning forward with his elbows on his knees. I slipped my shoes off and curled up in the corner of one of the chairs, massaging my feet.

"You're like a cat licking her paws," he said unexpectedly. "You have a cat's ability to take what's going and move on. I noticed that before. I hypothesized that feeding you might be a pleasure, and so it was."

"I'm glad it was good for you too," I said. "I imagine that you're rarely wrong in your hypotheses."

"There's a pattern to human behavior, and as such it's predictable in the same way that animal behavior is."

"So when you say no one meets anyone for the first time, are you talking in the animal sense? Like when a horse meets another horse, it's merely meeting itself in strange form. It should be already familiar with the stranger's horseness."

"Most people think I'm talking about the transmigration of souls."

"Is it useful to have people think you're dippy?"

"Yes," he said. "Is it useful to have people think you're stupid and greedy?"

"Sometimes. Sometimes it's annoying and a waste of time. Sometimes," I added, "it's entirely accurate."

"I don't think it would be profitable to proceed in negotiations with you on the premise that you are stupid."

I laughed at that. He blinked solemnly and paused. During the pause, the door opened and a man came in with a tray. He served me with a cup of espresso and glided out of the room, leaving Nash still poised on the edge of the sofa, looking earnest and anxious. While I, I hope, looked like a relaxed cat. It's always better to conform to your enemy's delusions about you.

Eventually he said, "So, you have money troubles."

I said, "You know I do."

He nodded. "I could handle those."

"With ease."

"But that's not all?"

"No. I have a beef with the labels and the publishers. They ripped me off. And before that they ripped Jack off."

He nodded again.

"And insofar as you are involved with the labels and the publishers," I went on, "you've ripped us off too."

"You believe I'm involved?"

"Yes."

"Then for the purposes of this conversation we'll accept that as true."

For once I say exactly what I'm thinking: "Well, Nash, that removes a whole layer of tedious accusation, denial, and justification."

"I told you, I abhor small talk."

"It wasn't going to be small," I say. "I have a stack of dodgy royalty statements which go back years."

"Let me have copies."

"You can handle that too?"

"It all depends on what you have to offer in exchange."

"Nothing," I say. I'm looking him straight in the eye when I say it, and he looks straight back. He's very difficult to read.

"Nothing?" he says, blinking slowly.

"Not while this conversation is being recorded." Well, it worked once, so it might again.

"I see," he says. No confirmation, denial, or justification.

We sit for a while in silence and I sip my coffee with apparent contentment. He looks perplexed, but I don't for one moment buy it. I recall Sasson's unease in the car: maybe he was aware he could be overheard by someone other than the driver. And I remember how quickly Nash kicked him out and how outraged Sasson was. Like someone carrying the can for someone else. Maybe Nash has a reputation for bugging his own house.

Nash begins tentatively, "If, for purposes of this conversation, we accept that as true, would you be more comfortable walking in the garden?"

"No," I say. "It's very late. There will be dew on the lawn. I don't want to spoil my shoes."

"Well, Birdie," he says with a helpless shrug, "it seems that we have met twice and I have silenced you twice. I'm devastated. The first time it was because I thought your conversation would be inane."

"Why did you want my company then?"

"You were beautiful and I was lonely. Why did you come?"

"I was fed up and lonely."

"With Jack?" This time, he looked genuinely perplexed.

"At the time, Jack was in the full flood of narcissism. Life is lonely with a narcissist."

"Why did you stay?"

"For the music." I sighed. "Besides, it's only a phase most rockstars go through. With any luck, they come out the other side."

Nash said, "Do you know how much courage it took to ask you out that time?"

"No," I said. "I've never asked anyone out."

"Then you've never been refused."

"That's a different question entirely. Of course I've been refused."

"I mean sexually."

"You didn't ask for sex. You asked for company."

"But if I had asked for sex, Birdie?"

"You didn't, Nash. That's what distinguished you."

"Did it? I always thought you wrote 'Walks Like a Spider' about me."

"You accept that I wrote it?"

"For the purposes of this conversation, I accept that you had a hand in it."

"It wasn't remotely about you," I say, lying through my teeth.

"You see, you were so sweet in person, but the songs were napalm."

"So much for being an inane conversationalist," I say lightly. The turn he has taken gives me the creeps.

"I thought about it a lot in the intervening years," he says. "Yes, I thought you were uninteresting. You said two things: the first was that money has a price, which is a truism. The way you said it made it sound trite rather than apposite. That, I now believe, was the effect of your appearance and a light girlish voice. Your voice has strengthened over the years and your delivery has more impact."

"It was still a truism," I say. "Even a cliché."

"The second thing," he goes on, ignoring me, "was, 'if you know a discreet way out of here, I'll allow you to take me anywhere.' I should have paid more attention. You were selling yourself very cheaply in those days. You held my hand for the price of a cinema ticket."

"When you say you abhor small talk," I say, "it's because you haven't a clue how it works. Did you record all your conversations even back then? And replay them, searching for hidden meaning? Nash, you don't get out enough."

"You are reputed to have a good memory," he retorted. "It's the same thing."

"No, it isn't," I say. "Memory is a reconstruction, of context as well as words." I'm beginning to feel as if I'm trapped in an elevator with someone I don't trust.

"Memory distorts and degrades more quickly than tape," Nash says. "Tape is accurate and absolute."

"Only if you take what's said at face value," I say. "Nash, I'm getting tired and I've an appointment at nine."

"Face value?" he says. "I thought you were accusing me of searching for hidden meaning."

"What if there was no meaning at all?" I say. "That's what small talk is."

"Of course there was meaning. I *knew* a discreet way out and you *came* to the movies with me. You didn't talk. I paid for the tickets. I did not grope, but I held your hand. The words were not without meaning; they were the basis of a deal."

"OK. There was a deal. But it was a long time ago."

"Nevertheless, what haunts me is that I missed something important—a clear equation between physical contact and money. If there was no meaning, why was the innuendo sexual? Why is it still sexual?"

"Still?"

"You said, only a short while ago: 'I'm glad it was good for you too.' Of course you were talking about the food, Birdie, but the reference was to that sordid question asked after carnal encounters."

"It was a bloody *joke*, Nash."

"No," Nash says. "The words mean something. They bring images to mind. Why do you conjure those particular images, Birdie?"

"Why do you receive them in that particular way? You're talking like one of those people who worry endlessly about song lyrics—even play them backward." As I say this, I realize with horror that Nash Zalisky, the *éminence grise* behind some of the loudest, weirdest recordings in rock history, is exactly such a person.

"Yes, lyrics," Nash says, "I was coming to that." He's still sitting on the edge of the sofa, his hands clasped anxiously between his knees.

I've had enough. I uncoil myself and get up. "Nash," I say, "don't start. This is a mistake. I'm playful with words. You aren't. Leave it at that. I'm going now."

"Please don't go," he says. "Nothing's resolved."

"There's nothing to resolve."

"You keep saying that, but you're wrong. I should have offered you my protection years ago—for more than just a few hours. I'm offering it to you now. There's a room prepared for you upstairs. If you're tired, sleep. We can talk again when you wake up."

"Thank you," I say. But I'd rather die. "I want to go home."

He doesn't move, an anxious boy with an un-dead face. I'm in Dorset, for Christ's sake. I want to be in London.

I say, "I need transport, Nash." I've been careless. Now I'm carless.

"Yes, yes," Nash says impatiently. "But you'll have to wait."

"You must have more than one car."

"But only one driver."

"I don't need a driver."

"Oh," he says. "You can drive?" He sounds astonished.

"Can't you?"

"I never learned."

We stare at each other. Impasse.

I say, "Please will you lend me one of your cars?"

"As a matter of fact," Nash says, "I don't even know where they're kept."

"I'll look." I walk away from him. I'm almost expecting the door to be locked, but it isn't. I leave him sitting like a decaying child and find my way through the hall to the front door.

The front door, however, is locked and I can't find any way to open it. The only other place I know how to get to is the kitchen. The back door is impassable too. I wander in and out of every room I can get into and find no way out. It's a huge house with many rooms. Some of them are empty of everything but books, some are completely empty. There is a small cinema and an indoor pool. There's a banqueting hall, a ballroom, a lot of suffocating silence but no exit.

I stood in the middle of the ballroom, feeling silly and angry. It was the one room Nash hadn't carpeted to death. The floor was a beautiful polished dancing surface. I tapped out an inaccurate para-diddle with my feet. There were two things going on, I thought. One of them has to do with what I want. The other is what Nash wants. Nash is a man and men are normally written in such big print that they're easy to read even by candlelight. But I don't know what Nash wants, and that is an unusual predicament for me.

If I didn't understand him, I wouldn't be able to bargain with him. I *have* to know what a man wants. I have to be able to give him at least the illusion that he's won before he'll give me what I want. All my experience tells me that.

I twirled on the beautifully sprung floor. I swung my hips and boogied by the light of the moon streaming in through the long windows. Then I said aloud, "Nash, in case you're listening, I'm in the ballroom. I hate being destructive, so please come along with a key before I break one of your elegant windows."

He appeared so quickly that I thought he must have been waiting just outside.

He said, "Why are you so desperate to leave me, Birdie?"

"Because I don't like the feeling of confinement."

"It's protection I'm offering you, not confinement."

"Thank you," I say carefully. "But sometimes the two can feel pretty similar."

He sat down cross-legged on the floor. "Did Jack feel that way too?"

"Yes."

"But it's a brutal world."

"All the same, I don't want to be cut off from it. Nor did he."

"He would have been torn to pieces without protection and so would you."

"That was a long time ago. Nobody's interested any more."

"You're wrong," Nash said. "You're causing a lot of interest at the moment."

"Not really. It's Jack. Some things don't change."

"Do the new tracks exist?"

I smile in the moonlight and shake my head. I say, "I'd love to talk to you properly. But I can't do it here."

"It's safe here."

"Where's your phone, Nash?" I say. "I'd like to call a taxi."

"Oh Birdie, Birdie," he says. "Have you any idea how much I could do for you?"

"If you want to do something for me," I say, "you could start by calling a taxi."

"Is that all you want from me?"

Yes it is, no it isn't, you lunatic prick. If you hadn't put the wind up me so badly, I'd have you tied up like a pet poodle by now.

I say, "I want a taxi and I want a fair deal for Jack. I think you can provide those. I don't know what your relationship is with Dog Records or Barry Stears, but I'm very wary of them. Once bitten, twice shy, and all that malarky. I have no cause to mistrust you personally, Nash, but you did once say you always wanted Jack on your label. If Dog's your label now, you've already got him, because Dog bought out both Cutz and Square Hole. If I'm reading the runes correctly, Mo'Zee is about to merge with Dog and that would give you the whole catalog. And Jack's list is still doing nicely. Why can't everyone be satisfied with what they've got?"

151

"I only wanted to talk to you, as a friend," Nash says plaintively. "I wanted us to get to know each other."

"We can do that," I say. "But not in a bugged house."

For a moment, Nash stops staring at me and looks at the moon instead.

He says, "Maybe I've always been a secretive man. Maybe I've always been self-protective. Great wealth, Birdie, allows one to take natural inclinations to great extremes. But you shouldn't mistrust me for that."

"I don't," I say. "But men have been telling me to trust them for years. And people have been using me to get to Jack for years too. It takes time to make friends, Nash, especially when you don't know what they've got on their shopping list."

"Ah," he says painfully. "Maybe I understand you better than you think I do. Wealth and power are like talent and beauty. You ask yourself: do they want me or do they want *it*?"

"Exactly."

"Do you want me to give you something for nothing, Birdie? As proof of my sincerity?"

"Yes," I say. "A taxi."

"Very well," he says. "But you must promise that we'll meet again soon."

"A promise isn't nothing," I say.

"Oh," he says. "I thought you meant nothing material."

"Nothing is nothing, Nash."

"You know," he says, scrambling to his feet, "you may not have wealth, but you do have power. I'll make a call for you. Wait here."

He skipped out of the ballroom in his tiny soft-soled shoes, and left me with a huge dance floor to prowl alone. I was glad the lights were off. I didn't want to see any reflection of myself. It's too late for bright lights, I thought, and I'm too old to stand them.

Nash comes out at sundown like Dracula, I thought, to suck the life and energy out of aging rock chicks. Exactly the opposite to rock musicians, who come out at sundown to give you all their life and energy.

Softly, almost under my breath, I sang "Love Lies Bleeding" to remind myself that I was alive. I danced flexuous steps to go with the sinuous melody line, reminding my feet that they'd soon be far away.

As I completed the circuit, I saw Nash almost hidden behind the door. A voyeur and an eavesdropper. If I ever agree to sleep in one of his beds, take me out and shoot me—I'll have become too gullible to be allowed to live.

"Don't stop," he said. "That was a great song. Did you write it?"

"No," I said. "That was pure, unadulterated Jack. And don't read anything into the word 'adulterated'—it was a slip of the tongue."

"There's no such thing."

I shook my head. "Do you remember that other song: 'Sliding Widows'?"

"No," he said. "Remind me."

"Well, that came from Jack misreading the side of a van belonging to the Sliding Window Company. He was charmed by his mistake, Nash. Mistakes make art."

"I didn't know that," Nash said, looking as if he'd like to take notes. "I wish I could remember the song."

"It would never have been written except for a slip of the brain."

We stared at each other for a moment, and then he said, "I'll walk you to the car—unless you've changed your mind."

This time, the front door opened at the merest touch of Nash's hand and we walked out into the setting moon. The black sky was beginning to fray at its eastern edge and he screwed up his eyes as if it were the brightest glare.

As we walked toward the car, he said, "I'll need some sort of tape or show reel. I'll need to be convinced you have something to sell."

"Did I say I had something to sell?"

"No."

"Anyway, I have no incentive. I mean, supposing I was to look through a trunk of old belongings forgotten in an attic or a cellar somewhere, and I happened to find a handful of Jack's demos or an old movie? Why would I tell you about them? If I did, you or Sasson or some tax inspector would immediately claim them and say I should've given them up years ago."

"There are ways round that."

"What ways?"

"Let me think about it."

"If there are 'ways' you can ensure that I benefit from what I own—that I own what I own—then I might be encouraged to look."

"Perhaps, sometime in the future, we could arrange an exchange of proofs."

"But Nash, I have no incentive to look for anything. Proof would only become an issue if I found something."

"What sort of incentive?"

"Cold cash," I say. "Something I don't have to declare."

"I see." He walks on a few paces. The car is in sight. It isn't a taxi—in fact, it looks like the same Bentley that made the outward journey. I wonder what happened to Sasson.

"Here's my problem, Birdie," Nash says. "I think you're being disingenuous when you say you need an incentive to look. Why should I pay you to look for something you've already found?"

"No reason," I say. "In any case, as you said, this was only a meeting between friends. So, thank you for supper, it was truly delicious. I'm delighted to have met you again."

We are beside the car. The driver gets out and opens a door for me. Nash takes my hand. He turns it palm up and kisses the inside of my wrist. I lean into him and kiss his withered cheek. His grip tightens in a spasm around my hand, as if an electric current has passed through him.

"*À bientôt*," I say airily as I wrench my hand out of his grasp and slide onto the car seat. I'm losing my mind: I can't tell if his reaction is desire or disgust.

I wave goodbye. That is one seriously fucked-up little man, I think, and I rub my wrist clean on the blond suede of the upholstery. Will he go back to the house now and furiously shower in boiling water the way I want to? Or will he search fruitlessly through Jack's catalog trying to find a song called "Sliding Widows"?

Good luck, Nash, and good night.

VI

Rolling Stone Magazine

"Hit The Road, Jack"
By David Palmer

27 Years Ago—Brighton, England
As the car draws up to the curb, two girls in silver hotpants leap into action. They come together, pubic bones grinding, knees between thighs. They strike a faux lesbian pose. The big one massages the small one's breast. The uniformed doorman looks on, expressionless. He's seen it all before.

Wearily, Jack climbs out onto the sidewalk.

"Wotcha doin', girls?" he drawls in that casual flat delivery only the British can muster at five o'clock in the morning.

"You," choruses the teen duo. The big one says, "We'll do you—any time, any place, anywhere."

Jack turns his back on them to help his companion out of the car. She is wearing a sunshine-colored silk maxi coat and little else under it. She's beautiful enough to be a slap in the face to Jack's teenage fans. They groan with disappointment.

The couple sweeps past and out of sight.

"Sorry, girls," the doorman says. "As you can see, Jack's got his hands full."

But the girls turn up again next morning at breakfast. Still in their silver hotpants and wobbling platform shoes, they teeter across the lobby to the cordoned-off area of the hotel restaurant where Jack's Pack, in varying states of hangover, are eating bacon and eggs.

"Who let them in?" Jack mutters to Connie McKenzie, tour publicist.

"I think they spent the night in Wills's room."

"Get 'em outta here. We got the bleedin' BBC coming. I don't want them around." Jack returns to his coffee and a copy of the *London Times*.

On the road with one of the great killer bands of all time, I discovered that the two would-be groupies weren't the only ones finding it difficult to gain access to the tour's inner circle. It was a raw March evening ten days into his punishing schedule of British venues before I found myself in the presence of kick-ass Jack.

In the two years since he last toured England, he has made so much of a reputation through album sales and concert tours in Europe and America that he finds himself somewhat in exile in his own country. Venues like the Lyceum Ballroom in Brighton (two matinées and an evening thrash, all sold out in three hours) are no longer big enough to contain him, and the security arm of this traveling circus is stretched to its limit. Isolated behind bouncers, photographers, managers, drivers, and business advisers, Jack has become inaccessible even to the members of his own band. Tempers fray. In the hiatus between soundcheck and performance, there is nothing to do but bitch.

All this will change in May when the tour hits the United States, and you feel that Jack's private army can't wait to stretch their wings and fly to open spaces where they'll have room to breathe.

"We'll be all right in Chicago," says Wills, bassist and long-time associate of Jack's. "They're used to people like us."

"Yeah, Mayor Daley loves us," croons lighting engineer Ken Castle. "He's so cool—puts us up in all the best hotels."

156

The room rocks with laughter. Last year in Chicago, half the road crew were arrested for possession of controlled substances and the tour would have been aborted without the timely intervention of Capitol Studios.

"Everyone wants us," says Wills, dragging on an untidy handrolled cigarette of dubious provenance. "Number-one attraction everywhere—that's us."

Meanwhile, Jack travels to the gig in a custom-built, heavily curtained bus. Inside, the bus is like a film set.

"In the style of a Tunisian bordello," Jack explains when, credentials double-checked, I am ushered down the aisle and past the oriental rug that serves as a door.

He is sprawled, pasha-like, across black satin cushions with his head resting in his lady's lap.

"How many Tunisian bordellos have you visited, Jacko?" she asks, tapping his forehead lightly with one finger. She is dressed in cream shantung with a skirt split almost to the waist. Her legs go on forever. Lack of access is not her problem; lack of privacy might be. In a decade when British rock stars are not in short supply, demand for this glamorous couple far outstrips their wish to meet it. Even during this short journey between hotel and hall, whenever we stop at lights or slow for an intersection, the drumming of hungry hands can be heard resonating through the reinforced panels of the bus.

"It's like *Suddenly Last Summer*," remarks Jack. "You wonder what they get out of it. Or rather, you sometimes wonder that they'd get out of it if they got in."

"You're supposed to be thinking about the arrangement for 'Adversarial Attitude,' " his lady reminds him, showing an unexpectedly practical side to her nature. June's asking which musicians to book."

Cleveland, Ohio. 27 Years On.
I never did find out what musicians were required for

'Adversarial Attitude'. Search through the most complete discography, and you won't discover a song of that title. As far as anyone knows, it was never recorded. Twenty-five years ago, the house that Jack built went up in flames and he with it. A three-month period of depression and spiraling drug-use ended in a blaze so hot and bright, they say it lit up the sky for most of the night. A casual remark made on a tour bus so many years ago serves only as a painful reminder of what might have been.

Today, at the conference preceding Jack's posthumous induction into The Rock And Roll Hall Of Fame, a panel analyzed the myths, the songs, and the influence of the music that is all that remains of Jack.

"We're interested in his cultural impact," said Teddy Wright, gruff-voiced guitarist whose virtuoso licks adorned most of Jack's *oeuvre*.

Interest in the singer's life and times is still avid on both sides of the Atlantic. A docudrama is slated for production next fall. Even more intriguing is a rumor that a collection of a dozen of Jack's previously unreleased tracks have turned up in the vaults of a London studio. They are to be cleaned up and digitally remastered for release in time for Christmas.

"This could be the most exciting discovery since the release of The Beatles' *Anthology*," said Rocky Netzdorf, author of the brilliant quasi-fictional *Escape Into Fire* (re-issued in paperback, Plume). "Facts are hard to come by, and spokespersons from Jack's record company are refusing to comment, but the vibe is there."

Made conspicuous by her absence is Jack's last partner, Birdie Walker, she of the long legs and insolently beautiful face from the tour twenty-seven years ago.

"Of course we invited her," said symposium head Richard Copeman, Rock Hall's Director of Education. "We would have welcomed her input."

The conference closed with a concert featuring, among

others, Jack's Pack and Friends, a reunion of Jack's sidemen with guest appearances by singers from a later generation of bands influenced by him.

"We bought all the albums, growing up in Red Lodge, Montana," said Skip Suskin of On-Line Animals. "The first thing we did when we formed our own band was to cover some of Jack's numbers. It's a blast to be doing them again."

'Adversarial Attitude' was not one of the numbers On-Line Animals would have been able to cover. But if the rumors prove true, maybe it is one of the songs that have been gathering cobwebs in a London vault. I hope so: twenty-seven years has been a long wait for the young reporter who first heard about the song in the back of Jack's own tour bus.

Sitting in a bar drinking a lonely toast to absent friends after the concert, I could almost hear Jack's flat London tones: "Wotcher doin', Dave?" he might have asked.

Waiting for you, Jack. You're twenty-seven years late.

VII

Love and Other Stuff

Someone is turning up the heat. The voice at the other end of the line is pink and perky: "Do you have a moment to chat?"

We were sitting around the kitchen table, Robin, Grace, Alec, and I, finishing supper, when the phone rang.

"It's for you, Lin," Grace said. "Someone called Imogen."

Imogen says she's a "researcher" from Median Films. She's the third in five days. They aren't all from Median Films: one was from the BBC and the other said he was with *Mojo*.

"This is for the new bio on Jack," Imogen says. "I need to check a few facts."

"Who gave you this number?" I ask.

"It's on file," says perky Imo. "I just wanted to ask you some background questions—like, how you met Jack, what he was like ..."

"That must be on file too," I say. "Look, I'm sorry, I'm not going to talk about this."

"If I've called at an inconvenient moment, can I leave you my number?"

"No," I say, and I hang up.

"What?" Robin asks. "What's the matter?"

"While we're all here," I say, "can I ask you a favor? If anyone from the media calls, please would you say I'm not here and you don't know where to find me."

"How do they get this number?" Robin's looking anxious, as she does so often these days.

"I don't know. And that's another thing. Please, if anyone asks you about anything to do with Jack or me, blow them off. I know you're

160

already aware of this sort of thing, Grace, but Alec mightn't have come across it before."

Grace blushes and Alec says, "I don't understand. What's going on?"

Robin says tartly, "They use anyone they can get their hands on to insinuate themselves into Lin's confidence."

"But why now?"

"Oh, there's always some excuse—some anniversary or other."

"But why don't you want to talk about it?" Alec asks. "Wouldn't it keep ..."

Grace interrupts, "Lin finds it all too painful."

"I'm sorry," says Alec, looking as if this has never occurred to him before. "But, if you talked to someone sympathetic, a friend, say, wouldn't it get the rest of them off your back?"

"No," Robin says. "It works the other way round. Talk to one, and the rest think it's open season."

"Say one word," I put in, "and it can come back to haunt you for the rest of your life."

"Can't you put the record straight?"

"No. It's all like that question, 'When did you stop beating your wife?' They start with a false assumption and you spend so much time and energy proving it false that everyone who doesn't say, 'You protest too much,' says, 'There's no smoke without fire.' Rumors and allegations stick, Alec. I'm sure you know that. You mess around on the Net. How much of what you've seen there would you say was true?"

Grace is blushing furiously now, but Alec says calmly, "Not much, but I'm sure if people knew the truth they'd stop inventing the rubbish."

"I don't think so. Which is the more interesting, Alec, Jack and Birdie met at a North London pub, or Jack met Birdie at a Tunisian brothel?"

Alec pauses for a moment and then says, "Assuming it was neither of those, where did you and Jack actually meet?" Oh dear. The slick little prick is catching on.

I treat him to my saddest, most open smile and say, "Yes, that's exactly my point. The truth, whether it's mundane or exotic, is the only thing I've got left that hasn't been thumbed through and fucked over by strangers. See, when you're associated with the entertainment business everyone thinks that your whole life is there to entertain them. That's what you are—a living breathing soap—and they have the right to include themselves in your life. You aren't real. You're just something to watch on telly. Every little thing is up for grabs: what *actually* happened, Birdie? What did it *feel* like? There's always someone who thinks they have the right to know the deepest, most sensitive details. Why? Because you're entertainment and entertainment is for everyone. It's like you made a contract to share every last thing with anyone who wants it. But you didn't."

If you prevent yourself from blinking long enough, your eyes will start to sting and a tear will form. If you're lucky, it will swell and roll gently over your lower eyelid and down your cheek.

Robin says, "It's all right, darling. Here, let me fill your glass. You'll feel better in a minute."

"Sorry," mumbles Alec looking mortified. Even Grace is staring accusingly at him.

I've shared my deepest feelings with him. Yes I have. But I haven't told him where I met Jack.

Meeting someone new is the best, the wildest time. The air crackles and hums with promise and I can be reborn. I can reinvent myself to become the perfect lover again. I'm a stranger in a foreign country— learning the language, discovering unfamiliar pleasures. I'm newborn every time. Breathless, restless, greedy.

Dumping an old love is like dumping an old identity. It isn't only the old love you're tired of—it's also the old you—what you became after close proximity to the old love. I slough off my old skin and stretch out in a warm new one which is so thin and sensitive it tingles at the lightest touch.

I was with an American called Cy Fuentes. He came over to record because London was the place to be at the time. He was handsome, talented, and jealous. We lived in a converted studio on Sydney Street. I was manifestly so uninterested in the domestic bit and he was so allergic to Bohemian squalor that he asked his sister,

Gabriella, to come and keep house. Gabriella was responsible for my meeting Jack.

She was thrilled to be in London, thrilled to be on the music scene. English musicians were so cool. English boys were peachy and Gabriella couldn't wait to gobble one up. She came across Jack while trawling the King's Road one evening.

Normally, her taste was for clean-cut kids in mod uniform, so she was afraid Jack would be as rude as he was scruffy. On top of that, she couldn't trust her own taste in music. Cy was always making fun of her bubblegum boys. So she took me along for a second opinion.

"Whaddya think, Birdie?" she said. "I mean, if he got his hair styled and wore a suit?"

"No," I said.

"But he could be gorgeous."

"Shhh!" I hissed. The hair on the back of my head seemed to shiver. Goosebumps came up on my arms. Because sometimes you hear a voice which you *know* can never be imitated or stolen. And then there's the rarest of all rarities—the unique voice with something to say. The real thing.

"He's got the cutest eyes," Gabriella jabbered. "Is he any good, do you think? He sounds kinda rough to me. I guess if he was any good he wouldn't be playing in a dim little club like this."

She wouldn't shut up, so I left her there and went home. I'd have to check him out when I was alone.

But the very next night Cy was playing at the Round House and at the end Gabriella brought Jack backstage to meet him. She wasn't showing him off so much as establishing her own credentials. She was saying, "Look at me—my brother's famous, he gets the prestigious gigs—I'm someone to know. If you're nice to me, maybe I'll do you a bit of good, introduce you to the big league."

Now, Cy was one of those hypochondriac musicians who go on endlessly about their health. His specialty was muscular aches and pains.

When Jack came in, Cy was surrounded by admirers and I was giving him a very public massage. Because that was another thing about Cy: he wanted to appear like a boxer after a fight, with a towel around his shoulders and his trainer—or, in this case, his hand-maiden—in attendance.

Cy was saying, "For fuck's sake, girl—it's where the Infraspinatus and the Teres major tuck under the deltoid—don't you know anything?"

Performers can be a real pain in the arse. But there were at least three hopefuls in the admiring crowd who would have cheerfully flattened me to get their hands on Cy's muscles.

I was in any case beginning to think Cy was too old for me. Too set in his ways. Too addicted to over-the-counter medicines. It was all becoming stifling and predictable. The world seemed full of older men who got their kicks from training young girls to be their own personal handmaidens.

That was the scene Gabriella dragged Jack into. She was saying, "Hey, Jack, meet my brother, Cy."

And Cy was coming over all anatomical about a kink in his shoulder. And the admirers were trying to show everyone their tits.

I wiped my hands on a towel and said, "I was never any good at geography. Find your own Teres major."

One of the admirers said, "Let *me*—I studied shiatsu in Wales."

"Go right ahead," I told her. "I was taught never to shiatsu on my own doorstep."

No one laughed except Jack. I looked up and saw him sniggering behind Gabriella.

He said, "Hi. Didn't I see you in the club a couple of nights ago? You walked out on me."

Gabriella didn't even bother to give me a name. She said, "This is my brother's girlfriend."

"Not any more," I snapped. "Sorry, Jack, I'm walking out on you again." And I grabbed my jacket and marched toward the door.

"Honey!" Cy protested, "come back. You know I think you've got great hands."

But I kept on walking until I hit the street where an undignified little scene developed. Cy was half naked, trying to mollify me. Gabriella was saying snotty stuff like, "This isn't the time for one of your sulks." The admirer was saying to Cy, "Take my coat—you'll catch your death." About a dozen fans were clamoring for Cy's auto-graph. And Jack was laughing his head off.

Eventually one of the admirer's admirers passed a big fat joint around and things calmed down enough for all of us to climb into cars and go to a party in Hampstead.

But the damage was done. Golden, laughing Jack made Cy look like a crotchety old man. The air hummed when I looked at him, and the walls shook when he looked at me. He danced with me once that night, slipping his arm round my waist and pulling me onto his lean hard body as if he was trying me on for size. The heat was almost unbearable and I had to push him away before we melted and became glued together, belly to belly, thigh to thigh.

He said, "You're not going home with him tonight."

I said nothing, but I knew it was simply a statement of fact.

"Because," he said, "that would be a shame and a crime, and a horrible waste."

So that's how Jack stole me from under Cy's nose. And that's how I stole Jack from under Gabriella's nose—depending on who's telling what to whom.

The Tunisian brothel story is much better because it's a direct steal from a tale about Messalina and it contains all the elements of hubris and come-uppance you could possibly want.

They say I took a bet with a famous whore as to which of us could service the more johns. Points were awarded for artistic merit and degree of difficulty. They say I was winning by a country mile when Jack turned up with his guitar. Then two things happened: I captivated him with my venerean artistry and he captivated me with his music. I pulled out of the contest and he paid my debt of dishonor to the famous whore.

They say this was where I caught the syphilis with which I infected Jack, driving him mad and causing his death and my own downfall at a single swipe. Yep, that's how the story goes. Whores and heroes, venality and venery, pride and fall. Great ingredients, and if they're still telling it about Messalina two thousand years later, what chance have *I* got?

At the time, running away with Jack was seen as a bad career move.

165

He wasn't rich and famous, like Cy. He didn't have the *trappings*. People suddenly talked about me as if I were a groupie and as if there were a recognized career structure for groupies. How unbelievably stupid.

Of course, what emerged, what neither Jack nor I recognized in his tiny shared flat with mattresses on the floor was that, as soon as Jack got me, he acquired the trappings. We became the subject of in-house, music-biz gossip. He became something other than just another young rocker. We were polluted from the very beginning, so to speak.

But I was only eighteen and Jack was only twenty-three. Babies. We didn't give a toss. When you don't know if you'll even last a single night together, when you don't know if you'll be having lunch with the one you went to bed with, how can you be accused of career moves? I could have blagged my way back into Cy's favor if I'd been interested in *trappings*. I'd done it before and I've done it since. Having my cake and eating it too was my specialty.

The miracle to me was that, at twenty-three, Jack was the youngest man I'd been with. His skin was as tight and supple as mine. He was someone I could *play* with. We could roll around like puppies. We could invent and shout nonsense at each other. We could dress up in freaky costume and hit the streets. We could tell secrets and giggle at grown-ups. We never did anything the same way twice.

Unlike all the others, Jack didn't have a ready-made world he wanted to slot me into. He didn't have a rigid attitude to music and life any more than I did. We could make it up as we went along.

I was astonished. I hadn't realized that even after leaving home and being kicked out of school I'd been hogtied. I'd been molded and shaped to fit into the adult world. Even the so-called anarchists of rock'n'roll had some sort of master plan I was being groomed for.

Jack, at the beginning, was a *true* anarchist. If he didn't like some-thing, he changed it. If he didn't like what was expected of him, he didn't do it. Onstage, he didn't play the entertainer. He sang what he wanted to sing in no particular order. He talked to the audience, fought with them sometimes. He quarreled with the band. He changed songs in mid-flight, leaving everyone else in disarray and scrambling to catch up. He wasn't afraid to fuck up.

It was undisciplined. It was irresponsible. It was irresistible.

Oh, and oh he smelled so sweet. He didn't smell like an adult. Even when his hair was unwashed, you could bury your face in it and swear he was a cat asleep in new grass. I didn't want a shower after I'd been with Jack—I liked the smell of his skin on mine. It was the smell of innocence. Beginnings are beautiful.

Now look what we're left with! Tonight, Grace comes into my room just as I'm turning out the light. She's weeping and she can hardly breathe for snot and tears.

"Oh, Auntie Lin," she says.

I hold the duvet back so that she can slide into bed beside me the way she used to when she was smaller than me.

"What's he done?" I say. Because no woman cries this way except for love. But Grace just cries and snuffles on my shoulder like an infant while I wait, getting wet and bored.

I wonder if Robin brought her kids up right. With our mother and father, howling achieved nothing but a slap and a period of isolation in our room. But Robin tried to make her kids' childhood a time of excitement and pleasure; above all, a guilt-free zone. She said she was crippled by the feeling that she was, in every way, unsatisfactory. Which, I suppose, was the burden a whole generation of English kids had to bear. So she gave her own children applause and encouragement and the sense that they were as important and valuable as the adults. It wasn't exactly that they could do no wrong, but wrong, once done, could easily be admitted to and just as easily forgiven. Which, as it turns out, is almost the same thing, because here is Grace, who clearly feels it is OK to come howling to my room after midnight. Not only is it OK, but she's confident that she will be welcomed and comforted. Even if the wrong she's done is to me.

"Don't make him leave," she gasps at last.

"Alec?" I say. "Why?" Because, for the time being, I don't want her to know what I know; at least, not until I know what she knows.

"Well, I knew he liked the music," she says, "and I knew he wanted to meet you. But I thought it was *me*. I thought he came here for *me*."

See what a sense of self-worth does? It's so much more of a bummer when you find out you aren't as important as you thought you were. Poor little Grace. I break out the tissues and pass a handful to her.

"Tell me about it," I say—comforting, neutral Auntie Lin.

"You'll never forgive me," she wails. She's never been unforgiven in her life—she's simply giving me notice that I must forgive her.

"He left his laptop in my room," she says eventually. "He was writing a letter, but he wouldn't let me see it. I thought it might be to an old girlfriend. He swore there was no one else—but, Lin, he's so special. Other women must want him too, mustn't they?"

"Sure," I say. That's another subject I have first-class honors in. "So you read his letter, did you?"

"He was different tonight," she tells me. "Not cold, but like he was thinking about something else. So when he went back to Jimmy's room I started thinking, what if it's some*one* else? But it wasn't. It was you. He was writing a report about you."

"Oh." Extraordinary—at last, the little sod has been careless with his security, but the wrong woman booted up the information.

"He's been following you," Grace says. "He's been recording your conversations. And I thought he loved *me*."

"He isn't following me because he loves me," I assure her.

"No-o," she says. "But he's fascinated with you."

"No, he isn't. He's doing a job."

"Oh Lin," she cries, "I thought you'd be furious with me."

"Why, sweetie? Because someone made a patsy of you?"

"Because I was indiscreet. I knew he wanted to meet you. I thought he was doing his doctorate on music journalism of the late sixties. That's why he was so interested in you and Jack. I should have told you, but I just wanted to help him. But I've let you down," she says, weeping more comfortably. "Can you ever forgive me?"

"I don't know," I say.

She looks at me, shocked. I was supposed to tell her she was my little Grace and everything she does is peachy and not her fault.

"How much damage is done?" I ask instead.

She pulls herself away from my comforting-auntie arm, and for a moment I think she's going to say, "I've apologized, what else do you want?"

But she's better than that. She says, "How much damage can he do?"

"Who was he writing to?"

"Mr. Sasson Freel," she says, "with a copy to a Mr. B. Stears."

"Ah." I sigh. "He can do quite a lot of damage."

She sags. "You're going to send him away, I know you are."

"Well, what would you do, Grace?"

"I ought to kick him out. I ought to wake him up right now and throw him out. But I can't. I love him, Auntie Lin. I really do. And I don't want him to know I messed around with his laptop."

So yet another generation of my family betrays itself for Jack's bright youth.

Part 3

THE MOVABLE MAN
AND THE MOVIE

"He's drunk, he tastes like candy, he's so beautiful.
He's so deep, like dirty water. God, he's awful."
                                                    Courtney Love

I

Peanuts and Promises

Alec Parry wasn't a bad man—he liked dogs and he tolerated children—but he loved the stories of young men who started out in the mailroom and went on to own the company. Which was a good thing because a post-graduate course in Media Studies opened the world of mailrooms to him.

He knew that the film and music business was a world where thousands of over-qualified young people applied for every menial job. The lucky ones were then brutally exploited by a system of internships where you worked like a dog for less than a living wage in the hope that, if you distinguished yourself, you'd be taken on as permanent staff.

Memo Movies was an independent music film company. It dealt in archive footage and classic videos, and every two or three years it made a film of its own based on the history of jazz, blues, rock, or the development of trip-hop. These productions depended heavily on Memo Movies' archive catalog because, when tracing the roots of any new movement in music, it's illuminating to show the influences on it with film clips of music history. Memo Movies' archive went back as far as an old film of Bessie Smith, made in 1927. It was a diamond mine for anyone interested in that sort of thing.

Before joining Memo Movies, Alec had never heard of Bessie Smith or Son House or Bill Broonzy or Howlin' Wolf or any of those legends who went back before the '60s. But he did like the music of the '60s and '70s—a fact he leaned on in his interview. After joining, he made it his business to become as knowledgeable as he could about the seminal bands of that era. And he was surprised how far back into history his research took him. He hadn't realized that even revolutionaries have a spiritual lineage, that they, too, inherit a tradition.

To do him credit, Alec made an honest stab at filling in the gaps in his knowledge. His motto might have been, "Blag your way in, become indispensable, and then stick like glue."

The problem was in sticking like glue. If history was anything to go by, when his six-month internship was up, Memo Movies would decide he was too expensive to take on full wages. They'd let him go and employ instead another monkey to whom they could pay the usual mixture of peanuts and promises. They would do this without appreciating Alec's potential. He was hard-working, ambitious, smart, well-educated, and resourceful, but he couldn't prove it in a menial job. If he wanted to be recognized, he first needed to be noticed.

So Alec became the helpful young guy who made himself useful to anyone who had a permanent staff job. If a consignment of videos went missing, he'd stay on the phone and track it down. If the coffee machine or the copier broke down, he was the one who badgered the repairman to have it fixed before the end of the day. If Production wanted to view material from Archives, he took it personally to the editing suite and made sure he stayed long enough to try to find out what the project was about.

A month into his internship, after he'd found out how jealous and close-mouthed all the people on the production side were, he discovered that Memo Movies' current project was Jack. So Jack became Alec's project too. He bought the CDs, he read the books, he watched all the film and video he could lay his hands on, and he trawled the Internet for references which the dinosaurs in Production mightn't have come across.

Then he had a stroke of luck: in a Jack chat-room he met **g.ace**. To begin with, he only monitored conversations, not wishing to join in. Then one day he came in on an exchange which ended:

metalman: to say hardcandy is not nosecandy, naïve.
g.ace: to say what u say, banal.
metalman: what, then?
g.ace: sex with minors h-c ref to taking candy from babies.
metalman: b***ox.

At this point Alec, who had himself been struck by the intimations of dirty sex in "Hard Candy" which, as Metalman clearly thought, ought to have been a song about drugs, interjected.

cela5 to g.ace: yes. thought so too—but ambiguous.

g.ace to cela5: all jax birdie songs ambiguous.

After a while, Alec concluded that **g.ace** was something of an expert and gave out his e-mail number. The conversation continued in private over the next week. He liked **g.ace's** style. There was wit and intelligence, and what looked to Alec like an inside track.

One day, he delivered a folder of video cover designs to the Managing Director's secretary and found the great man himself leaning over her desk. He'd never met the MD before and he couldn't let the opportunity go by.

He took a deep breath and said, "Good morning, Mr. Stears. I'm Alec Parry, an intern here. Sir, as I'll probably never get to meet you again, please may I ask you one question?"

Mr. Stears straightened, looking at first irritated and then indulgent.

Alec said, "Sir, they say downstairs that you and Jack were actually friends, so I wondered if you knew: is it true that Jack was a football fan, that he followed Tottenham Hotspur and he had a cockerel tat on the inside of his left knee?"

Mr. Stears's indulgent smile left his face. He said, quite sharply, "Where did you hear that?"

"Well, sir, I've been looking on the Internet for stuff about Jack which might enrich the current project."

"Who told you to do that?"

"No one, sir. I've been doing it for my own interest, in my own time."

"Then I must ask you to stop," Mr. Stears said. "Everything we do here is confidential. You must *not* discuss ongoing projects outside this building. Don't you know anything?"

"I'd never discuss a project," Alec said indignantly. "I was getting information, not giving it."

"Idle gossip could give rival documentary makers a head start."

"I don't gossip," Alec said. "I was simply encouraging someone else to. And I thought you might be the only one around I could check a *recherché* fact with."

Mr. Stears pushed his spectacles up his nose and gave Alec a hard stare. "*Recherché*, huh?" he said, "I think you'd better come through to my office and tell me what you've been up to."

Alec admired Mr. Stears's office. He admired the stripped maple floor, the Sheraton desk, the gothic windows, and the river view. But he promised himself that if—no, when—he ever made an office like this his own, he wouldn't spoil the effect by letting himself go to seed and getting overweight like Mr. Stears. He'd keep the Wurlitzer jukebox, though. That looked like a fun toy.

"OK," said Mr. Stears from behind the Sheraton desk. "Who gave you your *recherché* fact?"

Alec explained why he didn't know who his informant was, and he went on briefly to recount the conversation. He was encouraged by Mr. Stears's interest. If he wanted to be noticed, he thought, he'd lucked into exactly the way to do it.

"Let me tell you something," Mr. Stears said, after listening attentively for several minutes. "This correspondence could be dangerous. Do you want to know why?"

"Why?"

"Because the *recherché* fact in question is probably known only to a very few people. Intimates. Family."

"I didn't think Jack had a family."

"He didn't. I'm talking about Birdie Walker and *her* family. You must have formed an opinion about Birdie if you've been doing your research properly."

In truth, Alec had been keeping his eyes so firmly on Jack that, so far, Birdie was only the glorious appendage anyone would expect to see in the company of a rock god.

"Mmm," he said, in what he hoped was a judicious tone of voice, "tricky one, that."

"Tricky isn't the half of it," Mr. Stears said. "My concern is that if she gains even an inkling of what we're up to here, she'll block it any way she can."

"Why would she do that, sir?"

"Jealousy," Mr. Stears said. "Jealousy was always her problem. Jealous about Jack, jealous of Jack. Do you know, she even claims to have collaborated on some of the classic songs?"

"I didn't know that."

"Well, I suggest you find out about her before you resume your cozy little correspondence. You might be writing to a snake in the grass."

"I'll terminate the connection," Alec said. "I wouldn't want to compromise your production—that was the last thing on my mind. I had no idea it was so sensitive."

"Now you know," Mr. Stears said dismissively. "If you want to get on in this business, you have to learn that although networking is a tool of our trade, blabbing foolishly to anyone who seems to share your interest is one of the easiest methods of having your ideas stolen or blocked."

"I'm really sorry, sir," Alec said, thinking, maybe coming to the attention of the MD wasn't such a great idea after all. "But I promise you, I never said who I was or who I worked for or why I was interested. I was only coming off as a fan."

"I hope you're right," Mr. Stears said and turned away toward the river view.

Pudgy creepo, Alec thought as he left the room, four-eyed twat. Why did the wrinkly fat twats get the good jobs? Why did being a pompous prat get you the sharpest office? Everyone says, show them how keen you are. That's supposed to win you points, not lose them. I'll be fired before the day's over, and all because I used a bit of initiative. I'll have to dust off the fucking CV. Again.

But later, after lunch, he was summoned back to the river-view office.

"Sit down, my boy," Mr. Stears said. "Alec?"

"Alec Parry, sir."

"Well, Alec, I've been thinking—maybe you shouldn't terminate your connection. Maybe you're overlooking an obvious strategy."

"I am, sir?"

Mr. Stears took a couple of seconds to straighten his silk tie. He said, "Do you like working here?"

"Yes sir," Alec said cautiously. He was no longer certain how clever it was to show keenness.

"Would you like to work on a special project?"

"I really would," Alec said. This was more like it. This was way more cool.

"Then, perhaps you'd like to reconsider. If you were to continue this correspondence, in your own time of course, until you find out who you're writing to, you might have something to contribute."

"I'd like that, sir."

"But I can't stress strongly enough how cautious you must be. You must remember that you may be in touch with a member of Birdie Walker's family and it's impossible to overestimate how paranoid she is about media attention, how jealously she guards even those things of Jack's which should be in the public domain. Really, Alec, she's like the cobra coiled round the treasure chest."

"I'll be super-careful."

"And report back to me at every stage."

"To you?" Alec said, gleefully. "Personally?"

"I'll give you the number of my private line. And I'd like copies of the correspondence."

"That may be a bit inhibiting, sir."

"Why?"

"Well, I'll have to tell my informant a bit about myself if I'm going to personalize things. Sometimes you have to come on a bit strong if you want to intrigue people. I don't even know if I'm talking to a man or a woman."

"All right then, a *précis* will do. But be careful. Expose yourself, Alec, and we could all be shot."

War games, Alec thought, infiltrators. Spies on Level Four. And a foot in the door of the river-view office. When he left this time, he thought maybe Mr. Stears wasn't such a bad old fart after all—a bit slow, but he got there in the end.

A few days later, he found out who **g.ace** was. He called Mr. Stears immediately. "Grace Emerson," he said.

"Good God," said Mr. Stears. "The niece."

"Should I have recognized the name?"

"No. Better that you don't. At least ... no, let me think about it. I'll talk to you later." He hung up.

Alec was elated. He was really making an impression now, on all fronts. He was Mr. Stears's blue-eyed boy, and Grace thought he was

178

perceptive and sensitive. The dialogue with her quickly opened up to include books, movies, and politics. But not sport. Sport, he'd learned the hard way, could be a chick repellent. On the other hand, he confessed to a liking for sci-fi, because she would've expected something of the sort.

"dont give me a hard time on that," he wrote.

"nobody perfect," she replied. "ursulaleguin ok."

He liked her for knowing Ursula Le Guin.

"perfectwoman," he wrote, "dont tell me u married, 68, need walking frame."

"how did u guess?" she wrote back.

"u breakin my heart."

"got one? wow."

Sassy, good fun, he decided. She didn't immediately ask for his phone number when he flirted. He awarded her points for that. It kept the game alive.

The game picked up speed. Mr. Stears took him, in his chauffeur-driven car, to a Vietnamese restaurant in Soho, to meet a man who was introduced as Mr. Freel.

"This is Alec," Mr. Stears said, "the bright young man I've been telling you about."

Mr. Freel looked the part: tall, weighty without flab, intent, grave. Impressive. Alec tried to sit straighter. He found himself playing to Mr. Freel. Mr. Stears seemed to recede into the shadows.

Yes, Alec thought, the secret to being in charge was to look as if you're in charge.

Mr. Freel said, "It seems to me that you've used your imagination. You saw the potential and acted on it. I congratulate you. How happy would you be to continue?"

Alec gave himself a moment to look as if he was weighing up his answer. "To tell you the truth, Mr. Freel," he said with what he hoped was a thoughtful smile, "I'm enjoying myself. The Jack production is great and I'm glad to be involved. My own part in it is tangential, I know. But it makes me feel involved."

"It sounds to me as if this young man's a natural, Barry."

"Well, he's with us on an internship," Mr. Stears said, "so he's learning all aspects of the business. But he lacks experience."

"I should think, by the time this project's in the can, he'll have gained plenty of experience. You ought to take him under your wing, Barry. Or maybe someone else will snap him up."

"This is a slightly unusual situation, though," Mr. Stears said. "Most projects don't require this degree of subterfuge."

"Most projects, thank the Lord, don't require the cooperation of Birdie Walker. I expect you've included her in your research, Alec?"

"Yes, sir." Alec raised his brows and flicked his eyes to the ceiling. Both older men smiled.

"So are you willing to beard the she-wolf in her lair?" Mr. Freel asked, still smiling. "Because it might come to that. Somehow we have to find out, first, does the Antigua Movie really exist? Then, if it does, and we're pretty sure it does, it becomes a matter of persuading Birdie to let us have it. No small problem, I might add. I don't know how far you're able to go with the niece, but it could be very useful to have a line on a member of that family."

Alec waited, almost holding his breath. In fact, he'd already begun an absorbing fantasy starring himself as the subduer of the famous bitch-goddess. He was waiting for Mr. Freel to order him into the front line. But apparently that wasn't his style. So eventually Alec asked, "Is Grace anything like Birdie, do you think?"

"I only met her when she was a little girl," said Mr. Freel. "What do you make of her?"

"I like her so far," Alec said. "Which is to say, I like the persona she's sending."

"And does she like the persona you're sending?"

"We're still talking. If you don't like someone, it's easy to sign off."

"Tell me about her."

"Well, I think she's bright, funny, and sort of her own woman. It's hard to say. We talk about a lot of things. I didn't want her to think that Jack was the only reason I was interested."

"Very wise," Mr. Freel said. "Barry, it looks like you picked a winner here."

Being called a winner by someone like Mr. Freel gave Alec the sort of confidence he hadn't tasted since he left college. The real world, for him, had been a series of rejections. It was a place where nobody recognized him and nobody took the time to get to know him. Ultimately nobody would remember his name because nobody gave him the chance to be memorable. Now he was turning it around.

He gave Grace his phone number that night. She rang and they talked for two hours. He wasn't nervous about talking to her; encouragingly, she seemed much more nervous than he was.

"Well," she explained, "you meet a lot of weirdos on Jack's sites. Not you, of course."

She really wants to make a good impression on me, he thought, surprised and pleased. It's supposed to be the other way round, but she doesn't know that. It's me who's taking the risk, not her.

So he relaxed, and let her do the work. It's almost like a real relationship, he thought. Once started, the women take over and make all the moves.

Meeting was her idea. Going to her mother's house was her suggestion. Absolved of responsibility, Alec went along for the ride. It was during that period—of suggestions and possible arrangements—that she told him about her connection with Jack and Birdie.

"It's just a family thing," she said. "I didn't want you to think I was showing off."

"Why would I think that?" he asked, tense with excitement, staring down at the telephone as if it might be possible to see her at the other end of the line.

"Dunno," she said. "Some people get funny when they know you've got famous relations."

"Got me," he said. "I'm turning into a monster. You'd better call off our date—oh-oh—I'm turning green—oh, my fangs and claws …"

"Shut up," she said, laughing. "I didn't mean you. You're different."

Weird, he thought, how much more interesting listening to a woman was when you were waiting for her to say something important. He'd always found listening difficult, but learned how to fake it. With Grace, he was forced to listen properly. And the more he listened, the more details she gave him. It was quite a discovery.

She told him for instance that Jack was a major influence on her life. Not because of the music, but because of the damage drugs had done to him. "Everyone indulged him," she said, "but no one helped him. Birdie was the only one who tried, but she was too close to the problem. She just wasn't qualified. It damaged her almost as much as it did him."

"Grace is biased, of course," Mr. Stears said when Alec reported the conversation. "If you ask me, it was Birdie's extravagance and infidelity that tipped Jack over the edge. She led him a terrible dance."

Nevertheless it was the story of Jack's fatal instability that led Grace to study psychology at university. Now she was working for a rehab unit in Bristol. She wanted eventually to become a therapist, but that would be a long way in the future.

"I don't even understand my own past," she said. "The family dynamic is dominated by a tragedy Birdie won't talk about."

"Why won't she talk about it?"

"At first it was all too painful. Then she internalized, and now the wound has been left to fester for so long it would take a really skilled therapist to help her."

"Psychobabble," commented Mr. Stears. "If you want my opinion, the poor girl's had the wool well and truly pulled over her eyes. But that's Birdie—wool-puller *extraordinaire*. She doesn't want to talk about it because she won't admit to her part in the tragedy."

Mr. Freel, as Alec might have expected, took a more practical view. "Grace is confiding in you," he said. "Good work. Keep her talking."

By the time he met her, he felt he had the situation completely under his thumb. By that time too, he knew what his assignment was.

He cleared the decks. He told his mother and his girlfriend that he was being sent away on a junior management course and he wouldn't be in touch for a couple of weeks. He suffered an instruction session with Mr. Stears, and two much more enjoyable afternoons, organized by Mr. Freel, when he learned to operate the miniature equipment and tools he might need. Mr. Freel, he reckoned, was The Guy.

Yes! he thought, as he watched Grace walk through the barrier at Paddington Station, game on!

He stepped forward, smiling easily. She was kind of cute—he wouldn't even have to pretend.

"Hi, Grace," he said quietly, and watched her face relax and her lips part. She likes me, he thought, instantly. Oh you little angel, you like me. And she did.

If the watchful expression on her face had changed to disappointment or hostility he would've been, in the first nanosecond, blasted to stardust. He would have had to say—to Mr. Freel of all people—"She didn't like me. I don't know why. She just never gave me a chance."

It wasn't something he could plan for or avert. The groundwork was perfect but, with girls, groundwork counted for nothing. They either went for you or they didn't.

But she did. Her face relaxed, her eyes widened, and her soft lips parted.

"Hi, Cela Five," she said, and held out her hand.

Game *on!*

It was suddenly as if there had never been a doubt in his mind—like watching the ball sail into the back of the goal: ball, goal, destiny. What was intended, happened.

He wasn't even surprised to find Birdie at Grace's house. Him, Birdie, destiny. The stars themselves were playing into his hands. The goal was huge, the ball needed no persuasion. Alec was on a roll.

What did surprise him, though, was Birdie herself. He was expecting a towering figure. It wasn't that he'd imagined her to be unchanged from how she looked in the pictures he'd seen in Archives. It was more that he expected her to be … well, bigger—more imposing. When he saw Grace dancing with her, his first reaction was that Grace was the aunt and Birdie was the niece. No aunt he'd ever known danced like that.

He watched her, listened to her conversation with Grace, and couldn't believe she was of the same generation as his own mother. The talk was quick and spicy, peppered with laughter.

The mother was more what he expected: slower, vaguer, more out of it. He had to work at remembering she was in the room and including her. Grace had described her as a bit of an old hippie and she hadn't misled him. He felt he could safely leave the mother out of the equation.

"What d'you think?" Grace said, breezing into his room, her brother's room.

"We-ell," he began hesitantly, "kind of amazing for her age."

"Age?" Grace laughed indignantly. "Typical ageist orientation."

"OK, she's just amazing," he said. "And so are you. It's an amazing family."

"Amazing Grace," she said, striking a pose. "And don't you forget it."

Alec envied Grace her status with her aunt and her mother. If they never spoke of Jack, it was the only subject which wasn't acceptable in free-range conversation.

He liked Jimmy's room with its posters and the anarchy-colored quilt. Lying on his single bed, either alone or with Grace tucked into his armpit, he'd stare at the posters as if they were his private portrait gallery. All were emblematic figures and Jimmy had arranged them like a football team. Wittgenstein was in goal behind a defensive line-up of Stephen Hawking, Puff Daddy, Karl Popper, and Orson Welles. He wasn't afraid to put Mother Teresa in the midfield or to be childish and have Batman on the left wing.

Alec pictured himself among the strikers. Any team with him in attack would score. No argument. He had the juice.

Almost as proof, Jimmy had gone to Italy without coming home for the summer. I've never met the guy, but he's doing me favors, Alec thought. Now he could settle in and take his time. Only the mother missed Jimmy, turning quiet and somber.

Meanwhile, he spent his time gaining points with Grace and covertly studying Birdie.

She came and went without explanation. He followed her once while Grace was washing her hair, leaving early and, unbelievably, catching a bus. Alec noted the number but didn't get on. It was odd to see her, mythic traumatized bitch goddess, in a bus queue. He searched her room, opened her laptop, found notes for lyrics, chords, and arrangements filed under song titles, not in alphabetical order. He found accounts which seemed to make no sense at all. He couldn't find private letters—her filing system seemed random. Her clothes, too, ranged from massively expensive designer gear to scruffy jeans, all maintained with equal carelessness. She smoked sometimes, even in the kitchen, but at other times she didn't smoke at all. There seemed to be no pattern.

Alec didn't feel baulked or thwarted. Submerged somewhere at the base of his spine was an absolute confidence that all he had to do was be there. She would come to him. Like Grace, like Mr. Freel, she would spin into his field of gravity.

She liked him. He would walk into the sitting room while she was playing the piano, and she'd turn and smile. She would play a few lines especially for him and sing in a lilting tone, "Don't worry, be happy, every little thing gonna be all right." She thought, as Grace did, that he was anxious about finding a job. They thought he was looking for a job and a place to live so that he could stay in London and not go back to his hometown. Cleverly, he'd consigned his family to Hull—far enough away to be no threat.

He would drag a chair close to the piano and say, "Go on, play something else. It's amazing—no one in my family has any talent at all."

It wasn't flattery, he didn't have to fake an admiration he didn't feel. Truthfully, he felt that his own family would look lumpen beside Grace's.

"What d'you think?" she said. "Bass going, da di da dum-dum da-dum; drums going, pa-*tum tum* ti-tum; melody like this; harmony here; and a little descant line up here? What d'you think, Alec?"

"Sounds great," he said, in total ignorance, loving it.

"You must come to the club and see this band," she said. "You and Grace. I'd like to hear your opinion. You're the right age."

"Honestly," he said, "I don't know anything about music."

"Gut reaction—that's what I'm after—intelligent, sensitive first impressions. I *know* you can do that."

Yes! he thought. She *likes* me. "I'd love to," he said. And was rewarded by the smile. The intimate smile, brilliant blue eyes crinkling, the deep corners of her mouth stretching. He couldn't help smiling back. The laugh was even better. It was throaty and husky. It seemed to bubble up like soda in a bottleneck.

He could make her laugh, that was the wonder. He might come across her alone, sitting in the kitchen late at night, maybe with a glass of wine in her hand. She'd have that dreamy-sad expression she wore when she was solitary. He found she enjoyed it if he said

185

something a little cheeky like, "My dad always told me to beware of secret drinkers."

She wouldn't reply with something boring like: "What're you doing up at this hour?" She'd offer him the bottle and say, "Insomniacs of the world unite. Where do they keep the sleep in this house? I've searched everywhere."

And he said, "It's always on the top shelf, out of reach," surprising himself and making him glad to have his own imaginative riposte secretly recorded. Bit by bit, he was assembling a journal of her thoughts and memories, her comings and goings. Eventually it would be sent to Mr. Freel, and he didn't want his own part in the dialogue to sound lumpen. He wanted his part to be as light and kaleidoscopic as hers. He wanted to sound like the right man for the job. He wanted Mr. Freel to hear how Birdie was beginning to trust him.

"Don't let her seduce you," Mr. Freel had said. "She can charm the snakes out from under stones."

Well, listen and learn, Mr. Freel, Alec thought, and then tell me who's seducing whom.

II

Excerpts from the Antigua Movie

If you succumb to heat and magnetism and fuck someone you've only just met, sometimes you can find yourself irretrievably attached without sufficient information. You commit the grossest intimacies with a total stranger and then the wind changes, and you're stuck with it. No one with even a modicum of sense would buy a house or a car on such a basis. A puppy? Yes. Exactly the same lack of logic controls your choice of pet—especially if you're the soft-hearted type who chooses from an animal shelter. Unless luck is as blind as love, you'll find yourself devoted to a creature, riddled with ringworm, tape worm, and ear mites, who snaps your thumb off when you offer the healing hand.

Jack stirs the heavy air with an alien finger. He says, "Ripples." After a pause, he says, "I wonder how long before these ripples reach London." A longer pause, "I hope, by then, they'll be a cyclone. They'll blow the roofs off houses and tear the arms and legs off spidermen."

The blonde chick sharing his hammock says, "Assassination by cyclamen air."

From this great distance, in time as well as space, the ripple touches my cheek like a snowflake. This time, however, I can't actually *see* the disk-shaped whirlpool of rainbow molecules. I'm not stoned. But the picture is pretty: there is turquoise sea, cerulean sky, ocher sand, indigo shadows. There are two fallen angels tangled in a single hammock.

I stop the Steenbeck and say, "Can you lift a still photograph of this image?"

The technician says, "OK," and makes a note.

We go on, plodding frame by frame, into the past, illuminated by the dim light of an editing desk.

Some of the elements—"tearing the legs off the spidermen," the "cyclamen air," and the "cyclone"—found their way into "Walks Like a Spider," one of the cruelest songs Jack and I ever wrote—and, by the way, one of his most unlikely, melodic tunes. It took people a long time to recognize what a nasty song it was.

From this distance, his instability and his paranoia are obvious. But so is his beauty. From this distance, I say, "Don't touch him. Call an ambulance." I say, "Could you really see only the beauty? Did you really think you could heal this lost creature?"

But, when he found me, how was he lost? He wasn't lost. He was found. And so was I. Foundlings, both of us, and delirious with joy at the discovery.

Wouldn't it be ironic if I left this tedious editing room believing in arranged marriages? The belief tucked into the same envelope as half a dozen still photographs of pretty young lovers in an idyllic setting. The photographs will be strategically placed where another young lover can find them. Will the belief touch him too? He'll know what to do with the stills. But common sense in the matter of his personal affairs …? Oh no, that's still years and miles away.

Jack borrowed a small estate called South Winds. The house came complete with staff and groundsmen. But we never stayed in the house. We took first one, then two of the guest bungalows on the beach. Friends, hangers-on, the band, when they arrived, stayed in the house. It became crowded and the usual sniping and jealousy broke out.

To begin with, of course, we were alone. A sudden, mysterious departure caught everyone by surprise and we were gone before anyone could ask where we were going. We were gone, in fact, before we could ask *ourselves* what we thought we were doing.

"Got to get away," Jack said. Get away from what exactly? From the attention? Yes. But we'd courted that. We'd expended time and ingenuity on making Jack famous. He wanted success with every cell in his body and he couldn't be successful without being famous. He was a *performer*, for Christ's sake.

When a performer rejects attention, he rejects a large part of himself. The greedy, look-at-me shadow of the man goes hungry. Then the shadow wages war against the man and tears him up, searching for food.

"Got to get away," Jack said. "Gotta chill. We can talk and play. It'll be like it was: maybe we can *write*, y'know, like we used to when we were alone."

After only ten days, however, his hungry shadow found a bunch of American film students bumming around on the beach and employed them to watch us be alone.

Does it sound contrary? It sounded deeply contrary to me. But in those days I believed all the hype about simplicity and integrity. I hadn't accepted that nearly all men, women, and children are at war with themselves to some degree or another.

It wasn't that Jack's hungry shadow won the war. That would be too simple. But the fight became more personal and way more bitter.

Here is a nice little piece of film: here is Jack at table. It's dark, he's lit by a couple of fat candles, surrounded by plates, bottles, wine glasses. A roach smolders in the ashtray. His eyes are empty and sleepy. Hippie heaven. The simple life. The simple man with his simple wife.

"Yeah," he says, "tomorrow ..." But he doesn't go on. He looks up, directly into the lens. From here, from this distance, his slow candle-lit blink looks surprised. "Are you still here?" his bemused half-smile seems to say. "Gimme a break."

He dips his finger in the wine and begins to write on the table-top. The drifty blonde wraith at his side reads what's written in wine. She gets up slowly and wafts away.

The next shot is from outside. It shows the silhouette of palm fronds blowing in front of the lit window. In the shot after that, it is indeed tomorrow. And in between? The camera, this footage, implies that there was sleepy stoned love between the two shots, between the simple man and his drifty blonde. The appearance of two people, hand in hand, stepping off the porch into the warm sand in the morning confirms it. What you see is what you get.

What you don't get is what was written on the tabletop.

Jack wrote, "I am the eye. The eye is watching me. The camera is eating my eyes."

When the beaded blonde wraith read that, she got up, alarmed, and asked the Americans to stop shooting. Jack stayed where he was. He was literally paralyzed with fear.

Look at the drifty little wraith, so sweet, so young, and from this distance so ridiculous in muslin and feathers. Someone substantial, a down-to-earth woman, would have packed up then and there. She would've checked Jack into a private clinic and let the experts help him.

What in God's name did the wraith think was going on?

I can't remember. I know I was alarmed. And I know I thought in my simple-wife way that what Jack wrote was a metaphor. I thought he meant that the camera was destroying his ability to see himself as he really was, and he'd chosen a macabre way of saying so. I suppose I agreed vaguely with what he wrote, so I saw it as a sign of sanity. His fear was what frightened me.

In spite of what you see in those ninety seconds of film, stoned love was the last thing on Jack's mind that night. It took four-and-a-half hours and five tabs of Mandrax to persuade him even to lie down. He was rigid and gibbering with terror.

What did the wraith think? That it was an echo trip, or something? An incomplete metabolite of the previous day's acid? Oh yes, all that underground pharmacology—I remember *that*. We drank gallons of freshly squeezed orange juice next morning. How *very* effective.

But the soundtrack to this excerpt is interesting. A single acoustic guitar is playing the twelve-bar blues riff which was eventually elaborated and became the underlying theme for "Black Blonde" on the *Hard Candy* album.

I stop the film and turn to the technician. I say, "I want to change the soundtrack."

"OK," he says, making a note. "Give me what you want in and I'll see what I can do."

I hand him some old-fashioned reel-to-reel audiotape. He threads it onto the machine, and now the wraith is Jack's voice because this time there are vocals. This time, the single guitar picks out a sixteen-bar pattern. Half hummed, half sung, Jack's voice rasps,

190

"In the morning she holds me, she folds me, she opens the drawer by her bed. She breaks me, she makes me, the widow mistakes me for the man she keeps wrapped in her head …"

"Yes," I say. "Fade up there … fade out here. Yeah, that'll do."

The technician glances at me, puzzled. After all, "Black Blonde" was perfect for the job. Why would I want to cut it out?

"Both versions," I say. "I'd like a copy of both versions. On film. But I'd like the original version transferred to video."

III

Losing the Juice

It began to go wrong at the InnerVersions gig when Birdie led Grace to Dog Records' table to introduce her to Mr. Freel. Alec couldn't duck out because he was with Grace. He was sweating from the dance floor and not feeling at all like bright young executive material. Mr. Freel greeted him with a forbidding glare. Alec handled it rather well, he thought, by backing out and going to the bar to buy Grace a lager and lime. From then on, he avoided the record company table.

Avoidance meant dancing rather more often than he'd intended—which pleased Grace inordinately. Her pleasure was irritating, and worrying in case Mr. Freel thought he was a lightweight who couldn't keep his mind on the job. But he didn't have a choice.

Birdie, unnaturally it seemed to Alec, was keeping company with Mr. Freel and the bunch of guys who were clearly his subordinates. They were all easily distinguishable from the club crowd and, obviously, that was the way they wanted it. They were not there to have a good time. This was work.

Alec couldn't think of a way to signal to Mr. Freel that he was working too. The best he could do was to be unobtrusive. It was annoying. He wanted to be closer to the action. How could he shine and be unobtrusive at the same time? Not by dancing with Grace, that was for sure. Dancing with Grace defeated both objects. He tried to look cool, but her bounce and zest called for some sort of response, and he began to feel disconnected.

What kept him going was Birdie's amused encouraging smile, which he caught every now and then when he felt he was flagging. "Keep at it," her smile said, "you're doing fine." The problem was, he was forced to admit, that as she didn't know what he was doing she couldn't know whether he was doing it fine or not. All the same, he felt he had her approval.

She could, it seemed, move with ease between her family, the band and the company men. With Mr. Freel, she appeared to be polite but distant. She doesn't know he hates her, Alec thought once, standing on the edge of the crush at the bar, waiting to be served. The thought surprised him because, of course, Mr. Freel didn't hate her. He only wanted something she was unwilling to hand over. Mr. Stears was the one who hated her.

The music pounded into him like a jackhammer, making him light-headed and glad he'd decided early on to go easy on the booze. He wished he could hear what Mr. Freel was saying to the guy who'd pushed his way through the crowd to deliver a note. Mr. Freel read the note, folded it, and slipped it into his inside pocket. He leaned toward Birdie. Birdie nodded slowly.

"Isn't this great?" Grace said, taking a drink from his glass. "Let's dance."

But Birdie appeared in front of them, holding out the Volvo keys.

"Aren't you staying to the end?" Grace said, disappointed.

"I've got to talk to some people. Will you be all right on your own?"

"Don't worry," Alec said. "I'll look after her." He wanted to add, Unless there's something better I can do to help you. But he didn't.

"Isn't he perfect?" Birdie asked Grace. She gave Alec the keys.

A few minutes later, he saw Mr. Freel escort her through the club and Alec suddenly felt left behind. Mr. Freel's hand was on her elbow, urging her forward, and she looked small, almost fragile, beside him. Not a fair contest, he thought, unexpectedly. And with a pang, he realized that Mr. Freel, with his height, tailoring, and power, might charm, bludgeon, cajole Birdie into cooperating with him. Then he wouldn't need Alec any more, and Alec would be demoted back to office gofer at Memo Movies.

"Dance?" Grace shouted over the din. But now there was no one to watch, no one to avoid, and no one to approve or disapprove, and dancing lost its point. After a while, he feigned a twisted knee, and after that, there was no reason to stay.

"Are you OK?" Grace asked, a lot later.

193

"A bit tired."

"Is the knee still hurting?"

"A bit," he said and remembered to limp as he left her bed and went back to Jimmy's room.

He wedged his door ajar so that he could listen for Birdie's key in the lock. Maybe he could meet her on the stairs and suggest a nightcap. But the hours slid away and she didn't come home.

What the hell is she doing? he thought. She said she was going to talk to some people, but nobody talks all night. He could still see her walking away with Mr. Freel—Mr. Freel urging her, Birdie small and reluctant. I'm sure she didn't want to go, he thought. Leave her alone, Mr. Freel, she doesn't want to go and you're upsetting my game plan. She doesn't trust you. She doesn't even like you. I can tell. She never smiled at you once. You'll come on too strong. I know how to handle her. You don't.

The worst thing about that night was that he could sense the juice draining out of him. He was slowly being expelled from the zone—left unprotected outside the palace gate. What he realized, as the time dragged by, was that he was vulnerable.

He lay, scratchy-eyed, his ears ringing with the tinnitus that comes from dancing too close to big speakers, and realized that he'd invested too much in her. Birdie was way more vivid in his mind than Grace. Grace was Birdie's shadow, her echo. The correspondence on the Net, the sassyness and invention, was a correspondence with Birdie through the medium of Grace—Grace's mimicry of Birdie's style. As soon as he met the original, Grace receded. The most vivid thing about Grace had been the correspondence. Grace in person was only Birdie's niece.

But that was what was supposed to happen, he told himself, get to Grace through Jack; get to Birdie through Grace; get back to Jack through Birdie. Circle complete. Game over. But something got distorted. It wasn't a clean, simple circle any more. Maybe it never was. He should have added a tangent: get to Mr. Freel through Jack; get the pretty office, the Wurlitzer, the Beamer through Mr. Freel. But only if Mr. Freel doesn't take over and award all the prizes to himself.

Insomnia was not in the game plan. Anger, anxiety, and bewilderment weren't, either. Feelings were a pain in the arse. Alec saw them as blocks, chasms, snipers, and hidden explosives on his screen. His game hero was weakened and in danger.

Shut down, he thought. But instead he waited all night for the sound of a middle-aged woman's feet on the stairs, and it didn't come.

"What's up?" asked Grace, clear-eyed, glossy-haired. "You look dreadful." She plunked a bowl of muesli in front of him.

"Why, thank you," he said. "You look enchantingly dreadful yourself." But banter took too much out of him. He hadn't the heart for it.

"He's all worn out," Grace explained to her mother. "He's a maniac dancer, but he just can't take the Grace pace."

"Where's Lin?" Mrs. Emerson asked.

"Didn't she come home?" Grace said. "Dirty stop-out. These old people, staying out all night, worrying their children ..."

She was interrupted by the sound of the front door opening.

"Lin?" Mrs. Emerson called.

"Can't stop, sweetie," Birdie called back. "Got to shower, change, and be gone."

"At least have some breakfast."

"No time." Birdie's voice floated down from the top of the stairs. Doors opened and closed, water gushed, and twenty minutes later she vanished again without Alec seeing her.

"She'll wear herself out," Mrs. Emerson sighed. And then with unusual vehemence she said, "Sometimes I really hate rock'n'roll."

"What do you mean?" Alec asked.

"I don't know," Mrs. Emerson said more vaguely. "The way it builds you up and up till there's nothing left to do but crash. The way everything happens at night ... I don't know. How does she think she can survive if she stays up all night with one of her bands and then rushes off to an interview in the morning?"

"Has Auntie Lin got another interview?" Grace asked.

"I think so."

"You can't expect her to give up the music, Mum. She wouldn't be Lin if she didn't racket around at night. Can you *really* see her with a normal nine-to-fiver?"

"She'd be safer."

"Give it up, Mum," Grace said. "Besides, she's my role model whenever I think of growing old disgracefully."

"You don't know what you're talking about," Mrs. Emerson said. "And I hope you never do." She got up and drifted out of the room, leaving Grace biting her lip.

"Me and my mouth," Grace said.

"Why?" Alec asked.

"Because Mum thinks Auntie Lin's one of the tragic casualties of the rock'n'roll holocaust. Whereas I think she's a survivor."

"I thought you said she was traumatized."

"Of course. Aren't we all?"

Alec couldn't disagree with her that morning. So unaccustomed was he to fatigue that he placed himself in the front rank of the traumatized hoard. But after breakfast he went back to bed and slept till lunch.

In the afternoon, feeling better, he began to compose a communication to Mr. Freel.

"To Mr. Freel," he wrote. "The subject has, since I last wrote, been in touch with—1: BBC. 2: *Mojo* Magazine. 3: Virgin Records. 4: Mr. Ireland at your own company. 5: Sheeney TeleCine. 6: Inland Revenue. 7: Paul and Dahl Hair Salon …"

Grace swung the door open. "What're you doing? Let's go out."

"Where?"

"Anywhere. Who're you writing to?"

"Just a friend." Alec closed his laptop.

"You've got *friends*?" She stroked his hair and slid her hand under his shirt. "What on earth do they see in you?"

"Rat!" he said, grabbing her hand.

Insults and terms of endearment: Alec was grateful, and congratulated himself on the interchangeability of the two. There was no commitment implied in calling someone a rat. If it was interpreted as affectionate, no blame could be attached to him. Between him and Grace lay a shallow, frothy layer of jokes, puns, and innuendo. It was what they floated on. Underneath, he felt, was nothing at all.

Birdie blew in at dinnertime, but before she'd settled down there was a phone call from a film company called Median Films. Alec

196

knew about Median—it wasn't as big a company as Memo Movies, but it was a competitor. The call upset Birdie.

At first, Alec was glad because it meant that if Median was making a film about Jack too, and Birdie was upset, she wouldn't cooperate with them. But it made him aware of the urgency of his mission.

Then, she explained for the first time why she was so allergic to media attention. And for the first time, Alec understood that what seemed to Mr. Freel and Mr. Stears like a dog-in-the-manger attitude was self-protection.

The conversation, unlike most of the conversations at that kitchen table, was serious. And, suddenly, Alec felt the force of all three women ranged against him. Even Grace let him down. She, who had previously advocated the healing power of talking, turned tail and left him on his own—left him with a serious enquiry on his hands and what should have been her lines in his mouth: "Wouldn't you feel better if you put the record straight, if you talked to a sympathetic friend?"

And Birdie turned him down flat. If rejection wasn't bad enough, she made him feel that even his offer was wounding.

He'd been pushed into showing his hand too early by Mr. Freel's interference and Median Film's intrusion. The result was appalling: Birdie cried. Tears hung suspended from her long lashes, and he had to look away because he didn't want to see them fall. That was what happened when you got serious—you left yourself open to attack. Tears were sharp, raking weapons to be avoided if at all possible.

"Oh, don't worry," Grace said. "She'll come round. She's tired, that's all. She didn't get any sleep last night, remember."

He took refuge in the acid froth of their exchanges, but later, when she went down to watch TV, he stayed in her room to finish his letter to Mr. Freel.

How do you tell the Big Boss-man to butt out? "I do think," he wrote, "in view of the subject's reaction to Median Film's approach (tape to follow), that anything that might be interpreted as intrusion or digging should be discouraged. It only serves to harden her attitude ..." He was rather proud of that. It took him a long time to compose, but it sounded sophisticated and respectful while saying, "Fuck off, you're ruining my game."

Again, he didn't have time to finish. Grace said, "Still at it? Well, you'll be happy to know that Lin went to sleep in her chair. It might be because what's on telly's so boring, but I think, personally, it's because tears are cathartic."

IV

Excerpts from the Antigua Movie

Junior Moline sits like Buddha at the sound desk. On his right is a young beach bum with a lot of talent and attitude. On his left is The Widow Oats. Change focus, and you'll see what they see: the band— Jack, Teddy, and Wills, all with acoustic guitars—are sitting on the floor, working something out. Goff is tucked away behind a barricade of cardboard boxes to stop the drum sounds bleeding onto everyone else's tracks. A few more beach bums are building another baffle. What for? I can't remember. Over against the peeling back wall is an upright piano. Jack's blonde chick has her back to everyone and she's playing the piano, but you can't hear her. All the mikes are in the middle with the boys. The electrical gear—guitars, amps, etc.—is strung together like charms on a giant black cable bracelet.

It's *ad hoc*, it's messy. It's like a nursery school with all the toys on the floor. Lyric sheets flutter and fall whenever anyone walks by.

Everyone, it seems, is playing trains. They're stoking the engine, building up steam to drive the sixteen-beats-to-a-bar locomotive rhythm which propels the title song, "Hard Candy"—uh *huh* huh-hunh … Heads nod, feet pedal, knees pump, sweat rolls.

It's hot in there. The boys are stripped to the waist. The blonde chick's Indian shirt clings to her back.

Pull focus again, and you see the way Junior's shorts cut into his meaty thighs. The beach bum's frayed cut-offs sag low on his narrow hips. The Widow's bikini top supports nothing. It clings perilously to the unbelievable cantilever of her astonishing bosom—crimson on bronze. A tiny gold cross winks slyly, heliography from the foothills.

She calls herself Stella Splendens. The blonde chick calls her Offenses Against The Senses—Oats for short. Her perfume is too heavy, her makeup too thick, her colors too strong, her voice too brassy,

199

her breasts way too improbable. She strikes me, even now from light years' distance, more as a billboard than a woman. Constructed like a mantrap by the roadside.

What was she doing there? She looks all wrong in that ragged company. Someone brought her. Someone was doing a favor for the rich Widow Oats. But she was out of place on the island. She was a hanger-on, not a hanger-out. A bit of a joke, I thought.

"Out of it," Jack said. "Uncool." Then.

Later, when we came across her backstage, when Jack was touring *Hard Candy,* it was a different story. She didn't look so out of place in LA. She was built for LA. Built *in* LA, probably.

Never mind. She carried Jack away to her eyrie in the Hollywood Hills to sample her jacuzzi. Yeah, right! Which wouldn't have been too bad in itself, because shit like that happens on the road. Except that they were both such narcissists that they had to invite the paparazzi along to record the coupling. "Rock Rebel In Hot Water." Good headline.

"Birdie Flies" followed that, and "Sauce For The Goose"—yes, that was the banner caption to a picture of me and Homer Webb on a converted trawler off the Adriatic coast. Homer was lovely. He taught me to fish and he made revenge truly sweet. He didn't deserve what Jack said about him, either in the papers or in "Adversarial Attitude."

Widow Oats, on the other hand, deserved every word of what I said about *her* in "Sliding Widows." And, do you know?—Jack didn't even *like* her. He certainly never defended her and some of the unkindest lines in the song are his.

"I'll tell you how I feel about her," he said. "It's the way you feel about turkey the week after Christmas."

I would never have said a thing like that about Homer. In fact, I could've stayed with him a lot longer if Jack hadn't come to find me. He was sweet. His voice was too obedient and MOR for blues or rock, but it was nice, just right for his material—a ballad voice.

I go to see him sometimes, even now, and he's still sweet. Widow Oats got what she deserved: she married a Hollywood producer.

"Fast forward," I say to the technician, interested to note, in spite of this chasm of time between then and now, that The Widow still has the power to irritate the shit out of me. Actually, she didn't amount to anything in herself—it was the sight of Jack holing himself below the waterline on those titanic tits. It was so obvious, so show-biz. So disappointing.

Long ago, I believed that rock'n'roll wasn't show-biz. It was a way of life. It was somehow pure and exempt. I thought Jack and I were expressing real emotions—feelings which rejected show-biz bosoms as falsities, fallacies, falsies, false titties.

Maybe it wasn't fallible Jack who foundered on those improbable breasts, maybe it was me. There's no one so cynical as a disappointed believer.

It was Widow Oats who showed me the rock-rebel falling, not for the best, but for the biggest.

To be touched, to screw someone in heat or passion, is one thing—that happens—it isn't wonderful, but it's understandable. To fall for such a trite caricature of sexual attributes and to exploit it for publicity isn't understandable at all. Or rather, it's only understandable in show-biz terms.

In the next sequence, "Hard Candy" is coming together nicely. Jack is sitting on a stool. He still has the acoustic guitar strapped across his chest. Teddy and Wills have gone electric. Jack's chick is now playing a small organ.

Singer and organist are facing each other. There is intense eye contact between them. You might think that he is singing to her, that this is a moment of high romance. Don't be fooled by two beautiful kids' beautiful eyes locked together. They aren't romancing, they're counting. They're counting the vocals in so that stressed words fall on stressed beats. Complicated lyrics are being welded to driving rhythms.

Their slender young bodies sway and they look as though they're dancing. But they aren't. In each movement are the silent signals they're giving each other. Every swing of the shoulders, every dip of the head is a count or a signal. Nothing is done for effect. It's concentration, not show-biz.

It's Jack and his chick at their best. But, ah but, I say now in this dim editing room, it *was* being filmed. Doesn't that fact alone make show-biz out of concentration and a fallacy out of the notion of pure rock'n'roll?

I say to the technician, "Transfer this sequence to video, please."

I don't want to give the spidermen anything, but I'm forced to. If you want people to be jealous and acquisitive, they must have some inkling of what they've been excluded from. This sequence, at least, shows Jack and his drifty blonde chick acting like people who can be more than enigmatic and decorative. Even if the chick is only being used as a human metronome, at least she is being used for something—she isn't just floating around looking edible. Ah, vanity. Even now.

I love islands. But now, the sandy, scruffy wildernesses are mostly tamed and thatched. The dusty dirt paths are metaled, the miniature jungles and mangrove swamps are cut back until they're little more than herbaceous borders, and all the tattered, unruly kids are groomed to be desk clerks. We're running out of islands. Maybe there were too many movies showing sexy glamorous people like Jack and me getting away, cooling it, on undiscovered dots in the ocean. Eventually everyone wanted a piece of one.

I bet the shack we used as a studio was torn down to be a tiny part of a huge hotel, and tourist money destroyed what it existed to share in.

Jack and Teddy sit in the shade outside, leaning against the crumbling wall. Occasional sea breezes lift their hair away from young, strong necks. They are on a break. The kids have a desultory football game going with Wills and Goff. Now and then, the ball thumps against the wall. Nearby, an exhausted dog shares the meager shade, its emaciated ribs rising and falling in starved sleep.

With nothing better on offer, the cameramen film the band doing bugger-all while the soundman tries his hand at interviewing Jack. What was his name? Chip? Cookie? The credits will tell me, for unfinished, ragged, unruly as this film is the guys who made it stuck their names, big and bold, at the end.

Chip says, "What's your message, Jack? I mean, what's the point, man?"

Jack grins at him and raises a bottle of some local brew to his lips.

He blows a long hollow note across the neck and says, "Hear that lonesome whistle blow?"

"B-flat, I reckon," Teddy says, cupping one ear.

"That's our message," Jack says. "Be sharp."

"Yeah, man," says Chip. "But what're you telling the kids? Y'know, with the bomb and Agent Orange and shit?"

"Nothin' they don't already know," Jack says.

"Like what?"

"Live, love, and be happy," Teddy says, " 'cos tomorrow kerboom."

"Keep changing the light bulb at the top of the stairs," Jack says with infinite wisdom. "That's the one you need."

Jack has made mincemeat of professional interviewers, and Chip would give up right now if he wasn't too stoned to realize that Jack is being neither friendly nor gnostic.

"Yeah, man," Chip says in a wondering tone of voice, "the light bulb ... Like, ah, don't be left in the dark?"

Oh, this is wonderful. I turn to the technician and say, "This bit. Let's transfer this bit to video."

"OK," says the technician. "What the fuck're they on about?"

"Nothing," I say. "The message is that there's no message."

But Chip isn't ready to throw in the towel. He says, "But Jack, man, some of those songs are, like, so far out ... There's that one line, y'know, you were doing it over and over just now ... 'Hold me down when the hot wind shatters time ...' I can't get my head around it."

"Don't ask me," Teddy says. "I only play guitar."

"Jack?"

"I'll tell you," Jack says slowly and thoughtfully.

Chip waits. Teddy waits. And Jack gets up to retrieve the ball a kid has kicked at his legs. He doesn't come back. Teddy sits in silence for a few seconds. Then he says, "Yeah, lyrics, man. They're the things they use to break up the guitar solo, aren't they? Yeah, I thought so. Not much use otherwise."

Chip says nothing. Jack's gone. There's nothing left to say. Teddy knows this—it's why he hates Jack—but he sits there stubbornly until his wife, Christy, crouches down beside him and gives him a slice of pineapple. End of sequence.

That is the first and only time you'll see Christy in this movie. She's doing what she did many, many times—rescuing Teddy from the small, intolerable humiliations which are a second fiddler's lot. Nice woman. Good cook. Fiercely loyal until Teddy dumped her. I would have liked her if she'd liked me. But she didn't. Naturally.

I didn't have any girlfriends then—except Robin. Sisterhood as a universal concept rather than a family connection was a thing of the future. Suspicion was much more prevalent than support. Nowadays, I could have all the girlfriends I ever missed when I was Jack's blonde piece. Oh, yes—a drop in your estrogen level does wonders for your popularity rating with other women. But nowadays it is I who am suspicious. Where were these sisters when I was edible and supple? They were out spreading the whorey rumors and telling naughty stories about me to journalists. The *zeitgeist* was whispering a different message in those days from the one it whispers now, and women are very sensitive listeners to the *zeitgeist*.

"Let's take a break," I say to the technician. "Is there a decent pub within walking distance? I'll buy you a drink."

"OK," he says. "I'd better ring the girlfriend, tell her I'm going to be late."

She won't mind if an old broad buys her feller a drink, will she? Old broads aren't any threat. Estrogen and the *zeitgeist* are walking hand in hand a long, long way from island breezes and leggy, drifty chicks. No one will be betrayed tonight. Or will they?

V

Game Over

Alec dreamed he was in a playground surrounded by bright red and yellow swings and slides. Someone—his mother?—gave him something to hold. He carried the bundle up the ladder to the top of the tallest slide and let it go, intending to follow it down. But for some reason he didn't. He climbed up to a higher level and from there he saw, far below, a tiny baby rocketing, accelerating, toward the ground. The shawl it had been bundled up in blew away, leaving the baby naked and tumbling, skidding uncontrollably, down the glittering steel slope.

"She didn't tell me," he said, jerking upright in bed and seeing two giant female forms looming over him.

"Didn't tell you what?" Grace asked. The ceiling light was on, blinding him.

"Get dressed," Birdie said. "And be quiet. Don't disturb Robin. We'll be in the kitchen."

"Wha' ..." Alec mumbled, knuckling his eyes.

"The kitchen," Grace said, "and be quick."

He peered at his bedside clock. 03:18. He looked back at the door. The women were gone.

He was awake, sort of. He dressed in T-shirt and track bottoms, and stumbled as quietly as he could down to the kitchen.

Birdie was sitting at her usual place at the table. She was wearing a long red robe of some kind. Grace was making tea.

As he entered, Grace put the lid on the teapot and then came over to him.

He said, "What's up?"

For a second, she said nothing, and then she hauled off and hit him a stunning smack around the ear. As his face swung away from the

205

blow, his other ear met her other hand. Whack, whack. He staggered back. She pursued him and kicked him very hard on the shin.

He howled once and from his position, kneeling on the floor, he saw the hem of a red robe sweep around him and heard the kitchen door snap shut.

"Shut up," Grace said. "You'll wake Mum."

"What're you *doing?*" he gasped, crouching, trying to protect himself from the next stinging slap.

"That's *my* question," Grace said, delivering another one, two, three.

"Enough," Birdie said quietly. "I think the tea might be ready to pour."

When he looked up, Birdie was back in her place, calmly holding out a cup, and Grace just as calmly was pouring tea.

"You're mad," Alec said. His shin was throbbing and aching. His face was hot and stinging. His teeth felt loose. His ears rang.

"Too right, I'm mad," Grace said. "You used me, you bastard."

"You're rumbled," Birdie said. "Take it like a man."

"If that's what you are," said Grace.

He stared at them, his mind running like a dog trying to catch its own tail. What did they know?

"I don't understand," he said. "What am I supposed to have done?"

"Oh dear," Birdie said. "This is going to take for ever. We've got an asshole on our hands."

"No, really," he pleaded. "I don't understand."

"What don't you understand?" Grace said. "That cheating and lying and screwing a girl just to get into her house to spy on her aunt might upset me? Why should a tiny detail like Grade-A treachery spoil a beautiful friendship?"

"Look who's talking." Alec was short of breath and his eyes and nose seemed to be running, but he could still defend himself. He appealed to Birdie: "She was the one who started talking about you."

"Don't go down that road," Birdie said, sipping her tea. "That's between her and me. Concentrate on what's between you and her. You've got one chance and one chance only. Blow it and you're out."

"What chance?" Alec said.

"Don't talk to me. Talk to Grace."

"That's right, Alec," Grace said. "Explain yourself to *me*. And don't lie. You left your laptop switched on, so I know about Mr. Freel and Mr. Stears and 'the subject.' I know about your cameras and tape recorders. I know all that. Explain what you did to *me*. Tell me just who the fuck you think you are."

She was sitting very straight and tall. Her face was pale and as hard as china.

There was only one thing left to lie about. Alec said, "Oh Jesus Christ, Grace. I'm only a guy who wanted a job. I had no idea I'd feel this way." That was true—he'd had no idea he'd be standing on the rim of a chasm with his teeth wobbling and his leg half broken.

"I've had ten jobs since I left college," he said, "and it's been hard. I wound up at Memo Movies on a trial. They're making a film about Jack. I was just trying to get myself noticed. I was visiting all the Jack websites when I met you. You seemed to know everything, so I hung on to you. I didn't know who you were. I didn't know I'd feel this way about you."

"And how's that exactly?"

"Grace, I ..." Maybe this was the question he'd been avoiding all his life. His head felt like a toy box: he was scrabbling about, looking for something at the bottom, couldn't find it.

"Well?"

"Grace, I ... I just want to be close to you," he said desperately. "I want to be part of your life."

Miracle. For a split second, it looked as if the china mask might melt.

"What about your girlfriend?" she said, bone-hard again.

This time, his mind, like anxious hands, searched his hard disk. What had she seen? What had he written?

He shrugged hopelessly.

Grace and Birdie exchanged one of those terrifying, wordless female glances.

"I don't know what to say," he cried. "I lied to her too. I said I was on a management course. I'll have to tell her, whatever happens here. I can't go on with her any more. Not since you."

It felt true and untrue. His girlfriend was safe, and part of him would've given anything to be safe right now. Another part of him knew that she was from the lumpen past.

He fastened on to the bit that felt true. He said, "I've never met anyone like you before. I didn't know I could feel … this way. I think you've … changed me."

Grace looked at Birdie again. She said, "Do you believe him?"

Birdie, in her red robe, detached and almost judicial, said, "Hard to say, sugar. You must make up your own mind. Sometimes they luck into the right words. Sometimes they believe them—that's what makes it so hard. He seems to believe himself, but Grace, that doesn't mean that what he says is true."

"Well, I think I believe him."

"But remember, he came into this house like a spy. He courted you, cultivated you with *his own ambition* in mind. You were a convenience, a means to an end."

"It's true," Alec blurted out, "but I …"

"He kept it going," Birdie went on, implacable. "You have to ask yourself, would he *ever* have come clean if you hadn't rumbled him?"

"I've been going crazy," Alec said, to Birdie. "In the last few days, I felt I was splitting apart. I didn't know what to do. But, Grace, you've read my last e to Mr. Freel—you can see I was trying to find a way to make him back off."

Grace looked at Birdie again. "*That's* true, isn't it?" she said.

"Yes, but why, baby?"

"Why, Alec?"

"Because …" This was the big one, this was where you were expected to expose your throat. "Because what I was doing was wrong. Not just to you, Grace, although that was the worst. I was doing wrong to all of you." He turned to Birdie again. "They said you were a bitch … a sort of monster. Like you aren't really human. So, at first, I thought it was a sort of game. But they were wrong, and I'm so, so sorry."

Grace said, "Don't you believe him?"

"Believe what? That Sasson and Barry told him I was a bitch? Yes, I believe that. That he thought it was all a game? Yes, that too. That he's so, so sorry? Grace, honey, you have to think very carefully before you believe a guy who says he's sorry."

God, she was hard. Alec felt his eyes and nose running again. That's what always happens when you apologize, he thought. They throw it back in your teeth. He tried to wipe his nose on his T-shirt.

Grace said, "Well, I've thought about it and I believe him. I'm going to give him a cup of tea."

Oh you little angel, Alec thought. You *do* like me. You really do.

"Get him an ice pack while you're about it," Birdie said languidly. "Unless you'd still prefer to give him an ice *pick*."

"I *am* doing the right thing, aren't I?"

"Only you can say," Birdie said. "Only time will tell. It's a hung jury, but it's your vote which counts."

Blag your way in, Alec thought, and then.

"One piece of advice," Birdie said to Grace, "*before* you give him anything more than a cup of tea, if you want to know where he's coming from, make him take you to Hull to see his mother."

Oh shit, shit, shit, Alec thought. He could feel himself blushing. "Stanmore, actually," he said.

"You see," Birdie said, as if he hadn't spoken, "with relationships, you take things on faith which no way would you take on faith in business. If you don't want to get burned again, check his references. It's only fair. He's already checked yours—in fucking spades."

Grace looked at Alec.

"OK," he said reluctantly.

"Tomorrow? I mean today?"

"I suppose."

"*Now* you can give him an ice pack," Birdie said. "And Grace, if you're satisfied and you still want him after you've seen his mum, between us we might be able to come up with a plan to rescue his job. Because, as of this moment, he's lost all his points with Sasson and Barry, as well as with you. He's an embarrassment, and they won't be as kind as you when they find out."

"You're not going to make me quit?" Alec said in surprise. Mentally, he was already on his way to the job center.

"Do you want to?" Grace asked.

Key question. "Yes," he said. "They lied to me … about your aunt."

"They manipulated you," Birdie said, looking directly at him, the dazzling blue eyes almost pinning him to the wall. "What do you expect in show business? But if you have a choice, my advice to *you* would be, don't quit from a position of weakness. Wait till you're strong and then flounce. Whether you have a choice or not depends on Grace. I'm going to bed."

It was as if the spotlight had been switched off and he was left in the warmer, dimmer glow of Grace's hazel eyes. He sat down, carefully, and buried his face in his hands.

Now what? Exposed, humiliated, hurt. He should be toast. Why wasn't he toast? Because Grace saved him? No. Birdie *allowed* Grace to save his ass. Why? What for?

Ah. Alec saw a glimmer of light flicker across his screen. Game over? I don't think so—there's the double game to consider, the double infiltrator, the double agent. There's information and then there's misinformation. She *must* have thought of that.

And if she hasn't, Alec thought, I'll score points by suggesting it myself.

VI

Here Today Gone Tomorrow

Blackened redfish with some étouffée and jambalaya on the side, complementing the sweet potato—hog heaven. Junior gazed at his plate in ecstasy. On stage were Eddie LeJeune and the Morse Playboys—another rare treat. On the dance-floor, some of the best Cajun dancers in the city were executing the fancy footwork and controlled mayhem which went with the music. Traditional Cajun alive and kickin', Junior thought. Alive and cookin', he added, piling a little of everything onto his fork.

"You can't do better than Mulate's," he said, through the starburst of flavors.

Barry Stears nodded. "Perhaps a little spicy," he said, cautiously prodding the bulging area under his rib cage, preparing it for invading enemies.

Junior did the arithmetic: good music to listen to, plus good food to taste, plus good dancers to watch, minus Barry to deal with, equals ... Well, even with Barry alongside, he still came out ahead. Especially when Barry was picking up the tab.

"Where were we?" Barry asked.

"You're making a TV program about Jack and you want to interview me. For a fee."

"Right," Barry said, mashing étouffée into his potato. "How does that sound?"

"Fair enough," Junior said. "As long as it's here in N.O.—I don't want to travel, man. They're making the planes too small and they won't let you smoke. And as long as we talk about the music—I won't do the gossip. And as long as the fee's cool. I'll have to ask Sandrine."

"I'm particularly interested in *Hard Candy*."

211

"Yeah?"

"Not just the album," Barry said. "You went to the Caribbean, didn't you, when they were doing the demos?"

"Yeah, six weeks. We worked most nights and slept most days. I didn't come home with much of a tan."

"What do you remember about it?"

For a moment, Junior held his loaded fork suspended between plate and mouth. "Making do," he said. "It wasn't a proper studio—we had to build a lot of it ourselves. There were people everywhere—wives, friends, girlfriends, kids off the beach. Sometimes they'd have the kids singing and playing too. Dustbin lids and spoons. Nice stuff, lots of fire and invention."

"And a film crew?"

"Yeah, a handful of young guys. It was a mess, but we got the job done."

Barry reached into his inside pocket and pulled out an envelope, which he placed next to Junior's plate.

"What's this?" Junior asked.

"Photographs. I wonder if you'd look at them and tell me if you think they were taken then."

Reluctantly, Junior put down his fork and examined eight rather sludgy color stills—Jack and Birdie playing in the surf, Jack and Birdie sharing a hammock, Jack on a shady veranda rolling a joint.

"Yes, look—that's the studio," he said. "See what it was like? Jerry-built. No proper sound-proofing. Where did you get these?"

"They're stills from the movie," Barry said.

"What movie? Oh, *that* movie. Is this the thing Teddy came to see me about?"

"It might be," Barry said, collecting up the photographs and restoring them to his pocket. "For a long time, I thought it'd been destroyed."

Junior looked at Barry, taking in his tailoring and trendy tie, so tight-assed and out of place among the jeans and epigrammatic T-shirts. He realized for the first time that Barry wasn't drinking. Uh oh, hassle. He said, "Look, I told Teddy—I never saw the movie, and Birdie never stored anything with me."

"No, no, old man," Barry said. "I know that. We're a few steps farther on now. I'm only here to persuade you to participate. You were pivotal to the most important recordings."

"Yeah, I was, wasn't I?" Junior said, taking a long swig of beer.

"It's a serious program we're making—an evaluation—about the times, the innovations, influences. How that unique sound came about, its impact on the present day."

"Sounds OK to me," Junior said. "Just as long as it doesn't turn into a hatchet job. There's been too much said ... y'know, personally."

"Absolutely not," Barry said. "I know you've remained friends with Birdie, and I respect that. I wish I could say the same—after all, Jack was my very best friend and I would've liked to have stayed in touch with her after his death. Maybe if things had been different I could have helped her—stopped her going off the rails."

Junior took refuge in the food. Good food represented comfort in times of stress.

"I'm still hoping I can prevail upon her to contribute. But I'm not holding my breath. And I'm not asking you to use your influence, either."

"That's good," Junior said, " 'cos I ain't got none to use." He was relieved to see that even if Barry wasn't emptying his glass, at least he was clearing his plate.

"I was wondering," Barry said, "it's a long shot, I know, but did you keep any of the production notes?"

"For *Hard Candy*?"

"For instance."

"The record company kept all those."

"I mean what you did in Antigua. For the demo. There was stuff on the demo which didn't appear on the album, wasn't there?"

"Sure. Some of it came out on the next album. But I wasn't involved with that."

"I know," Barry said, "and I've never understood why."

"Lots of reasons. Everyone fighting. Anyway, Jack wanted to produce himself. He'd got so's he thought everyone was trying to take things away from him, bend him out of shape. I couldn't deal with it. I came here."

213

Barry nodded in approval. "I can see why. But it'd be useful, for the purposes of our program, if you could remember what was on the Antigua tapes. We'd like to be able to reconstruct the decision-making process—why certain songs were on *Hard Candy*, why others were held over for *Hard Time*. If you kept production notes, it'd be a great help."

"Mmm," Junior said. "I don't know, man. I could go through my records, see what I still got."

"Good," Barry said. "That's all I ask."

"It was a long time ago."

"Don't I know it," Barry said, petulance creeping into his voice. "I've been talking to the guys—Teddy, Wills, Goff—trying to reconstruct what you all did in Antigua. Do you know, none of them remembers the same things."

"I'm not surprised, man," Junior said. "There was a bucket-load of mood-enhancing substances floatin' around."

Barry sighed. "God, I wish I'd been there. *I'd* have kept accurate records. Stoned musos are a historian's worst nightmare. That's why notes would be a godsend—anything you've got in black and white. I'd be prepared to pay generously for them." He leaned toward Junior, suddenly confidential. "There's something else," he said. "There are other film companies on the prowl and I don't want anyone but Memo Movies to talk to you. As I say, I'll pay very generously for any help you can give me, but it must be exclusive help. Is that clear?"

"OK," Junior said. Barry's breath was tickling his ear, making him uncomfortable. "But exclusive ain't cheap."

"It will be built into your fee."

"That'd be useful," Junior admitted, noticing with regret that his plate was empty. Production notes. What you did. When. Who was playing which instrument. How you achieved any particular sound on which numbers. Levels. Keeping track of tracks. Very organized. In theory. He said, "I never thought what we did would have any significance two weeks later, let alone two decades plus. It was a here-today-gone-tomorrow thing."

"Except it wasn't gone tomorrow," Barry said. "Or the day after that. It just went on and on, gathering significance and value as time passed. Even the out-takes—the tracks Jack rejected at the time—if we could lay our hands on those, they'd be worth a fortune now."

"What tracks?"

"That's why we need production notes. To see if there were any numbers which didn't make it into either *Hard Time* or *Hard Candy*."

"Right," Junior said. "Well, I don't remember any offhand. You should ask Birdie. She's the one with the memory."

"And she's the one with the negative attitude. But her loss is your gain, if you see what I mean."

"No," Junior said.

"Well, if she was cooperating, your contribution wouldn't be half as valuable."

"Oh."

"Damn right," Barry said. "Think about it."

"It's a pity you can't lay your hands on any of the working tapes," Junior said. "Jack used to come to the studio with some really fizzin' guide tracks they'd put together themselves. But I guess that was the sort of stuff which went up in flames. That really *was* here-today-gone-tomorrow."

He looked at the dancers—watching with pleasure the intricate couple movements, one configuration leading to another, speedy precise footwork. When the number closed, everyone clapped and went back to their beer. All gone, all the activity and artistry disappearing into silence. No reminder of their skill remaining unless you counted sore feet. Live music, live performance, existing one time and one time only. God bless 'em all, Junior thought, anything else is like pinning butterflies to corkboards—you got a dead butterfly, but you ain't got what moves you.

Part 4

GOING DOWN

" 'Cos you paid the price to come this far—Just to wind up where you are …"   Ry Cooder

I

The Blues

Hard cash, cold cash, cash on the nail. Nash Zalisky came through with a finely judged amount. He hadn't lost his touch: his judgment was so admirable it made me laugh. It was banknotes of a number a hard-working person would save for the trip of a lifetime—the sum needed to travel halfway round the world in comfort, stay somewhere comfortable for three weeks and then come home. Comfort is the key word, not luxury. If you traveled first-class, you'd blow it all in two days.

It was an amount which wouldn't pay off the mortgage or buy a new car or put the kids through school. You couldn't go mad on it except for a very short time. But it wasn't insulting, either. It was perfect, windfall cash.

I packed a bag and told Robin I was going to the States for a couple of weeks. Modestly I took the shuttle to Heathrow, Terminal Four. It was a long way to go to use a telephone, but details matter in this game.

When Nash came on the line, I said, "Thanks, Nash. I hope I'll have some good news for you soon."

"Good, Birdie, good," said his fussy little voice. "Where are you?"

"On my way." At the same time an announcer said, BA flight blah to Boston and blah …

I said quickly, "Listen, Nash, I wanted to ask, if I run out of time or money, can you …"

Bing-bong. "This is a security announcement …"

"I can wire you a reasonable amount any time, anywhere in the world," Nash said. "But Birdie …"

"My phone card's running out," I said. "I'll be in touch."

"Birdie …"

I cut the connection and yanked my card. Then I took the shuttle back to London and went to Maida Vale. Call me paranoid if you like, but from now on I don't want Nash to know my mobile number or which phone company I use. A weasel like Nash can insert himself into the smallest gap in your security system. Communications are his specialty.

Years ago, there was only one phone company and it was relatively easy to buy your target's number. I know, because Jack had to change his every two weeks or so. Now there's a whole tangle of landlines and satellite junk. More ways to communicate, but more opportunities for people like Nash to eavesdrop or tap into revealing little items like your telephone bills. I wonder how long it takes these days for the freaks to buy the stars' phone numbers?

There's no phone at Maida Vale. It's a wretched little flat and it isn't mine. But it's free and I have the key. Narrow dark stairs lead to a narrow dark hall and then this wretched dark space. I can put up with it for a short while when necessary but, oh, it dampens my spirit and cramps my style. The worst of it is that I know it's the only place I could afford if I were ever to consent to living within my means and having my means determined by the spidermen.

The place is filled with boxes and, again, most of them don't belong to me. They belong to a woman called Marielle, who used to dress a glittery-glam guy I knew years ago. She ran the wardrobe and the laundry for him when he went on tour. I refused to go on tour with him after the first time. But I liked her, and while she was away I watered her plants and fed her cats. Now, many miles down the pike for all of us, her cats and plants are dead and she is in an old folks' home with premature Alzheimer's, as alone and scared as a body can be. One day she'll die, alone and scared, unable to remember her own name. Everyone's a stranger to her and every step she takes is into the unknown. At the mercy of badly paid professionals, she is allowed only four fresh incontinence pads a day. Soon, resenting even this extravagance, they'll strap her to a commode. You'd think the glitter-glam guy would help her out. But he's driving a cab in Manchester and can't even pay his own kid's maintenance. It's just another rock-biz story

220

playing itself out. And meanwhile I still have the key and a place to hide in.

If it all goes wrong, I could end up living here permanently with nothing much to do except reflect on how cruel life is to insane, incontinent old women, and how the older you grow, the harder it is to pick up the pieces and start again.

The beautifully judged mad money Nash has bestowed upon me, if it's all I make out of this, will not see me into a comfortable old age. It won't protect me from being scared and alone, nor will it buy a lifetime's supply of incontinence pads. Because, walking through this narrow doorway, that's what I think I'll need—one step into this wretched little world, and already I'm shitting myself.

I look at Marielle's cardboard boxes and I think: is this all there is? She started packing, unpacking, packing, long before anyone knew something was going wrong. Bundling up her life into smaller and smaller boxes for the trip of a lifetime to a foreign country where she would be a perpetual stranger even to herself. Her life is in these boxes, not in her head. There's more of her life in my memory than there is in hers. I can tell stories about her. She can't. It's all wiped off her screen. Blanked.

Terror-struck, I realize that the process began when she was only a couple of years older than I am today.

I jam Taj Mahal's *Natch'l Blues* into my personal CD player and clamp the earphones around my head. I press, crush, the cans against my ears as if the strength of my arms will ram music into my brain. I close my eyes tight and wait for the moment when music becomes thought and thought becomes music, when my hips move of their own accord, when pulse equalizes with beat and kick-starts the heart.

It's what the Blues are for. Courage. When circumstances are crap, when you can't face life, when you can't face yourself, when you're sinking, the Blues give you grit.

Without music and money, you might as well fade away and die.

II

Soft Touch

These days, when George Adler walked into the office in the morning, he walked with the lightest step a heavy man is capable of. He enjoyed seeing fresh flowers on the reception desk. When he came in early, arriving before Tina, he would find that although Linnet was absent, the overnight calls had already been logged and the coffee machine was primed and ready to switch on. Then he could sit alone with a steaming mug in his hand and recover from commuting, mulling over what was to be done that day, even reading the morning paper.

George was good in the early morning. Tina wasn't, she built up steam as midday approached. And Linnet was best in the afternoon and evening. As a team, he thought, the three of them worked an eighteen-hour day in shifts. He went home early, Tina a couple of hours later, and Linnet would clear everyone's desk, organize the next day, and lock up.

Today, though, when he arrived, he found the office already open for business and the coffee ready to pour.

"Hello?" he called, and went to his room to unpack his briefcase. These days, he rarely had to take work home, so his briefcase usually only held the morning paper and a lovingly prepared packed lunch.

"Morning, Linnet," he said when she came in with his coffee. "You're early. Something special on today?"

"I couldn't sleep."

Her smile was so warm that he nearly missed the pallor and the shaky hand.

When she came back half an hour later with the opened mail, he said, "Anything urgent in that?"

"No," she said. "Routine. There are a couple of things waiting for signature, but otherwise ..."

"Are you feeling all right?" he asked, because although she was as quick as usual he sensed an uncertainty about her.

"Yes," she said. She turned to go and then stopped in the doorway. "Yes," she said more slowly, "but I do have a problem. George, would you mind if I took off my employee's hat and signed on as a client for a moment?"

"A client?" he said, surprised. "What's up?"

She sat opposite him on the client's chair and said, "I'm afraid it's one of those stories where past and present collide. But the immediate difficulty is that I'm being followed and I've been forced to move out of my house. Also, I've had some things stolen."

Later that afternoon, talking to Tina, George said, "I could scarcely believe what I was hearing. I mean, I knew she was different. I said from the first, didn't I, that she was a bit special?"

"At length," said Tina.

"Please," said George, "don't mock. I'm only saying I'd never've guessed that our wonderful Ms. Walker had a story like that up her sleeve. Even *I* have heard of Jack."

"Gosh," Tina said. "And I bet you've heard of Elvis and the Beatles too, you trendy old raver."

"All right already."

"Well, me old dear, you *are* coming over a bit star-struck all of a sudden. However glamorous the setting is, she's our Ms. Walker, a middle-aged woman with a problem, needing a bit of advice. *Pro bono*, unfortunately."

"She did offer to pay, of course."

"And of course you declined."

"You're giving me that look," George said. "I am not a soft touch."

"But you do have a soft spot for Linnet. Admit it."

"The point is," George said, huffing gently, "are we going to help her? Or are you prejudiced against her because she's had a racy past and a lot of people have said bad things about her?"

"Racy's putting it a bit mildly," Tina said. "But no. Handsome is as handsome does, and I've got to admit that she's done handsomely by us."

"So?"

"So, all I'm asking is that you look at it coolly. Break it down. Take the drama and emotion out of it and what've you got? Just an ordinary middle-aged woman who's afraid she'll be ripped off."

But George was having difficulty seeing Linnet as an ordinary middle-aged woman. Had he ever? If he was brutally honest with himself, he'd have to say that he'd never seen her as ordinary. There was a part of him that had always felt that they were using a Rolls-Royce to deliver the milk.

"Tina doesn't seem to see that this is both qualitatively and quantitatively different," he told Fay over dinner that night.

"Maybe Tina resents having employed someone under false pretences," Fay suggested. "More pie?"

"Ah, but where were the false pretences?" George asked, holding out his plate. "She told us her name. If I was of a generation too old for it to mean something, and Tina was too young, that's our look-out, surely."

"She gave you her proper name," Fay pointed out, "not the name she's known by."

"How long can a grown woman live with a sobriquet like 'Birdie'?"

"A linnet is a bird too," Fay said, as if it were highly significant.

"The point is," George said, irritated, "there's something rather gallant about a woman trying, all by herself, to protect a dead lover from powerful, acquisitive forces."

"Isn't that a rather romantic way of seeing it?"

"Romantic?" George said, startled. He stared at Fay, but she was looking back at him with nothing more than amusement in her eyes.

"Maybe it's the thought of a *pro bono* case," he said, recovering quickly. "Tina's very hard-headed about expenditure. The business is only just beginning to turn the corner, after all."

"What does Linnet actually need?" Fay asked.

"I don't know yet. I'm still thinking about it."

"You like her a lot, don't you," Fay said, musingly.

"Yes I do. So does Tina."

"Does she?"

"Of course." He watched Fay covering the pie dish with foil, carefully tucking down the edges. Did Tina like Linnet? Why was it important for him to tell Fay that she did? Why was he asking himself these questions? It was because of a curious expression that Tina and Fay shared. It reminded him of his mother. The saying, "There's no fool like an old fool" popped, unbidden and unwelcome, into his head.

"Oh, for God's sake," he exclaimed, and stumped away crossly to watch tennis on TV.

Ten minutes later, Fay came in with two cups of peppermint tea. She settled beside him on the sofa and asked him the question he'd been asking himself. "Dear," she said, "why are you being so defensive about this? It's most unlike you."

"I don't know," he said with a sigh. "I think it's because both you and Tina seem to be implying that I'm emotionally involved."

"What's so bad about that? After all, Linnet has made your working life bearable—if not a pleasure—so it's understandable that you wouldn't want her threatened."

"Exactly," he said with relief. He sank back into the cushions, prepared to let the matter rest. But Fay was still waiting.

"What?" he said.

"Maybe," she said gently, "Tina and I are wondering about the woman who gave you some rather iffy references and yet can still make you act out of character."

"I'm not acting out of character," George said, annoyed. "Do you know, Tina accused me of being star-struck."

"No!" Fay said. "How very insulting!"

"This isn't a joke." He got up and stamped away to bed, leaving his peppermint tea untouched.

III

Sex and Suicide

"The lady's a spring chicken," Jack sings. "No meat on her bones, slim pickings. Sleeping on my dirty floor, she says to me, she says, 'no more' ..."

I look at Marielle's dusty carpet. I couldn't bear to sleep in her bed, so I laid a mattress on the floor.

In the beginning, Jack and I slept on a dirty floor next to the kitchen with its creeping detritus and dripping taps. The others had to step over us to get to the cornflakes. We didn't give a toss. But we wanted to be alone, so we rented a flat a couple of blocks away and we bought a bed. No chairs, no tables, just a big second-hand bed. We didn't care who'd been born, who'd died, who'd lain sleepless in it. Quite soon we bought the Camden Hill house.

Jack's graph was on the rise. Slowly at first and then steeply, up, up, and with it we rose through the lower strata of property—a sort of rake's or rock's progress—until we reached the big house in the home counties with its protective wall and gate. If the graph had continued in the same trajectory, the next step would've been to the big house in a tax haven—France, Switzerland, or the Caribbean, and apartments in all the cool cities. But it didn't. The trajectory ended in tragedy and here I am back on a dirty floor. Oh yes—the yo-yo motion of real estate in rock-biz—nine times out of ten, you'll find yourself at the end of your string.

Blackwood Park was the house that Jack burned down. The protective wall and gate prevented the fire brigade from getting straight to it. Precious minutes were lost while panicking grounds-men searched for the spare key. The housekeeper and her husband ran around in their nightwear like headless hens, trying to save their own valuables. Outside the gate, with the fire brigade stalled, the little group of fans who had set up a semi-permanent campsite on the verge cried and wailed and tried to scramble over the wall. To do what? To save Jack? Or to ask him for his autograph?

I don't know. I wasn't there, so I only saw the pictures like everyone else. And everyone else saw pictures of me a day later gazing, stunned, at the wreckage. "Ladybird, ladybird, fly away home," jeered the caption. "Your house is on fire and your meal ticket's gone." There's nothing so cuddly and comforting as the British press.

At the inquest, the housekeeper inaccurately said Jack had been drinking. She told the coroner that she'd served supper at ten-thirty but that Jack had eaten very little. She said he'd been "down in the dumps." She prepared a tray of sandwiches and snacks with a thermos of hot coffee, which she left in the sitting room. She went to bed at eleven-thirty and heard nothing till the smoke alarm woke her and her husband at four in the morning.

Her husband said that after supper Jack went down to his studio in the basement. Jack was working, he said, and seemed vague, "not quite himself."

The chief officer of the fire service said that the blaze had been started in the basement with some sort of accelerant like lighter fluid or kerosene. He said that the beams and joists burned away and that by the time his crew got to the scene the ground floor and an upper story had collapsed into the basement. It took them several hours to control the fire and a further two days to recover the body.

Jack's doctor said that three weeks previously he'd prescribed Valium for Jack because he appeared to be suffering from depression and stress following an arduous tour of the United States. As far as he knew, Jack seemed to be a sensible sort of chap who could be trusted with prescription drugs. Laughter from the press gallery was quickly silenced by the coroner.

Jack's shrink said that Jack was experiencing paranoid delusions and that he had prescribed Mandrax because of stress and fatigue. He had been seeing Jack for six months on a regular basis—when he was in the country and when he remembered to turn up for his appointments.

No one asked for my unqualified opinion about the state of Jack's mind. All they wanted to know was why I'd left him alone, why I hadn't burned to death too—keeping him company like a good wifey. It was, by that time, already well known that I'd been at a party on board a launch on the Thames. There were pictures of me dancing with a couple of minor aristos, James Coburn, and Björn Borg. Ho-ho.

I said that we'd both been invited, we'd both planned to go, but Jack pulled out at the last moment. I went because it would have been impolite for us both to bail. I didn't hear about the fire until the boat docked and we disembarked for breakfast.

The crowd outside the court booed and threw flour, eggs, and vegetables when I came and went, telling me clearly that the wrong one died. It was a bad mistake to shack up with the man everyone else loves, and it was worse than a mistake not to throw myself on his funeral pyre.

A journalist once asked me what it was like to be hated by just about everyone, and I didn't answer. What could I say? It's a way of life? It's a cherished facet of my complex identity? Or should I have asked in return: what should I do to make everyone love me? Dump Jack? Mutilate my face? Go on a chocolate binge? Have two-thirds of my brain surgically removed? Die?

Actually, the question is more interesting than it appears to be, especially in the UK, where brains and beauty are commodities you're supposed to conceal and apologize for. You can get away with beauty if you turn yourself into a joke blonde with big boobs and a generous heart. And you can get away with brains if you can dilute them with large helpings of the common touch and humility. But if for any reason you lead a public life and you don't butcher your natural attributes, you'll face tremendous hostility. Simply by being who you are, you'll antagonize the majority of the general public.

People need to feel sorry for you or superior to you, or they won't accept you as one of their own. If they don't accept you and you commit further crimes, like shacking up with the sexiest man in the country and being seen to live a glamorous life, you will be treated like a thief. You are seen to be stealing something which rightfully belongs, not to you, but to them.

So Jack died horribly in a fire and left his arrogant blonde piece alone without protection—tally-ho, open season.

Unfortunately, the people who came to help Jack's arrogant blonde piece were the people who understood and had themselves suffered from the boom and bust cycles of media attention—those who were themselves very rich, very famous, or very both. Thus the blonde piece was seen to be *profiting* from Jack's horrible death— double scoop of tally-ho, open season.

I wonder, if they saw me now, on a little camp bed, with my nose six inches from a dirty floor in a dark and wretched flat, would they forgive me? Nah, probably not. They'd say I was getting my come- uppance. And who knows—they might be right. Distinction deserves punishment. We all strive for equality.

Why couldn't they wait? Age and Alzheimer's, after all, do the same job pretty completely. We all end up in a similar place. Where will the dangerous distinction be then?

So much for my problems, such as they were. What of Jack's? Did he have any? He was beautiful, talented, rich, and famous— obviously no problems there. On top of that, he was loved. No one hated him. He had the most efficient lightning conductor money could buy to divert hatred. He had me. I protected him from being struck by jealousy and hatred. He was safe while he walked under my umbrella.

Lucky Jack—all those gifts, all that unconditional love and approval. That's what everyone wants. Well, maybe, but it destroyed Lucky Jack.

After all, Lucky Jack started out as a rebel rocker. His hair, his clothes, his demeanor were, at that time, an outsider's slap in the face for the establishment. His songs had some hard things to say about the narrow constraints of England, about po-faced, joyless morality, about the land of hope and glory with its impotent militarism and xenophobia. His very existence was predicated on opposition.

He didn't see himself as speaking for a generation. He was speak- ing for himself, and then he was adopted by a generation.

When that happened, he found himself in a position of leadership, bearing the weight of millions of hopes and fears. He couldn't speak for himself any more. He was representing his generation. And he found he didn't have the freedom any more to fuck up.

He was loved, and it's a lot harder to dismiss love than hatred. I, at least, had the freedom to despise and fight against the people who hated me. He was not allowed to show the slightest contempt for the people who loved him. Slowly but surely he was suffocated by love and approval.

The night he blew it all away, we were both supposed to be on the launch chugging around Marlowe, Cliveden, and other significant landmarks on old father Thames. We were supposed to make merry with the hereditary hoorays and their henriettas, with safely selected elements of show-biz and sport. I could go. I could take what they had to offer in a spirit of detachment, like a thief at their table, well aware of their contempt.

He couldn't. They were offering him a place at their table without irony or contempt. We love you, Jack, you're one of us.

He wasn't one of them. But they loved him, so they were adopting him too. Lucky Jack.

I went to the party and he went out of his mind.

He thought they were stealing his soul. Along with the trinkets, the clothes, records, ideas, photographs, time, which everyone was already pinching with impunity, now they were stealing his beliefs and appropriating his rebellion.

Even now they're still at it: the tele-cine lab I was secretly working at was broken into, and a reel of film—images of Jack, sounds of Jack—was stolen. Someone believes that what belongs to Jack, Jack himself, is their own property. He's loved and desired, even now. So many years later, he must still give himself freely. Lucky Jack.

The last thing he said to me before I left for the party was, "You smell of sex and suicide."

And I said nothing because I was pissed off with him.

Sex and suicide are not concepts you talk about in a coroner's court unless you want them aired and analyzed in public for weeks afterwards. I kept Jack's last words to myself.

The coroner asked, but I told him that Jack simply said, "Goodbye, have a ball."

I tried to imagine what would've happened had I told him the truth: "He said, 'You smell of sex and suicide,' but that was normal. Jack was always coming out with stuff like that. That's the way drug-crazed rock stars talk."

And yet I could've said that. Sex and suicide are two good s-words. They sound well together. Who knows, maybe Jack was trying out a line—they have an end-of-chorus ring to them. I wouldn't have been surprised to come home to find Jack asleep with a partially completed song called "Sex and Suicide" crumpled next to his elbow. Waiting for me to finish it for him. Certainly, I'd have been less surprised to find a song than to find the smoking wreckage of his mansion on the hill.

Speaking of mansions on the hill, I've given that soul-snatching spiderman enough time. I'll ring him from a public call box in the West End tonight after work.

"Nash," I say. "I might have something for you."

"Have you, Birdie?" he says. "Why am I not surprised? What've you found?"

"What have you arranged?"

"Ah, Birdie, Birdie, why won't you trust me? Haven't I already sent you ample proof of my good will?"

"Not ample, no," I say. "Sufficient but not ample."

"Sufficient is ample," Nash says fussily.

"Trust is expensive."

"No, Birdie—trust is free. *You* are expensive."

I laugh and wait.

Nash says, "I want to see what you've got."

"A sample," I say. "I could arrange to show you a sample—pay per view. Maybe."

"I've been giving your problems a lot of thought," he says. "I'd like to be able to clear up one small matter for you."

"How kind," I say. "Which small matter is that?"

"Tax," he says. "A representative of mine has been talking to the

231

Inland Revenue. He says that they'd be willing to do a deal. You could start again from scratch for seventy-five per cent of the total bill if it were paid in a lump sum."

"That's sweet of you, Nash. But I couldn't pay it if it were seven per cent."

"Well, of course not. That's why you're in such a mess. It's so sad, Birdie. I wish you'd come to me before. I can sort this out for you with a single phone call. Think about it—you could come back to the UK to live, you wouldn't have to wander like a gypsy and work for gangsters."

"Are you calling Sasson a gangster?"

"I'm talking about a Malaysian gentleman who owns a chain of night clubs. I understand you were reduced to booking acts for him."

"He wasn't a gangster as far as I was concerned," I say. "He paid me well and he kept all his promises. How do you know about him anyway?"

"I'm *interested* in you, Birdie. I wish you'd believe that. I want to help you. And to prove it, the minute you show me whatever it is you've found, I'll make that call to the Inland Revenue. There should be no more secrets between us."

"You're going too fast for me, Nash," I say. "It's unnerving." It's true, I am unnerved. He's been talking about my affairs to some bastard in the tax office. He's been checking up on my contacts. I can feel him crawling all over my life.

"Let me think about it," I say. "It's true that the tax bill has been an impossible burden, but it doesn't solve the problem of future earnings and ..."

"Come here," Nash says impatiently. "Bring your sample or whatever you call it. Show it to me and I'll make the call."

"No," I say. "Wait. I'll make the arrangements." I will not go back to his house unprotected and I'll be damned if I'll show him so much as a nail clipping on the mere promise of a phone call. I hang up.

IV

Show Time

"Who's paying for this hotel room?" Tina asked.

"Linnet," George said. "She gave me cash."

"This is weird. She should be here." Tina twitched the curtains and looked down over London rooftops and half-hidden streets. "Cash payments," she said, "fingers on phone buttons. It's like buying back kidnapped children, or extortion or something."

"Well," George said, "I advised her not to be here, and you wanted someone in the office." He turned the TV round so that it faced one of the easy chairs while Tina tested the video.

"A poncey hotel room!" she said. "We could've done this in the office."

"Not if Linnet wants to keep her place of work confidential."

"It won't be confidential for long," Tina said. "This bloke's going to check us out quick as a fox."

"But not before this meeting."

"And we'll be a bleeding sight easier to check out than he is," Tina continued, looking at her watch. "He's big-time."

"Exactly," George said. "This makes sense. Don't tell him the venue till the last minute and don't tell him the room number till he arrives."

"It makes sense," Tina agreed, "but only if you're totally paranoid about him bugging the room and re-routing phone calls. Bloody hell, George. I feel silly. It's only a bloody video."

George sighed. He'd made up his mind not to defend Linnet or any of the decisions they'd made jointly, but already he was acting like her advocate. "Look," he said, "we all agreed. So let's just stick to the plan and get it over with."

"Amen," said Tina, and the phone rang. She picked up the receiver, listened and said, "Thanks. Would you send them up."

"Them?"

"Visitors," Tina said. "Didn't say how many. Come on, George, don't look so anxious. It's show time."

A few minutes later, there was a tap on the door. Tina opened it and admitted a short, stocky man in a pale raincoat.

He said, "Good afternoon. I'm Mr. Zalisky's assistant. Would you mind if I look round? It's only a formality—just a routine we go through whenever he goes anywhere."

"Be our guest," Tina said, standing aside and glancing at George.

George watched. The stocky man was practiced and thorough. Bugs, bombs, or bandits would've stood no chance.

"Amazing," Tina muttered. "Looks like we've got paranoia on both sides."

It was real, George thought. Up till now, a secret part of his brain had thought he might be indulging Linnet.

He was pleased to see Tina follow their unexpected guest to the bathroom. They both watched while he closed the window and the curtains, cutting all the daylight out of the room.

"OK," the stocky man said. "Thank you." He punched a button on his walkie-talkie and said, "Everything's fine." Then he stood in the middle of the room. "Terrible summer we're having," he remarked pleasantly. "I like to play a round of golf myself, but I've hardly had the chance. Oh, by the way, by all means send down for coffee for yourselves—Mr. Zalisky always brings his own."

"I don't think we'll bother," Tina said.

"Don't blame you," the stocky man said. "Who do you work for, if you don't mind my asking?"

"Whoever the client is," George said. "In this case, Ms. Walker."

"I mean, what's your outfit? What's the name of the firm?"

"Oh, I see," said George. "It's a small South London firm. You wouldn't have heard of it. Why? You looking for a job?"

"You never know these days," the man said. "Got a card?"

George patted his pockets. "Somewhere," he said. "Tina?"

"Tell you what," Tina said, "I'll look one out and give it to you before you leave."

"OK," the man said. "I must say, I don't think Mr. Zalisky was expecting professionals. He thought he'd be ..." He broke off as a knock sounded at the door.

Tina opened it to a little man dressed all in black. He blinked at her nervously through thick steel-rimmed spectacles as if his mother had sent him next door to borrow a cup of sugar and he wasn't at all sure of his reception.

"Where's Birdie?" he asked plaintively.

George said, "I'm George Adler and this is my colleague, Ms. Cole. Are you Mr. Zalisky?"

The little man nodded, and George went on, "Ms. Walker sends her apologies. She's asked me and my colleague to represent her in this matter."

"Oh dear," the little man said, opening his hands helplessly. "I don't know ... I was expecting to see her. This is most disappointing."

Tina said soothingly, "Ms. Walker has given us detailed instructions and a video to show you."

Her tone was so maternal that for one moment George thought she was going to pat the little man on the head. He said, "Would you like to take a seat, Mr. Zalisky? Shall we get on?"

But Nash Zalisky dithered in the doorway until the stocky man opened his bag and brought out two pillows and a handful of clean white napkins. One pillow went on the seat of the chair opposite the TV. The other rested against the back. Napkins were spread over the arms and back like antimacassars. Only then did the fussy, anxious little man consent to sit down. The stocky minder stood behind the chair like a soldier at ease.

"The tape, the tape," Nash Zalisky said, fluttering his hand.

Tina picked up the remote and pressed the play button. The screen lit up to a picture of sun and sea. Surf was rolling in, small black kids were playing beach soccer. In the background, a guitar played. The camera scanned the horizon, turned, and came to rest on a hammock strung between palm trees. Two young people were sharing the hammock. They looked like a pair of film stars. The

235

camera crept closer. The man had one arm round the girl. His other hand made circles in the air.

"Ripples," he said. "I wonder how long before these ripples reach London."

Tina touched the pause button and the image of the handsome man stuck trembling to the screen.

George said, "Is this the video you want to see, Mr. Zalisky?"

"Maybe," Nash Zalisky said. "But how do I know this isn't all there is?"

"Shall I fast-forward?" Tina asked. "You can tell me when to stop."

Images raced silently across the screen. "It's all here," Tina said. "We haven't substituted Tom and Jerry."

But on the screen people scampered and chased each other through the sunshine, speeding through dawn to dusk like cartoon characters.

"Stop!" Zalisky cried, and the headlong rush halted suddenly in a candle-lit room. The shuddering picture showed George a close-up of a heartbreakingly young Linnet with dim light gleaming off unruly fair hair.

"Can you go back?" Zalisky said. "I want to see this bit."

"I'm sorry," Tina said. "George?"

George dragged his eyes away from the screen and said, "I'm afraid, at this stage, we're only authorized to confirm to you that the footage exists."

"Just a couple of minutes," Zalisky pleaded. "Surely there's no harm in that?"

"I'm sorry," Tina said. "Our instructions are explicit: we can only go on when the money's been transferred."

"What absolute nonsense," Zalisky said. "Why doesn't she trust me?" He was staring at the screen as if he thought he could persuade the blonde child to change her mind. Still staring, he held out his hand and the thickset man placed a mobile in it.

He punched a number, and said, "Yes, this is he. Would you call Mr. XYZ and confirm the arrangement we made this morning." He snapped the phone down and turned to George. "I'm here to *help* her," he said. "Has her life been *so* full of betrayal that she can no longer tell who her real friends are?"

George found himself disliking the little man so intensely that he couldn't answer. He picked up his own mobile and called the office. "Hello there. Just to tell you Mr. Zalisky has made his call."

Linnet's soft voice replied, "Thanks, George. I'll check that and ring you back."

Zalisky said, "Is that her? I'd like to speak to her."

"I'm sorry," George said, "but she hung up." He cut Linnet off.

"Now we'll have to wait," Tina explained. "Ms. Walker wants to make sure all your arrangements are to her satisfaction."

"This is ridiculous," Zalisky said. "I hope you can see how unnecessary all this is."

"I'm sure you're right," Tina said.

"Then …?"

For a moment, George thought the little man was going to make them a counter-offer. His eyes flicked between the two of them with something like hope, but then he shrugged helplessly. The thickset man rummaged in his bag and produced a flask, from which he poured a single cup of black coffee. Zalisky accepted the cup and returned to his scrutiny of the face on the screen.

The face on the screen, George thought, was extraordinary: eyes lowered, shadowed by long lashes, lips parted as if she were about to speak, luminous skin, the whole framed by gleaming, coiling hair. She seemed to be emitting light. She could have had a career in the movies, he thought, and wondered why she hadn't.

Electronic interference slashed jagged lines across the immobile face. But the horizontal lightning was powerless against such a potent image of perfect, dewy youth. The youth, the sheer lack of years, got to George and made him feel he was protecting a child, any child, his own child, from whatever harm life had in store for her.

Whatever was in store for that face had already happened. He knew that, and it almost brought a lump to his old, experienced throat. But he wondered, suddenly, if it was the same illogical emotion which was driving Linnet. Wasn't she trying to protect Jack, the young handsome subject of the film, from further harm?

After the call came through and Tina rewound the tape to the beginning, he watched Linnet the child wander through ten minutes of excerpts, barely saying a thing. She was clearly Jack's adornment, Jack's medal, first prize for simply being Jack. There was little to see of the Linnet George knew, and he wanted to stop the film and lecture the child as if she were his own daughter.

"Say something," he might have said. "You're worth more than this. Be yourself. If they don't like it—tough; that's their problem, not yours."

But the only time he saw the real Linnet break through the blank mask of beauty was in a short scene near the end, where she was playing a keyboard and Jack was singing. Then he saw the astonishing eyes focus, concentrate, and communicate the way they did every day years later in the office. That was the only time, though, and when the scene came up he was surprised because he didn't know she could play piano. In fact, with only the film as evidence, it was surprising to find out she could do anything useful at all.

At the end, when the screen went black and Nash Zalisky said, "What a loss, what a waste," George had to make an effort to realize that he was talking about Jack. The film was about Jack, not Linnet—Jack, Jack, Jack, all the way. George's inner dialogue with the child Linnet was irrelevant.

Tina rewound the tape but left the cassette in the machine. She said, "The next step is to ask you if you wish to buy the cassette with no transmission, publication, or reproduction rights attached. It would be for your own personal use only."

"It's a sample," Zalisky said. "A sample of what?"

"Of a film of about ninety minutes' length," Tina said, "and some unedited footage which survived after the film was edited."

"Do you know for a fact that the film and the extra footage exist?"

"Yes," said George, carefully avoiding Tina's eyes. Neither of them had seen it.

"Have I your word on that?"

"Yes."

"You see," Zalisky said, "we have a problem. Of course I want the cassette. I want to examine it at leisure and I need to show it to my consortium of backers. But the consortium feels that the price we discussed prior to this meeting is too high. I've already paid heavily just to view it here."

"The price," Tina said, "is not negotiable. Neither Mr. Adler nor I are authorized to negotiate. We're simply here to carry out Ms. Walker's instructions."

"What the consortium has in mind," Zalisky said, as if Tina hadn't spoken, "is an exchange." He turned to look at George. "This is difficult," he went on, clasping his hands between his knees. "As you know, I'm trying to be a friend to Birdie. I'm trying to protect her—to safeguard her future. But my backers have other ideas. I, too, have instructions to carry out. You must understand that I'm representing money and interests that are not my own. This, unfortunately, is business."

"Even so," Tina persisted, "we can't negotiate with you."

"What the consortium proposes is a simple exchange—one cassette, plus those reproduction and transmission rights which Birdie wants withheld, in exchange for another cassette." Zalisky held out his hand and the stocky man behind his chair gave him a video cassette of his own. "I'm afraid," he said, "that when Birdie finds out about *this* piece of tape she'll want to rethink her strategy. As I say, this is not my idea, and I'm quite devastated about it. But you'll have to see it so that you can make Birdie understand that the consortium means business."

"Hold on," Tina said. She looked at George. "We should discuss this."

"What's on the tape?" George asked.

"I haven't seen it," Zalisky said, licking his dry lips fastidiously. "But I am assured that it's unpleasant. Birdie won't want it in circulation."

"I'll ring her." George punched his radial button and a moment later heard Linnet saying, "Hi, how's it going?"

"There's a snag," George said, keeping his voice neutral. "Mr. Zalisky wants the cassette, plus all the rights, in exchange for something you won't want to see in circulation. It's another video cassette."

There was a short silence and then she said, "Have you seen it?"

"Not yet. He wants to show it to us."

More silence. George looked at Tina for help, but she was watching Nash Zalisky with narrowed eyes.

Linnet said in a small voice, "George, do you think he's bluffing?"

Without warning, George felt his knees begin to tremble. He said, "Talk to Tina, maybe she knows."

Tina took the phone and George sat down on the edge of the bed, staring at the blank TV screen.

He heard Tina say, "I think it would be wise to find out. OK, talk to you later." She turned to Zalisky and said, "We'd better see what we're dealing with."

She took Linnet's cassette out of the VCR and substituted Zalisky's.

Zalisky accepted the remote and said, "I think I'll use your fast-forward technique. I don't think any of us will want to view this in real time."

What followed ripped through George's brain like an express train. It was black and white footage shot from a fixed camera position. The location was a hotel room with the bed in the center of the screen. A man and a girl trotted jerkily in, dancing to and fro, tossing drinks down their throats, tossing clothes onto chairs, their bodies emerging rapidly from their colorless garb like trees stripped of leaves by a strong wind. A brief scene of jolting coupling was followed with barely a pause by another in a different position.

Zalisky stopped the film at a place where both faces were turned toward the camera. The man was at least three times the girl's age. He was heavy and balding. His meaty hands gripped the girl's slender hips holding her immobile on her knees. There was no expression whatsoever on her face. It was the same blank mask of immaculate young beauty she had shown George on the previous tape.

Zalisky said, "Sadly, I think we can all agree that we're looking at Birdie. What a shame. It really does undercut her bargaining power."

George crossed to the window and opened the curtains. Outside, the sky was as gray as the picture on the screen. Behind him, he heard Tina clear her throat.

"Let me get this straight," she said. "What are you proposing to do with this tape?"

"Nothing," Zalisky said. "For myself, I'd burn it and all the existing copies. Unfortunately, it isn't within my power to do so, and the owner of the tape has already received an interesting offer for it from a multimedia group. He would, of course, reject the offer and destroy the tape if we can come to a sensible agreement with Birdie regarding the Antigua Movie and the audio material she claims to possess."

"I see," Tina said. "So you'd like us to relay this offer to Ms. Walker? She should give up all materials and rights to them in return for a promise to suppress a few minutes of pornographic film. Is that the deal?"

Zalisky replied, "I'm sorry to say that it isn't simply a question of pornography. If you force me to continue, I'm told that we'll see the ingesting of cocaine, and at the end there is clear evidence that this was a commercial transaction."

"I should bloody well hope so," Tina said. "No one goes with a pig like that for the fun of it."

George turned to face the room again just in time to see Zalisky blinking in surprise. He said quickly, "You'd better call Ms. Walker again, Tina, and see how she wants us to proceed." The anger in Tina's voice calmed him, made him feel that his own emotional reaction was not entirely foolish.

While Tina was making the call, Zalisky said, "This pains me. It really does. Please, please, assure Birdie that I'm doing everything I can to protect her. If only she'd *talk* to me, I think she'd realize that I'm the only friend she's got. I do urge you to explain to her that where Jack's image and recordings are concerned we are the only game in town. No other record company will touch them once the contractual situation has been disclosed. And with this ... er ... pornography extant, I don't think anyone else will take her claims to title or copyright at all seriously. I would so much like to shield her from inevitable rejection and disappointment."

George considered picking the fussy little man up by the scruff of his neck and dangling him out of the ninth-story window until he shut up. Instead, he clasped his hands behind his back and rocked gently on his heels. The stocky man, who was still standing at Nash

241

Zalisky's elbow, seemed to be transfixed by the dirty gray image that was still shuddering on the TV screen.

Tina put down the phone, stepped across the three men, and switched the TV off. She said, "Well, Mr. Zalisky, you've given our client a lot to think about. In the meantime, thank you for coming. We'll be in touch."

Zalisky said, "Is that all? Doesn't Birdie at least want to exchange tapes? I wish you'd let me talk to her."

"Our client is very disappointed with your counter-offer." Tina sounded as if she were reciting lines. "She instructs me to say that she needs time to think it over."

"She has forty-eight hours," the little man snapped. "Even I can run out of patience. She'll have to learn to take the hand of friendship and not to scratch it." He rose to his feet and darted waspishly out of the room, leaving his minder to scuffle around collecting pillows and napkins. The minder's last act was to snatch the video out of the machine and stuff it in his pocket before hurrying into the corridor.

"Well, cheerio and *hasta la vista* to you too," Tina said to the closing door. "Jesus Christ, George, what a bust! I apologize. Paranoia, in this case, is entirely justified."

George sighed and sat down on the bed. "What did she really say?" he asked.

"She was pretty upset. But what the hell—she got all her back tax paid. That's not bad going for letting that little prat watch a ten-minute video."

"We've still got it, haven't we?"

Tina patted her shoulder bag. "Right here," she said. "I wouldn't give that extortionate little pile of parts a kick in the pants, let alone something he really wants."

George allowed himself to smile at last. The afternoon had gone very badly, but at least he felt Tina was on the team. "I thought you were going to have one of your famous lapses of good nature," he said.

"Did you see his face?" Tina asked indignantly. "I thought he was going to lick the screen. You know what's really pornographic, George? It's men's expressions when they're watching it. Not yours,

242

though. You looked as if you were watching a tragedy. Which maybe you were. Oh, fuck it. Let's pack up the VCR and get out of here."

"I wonder what she'll do now," George said, watching Tina fiddle with plugs and cables.

"Mr. Zalisky's one hungry little bastard," Tina said from behind the TV set. "He'll be in touch again. Linnet's got something he wants. He isn't going to leave it there."

V

Serenity

There's a rock'n'roll cliché which goes, "If you screw up really badly on stage, pretend it's part of the act and carry on." I tell all my baby bands that one. I also tell them not to be afraid of rock'n'roll clichés—they're there for a reason: they work.

Carrying on isn't always easy, especially if you need to carry on *con brio*. You can't buy *brio* in a supermarket. You can, however, buy it from a dealer who might call it by another name—like amphetamine sulphate or cocaine. That's another rock'n'roll cliché—one I tell my baby bands to handle with care. I'm in no position to advise not handling it at all, and besides it'd be a waste of breath. Bands do drugs or they don't. They pig out on them or they don't. It all depends on availability, personality, and peer pressure. It does not depend on sensible advice from a woman old enough to be their mother.

A little white candy gives you time and space. It clears your head and returns all the *brio* you lost during the course of a horrible day. A sensible woman knows better than to take more than a little. A sensible woman knows the difference between *brio* and bouncing off walls. Besides, this particular woman only had a little. It was in her first-aid kit and it was there for emergencies.

I thought I could go home to Robin's house, to warmth and light and company. But after the way Nash turned my plans upside-down a sensible woman would keep her bolt-hole a secret and her family out of the firing line.

I am a sensible woman, so here I am, back in the wretched dark place Marielle used to call home, with only my first-aid kit for company.

Like cocaine, loud dirty music is a good antidote to a busted day. It courses through the veins, racing from hips to fingertips, chasing frustration and depression out of your system.

I look in the trade papers, I search through *Time Out*, but I can't find the music I'm looking for. So I go to see InnerVersions play upstairs at the Fleece and Firkin instead.

I'm late and the first set is almost over. There's something wrong with the band—they're all isolated from one another, heads down, not communicating. The silly, baby-bastards have been fighting again. This band does not know how to use its negative energy. Great bands do. Great bands do not go into sulks and take it out on their audience. Great bands explode from inner tensions—they do not implode with a sad farty sigh. However bad a great band is on any particular night, it does not depress its fans, bring them down, or send them home cold.

InnerVersions piss me off. I leave in disgust, but on the way out I have an idea—an old idea, but it makes me laugh. I walk down the street till I find what I want at an all-night deli. I buy a packet of trickery and half a pound of flim-flam—the fixings for a bitch-brew.

Back at the Fleece and Firkin, I make sure the band has seen me but I don't join them. They're doing what they do best—which is avoiding each other in a collective huddle like a dysfunctional family on holiday. They see me and clearly they think I should come over. What do they expect me to do? Give them a pep talk? Use all *my* charge to top up their batteries while they bring me down? No, thank you, I'd prefer to sit in a dark corner and work any magic I still possess for my own benefit.

After a few minutes, Sapper comes over. I knew it would be him. He begins with some tedious complaint against Flambo and Dram. I smile at him—warm, affectionate, amused. It's a good smile and it puzzles him because it's such an inappropriate response to his whinging. Mysteriously, while smiling, I'm cutting slits in sultanas with my little silver penknife and I'm doing it secretively under the table.

"What're you doing?" he says, craning his neck, trying to see.

"Shhh," I say. "Don't be uncool."

"Oh," he says as if he understands, and while he's watching I slice a fragment from a small shapeless cake of a grey-brown substance. I stuff the fragment carefully into the slit in the sultana and then surreptitiously I put it in my mouth. I chew slowly and sip a little dark rum. My splendid smile becomes heavenly.

"What is it?" Sapper asks.

"Shh," I say again. "Serenity. Haven't you heard of it?" A good question to ask a young man who's both arrogant and ignorant.

"Isn't that something they took in the '60s?" he asks.

I say vaguely, "It went out of style when the heavy chemists took over."

"What does it do?" he asks.

"What is it called?" I counter. "That's what it does. Nothing spectacular. It's a natural substance. It just makes you feel better."

"Well then, lay some on me," he says. "I'm ready."

"Sure?"

"Bloody Flambo," he says. "He really gets up my nose ..."

While he's complaining and watching like a hawk, I repeat the procedure with the tiny brown fragment and the sultana.

"Chew it very slowly," I say. "Keep it in your mouth as long as you can—especially under your tongue. A sip of rum helps bring the sweetness out."

It's truly amazing what people will put in their mouths if someone tells them it will make them feel good. Sapper only has my word for it, but he takes his medicine like a lamb. I have expertise on my side, a little silver knife, a dexterous way with a sultana, and a sliver of substance X. It looks like '60s arcana, it tastes good, and, by golly, it'll do him good.

"Now shoo," I say, waving him away like a child I've indulged with a treat, "and don't come back till you're in a better mood." I send him off, an advertisement on two legs.

Sure enough, after only five minutes, first Corky, then Karen, Dram, and Flambo drop casually by for a taste of mama's little helper. Not only them but also their friends and their friends' friends. Word is out. Everyone wants a hit.

The band excepted, I make them pay. No one appreciates what they get for free. Besides, magic never comes cheap.

I do very good business. It cheers me up no end. The very novelty of it! I mean, whoever heard of a middle-aged lady dealing? It just isn't done. There's a dance in the old dame yet, and that's no lie.

The real joke of it is that when the band got up for the second set they were relaxed, grinning like lunatics and playing their tiny hearts out. They gelled, they yelled, and, clearly, from the audience's reaction, they hit the sweet spot. Oh yeah, I'll have them singing "All You Need Is Love" if they don't watch out.

Drugs do what you expect them to do. You are told what you're going to feel. Everyone else tells you what *they* are feeling, so you wait for it with suspense and anticipation. Hope and expectation make you feel what you think you should feel. In this case it's serenity.

Do you know that in the '20s and '30s they referred to the effects of good ol' peace'n'love marijuana as "reefer madness"? Who knows why. Maybe people just acted the way they thought they should act. Reefers were marketed as go-crazy stimulants, so people dutifully went crazy. Nowadays, Sweet Mary Jane is a chill-out soporific. Same drug, opposite effect. It all depends on marketing. So if you want a mellow evening, invest in a packet of sultanas, stuff them with scraps of diced shitake mushroom, and call your product Serenity. It's all in the name. No wonder Ecstasy took off like a rocket.

I wish I could have pulled the trick on Jack. But he knew me too well. Or maybe it only works on recreational users because, in the main, they're inexperienced and highly suggestible. Heavy users are neither.

But I don't want to think about failures tonight, so I put Jack out of my mind and concentrate on the band. They're doing a song called "Half Empty," and something nice is happening. Usually, Karen does the harmony, almost unnoticed, from behind the keyboard. Tonight, under the influence of Serenity, her voice melds with Sapper's in almost mystical exactitude. The most surprising thing of all is that Sapper—for once—is listening. He turns toward her and then goes over to the keyboard. They sing together, breathe together, and their voices make a perfect chord.

Ozzy Ireland appears and comes over to my table. There's rain on the peak of his baseball cap and an inquisitive look in his eye. "Staff meeting at Dog," he explains. "What's going on? Have you signed? They are talking *openly* about a Jack retrospective with ten new songs. There's a huge buzz on the top floor."

"Listen," I say, pointing to Sapper and Karen. "Sounds good, eh? Maybe, when InnerVersions fragments, you could build a new band around just those two."

While he's engaged, I slip away. The last thing I want to talk about is Dog and how confident Nash, Sasson, and their cronies are feeling.

VI

A Grotesque Suggestion

"And this," Barry Stears said, "is Alec Parry, who's done such sterling work for us. Alec, meet Mr. Zalisky."

Alec stepped forward ready to shake hands, but Mr. Stears blocked him. Mr. Zalisky, it appeared, did not want any physical contact.

"Alec has been our eyes and ears," Mr. Freel murmured.

Both men, Alec thought, seemed buttoned-up. Breath was being held. He was excited by the tension in the room. The whole huge house seemed to be whispering, Hush, let's have a respectful silence for the concept of wealth.

Brought up on magazine articles and TV programs about lifestyles of the rich and famous, Alec felt he should be more blasé, but now he was here what overwhelmed him was the simple fact that one man owned so much space. Here, the notion of conspicuous consumption was turned on its head: trophy possessions like antiques and Wurlitzers were booted out like so much catalog junk. The real prize was space and other men's time. While apparently doing nothing and being nobody, Mr. Zalisky commanded and received, at a moment's notice, the presence of two important, busy men. How the hell, Alec wondered, did a wizened runt manage a trick like that? It wasn't as if Alec was the only one who had been left to cool his heels for an hour in the cavernous hall. Mr. Stears and Mr. Freel had to wait their turn too. Astonishingly, neither man complained.

Of course, Alec was the last one in and would probably be the first out, but in the meantime, here he was at the center of the cabal. Birdie called them "the troika."

Alec sat in the only vacant chair, completing a square around a glass coffee table. The meeting wasn't even taking place in a proper

249

office. They were in a vast, bare room with a deep, deep carpet and thick brocade curtains which shimmered in dim light.

Mr. Freel began by saying, "Well, Alec, my boy, Mr. Zalisky wants to ask you a few questions." He then went on to ask them all himself, with a few interjections from Mr. Stears. Sir, it seemed, didn't even have to use his own vocal chords.

"I wonder if you'd go through the events leading up to our acquisition of a small can of film," Mr. Freel said.

"Well, as you know," Alec said, "I'd been monitoring phone calls made to and from Mrs. Emerson's house, and I noticed quite a cluster for Sheeny TeleCine. I reported the fact."

"This was before Birdie left the country?" Mr. Freel asked.

"Yes, sir. So I went there. It's a scruffy place in Brook Green. They specialize in transferring film to video. I think most of their business comes from people who want to look at their old home movies on TV. They do titles and graphics and other odds and ends. Anyway, Mr. Stears was looking for a film, so a tele-cine lab rang a few bells."

"Could Birdie have known you'd found the place?" Mr. Freel asked.

"I don't see how, sir. It wasn't as if I followed her there, or as if I talked to anyone who could have told her. I just had a look at the building and reported back to Mr. Stears."

"Now, the photographs you brought us," Mr. Freel said. "The ones you thought might be stills from a movie. Has anyone noticed they're missing?"

"No one's said a word. They came from a shoebox at the bottom of Mrs. Emerson's wardrobe. She ... I don't know, sir, she collects things. There's all sorts of stuff that looks as if, well, as if she'd only keep it because it had something to do with Jack. It's a real jumble. I only noticed because the envelope had 'Antigua' written on it."

Mr. Stears turned to Mr. Zalisky and said, "Apparently, Birdie's sister carried a torch for Jack. Her bedroom's something of a shrine to him."

"I'm sure she would be really upset if she knew anything was missing," Alec said, "and she hasn't been upset."

"Fair enough," Mr. Freel said. "We're simply trying to establish whether or not you've aroused suspicion."

"I don't think so, sir." Alec carefully prevented himself from blinking. "But the, er, burglary happened after Birdie went away, so I don't know how she reacted when she heard about that."

"Right. She packed up quite suddenly one night and left the next morning?"

"Yes, and I don't know why. A hand-delivered package arrived. It seemed to be something she was waiting for. It might've been money, but I don't know."

Mr. Freel and Mr. Stears glanced at sir, but sir remained silent.

"Where did she go?" Mr. Freel asked.

"I don't know. Nor do Grace or Mrs. Emerson. That's what she does—just blows without saying where. It's a bit of a joke in the family. I've looked at her passport, of course. There are immigration stamps from airports all over the world. But if she went abroad, she's back now. She called Mrs. Emerson from a public phone in Maidenhead last night."

The troika nodded. They already know that, Alec thought, disappointed.

They already knew a lot, Alec told Birdie later that night. "What they seemed most interested in was where you go. Where are you now, by the way?"

"In Devon," she said, the husky laugh making his ears tingle, "but don't tell anyone." Their secret.

"They speculated for a long time about whether you knew that I knew about the lab. And there was a lot about if the lab could manipulate sound and images. Which I couldn't really answer. Mr. Stears knows more about that than anyone."

"What conclusion did they come to?" Birdie asked.

"Well, Mr. Stears said he couldn't tell without seeing the video. He said the film he had was clearly made from the original negative, but obviously anyone could switch soundtracks if they had the original material. He said he'd have a better chance of diagnosing it if he could compare the film with the video. Mr. Freel said that obviously it was the video which was manipulated because that was the one they were intended to see. But he said that ultimately it didn't matter." Alec paused, then he said, "I'm muddled, Birdie. Did you manipulate the video?"

251

"There were two versions," she said, "with different soundtracks. They stole one—with your help. I showed Nash the other. Don't worry about it, Alec. I'm just keeping them on their toes. What did Nash say?"

"He didn't say anything. He just sat there fidgeting and making everyone really nervous."

Birdie laughed again.

"So there was a lot of talk about what you might have done in the lab and, especially, how much time you'd had to do it." Alec was wondering how to tell her the rest. He didn't want to upset her even if she was in Devon. But he had to warn her.

It had come unexpectedly after Mr. Freel said, "Does it really make any difference if the video was doctored? That's Jack's voice we heard on the soundtrack. We're all in agreement about that, aren't we? So we have concrete proof there is at least one brand-new song—and it's unbelievably good."

Mr. Stears said, "I know you'd be satisfied with a few extra tracks, but I've got a far more exciting idea in mind. I went over it again and again with Junior Moline. He looked up all his old notes—such as they are—and nowhere can he find any reference to a song called 'Sliding Widows.' He doesn't remember anything like it. Nor does Teddy."

"That doesn't mean a thing," Mr. Freel said. "We know Jack was planning a new album several months before he died. David Palmer mentions it in that *Rolling Stone* article. Jack kept writing up to his death."

"But that doesn't explain the quality of the sound—especially if Jack was recording himself at home," Mr. Stears argued. "Junior couldn't explain it either. He thought at first that it was a *digital* recording. He was convinced. But then he said it couldn't possibly be because digital recording simply wasn't around then. But he kept saying the quality of the sound was too good to be analog. Digital didn't exist then, Sasson. But it does *now*."

"You're crazy, Barry," Mr. Freel said. "This is a complete red herring. This is where those 'Elvis is alive and well and living on Mars' stories come from. The important thing is that we now have evidence that previously unreleased recordings do actually exist. Besides, Junior had nothing to do with any of Jack's production after *Hard Candy*. Jack produced *Hard Time* himself, working with other engineers. Maybe Birdie had the soundtrack digitally remastered. That's done all the time."

It was as if they'd forgotten Alec's presence and were continuing an old argument. The only one to remember was Mr. Zalisky. He spoke up for the first time saying timorously, "Maybe this isn't the time or place for such a discussion?"

It was comical to Alec that an interruption as weak and uncertain as this made Mr. Freel and Mr. Stears shut up like school kids caught shouting in chapel. That was real power, Alec thought, when you didn't even have to raise your voice or sound halfway confident but you could still make grown men stand to attention.

Reluctantly, he reported what Mr. Stears had said. There was a moment of silence. Then Birdie said, "Oh Alec, that's grotesque." Just four words from a long way away, but he could hear a lifetime of sadness in her voice. They continued to speak for a while longer, but when at last he rang off, Alec felt heavy with her distress. He looked across the room at Grace, who was curled up in a chair pretending to read *The God of Small Things* but actually listening to his side of the conversation.

"What did she say?" Grace asked.

"She said, 'That's grotesque,'" he told her, imitating Birdie's tone of voice.

"Well it *is*," Grace said angrily, "really stupid and cruel. Lin's right—whatever you give them, they always want more."

"I know," Alec said. He was hiding his exhilaration, even from himself. He wished he still had the piece of film Mr. Stears was so excited about. He wished he could use his own ears to compare the quality of the sound against a digitally remastered copy of *Hard Candy* or *Hard Time*. There must be some way, he thought, of distinguishing a track which was digitally recorded from an analog track which had been digitally remastered. If anyone could say for sure that it was a digital recording, then Mr. Stear's "bigger prize" would be within his grasp. What if Mr. Stears was right? What if that was Birdie's big secret? She'd go to any length to protect Jack if he were still alive.

253

"It's so absolutely dumb and off the wall," Grace said, as if she could read his thoughts. "If Mr. Stears is hinting Jack's still alive, he's out of his mind. Wouldn't I know about it? Wouldn't Mum? I hope he keeps shit like that to himself. Poor Auntie Lin."

"Don't you get sad too," Alec said. He went over to her and sat on the arm of her chair. "It's all right. Mr. Stears is an idiot."

Grace nestled against him. She was, he thought, both harder and softer than she had been before the night of the big bust. He never quite knew what to expect.

She said, "If it wasn't so tough on Mum and Auntie Lin, I'd say I wish he'd say it out loud and get so much egg on his face he'd never be able to show himself in public again."

"May he die of lingering humiliation," Alec said.

"Then we'd appoint you Managing Director of Memo Movies in his place." Barry Stears, since the big bust, had become the scapegoat, the author of Alec's corruption. Grace, in particular, seemed to find Barry Stears a useful excuse for all his wrongdoing. Long may it last, Alec thought, grateful that she needed an excuse as much as he did. She likes me, he thought for the hundredth time.

"What does your Auntie Lin do in Devon?" he asked, stroking Grace's hair.

"She goes fishing," Grace said. Her cheek was resting on his thigh. "She's got an old friend down there. An old boyfriend, Mum says."

"Fishing? I can't imagine Lin up to her thighs in cold water."

"You'd be surprised," Grace said. "She says it's the most fascinating occupation in the world. She's quite zen about it."

"Is she zen about the old boyfriend too?" Alec coiled a lock of Grace's hair round his forefinger and held his breath.

"She never says a word about him. You know what they say about old flames, don't you? They never die—they just cool off. But all you have to do, if you want to revive them, is to blow on them. Shall I show you?"

"Ooh, yeah," he said, "go on then."

Devon, Alec thought as he tumbled onto the floor.

VII

Thank God for Lipstick

Every song has to come to an end. While you're recording, if you can't think of a proper ending, the fade will save your ass—repeat to fade. On stage live, however, you need to find a way out and hit it with conviction. Give the audience something to applaud. Of course, that can cut both ways: you might be giving an audience the perfect chance to boo and chase you offstage with flying beer cans and other messy missiles. You can find yourself after a gig, cowering in your dressing room, swearing to give up music forever. If you don't like risk, I tell my baby bands, get a job in a dry cleaner's. It's much, much safer.

Real life, sometimes, is like playing live. There's no graceful fade when you run out of steam. You either have to carry on carrying on or you have to come to a dramatic conclusion. For all the planning you put into a certain phase of your life, it's hard to see how it will end. Will you be taking encores, or will you be shivering in your dressing room? It all depends on whether or not you've made your audience dance to your tune. Have you been able to please a hostile crowd? Or have you not?

I knew when I began this phase of my life that I was facing a very hostile crowd. Now, it doesn't look as if I'll be able to get offstage without beer in my hair. There was a message on my voice mail from Tina Cole, which said, "Linnet, sorry to ring you so late. I don't know how he got my home number, but I've just had a call from Mr. Zalisky. He wants to remind you that you only have twenty-four hours left to come to an arrangement with him. He says that you should present yourself and *all* the materials, both audio and visual, at his home. You may bring representatives, but you must come in person. I said I thought it was unlikely that you'd agree to an arrangement like that, but he ignored me completely. He said if you don't deliver, you will get nothing but grief. That's all."

I lay down on the canvas lounger and wondered what smart-as-a-whip Tina Cole would do now? No advice from her. She thinks he's just saying put up or shut up, when actually he's saying, Birdie Walker, I've got *your* number. You're nailed.

It's interesting that Nash picks Tina's home number, not George's, to demonstrate his infallibility. I bet he had a choice. I bet he thought about it and decided she'd be the more objective conduit for his message.

Karen tells me she has dreams sometimes of standing onstage in front of a packed house, playing a number she doesn't know on a keyboard which is slowly turning into a tablecloth. Every time she moves her hands, another couple of keys have become useless and she'll soon be reduced to playing with one finger. Maybe Karen is dreaming for me.

I slide headphones over my ears and listen to one of the great rock'n'roll dreamers until I find enough consolation to think about sleep. It's five in the morning and dawn's breaking. For most of my life, I've gone to bed with the lark. Take that how you will—I'll take it lying down.

I remove the headphones just in time to hear someone hammering on the door downstairs. Hammer away, I think, there's no one at home. Marielle's not here, and nor am I.

Then, as the knocking continues, a lifetime of training kicks in. I get up and flush the contents of my first-aid kit down the toilet. I brush my hair, powder my nose, and put on a good pair of shoes. Trapped in Marielle's wretched apartment, if someone comes in, I can neither fight nor bolt. In any case, as the song says, I'm a lover not a fighter. If someone comes in and I am, as Nash hinted, nailed, I want to greet the intruders looking good.

I won't make it easy. I won't open the door for them. But whatever weapons I have, I'll use. Unfortunately, my best weapons are useless against brute force. A smile, wit, charm, and good shoes only work against those who are vulnerable to them.

The hammering increases in volume and ends with a splintering crash. Heavy footsteps on the narrow stairs come to a halt at my door. Then the cry: "Police. Open up."

Police? Unbelievable—pull the other one.

But it is, indeed, the police. "We have a warrant to search these premises."

"What on earth for?"

"Illegal substances."

"Please tell me this is a joke," I say. "What illegal substances?"

"We must ask you to accompany an officer to the police station."

I am stunned. I refuse. But, as the song goes, "When the Lord says 'Get ready,' you gotta go." So I went.

Here is the kicker—as I went out onto the early-morning street with a policeman on either side of me, two flashguns went off in my face. I wasn't expecting them and I didn't have time to turn my head. I was, as Nash implied, nailed. When the police and the press are in cahoots, there's nowhere to run, nowhere to hide.

The story broke in the first edition of the evening paper the very same day. There was a picture of me on the front page. I'm flanked by two smug cops and I'm looking straight into the lens with a defiant expression on my face. Thank God for lipstick, I say, because, cruelly, the picture editor also inset an old photo of me dancing with Jack from over twenty-five years ago. There we were, supple and slender, bright hair flying, without a care in the world. And here she is now, old superbitch in a raincoat, allegedly caught dealing drugs to school kids at a nightclub—the woman the British public most loves to hate.

Yes, yes, they rifled the archives and resurrected my history. They reprinted bowdlerized versions of the worst stories. They said that my fight for control of Jack's fortune had ended in failure and that, after my looks faded, I'd been reduced to prostitution and drug-dealing to make ends meet.

I shouldn't have been surprised. When they really want to hurt a woman, the media always accuses her of faded looks, sexual depravity, and vice against children. No, I really shouldn't be shocked or upset. It is, after all, only more of what I was so accustomed to when I was young.

The funny thing was that when I saw the pictures and read the article, I was tucked up in Tina Cole's spare bed with a glass of her best Scotch to calm me down. Free. The police didn't charge me with anything, because of course there was nothing to charge me with. They couldn't put me in jail for sharing a packet of sultanas with a bunch of kids.

Eventually, they admitted that they'd been misinformed. But they didn't apologize. They said that they did not alert the press. I pretended not to believe them, but I do. That piece of planning has someone else's fingerprints all over it.

The police never apologize; they simply release you into an indifferent world without a stain on your character. The world is indifferent because it is only interested in stains. Clean is boring. Clean does not get your picture on the front page.

"It's not such a bad picture," Tina says. "You don't look like a criminal."

What does she know about good or bad pictures? She's never had photographers hiding at the bottom of her stairs or under gratings trying to see up her skirt. She's never had to use kitchen doors, fire exits, or lavatory windows when she wants a little privacy. I can't imagine her covered by a blanket on the floor of a car because she's had a little too much to drink at a party and doesn't want it splashed all over the papers the next day.

She's still trying to come to terms with the notion that her reliable, organized Ms. Walker is a woman with a past and a debatable reputation. She is, herself, a straightforward person. What you see is what you get. She can't quite appreciate that in me she got unimaginably more than what she saw. She wanted efficiency and know-how. Well, be grateful, Tina Cole—that's exactly what I gave you. Don't blame me because you saw only what you wanted to see.

She says, "I don't understand why the police thought you were dealing drugs."

"Because they were told. Someone must've seen me with the band. But this has nothing to do with drugs, Tina. It's about searching the place where I was staying. It's about reducing my bargaining power. It's about what's done to notorious women."

258

It's so strange, isn't it, Tina Cole, to find out that your quiet Ms. Walker, with her respectful manner, mixes with rock musicians and kids in clubs. It isn't dignified in a woman her age. OK, so maybe we all went a bit crazy when we were young, but most of us grew up and hid the Strat in the cupboard under the stairs. Most of us got married, bred, and paid mortgages. Most middle-aged women would rather stay home and watch *Love Story* than racket around in clubs after midnight. Or would they, Tina Cole? Maybe older women do what's expected of their age group rather than what they'd like to do.

Which is worse, Tina Cole, a woman suspected of dealing drugs or an older woman suspected of dealing drugs? A woman racketing around by herself in a club or an older woman doing the same thing? It's a fine point, but a telling one. If you want the question answered, read the evening papers—they'll tell you exactly what to think about your oh-so-respectable Ms. Walker.

My two worlds have collided in a way I never intended.

She says, "These new songs, materials, whatever it is Mr. Zalisky wants—what's happened to them?"

I sigh, and tell her simply that they're safe. But she's read the article. She's read the paragraph which said, "A leopard does not change its spots and it seems that Birdie, after so many years in the wilderness, is still trying to feather her nest at a rock legend's expense. A spokesperson for a well-known record company today said, 'She approached us several weeks ago with tapes of dubious provenance that she claims are Jack's last work. If true, this would be of inestimable interest to the record-buying public. But as no one has yet been allowed to verify the quality, or indeed the existence, of these songs we cannot comment.' With the twenty-fifth anniversary of Jack's death coming up, we shouldn't be too surprised if many such claims surface. There is still a fortune to be made from the sales of records by dead rock stars." The article then went on to evaluate the posthumous worth of everyone from Elvis to Kurt Cobain, giving them marks out of five and using little money-bag symbols as counters.

Without a doubt, this article is killing several birds with one stone, and I am the least of them. I don't have to rack my brains to decide who gave the journalist this information. Or why.

Tina says, "Why does the record company spokesman say the tapes may be bogus?"

"Because he wants to say that I'm bogus. He wants to say that my ownership is bogus. He wants to create a buzz and drum up controversy—is this the real Jack or is it a clever fake? One way or another, it's great advertising for the record company and terrible publicity for me."

"It's sneaky," she says, nodding.

" 'She approached us,' " I quote. "Doesn't that sound shady? Isn't it a wonderful choice of words? 'With tapes of dubious provenance.' Peddling dodgy bootlegs in car-parks. You'd never guess from that who's been importuning whom, would you?" I sigh again.

"Well, look, why don't you get some rest?" she says awkwardly. "We'll sort something out later."

"I'm not asking you to sort it out," I say. "It's way too murky. Besides, I know what you charge. I work for you, remember. Or I used to work for you before I got my picture in the paper as a drug dealer. That won't look too cool, will it, in your line of business?"

"Oh, bugger that," she says. But she's thought about it. She'd be a fool not to think about it, and she's no fool. She leaves, closing the door softly as if I'm an invalid—an unemployed invalid.

I sit on her spare bed and massage my feet with hand cream. The good shoes, which made my legs look long and slim in the photograph and which caught the eye of a detective inspector, have crippled me. They were never designed to be worn for fourteen hours straight. They're impress-the-punters pumps, which should be removed before your feet swell and you need a can opener.

Someone ratted on me. I think about lines of communication and who is in touch with whom. I think about my baby band. My mind settles on Flambo: not only is he a piss-poor drummer, but he blames me for rearranging InnerVersions, rearranging their sound, and consequently for marginalizing him. He got high on Serenity. Therefore Serenity, for him, is a real drug and I am a drug dealer. If he wants to get rid of me, ratting on me to Sasson might be the way to do it.

I noodle on it sleepily. If Flambo were not such a piss-poor drummer, would I be so quick to call him a rat? Even now, after all

260

these years, I'm still liable to believe that good musicians will be better human beings than bad musicians. It's been proved to me a thousand times in a thousand ways that good art does not, *per se*, come from good people. And yet, and yet ... Maybe I will always be susceptible. If Flambo were a shit-hot drummer, I would not automatically suspect him of being a rat.

And anyway, it doesn't fuckin' signify who ratted on me. The only person to blame is myself. I disobeyed the first law of bunko—which is never, never, never pull a stunt on your own doorstep.

On the other hand, maybe that doesn't signify worth a damn either—if the troika wanted to hang me out to dry, they'd have found a way without Serenity.

Part 5

AIN'T GOIN' DOWN

"She's sweet—does she mean it? … She's mean—
I think she means it."   Jack

I

Patchwork

In a drawer beside Robin's bed was a rose-colored silk sachet. The rose silk was shot through with gold and silver thread. It came from a Kashmiri scarf which Jack once gave Lin and which Lin once left behind after a flying visit. Robin appropriated the scarf. It was her favorite, she wore it all the time. But small children who experiment with paint and scissors are very hard on favorite garments. The scarf retired, injured. Robin was never a woman to give up on beautiful favorites, so pieces of it appeared in one of her layered hippie skirts, in a tiny waistcoat she made for Grace, and a sachet she made to hold potpourri.

Now, as well as potpourri, it held an ugly shapeless lump of metal—a gift, again inadvertent, from Lin. She came home in the dead of the night, after that dreadful, empty day, her face scraped bare with shock and grief, her clothes smelling of charcoal and her hands balled into fists. Robin, utterly bereft herself, badly needing comfort herself, with no words, no consolation to offer, simply opened her door, her arms, to her widowed sister. And Lin opened her clenched fist to show the ugly fragment hidden there.

"The Egyptian ring," she said. "He was wearing it. Oh Robin, there was nothing else. Keep it for me. I've held it for hours. I know it's insane because it's been through fire, but I've been trying to keep it warm. And I can't. It used to be lovely. Now it's hideous, but it's all I've got."

So Robin kept it. And with it she kept the smell of charcoal and ashes, of killing smoke, of soot and smuts, trapped in a misshapen lump which had once been bright Egyptian gold. Every so often, she changed the potpourri because, even now, she sometimes woke up

265

with tears in her eyes, certain that she could smell smoke. Lin never asked for it back.

Robin was sure she hadn't forgotten—how could anyone forget a thing like that? But that end had been the beginning of a rootless, drifting existence for Lin, with never a place to call her own, never a place to settle down and gather treasures around her. Because a week later she disappeared, chased out of Robin's house by door-steppers, unceasing phone calls, and envelopes dropped through the letterbox.

Twenty-five years ago, Robin thought, and it seemed like yesterday. Especially now. She peered through a crack in the curtains and could identify at least half a dozen strange cars in the street outside. She couldn't answer the phone and finally Grace unplugged it.

"They're mad," Grace said. "Auntie Lin pushing drugs? Why are they saying these things?"

All Robin could do was shrug helplessly. "They've always said terrible things about her. I don't know why."

"I bet there are whole chapters about it in feminist psych books," Grace said. "Punishing famous women or something like that. If there aren't there should be. Maybe I'll write one if I stick to psychology."

"Why wouldn't you stick to psychology?" Robin asked anxiously. "Is it Alec? Is he telling you to give up your job?"

"Don't be silly, Mum. But women's lives seem to go where the wind blows, and it might be more fun to blow back to London. Maybe I'm tired of serious subjects. A job in film or TV ..."

"I thought you liked psychology."

"I did. I do. But at the moment all I'm doing is helping no-hopers. I'm like a junior social worker. You can't expect me to stick with a career I've grown out of."

"Have you grown out of it?" Robin asked quite tartly. "I'd have thought a little understanding of human behavior might be pretty useful to you."

"It's Alec, isn't it? You've never liked him, have you?"

"I never said that. But I do think he could've been more honest with us."

"Well he's being honest now," Grace said, "and if that isn't good enough for you, we can both leave."

Why did everyone always leave her or threaten to leave? It seemed to be everyone's ultimate weapon. And it worked. The thought of the people she loved dropping out of her life frightened Robin and made her obedient. It caused no end of trouble too. Even the threat of putting her crazy old mother in a home where Robin couldn't keep an eye on her had driven her into an action which exasperated her husband. Me or your mother, he said. Choose. She couldn't choose, and her husband left.

She wanted everyone. She knew what it was like to live with a gaping hole in her heart where a loved someone had been, and she didn't ever want to repeat the experience. Even if it means a lifetime of … of what? Servitude? The word "blackmail" fell with a thud into the back of her mind.

Without thinking, she reached out her hand and plucked a white Venetian mask from the top of her chest of drawers. She held it in front of her face and said in hollow, theatrical tones, "Go, my child. If you have learned all I have to teach you, then go. A strong woman has no need of her mother. My work here is done. Go, and," she added, running out of invention, "may the force be with you."

"You're a nutter, Mum," Grace said, laughing uncertainly.

Robin tied the mask securely onto her head and opened the curtains. All at once, a man with a camera popped up from behind the hedge and took her picture.

"Come away," Grace said. "They'll think you're Auntie Lin."

"Tough," Robin said. But she stood back from the window. She kept the mask on because she didn't want Grace to see the heads of sweat on her lip or the fear in her eyes. Even joking, she couldn't tell Grace to leave without paying a heavy fine.

"We're going stir-crazy," Grace said. "When's Alec going to come back with the bread? Where's Auntie Lin?"

"I don't know," Robin said. "She can't phone 'cos she knows I won't answer and she won't come here with all these idiots on the doorstep."

"Maybe she's gone back to Devon."

"Maybe."

Twenty-five years ago, there had been islands and villas and yachts to escape to, Robin thought. Where were they now? She couldn't imagine any of those rich stars, made respectable by longevity, swooping down like knights in shining armor to scoop Lin up and spirit her away this time. Not after this latest sleazy, seedy, slimy smear. Which no one was bothering to retract. Lin no longer looked the part, no longer looked like the child princess in distress. All the aging knights and princes had grown-up families and supermodel brides to support. This latest slur cast Lin as the wicked old witch. Princes don't gallop up on white horses to rescue wicked old witches. Wicked old witches burn in their own ovens, Robin thought. Only the young and lovely are fit to be rescued. Even aging princes knew that. Especially aging princes. The old and the wicked must, perforce, rescue themselves, if they could. Or burn if they couldn't.

The smell of charcoal and smoke mixed with potpourri drove Robin out of her bedroom and up to the attic to work on a garment fashioned from a thousand pieces of silk remnants. Somewhere, she thought, there was still a square of the old rose-colored scarf. She searched through her boxes.

If I find it, shall I use it? she wondered. No. Or only if I make this into a dress for Lin. Lin's scarf was Lin's past. No one else deserved it. However much a private client was prepared to pay, Robin knew she couldn't sew a remnant of Lin's story into a garment which Lin wouldn't wear.

Bugger that, Robin thought. And bugger the rich private client. I'll make this silk patchwork into a dress for Lin. I'll clothe her in her own beautiful youth, in her fairy-tale past.

Robin paused for a moment, picturing Lin swishing into a room wearing the riot of glowing colors. She nodded, and Lin smiled back at her. Yes.

Swirling Lin morphed into spinning Jack, strutting in front of thousands of screaming fans in a coat of many colors. Robin made the coat for him and he wore it on his last tour. Perfectly cut to swing and shimmer under spotlights, to be seen from the back rows of theaters and stadia, to let his fair skin breathe in the heat and frenzy of per-formance—it was Robin's best work. And like Jack, it went up in flames twenty-five years ago. Gone.

Time tangled itself in a knot and Robin sewed, pinned, and cut till lunchtime. A shape was forming in her mind, a queenly shape, a garment to be worn with pride. It must have a high collar, she thought. Lin, you won't hang your head in this frock, no way.

Downstairs, in the kitchen, she found that Grace and Alec were making toast. Some of yesterday's chicken soup was simmering on the stove.

"Sit down, Mum," Grace said. "Alec wants to tell you something."

II

Negative Energy

"No," I say, "no, no, no." Oh I have power—the power of refusal. I can't make stuff happen the way I want it to, but I can stop it happening.

"Your forty-eight hours," Tina reminds me.

"Not mine," I say. "Forty-eight hours was arbitrarily and unilaterally imposed by Nash."

"Haven't you taken enough stick?" she asks reasonably.

"Yes," I say, equally reasonably.

We're sitting in her living room. Three of us. The curtains are closed. Outside, lurking, is a handful of reporters. Someone whose name we can only take a wild guess at knows I'm here and has leaked Tina's address. She, in spite of her reasonable tone, is angry. George is worried. He sits in a deep armchair, his fingers playing nervous scales on his ample shirt front.

"But if you talk to Nash," she says, "won't he call the dogs off?"

"He can try," I say. "But I think his understanding of dogs is incomplete. They're harder to stop than to start. Please take my word on that one."

"Isn't it worth a try?"

"From your point of view, it is; from mine, it isn't. I can solve your problem by finding somewhere else to stay—which I will do; this is no way to thank you for rescuing me from the police station."

"Stay with me," George says.

I smile at him—he's very sweet. "Thank you, but that'd only transfer this gig to another venue."

"I don't think Fay would exactly rejoice," Tina says.

"She wouldn't," I agree, "and I'm not going to do it."

"Well, what *are* you going to do?" she asks. "It seems to me that there are two ways to go: one is talk to Nash Zalisky, and the other is talk to the press."

"The third is leave the country," I say. "That's what I usually do in these circumstances."

"You'll lose everything," George points out. "Plus you risk having that pornography released on the Internet or whatever Mr. Z plans to do with it." He shifts uncomfortably. "I wish that damn lawyer would pull his finger out and get here."

That damn lawyer is someone he and Tina trust. Their inexperience is most obvious here. The lawyer is not a music-biz lawyer—he has that in his favor, but he has that against him too. Talk to a lawyer. Talk to Nash. Talk to the press. All reasonable suggestions—if you don't know lawyers, Nash, and the press like I do.

I am tired. I drank too much Scotch last night, hoping it would help me sleep. Fatigue and hangover are sitting between my ears like twin incubi, jabbing my brain and giving me visions of other times when it all went wrong. They winkle out the memories of loss and theft, of impotence and humiliation. They speak through my mouth and say "no" to every suggestion. They have hidden all my chutzpah in their deep dark pockets.

"I'll make some coffee," I say, and I leave Tina and George to make their naïve suggestions to each other. I go to the kitchen, pretending to be quiet, efficient Ms. Walker. She may be in a jam, she may be causing a jam, but she's ever so helpful and she uses real beans. Her mask is perfect: she's useful, tidy, organized. She expends her energy in the service of others. And she doesn't cost much.

Birdie grimaces behind Ms. Walker's tidy mask.

The phone rings and is answered. A moment later, George comes through to the kitchen. He says, "It's Mr. Z. Tina's talking to him."

I let him carry the tray and follow him.

Tina shields the mouthpiece with her hand and says, "Mr. Zalisky is summoning you to Badlands. He's sending a car."

Tidy Ms. Walker says nothing. She begins to pour the coffee.

"Linnet?" Tina says. "You don't have to go alone. I'll come with you."

"So will I," says George. "So will that damn lawyer when he bloody gets here."

271

"Mr. Zalisky says that you'll have all the protection you need from the media at Badlands."

Ms. Walker hands George a cup. Black, no sugar. She knows what he likes. She places a cup on the table beside Tina. White, one sugar. She considers Mr. Zalisky and his summons. She knows what he'd like, too.

"Linnet?"

I say, "Tell Nash thanks, but no thanks. Tell him that Ms. Walker will be making a statement to the press—the sort of statement which will have the media camping on *his* doorstep within half an hour of its release. And press helicopters flying over his house. Tell him especially about the helicopters and how noisy they are. If he can lie about me, I can lie about him. And I'm *way* more inventive than he is. Tell him further that I've put up with shit before and I can do it again. He isn't hurting me, he's just raising my price."

"But he *is* hurting you," George says.

"As for his forty-eight-hour deadline," I say, smiling pleasantly at George, "here's one of my own: tell Nash that unless he comes up with an acceptable offer within forty-eight hours I will call a press conference in Hyde Park, at the site of Jack's last free concert, and I will explain the situation and then publicly burn all the materials, both audio and visual. If I can't do one last honest deal for Jack, the whole lot goes up in smoke. The symbolism will be very clear."

"For God's sake, Linnet," Tina says. "You won't do that."

"Try me," I say. "What have I got to lose? Money? If Nash has his way, I'll be robbed blind anyway. My reputation? I never had one. Tell Nash, it's cash or conflagration. His choice."

Tina looks at me as if I'm a child having a tantrum. Mature women negotiate reasonably. I walk away and go to the spare bedroom before she can talk me down. That was my message, Tina Cole. Deliver it.

Ten minutes later, they come to find me, and by that time my bag is packed. I say, "The usual procedure is a decoy car at the front door and a greengrocer's van at the back—in the absence of which, I'll call a cab. I'll contact you at the office later."

"Stop it," Tina says. "Let's talk about this."

272

"All right, but there isn't much alternative. I know you think I'm being destructive and unreasonable, but this is an unreasonable situation. Mature, reasonable folk with mature, reasonable aspirations don't succeed in rock'n'roll."

"So you put a gun to your own head and say, 'If you don't give me what I want, I'll pull the trigger,' is that it?"

"Sounds pretty much like it," I say, and start to laugh. "What did Nash say?"

"He said you were willful and cutting off your nose to spite your face. Then he hung up on me." She thought about it for a moment and then said, "Willful? I haven't heard that one since I was about five years old. He really does think you're a moron, doesn't he?"

"Well," I say, "he thinks I'm a hysterical, greedy woman. Same thing maybe."

George says, "Did you mean any of what you said?"

"Oh yes."

"Then start with the press release," he says. "I wouldn't mind seeing Mr. Z take a dose of his own medicine."

"Right away, Mr. Adler," I say, "as soon as I get settled. It's top of the list."

"Where are you going?" Tina asks. "Look, I know I'm pissed off with the twats outside, but I think you'd better stay. George won't forgive me if I let you go."

The phone rings and she goes to answer it. George looks at me and says, "She's right—I won't. She isn't asking you to leave, you know. I know you think you should, but it isn't necessary." He has a relieved, twinkly look in his eyes. I know that look. I've done something which pleases him. What is it?

He says, "The thing about Tina is that she's very concerned with fairness. Unfairness makes her angry. She isn't angry with you."

Ah, that's it. Efficient Ms. Walker has behaved like a child throwing a wobbler, which you'd think was a great big turnoff. But, in fact, sweet George digs it. It allows him safely to hold my hand, protect me, and explain the world to me. Essentially, it has allowed him to become parental in his relationship with me. He can act in the mask

273

which suits him best—the Good Father's mask. Yes, sweet Mr. Adler is at his most comfortable as the Good Father.

"Tell me about the tapes," he says. "Are they really so valuable?"

"Yes. And no. They're just songs taped on a little four-track. They were only meant to be guide tracks. But death and age have given them enormous value. There's a mystique too. It's all part of the unfairness. Why does one singer gather mystique and value and another drop out of sight? Why is fame and success splashed so liberally on a few and not on others? It's neither fair to the famous nor to the forgotten. Value doesn't necessarily have anything to do with quality. Jack's tapes are extremely valuable because so many people want them."

"And for no other reason?"

"They're good songs," I say. "But that's not what's causing all the fuss, is it?"

"No," he says. "Fame and notoriety are causing all the fuss. What I want to know is how valuable are they to you?"

"I can't say." I think about it. "If your house was on fire, and all the people you loved were already safe, what would you rescue?"

"Ah yes, that question," he says. "But you say you'll destroy them."

"Yes."

"Wait a minute," he says, "something's coming back to me. In olden times, some parents would murder their own children rather than let them be taken into slavery. I don't agree with it, but you can see their point."

If you let a man answer his own question, he will find an answer he understands. He may not understand *you*, but an answer is generally a satisfactory substitute for understanding.

Fortunately, Tina returns before the dear man's answers become even more absurd. "Well, well, well," she says, "your lousy reputation's working in your favor for a change. Mr. Zalisky seems to think you're capable of acts of vandalism and self-destruction beyond my wildest dreams. What a way to do business!"

"He believes her?" George asked.

"We-ell, maybe he thinks he can't afford to disbelieve her. Linnet, what did you ever do to the man? He's very, very weird about you."

"I went to the movies with him once a long time ago," I say. "But it isn't me. He's weird about Jack. It's that old mystique again. Jack had it in truckloads."

"No," Tina says. "he's weird about you. Why do I think he's a pervert?"

"A pervert?" says Good Father George.

"I want to send myself to the laundry after talking to him. Why?"

I just smile and shake my head.

"And how did he get to be so rich and powerful? He's such a warty little shrimp."

"He does challenge evolutionary theory, doesn't he?" I say.

"It really frightens me when two women discuss a man they don't like," George says. "So would you mind sticking to the point. What did the warty little shrimp agree to?"

Tina consults her phone pad. "Well, subject to Linnet's approval, the suggestion is that we send our lawyer over to talk to his lawyer."

"Lawyers," I say. "He's got them in football teams. We've got to discuss that."

III

Q BIRDIE WALKER: As mad and bad as ever. "Jack did what Jack did. Shit happens." Now the face that launched a thousand hits takes on Super Spider. Who's your money on?

Words: Ty Casparo

Photographs: Roy O'Brien

It is one of those soft late summer days and the overgrown garden behind the Chelsea Arts Club is suspended for a moment between sunshine and showers. Ms. Walker sits on the terrace with a glass of wine in her hand, treating the aging hipsters to a rare glimpse of Birdie unbuttoning.

"Rule number one," wannabe music scribes were taught back in the bad old days, "Birdie walks, but she doesn't talk." Those were the days when rock chicks were mad, bad, and dangerous to know. So how's she feeling today? Bad? Not so's you'd notice. Dangerous? Well, you might want to avoid those Ibiza-trash heels. Mad? Ah, now you're talking! "Mad as hell," she steams.

She is not, as you might suppose, referring to her recent arrest for allegedly dealing mind-altering substances to minors. "If it weren't so stupid, it would be funny," she says loftily. "It's not my fault if someone can't tell the difference between a handful of sultanas and Class-A drugs." Not something you could accuse Birdie herself of. "History," she retorts with a flick of the once-famous golden mane. "I'm not apologizing for the past."

But wasn't it the excesses of yesteryear that added her legendary lover Jack to the list of drug fatalities? "Jack did what Jack did, and he didn't do anything by halves. Fame, drugs, and paranoia can be a destructive cocktail. Shit happens." Shit happening seems to be on the Bird brain today and that's what's making her so mad. "Jack was convinced the record companies were ripping him off and, surprise, surprise, they still are. More than ever now with Jack's anniversary coming up—all the old stuff repackaged, prepackaged, your usual multimedia T-shirt, Jack-on-the-rack culture—coordinated by Super Spider."

Super Spider, it seems, is Birdie-speak for Nash Zalisky, the eccentric, reclusive mogul behind many of the pipelined Jack projects. "He always wanted to lure us into his web," Birdie shudders. "If Jack hadn't died, Super Spider would've sucked him dry. Not many people know that Nash was totally obsessed. He still is. He's been searching basements and rubbish bins for anything to do with Jack: photos, nail clippings—you name it. So he comes to me and says, 'What've you got?' And I'm like, Whoa! I'm not into the necrophilia thing. Besides, why should I give him anything of Jack's? New stuff, new deal—or no deal."

Hold on a minute! New stuff? Can the original Rock Widow mean that there's a secret legacy snatched from the grave? It seems she can. A forgotten stash of demo tapes and some unique sought-after movie footage have miraculously surfaced just in time for the eagerly anticipated Jack-fest. But we aren't talking about mere nail clippings now, are we? "We are not. Dog spokesmen want to downgrade what's been discovered, but that's for the usual exploitative reason: they want to own it, but they don't want to pay."

Almost from the start, Birdie claims, corporate double-dealings left Jack with the lifestyle of a megastar but practically zilch in his pockets. "It's a rockbiz cliché," she seethes. "The people who take the profits aren't responsible for the losses. They take the bread and the people who make the music live on the crumbs. Jack didn't even own his house or his car. What's worse, he didn't own his music."

So who does? "I do." The brilliant blue eyes gaze out defiantly. "It's something the record companies never accepted. But I worked with Jack and I can prove it."

Quite a claim. True or false? Someone who worked extensively with Jack, and witnessed relations between the glamorous couple, told *Q*: "He'd start a song; she'd finish it. She'd come up with a line; he'd construct a whole theme from it. Being in the same studio as those two was like watching a game of ping-pong. They were almost inside each other's heads. But, of course, Jack was the star, so Jack got all the credit. That's the way it was in those days."

Not everyone interpreted the relationship in quite the same way. "She was riding on his back," one source close to Jack's band informed *Q*. "He was the golden goose and she had a taste for *foie gras*."

The face who reportedly launched a thousand hits doesn't deny it. "Sure I enjoyed the high life," she admits. "Who doesn't?"

It's a lifestyle that she may enjoy again if the contractual mare's-nest of the past twenty-five years can be resolved. But without a new deal, she insists, there will be no new music. "It's great stuff, but I'd rather burn the lot than sell Jack into slavery again."

Birdie, if anyone cares to remember, is no stranger to the tragic results of fire, so you're forced to the conclusion that she means what she says. Behind the blonde hair and innocent blue eyes, there's a core of pure steel. "No, it's not an idle threat," she chirps. "I haven't come all this way just to make things easy for someone I think of as a prime case for natural deselection."

Ouch! Watch out, Super Spider, Birdie Walker sharpened her talons long ago, when rock chicks *really* knew how to be mad and bad. She wrote the book on dangerous-to-know back in the days when such things mattered. Today, it seems, she's going by the book.

IV

Feel Like Shit and Ashamed

My sister has made me a dress. And what a dress! There's nothing else like it in the world. It is unique and when I put it on I am unique too. There are no designer labels and it cost her nothing but time— by which I mean that it cost her the whole of her life and experience, her hands and her eyes.

Years ago, I took her gift for granted. "Oh, Robin will make you something," I said to Jack when he wanted a certain kind of stage costume. Anyone can sew if they've got the patience and nothing better to do. Robin's patient and she's got nothing better to do than run you up what you want. I knew she'd make him something marvelous because she adored him. Adored him but bored him. There was always something abject in her devotion. Sugar and no spice.

Oh, but there's spice in this dress. And wit. Look at the collar— it rears up and then curls gracefully over, below the ears. It's a collar which forces me to hold my head high and stare into the mirror-mirror-on-the-wall. This is a dress for me *now*. Today. It is not feathers for a bird-brained chicky-babe.

Tina taps on the door and comes in. Her eyes say, "Wow!" when she sees what I'm wearing, but her mouth says, "Are you ready? I was going to call a cab, but someone's sent a car."

"Call a cab," I tell her through the mirror. "Send the car away."

"But it's a Rolls," she says wistfully.

"Nash bugs his cars. But keep it outside your door if you want to look good."

"I'll get rid of it," says puritan Tina. No ostentation without good reason. "But we ought to get a move on, or we'll be late."

"Exactly," I say. "We're going to be late. Relax. Make a cup of tea and chill."

I have my reputation to consider. Am I the type to turn up dutifully, on the dot, and then wait patiently for the honchos to get their act together? I am not. Nor is this dress. Robin has made a garment worth waiting for. Nash sent his car, but it is not, as Tina thinks, a mark of respect. He wants to know where I am, and when I will arrive. It is a symbol of control. Go suck your tiny thumb, Nash. I'll come when I'm good and ready.

Tina is uneasy. In her world, they're punctual and reliable. They prove their worth by doing what they say they're going to do when they've said they're going to do it. In my world, you prove your worth by winning the status games. Hurry-up-and-wait is a losing gambit. All it will do is prove to the opposition how easy you are to control. If I showed up on time, I'd be telling Nash he'd got me beat, that I'd been frightened and brought down by public exposure, that my own threats had no sting. Whereas what I want to tell him is that time's on my side. I've got Jack in my pocket, the way I always had, and if he wants Jack he'll have to deal with me. I am Rainbow Woman, Nash Zalisky, fuck with me and you'll never see your pot of gold. What a difference a great frock makes!

I sit in the cab while George pays the driver, then I get out and sweep into Dog Records' lobby in one fluid swoop. I leave my briefcase in the cab, forcing Tina to retrieve it and hurry after me, carrying it. We meet our two lawyers.

I have four in my entourage. Not as many as I'd like, not as many as I used to have, but four more than I've had for ages. Two lawyers, one security man, and one PA to carry the bag. That's how it will look. Tina tries to return the bag to me, but I ignore her. Silly woman—whatever is she thinking? Rainbow Woman doesn't carry her own bags.

We go up in the lift to the top floor and find Sasson waiting to greet us. Good—that's more like it.

Now here is a strange thing: Sasson takes my hand and kisses my cheek. "God, Birdie," he says, "you look stunning."

He waves my party of four into the boardroom, but he delays me. Now we will have to enter the meeting together—which will indicate, to those present, an alliance or friendship. Sasson cannot be ignorant of the visual language of meetings.

He says, "Birdie, whatever happens, please believe that I was not responsible for the smear campaign. I wouldn't do that."

" 'Whatever happens'? What *is* going to happen, Sasson? Any more tricks up that midget sleeve?"

"Not that I know of. I think your legal team's done a good job— a better job than I'd personally like."

"You mean it's a straight deal?"

"I mean, Birdie, you don't want to make the pips squeak over every damn percentage point. There's such a thing as being *too* tough, you know."

"I just regret not getting tough years ago when Jack was alive."

"Ah yes," he says, just for a split second looking like young Sasson.

I wonder how much he allows himself to remember. Is there a tiny corner of his memory which makes him feel that he let Jack down? Or has he armored that tiny corner and remembered only the fiction: that I drove a wedge between him and Jack.

He says, "Birdie, before we go in, is there anything I should know?"

"Like what?"

"I don't know—anything else you're hiding, another ace in the hole that'll up the ante again. I've got a lot riding on this deal. I'd like to think, now we've got the finance sorted out, we could work together."

I don't get a chance to answer because Nash bustles out of the elevator with his bodyguard. However late I was, he wanted to be later. I laugh. I look at Sasson and he can't resist it. He laughs too.

"What? What?" Nash asks, suspicion flaring behind his glasses.

Sasson straightens up first. He says, "Nash, good of you to come. Shall we go in now?"

"I don't know," Nash says warily. "I had a terrible dream. I nearly didn't come. I nearly didn't get out of bed. Birdie, have you ever had a dream so bad that you feel the whole day will be cursed? Remind me to tell you about it. What a beautiful dress, Birdie. Did I buy that for you?"

"Not a chance," I say, letting the old laughter linger in my voice. "This is a dress no mere money can buy."

"Oh," he says to Sasson, "we've been paying her too much."

"We'll see," Sasson says. "I can't wait to hear the new tracks."

"Why are we standing out here?" Nash says plaintively, and Sasson leads us into the boardroom.

I slip into a chair between George and the more savvy of the two lawyers. Nash sits at the center of an army. Sasson, as host, sits at the head of the table with an array of board members and advisors. The only one not present is Barry Stears, which is strange because the deal involving the movie is with him.

Everyone turns and watches me sit down. I am the show, the girl in the spangled tights. Roll up, roll up, the notorious scarlet woman has just made her entrance. Watch her balance on the wire—soar or floor—it doesn't matter as long as there's a spectacle.

I lean toward the savvy lawyer and whisper, "Where's Barry Stears?"

"I'm told he had to go to the US suddenly. That's his proxy over there." He indicates another gray spidery man with the smallest flick of one finger. The savvy lawyer has played this game before: he knows the value of *sotto voce* conferences with his client. Nothing important is said. Sometimes, at a strategic point, he leans toward me and says something idiotic like, "Bit warm in here, isn't it? I wish they'd turn the air-conditioner up." And I look down at his unreadable notes, nodding sagely. The secret agenda: you've got to have one even if you haven't got one. Otherwise, I sit back, nonchalant, relaxed, legs crossed, shimmering in my rainbow garb.

The main deals are these: first, the new Dog album; sub-clauses, my participation in arranging and producing it, publishing, copy-right, the videos, reproduction and mechanical rights. Second, Memo Movies' film; sub-clauses, visual material to be supplied by Ms. Walker, soundtrack and rights thereto, interview fees, etc. Third, the authorized biography; sub-clauses, Ms. Walker's agreement to be interviewed and supply previously unpublished photographs.

Hanging over all this is Nash's deal with Dog and Memo, giving him TV, Radio, and CD-ROM/e-commerce rights. In other words, Nash wants the world première on everything, because he is number-one spider, and he can afford it.

Most of this was thrashed out by gray men, including my gray men, over the previous few days. From my point of view, the offers are now adequate and the payment schedule is satisfactory. Even better, my lawyers have set up a private bank account for me with a subsidiary account in … wait for it … yes, in the Cayman Islands.

With this account in place and the knowledge that I've forced all three parties to do separate deals rather than allow myself to be bundled tidily into one all-encompassing contract, I can afford to sit back.

In fact, I am secretly jubilant. I have brought us to this stage without ever letting the opposition have a proper sight of what they're buying. The old-fashioned method of seduction has a lot to recommend it. Do not display your wares because to do so would cheapen them. Conceal and hint. Build hunger, and then in a carefully contrived accident, flash a little flesh. Ooh, yeah—I've gone back to long skirts and petticoats for this deal.

From across the table, I catch Nash staring at me. I lower my eyes shyly and think, yep, attempted rape only drives the bride price up, I wonder if he understands that now. I hope not. Let him think he's forced me to this table. Let him think that my counter-threat began as a tantrum and ended with one mildly snide article in Q magazine. Now he thinks there's a chink in the wall—I've broken my silence once, so I'll be easy meat for any interviewer he chooses to feed me to. I have all the stories, the essence of Jack, locked in my head; let him think he's found the key and I'll spill my precious load into his waiting hands. Well, Nash, we'll have to see about that.

But eventually, the time comes when even Rainbow Woman has to show and tell. All parties, including mine, are satisfied so far. Now they want to see the bride's face.

I ask Tina for the tape cassette and the video cassette. She gives them to me with a rather sour look. I expect that while this meeting

283

has been grinding on, she sat there silently, wondering what the hell she's doing. Good Father George isn't wondering. He knows he's here to protect me. But Tina, being rather more skeptical, has probably come to the conclusion that her only purpose is to look like a personal assistant and bag-carrier to the woman who used to tidy her office. Tough break, Tina, but that's show-biz.

"What do you want first?" I say, turning to Sasson, "music or pictures?"

"Music," he says. "Do you mind if I ask my chief engineer in to hear this? I know we won't be listening to the masters yet, but I'd like him in on this as early as possible."

I smile and say, "Of course." I'm pleased with Sasson. He's provided the dramatic pause. During it, I get up and walk over to the sound equipment. I keep the tape and video in my hand. Even these simulacrums of the real deal are too valuable to give to anyone else.

I look at the sound system, the giant speakers, the Star Fleet control panel. Mooching, figuring out how the system works, I have separated myself from my team, from the ranks of suited spiders. I am music, they are business. Music versus money. Romance against finance.

The silk rainbow swirls against my thighs as I walk to the window, turning my back on the table, looking out over the Soho rooftops to the clouds beyond. There are faces and fungi in the clouds. It is a dreamer's sky, full of morphing images. No two people will see the same picture on the cloudy canvas. No two dreamers will dream the same dream. That is the art of clouds and dreams. Those are the clouds and dreams of the artist. And these are the thoughts I can't afford to be thinking in the company of spiders.

I turn back toward the room and find that every eye is upon me. Nash is getting out of his chair to join me at the window. Oh no, that'll never do. I let him commit himself and then I glide around the other side of the table and out through the door. Leaving the boardroom without explanation, carrying with me the cassette and video. I cause pandemonium. Unbelievably, several of them chase my skirt as it flicks out into the corridor.

In the open-plan office at the end, I stop at the first desk and ask for the ladies' room. The chasing posse is there to be ignored. I sashay into the ladies room and lock the door.

It is extraordinary. Am I a rogue elephant or a psycho? No one, it seems, has the slightest idea of what I'm going to do next. Am I really so unpredictable that I cannot avoid Nash and go to the ladies room without being treated like an absconding prisoner?

In the mirror, I look at my reflection and smile. Unpredictable, exotic Rainbow Woman is still, for the time being, in charge of the goldmine, the means of production, the wealth of the gray nation. No wonder they're scared shitless.

By the time I return, the gray nation has assumed some semblance of dignity, leaving just one scout by the elevator to make sure I "don't get lost." But I cannot sit at a table with them any more. I need the separation, especially if I am to listen to Jack's voice. After I've slotted the cassette into the deck, I go back to the window and turn my back on the audience.

Jack's voice begins, husky with cigarette smoke, "Gimme time, gimme one last chance …"The opening line of "Adversarial Attitude." There is solid rich rhythm guitar under his voice and some honky-tonk piano providing the fills. It's the timeless song of the ill-treated man, his stone-hearted rival, and the stolen woman. It's violent and insulting: "She says he's steady, kind, and sweet—I know the whoring, boring man who beats his meat …" Jack calling poor Homer a wanker in his own inimitable fashion. Anger stretches his voice and gives it the hornlike power which can cut through any rock'n'roll band, however loud, and dominate it. If you heard that voice only once, even if you never heard it again, you wouldn't forget it.

I stare out at the clouds, remembering how the hair on the back of my head prickled when I first heard Jack. I remembered thinking that no one could possibly mistake that voice for any other. And how he stuttered on some of his consonants, "My b-baby," partly playing for time if he came in a breath too early, partly the result of taking speed. Whatever. It was impossibly sexy. Standing alone, staring at clouds, remembering, I can feel even now the lurch I felt long, long ago.

The tape rolls on. I left a couple of false starts in. Jack says, "Fuck it, babe. What're we doin' here?" And I say, "G, A minor seven, and

G. Split bars, remember?" "Yeah, right," says Jack and begins "Hopeless Case" again.

Another time, he says, "What's it say here, Birdie-bird? I can't read your writing. Whadya mean you don't know? It's your fuckin' song—I'm just the poor bleedin' singerman."

Once he says, "Take three, fuck it. This time, doll, skip the harmony except on last words and the last line of chorus." And I say, "*Thank* you, Maestro," in a sarcastic tone as if that's what I'd been telling him all along.

Mostly though, I've been very kind to the gray nation—apart from three superficial interruptions, I've given them ten good takes of pure Jack. I do not want to belabor the point I'm making. Which is that they must not assume that Jack wrote alone or worked unaided. They must not assume, as they always used to, that little Birdie-bird was there simply to roll his joints and warm his chilly toes.

The tape rolls on until there's nothing but audio hiss to listen to. Nobody moves. Nobody says anything. I don't bother to look at their faces, but I leave the window and eject the tape into my own hand. Then everyone starts talking at once.

This is a charade of my own making and I can't blame anyone but myself. I feel like shit and ashamed. That's one of Jack's lines in "Coal Dirty Soul"—"Feel like shit and ashamed, rode the roller 'til I went stone blind ..."

Now is not the time to walk away. I should've done that years ago. But I didn't, and now I have to stand here like a huckster in the market place with my goods in my hand, peddling what can never be paid for.

Maybe you can't bridge the gap between art and money. Maybe you can't ever sell what's precious to you without feeling like shit.

Ah fuck it, I think. We've been here before. If you feel like a slut, make 'em pay through the nose. We all sell whatever we've got to sell—skill, muscle, time, sex. We don't have to respect the buyer, but we've all got to eat. Jack wasn't pure. Only his voice was pure.

Sasson comes over to where I'm standing, contemplating the cleanliness of clouds. He lays his arm around my shoulders and says, "Well, well, Birdie dear, you *did* have something to sell, didn't you?

That was the real McCoy. Very good quality for cassette tape. But you do have the masters, don't you?"

"Of course."

"I won't ask you where you found them."

"No. Pointless."

"But if there's any more ..."

"It's never enough, is it, Sasson?" I shake off his arm and turn to face him. "What more do you want?"

"Nothing," he says quickly. "Really, Birdie, nothing more. It's just that I didn't know anything about these songs. They aren't leftovers or make-weights. They're fresh and whole and alive."

"Unlike the poor singerman," I say. "You don't have to sell them to me, Sasson. I'm selling them to you."

"And I'm ready to sign," he says. "I don't mind telling you, Birdie, a couple of days ago I thought your agents were pushing too hard. But now I'm not so sure."

Nash calls out from his side of the table, "Are there cue-sheets?"

I say, "Yes. I'll give them to Sasson with the masters."

"I'd like to see them now," he says waspishly.

"No can do," I say. "Besides, the music deal's with Dog."

"Who do you think owns Dog?"

"I think you own the whole world, Nash, but you'll get the cue-sheets when you get the masters."

My savvy lawyer butts in to remind Nash of the payment schedule: front money first, contract second, materials third. But Nash silences him. "When were these songs written, Birdie? Before *Hard Candy*, after *Hard Time*?"

"Before, during, and after," I say vaguely.

"Aren't there any production notes?"

"There wasn't a producer, Nash. Just us. We didn't make notes. We didn't write a diary. And before you ask, there aren't any hand-written, dated, lyric sheets either. I made the cue-sheets when I transferred the master to cassette."

"And when was that?"

"After I found the masters. What's the matter, Nash? Are you afraid I'm holding out on you?"

He looks up at me like a worried gnome who's about to burst into tears. "I don't know, Birdie. You never tell me anything."

Sasson says, "Shall we move on? We should take a look at the visuals now."

Blinds are drawn, lights are dimmed, and I am denied the consolation of clouds. But I'm less in need of consolation for visual images. Images of young Jack and Birdie do not move me with anything like the force that Jack's voice does. I am hardened against pictures of myself, and pictures, in any case, have less power over me than music does. I'd give you my eyes to save my ears any day.

Pretty people in pretty places—so what? Picture postcards. Flick through, see Jack walk and talk. Amazing, huh?

Around the boardroom table, the gray nation watches Jack turn his head to look out to sea, and yes, it's such a pretty profile. There's sun on his face and wind in his hair. Good ol' Jack—forever young and beautiful—one of the world's most marketable men. He had it all in an age which wants it all. The singer's a genius: fine, yawn. The singer's a beautiful young genius with a lop-sided sexy smile: woh-yeah, now we're cookin'. Video did indeed kill the radio star. It gave birth to a whole generation who could only listen with their eyes.

The Memo Movie team are all leaning forward, watching intently, and again I'm surprised that Barry is absent. This was what he wanted. Sasson at the head of the table is taking notes. Nash, who has seen some of this before, is watching me.

I go back to my seat between George and the savvy lawyer. George whispers, "How're you holding up?"

"OK," I say. "I wish it were over."

The savvy lawyer says, "Don't worry, everything's fine. We've covered all the bases."

From across the table, Nash's reptile eyes blink slowly and my hand, in response, closes tightly round the audio cassette. He will have recorded my recording—of course he will—in spite of the veto my lawyers put on copying. But a copy of a copy won't help him much. It will just join his collection of stolen property.

Soon, the lights are switched on and refreshments are brought in. There's tea and coffee, sweet and savory nibbles. I notice, on the bottom tray of the caterers' trolley, ice buckets with bottles of a very good champagne in them. All you can eat and free champagne, just sign on the dotted line.

The Memo Movies men bat me questions about film stock, format, and the condition of the materials. My savvy lawyer and his honest but inexperienced colleague field them. One of Nash's representatives asks for and receives a handful of photos. He asks if negatives are available. They are. My savvy lawyer shows them. He collects the video from the machine, he brings the photographs back to our side of the table. The small hoard still belongs to me. So far, I have signed nothing away.

The lawyers buzz around in circles, comparing amendments, inclusions, and deletions, shaking crumbs off the contracts. We are almost ready.

Sasson says, "I suggest we begin with the music."

Everyone shuffles back to their places. Sasson is straining at his tether and chivvying.

I whisper to the savvy lawyer and he raises his hand. "My client would like to begin with her agreement with Mr. Zalisky."

"Birdie, *please*," Sasson says impatiently. "Surely the music is at the top of the list."

I shake my head and my savvy suave lawyer digs his heels in. Birdie is being capricious again. She won't budge.

Nash turns the pages of his copy of the contract as if he's never seen one before in his life. It's as if the decaying little boy is rummaging through birthday wrapping paper, searching for a present he might have missed.

"Nash?" Sasson says. "Would you mind kicking off?"

Nash hands the contract to one of his lawyers to tidy. He looks at Sasson and me. The lawyer shows him where to sign and hands him a pen.

He puts the pen to the paper and waits for me to do the same. As I start to write, he puts the pen down and sits back in his chair. His expression is sulky and dissatisfied. He says, "I don't know. I'm still not sure."

Sasson turns his impatience on Nash. "What aren't you sure of, Nash? We've heard the tracks. Everything is as Birdie said it would be. Now, please, may we get on?"

"Oh, well, yes," Nash says uncertainly. "The tracks. Magnificent, of course, but I keep asking myself, are we contracting ourselves to the wrong party?"

"What on earth …?" says my savvy lawyer. "We've spent hours, days, establishing title."

"Nash," Sasson says warningly, "you gave me your word."

"Well, I suppose I did." Nash dithers with pen and contract. Then he drops the pen again. "It's no good," he whines, "I can't quite bring myself to do it. I'm sorry, Sasson, but what if Barry's right? Wouldn't we feel just awful if we signed this extortionate deal with Birdie when we should be signing with Jack?"

A thick silent fog drops on the room. People peer at each other, eyebrows raised. They look at me.

Sasson says, "This is absurd. Birdie, I'm so sorry. This wasn't supposed to happen. Barry thinks Jack is still alive. He's gone to the States to look for him."

I cannot think of a thing to say. I glance around the shrinking room. The walls are creeping toward me. The gray nation's gray faces sway in my direction like giant mushrooms.

Nash's slitty little mouth moves. His voice sounds like an owl hoot. "I could've spared you this, Birdie, if only you'd come to me. I don't really understand Barry's reasoning and I'm sure neither Sasson nor I concur with him, but there you are. He's convinced. What could we do?"

"You could've tried harder to talk him out of it," Sasson says disgustedly. "You didn't have to lend him your plane. And you certainly didn't have to introduce the subject now."

"Ah, but Sasson," Nash hoots, "keen as we all are, we cannot be party to a fraud."

Only my sister's clever dressmaking keeps my head erect.

"Yes, Birdie," Nash says, his frog-spawn eyes magnified behind his glasses. "I'd love to sign, believe me. You know I have your best interest at heart. But Barry, well, he was always such a *fan*, don't you think? He's sure he'll find Jack alive on a small island off the Florida coast. I hope you won't be too upset, but we'll have to postpone the signing till after his return."

My two lawyers are on their feet, arguing. Nash ignores them. He says, "I wish you'd trusted me, Birdie. Mistrust, you see, breeds mistrust. And now look what's happened. Barry is utterly out of control. Do you know, he's so certain that he's found Jack's location that he's taken your sister, Robin, along to help him with the identification."

"Catch her," George's voice booms in my ear, "I think she's going to faint."

V

What's Done in the Dark
Will Come to the Light

In the night, Robin listened to the roar of the engines. It filled her head, driving cotton wool thoughts into a stampede. Everything was too loud: jet planes, cars, baggage carts, human voices, all chewed up and blended in the air-conditioner.

Robin was not a good traveler. Nervous of flying, prone to air sickness, a martyr to jet lag, she always felt she'd left three-quarters of her brain at home with all the other essentials she'd forgotten to pack. And nowadays she could add swollen ankles to her list of miseries. Swollen ankles and disillusionment.

Flying in a private plane should exempt you from the discomforts of coach-class travel. There was a bathroom, with scented soap and face spritzers, so why did her skin feel oily and bloated? Why were her fingers puffy and clumsy? The food was freshly cooked in the galley and presented with an elegant vase of flowers, so why was her stomach bubbling with gas exactly the same way it did when she couldn't distinguish fish from foul fowl on normal flights. Surely millionaire moguls should have solved the problems of earache and flaky elbows in their private transport.

Oddly though, discomfort was a comfort to Robin. It filled her mind with small, pressing spikes and distracted her from a huge and terrible vertigo. If she opened her eyes and looked ahead, she would certainly see where she was going, and she'd know that although the jet was flying, she was falling.

Without indigestion to concentrate on, she would have felt like thieving Judas—stealing her sister's life. Lin's life was planes and travel. Lin always said, "Gotta go," and then hopped it without explaining. Robin was the one left behind. Lin rang up from Paris, LA, Bangkok. Robin was there to take the call. Strange men sent cars to carry Lin to strange places. Robin left a covered plate of food in the fridge for when she returned.

Robin still wore her ex-husband's ring years after he emigrated to New Zealand with his new family. Robin kept Jack's Egyptian ring in a sachet next to her bed for twenty-five years. She did not fling down her life, leave her daughter alone with a stranger, abandon her sister at a difficult time, and whizz off to the other side of the world at the word of a fat man she didn't trust.

Barry Stears, the pickpocket of rock music, always trying to squeeze into the same frame as the talent, jealously eyeing his neighbor's plate, receiver of stolen images—he had told her a theory so unbelievably laughable, so laughably unbelievable that, if it were true, it would turn the last twenty-five years of her life into a mockery.

"You're insane," she said. "You're pathetic."

"No, listen," he said.

"Get out of my house," she said.

And here she was unable to sleep or think. Because she was going to squash the cruel story flat. Laugh it into oblivion and save Lin the trouble. Really.

Really? Wasn't it just as likely that she was a pitiful straggler climbing up Glastonbury Tor on midsummer eve, hoping for a glimpse of King Arthur's ghost? Arthur lives and is watching over England. One day he will return to lead his people and all that crap. UFOs. Atlantis. The Second Coming. Pitiful.

But something sick and triumphant made Robin write a note to Grace: "I'm off to the States. Shouldn't be gone for more than a couple of days. Look after yourself." Borrowing Lin's attitude, Lin's handwriting almost. Gotta go. See you soon. Love.

Alec, furious, dropped a bottle of milk on the kitchen floor. Shattering glass, milk splashing on his shoes and trousers, allowed him to swear—fuck, fuck, fuck, fuck, fuck.

"Just mop it up," Grace said, irritable too, but for a different reason. There was no reason that Alec could see. So she had to make her

293

own breakfast once in a while. Big fucking deal. It wasn't like she'd been kicked out of her own game, back to level one, after doing all the work, and having all the inspiration which should have taken him to level ten. To the airport. To the States. Grace wasn't the one who'd cooked up all the arguments that had allowed Mr. Stears into the house and kept him and Mrs. Emerson talking. All she did was look at him narrowly every now and then and say, "Whose side are you on?"

"Yours," he'd say every time. "Yours, a hundred and twenty-five per cent. Don't you see? This is for you. It's like an abscess. It needs to be lanced."

"If it's true," she said. "But it isn't true."

"Then Barry needs to be zapped before it gets any farther. One way or the other, we've got to get involved. Don't you see? We can't let him run around like some renegade. We've got to know what he's up to."

Playing both sides wasn't a game for amateurs, he decided. Make one little mistake and both teams would come down on you like a ton of rubble. And now, on hands and knees, sloshing around in spilled milk, he seriously considered packing it all in and heading for home.

Devon was my error, he thought. The old bloody boyfriend in Devon.

"Devon?" Mr. Stears said, perking up. "Are you sure? Why didn't you tell me before?"

"I didn't know what you were thinking," Alec said. "And besides I only just heard about it."

"An old boyfriend? Does she go regularly? How long does she stay?" Mr. Stears seemed excited. "Good work, Alec. See what else you can find out."

But a day later he said, "Absurd, what on earth made you think Devon was the target? Don't you know anything about Birdie yet? If she says southwest, the best place to start looking is northeast."

I bet you didn't come up with that one all by yourself, Alec thought, annoyed. He said, "But she does go to Devon, Mr. Stears. Grace is sure of it."

"Well, of course she does," Mr. Stears said tetchily. "Homer Webb has a farm there."

"Who's Homer Webb?"

"He's one of Birdie's old boyfriends," Mr. Stears explained with exaggerated patience. "But he's the wrong old boyfriend."

You might've remembered that yesterday, Alec thought.

"I know there are a lot to choose from," Mr. Stears said, "but you'll have to do better than Homer Webb."

Like this whole Jack-hunt was my idea, Alec thought. But he did come up with something better. And it was something that had been staring him in the face ever since he came to stay in Grace's house. Every morning. It was one of the things that was so different from his own lumpen family. Mrs. Emerson made coffee with real beans and, here's the cruncher, she juiced real fresh oranges—the Produce of the State of Florida, USA.

"I'm glad you like it," she said when he complimented her—as he was always careful to do. "They're the best juice oranges in the world. Lin sends me crates of them."

It was an unremarkable tidbit of information which went un-remarked for weeks while Alec was supposed to be tracking down old movies, film labs, and soundtracks. But suddenly bells rang when he began to search for traces of Jack.

Florida oranges. Crates of them sent by Birdie to her sister in England. Why would Birdie go to Florida? Not for Disney World, that was for sure. He wanted to ask her, but she wasn't around to be asked. She'd abandoned him, got herself arrested, and made him feel he'd picked the losing side.

One morning after breakfast, without any purpose in mind, Alec examined the box of oranges and discovered that the original order had come from an insignificant little island off the Gulf Coast of Florida. More to revive Mr. Stear's flagging approval than anything else, Alec suggested the notion of a secret island hideaway. A really ace idea. It should've put Alec on Mr. Zalisky's plane, not Mrs. Emerson. A move like that deserved a better reward than milk-soaked trousers.

The car was huge. Alicia, the driver, was tiny. She sat on a cushion, but even so Robin worried that she couldn't see over the dashboard.

295

Robin worried about a lot of things—the heat, the glare, not having dark glasses, Alicia driving with only one hand on the wheel. She didn't want to die on the Tamiami Trail in the company of a dwarf and a slug. Tiny people shouldn't be put in charge of outsize cars. Slugs with jet lag shouldn't be put in charge of conversations.

After a stop for coffee and doughnuts, Robin moved to the front of the car to get away from Barry. Alicia talked nonstop and Robin found her hard to follow. But she gathered that Alicia was the agent's wife. The agent was on the island and he worked real hard. There was this phone call at three in the morning, and Guido had been workin' on it ever since. Alicia hadn't seen Guido for days. Presumably because he was on the island. A big agency in Tallahassee called Guido. Or was it a big legal firm who did stuff for Disney in Orlando? Anyways, with Guido on the island, there was no one else to hire the car and meet the nonscheduled flight in Tampa except Alicia. But, hey, that was cool, she liked driving, and they were going to the island, so, what the heck, she just put a coupla clean shirts for Guido in the trunk and here she was. Neat, huh? England was neat too. Alicia went there once when her older sister's husband, who was in the air force, was stationed in Essex.

Robin smiled. Barry had been under the impression that Nash would lay on a chauffeur-driven limo, and he couldn't come to grips with this tiny woman who insisted on eating her chocolate doughnut at his table and who talked a blue streak. He slumped in the back seat and tried to maintain a dignified silence.

"This glare's killing me," Robin said. "I forgot to bring dark glasses."

"No problem," Alicia said. "There's a Wal-Mart in the next plaza. We'll do some shopping."

Robin bought a black T-shirt which said "Oh shit, sharks!" for Grace, and another one for Jimmy which said "And now I'm going straight to hell" in gothic script. Then she bought a straw hat and dark glasses for herself. Buying presents for the kids made her feel more normal.

"What's the matter with you, Robin?" Barry snarled from the back seat. "We aren't on holiday, you know."

છ છ છ

"You've got to come home," Grace said to Jimmy on the phone. "Everyone's gone crazy. Auntie Lin's in trouble. Mum's flipping out. She just ran off without telling me. Some stupid, stupid bastard's gone and convinced her that Jack might …"

"That's why I'm ringing," Jimmy said through a lot of static. "There was a picture of Auntie Lin being arrested in one of the Italian gossip mags. I couldn't believe it, sis. What's the old raver been up to now?"

"She was set up by a bunch of rock-biz dirt-bags. And she won't come home 'cos of the tabloids door-stepping this place. It's like the old days, Jimmy. It sucks, it really sucks."

"Oh for God's sake, Grace," Jimmy said. "What're you talking about? You don't remember the old days—you were just a baby."

"You'd be surprised," Grace said loftily. But in spite of what she told Alec, Jimmy was right. She couldn't remember Jack at all. She didn't want to admit it, though. Jack was her one and only claim to glamour and she wouldn't let him go without a fight.

"Anyway," she said, "that's what Mum told me. She said history was repeating itself. And now she's freaked out and gone to the States to look for Jack …"

"She's done *what*?"

"I told you. This fat creepo Alec works for turned up and gave her a song and dance about Jack being alive and Auntie Lin hiding him out on an island, and she fell for it. She *fell* for it, Jimmy, and she pushed off to the States while Alec and I were at the movies. Please, Jimmy, you've got to come home."

"Maybe I'd better," Jimmy said. "It sounds like you've all lost your marbles. Does Lin know what's happening? Or is she still in chokey?"

"She's undercover somewhere. I can't talk to her because the phones are all bugged."

"Oh Grace," Jimmy said wearily, "please tell me you're joking."

"They're bugged," she said firmly. "Alec did it himself."

"Then tell him to undo it. Is this the guy Mum put in my room?"

"Sort of," Grace said. She felt stupid and depressed. She shouldn't have mentioned the bugged phones, not on the phone. Things were falling apart.

"Where is he? I want to talk to him."

"He's out." Where? Alec was in a foul mood. That's why she was so glad Jimmy had called. She was in need of someone to talk to. She was feeling unusually insecure.

"This stinks," Jimmy said with authority. "Go out to a public phone box and try to get hold of Auntie Lin. She's a tough old bird—she'll know what to do."

"She'll freak."

"She's nowhere near as fragile and romantic as you think she is. She's survived all sorts of shit."

"But they're trying to turn Jack into Elvis. It's horrible and grotesque."

"They probably think it'll sell more records. I'm sorry they've sucked Mum in, though. She's the one who'll freak."

"Are you coming home?"

"Hell, yes," Jimmy said. "You're making a right dog's dinner of this. Anyway, I only rang to see if Mum would send me some dosh. Italian campsites suck and I'm going broke."

Thank God, Grace thought, someone's coming. It was only Jimmy, but it broke the isolation. It occurred to her that she'd never been alone in the house for more than an hour or two. It was her home and her mother was always there. Always. She worked in the attic and she rarely went out, except to go shopping or make deliveries. This was her mother's domain. She was never more than a yell away. Everyone else came and went, but Mum was a constant.

It never occurred to her that her mother might even own a suitcase. Now she was gone, and without her, oddly, Alec seemed to lose his charm. He suddenly became a stranger. Nice-looking, yes, but a bit self-centered and sort of unsafe. Like, she could trust him when Mum or Lin was there, but alone, she felt weird about him—like, she couldn't see the point any more.

The place was extraordinary, Robin thought. You drove down a long straight road behind all the slowly cruising Chevies and Buicks. On either side of you were golf courses and condominiums with names like The Beach Place, The Verandah, Buttonwood Harbor, all sticking up clean and white like false teeth. Behind the false teeth, the Astro Turf grass and sprinklers, the sea winked and glared.

Then you turned right into Bowsprit Lane, past a line of tidy bungalows with mail boxes shooting laser beams of reflected sunlight straight into your eyes. The lane petered out into a turning circle and then became a sandy track which disappeared into dense dark undergrowth.

She was barely a hundred yards from the main road, scarcely five hundred feet from the twin rows of holiday bungalows and, without warning, she was about to step into a tangle of wild oak, unrecognizable tropical trees and vines.

The sun couldn't penetrate the twisted unrestrained greenery. It was dark. She took off her new sunglasses and peered into the gloom. She could just distinguish the outline of a screened porch. The timber was the same grey color as the tree trunks, and thick exotic foliage pressed up against the mosquito netting, making it look like a forgotten, overgrown aviary.

"This can't be it," she said out loud, almost making herself jump. "Lin would never own a place like this. Not here. It's all wrong. Just not Lin at all."

She turned back to Barry and Guido. "Really," she said, "this just isn't Lin. There's been a mistake."

Guido said, "Yes, m'am."

Barry said nothing. He was looking extremely unsure of himself.

Guido said, "Shall we go sit in the car? I'll get a coupla cans from the cooler. I got beer, Diet Coke, or Sprite."

"Sprite," said Barry.

"Beer, please," said Robin. She needed a drink. There was something unnerving about the coiling distorted vines and trees—the unexpected darkness. It was a vestige of primeval forest, forgotten by the planners and architects and landscape designers. Forgotten by progress.

Guido was only an inch or so taller than his wife, but poking out from the sleeves of his crisp short-sleeved shirt was a pair of arms which would have made Popeye the Sailor Man proud. He and Alicia drank Diet Coke. After a pause, he said, "See, I was surprised

299

as you. But I checked twice at the Land Registry *and* the post office."

Alicia said, "He always double-checks, Robin. He's known by it."

"I didn't mean to be rude," Robin said. "It's just … well, I know my sister."

"Sure you do," Alicia said.

Guido cleared his throat politely. "The property was purchased twenty-seven years ago and it's registered to the Eagle Holding Company, sole proprietor, Ms. Linnet Walker."

"Who pays the property tax?" Barry asked, sounding confident again.

"Eagle Holding."

"No, no," Robin said. Lin pay property tax? Surely not. Lin didn't *do* taxes. Lin wasn't a resident anywhere. She never even had a place to hang her hat unless it was Robin's house.

"Have you spoken to the neighbors?"

Neighbors? Robin looked round vaguely. Of course there were neighbors, close neighbors, on this tacky, *nouveau riche* playground of an island. But this corner of nightmare jungle seemed to have been picked up from the set of a film about mad swamp dwellers. The darkness, the silence, argued for total isolation.

"See, there's a problem," Guido said. "This part of the key ain't residential. People own property, sure, but, like, it's vacationers—they just come for the season to play tennis or golf or for the sailing. Hardly no one lives here all year round except the people who work here. And most of them come in daily from the mainland."

"Regular folks wouldn't live here and raise families," Alicia concurred. "No regular folks, no regular neighbors."

"But I talked to the Quaker lady at the post office," Guido said, "and a guy who's been at the pharmacy in the Avenue Mall for years. They say there's a guy here who was wounded in 'Nam. He don't never come off the property, never shows his face. He don't get no deliveries and he doesn't own an automobile. They say there used to be a black woman came a coupla times a week, but nobody's seen her in years."

"Are you listening, Robin?" Barry said pompously. "Doesn't ever show his face. Maybe wounded in Vietnam. Or maybe suffered serious burns in a fire twenty-five years ago. It adds up."

300

"But that's as far as I can go," Guido said. "I can't sit here and watch the house 'cos that's what the Sheriff's Department here don't like. You hang out here for a spell and just see if they don't slide on through to check out where you're at. People here dial 911 if they see a bicycle in a no-parking zone."

"It's that kinda place," Alicia confirmed. "Exclusive."

"Way I see it," Guido went on, "only thing you can do is walk on up to the door and talk to the guy straight up."

"Oh dear," Barry said.

Talking to people straight up was not one of Barry's strengths, Robin thought. She'd had twenty-four hours of his hints and sly rummagings for information.

"Only problem with that," Guido said, "is the dogs. Guy got a coupla mean suckers in there. I saw 'em night before last. Pit bulls or something. Came out after racoons, I guess."

"Pit bulls?" Barry said.

"What do you want to do?" Guido asked inexorably. "'Cos I suggest you don't wait till after dark. If the dogs don't get you, the bugs will. This guy doesn't spray—he got mosquitos here big as dinner plates."

Guido's getting a kick out of this, Robin decided. He's treating us like greenhorns in the wild west. She looked at Barry dithering, playing with his Sprite can, rolling the cold surface over his pink cheeks and between his plump palms.

She said, "Well, Barry? This was your idea. What're you going to do?"

Barry's buttocks writhed against the car seat. He said, "Robin, look, I mean, Jack was virtually your brother-in-law."

"Yes. And I've been listening to twenty-four hours of you saying he was your best friend."

"But if he's scarred, Robin? If he's mad ..."

"If he's scarred and mad, he's still Jack." Robin opened the car door and waves of wet heat rolled in. She said, "Come on. We've got to find out, one way or the other."

The picture of the bright angel on her wall, the one who greeted her every morning, beckoned. And summoned, Robin walked forward into the gloomy tangled jungle.

When I think of all those stories of people looking where they've been told not to look—Orpheus in the underworld, Pandora and her forbidden box, the foolish bride in Bluebeard's Castle—I see initiative poorly rewarded. Loss and death follow the curious. Don't look, they say. Don't be too clever. Don't ask too many questions. Death stalks the detective. But the human condition is to ignore warnings, to go where you're not welcome. That's how new worlds get populated. The naked ape isn't satisfied with the tree he was born under. "Gimme more," he says as soon as he learns to speak. Greedy little bastard.

Good. The globe is crawling with greedy little bastards. I know, because I proudly count myself as one of them. My gimme-more gene is highly developed, so in that respect I understand Nash, Sasson, and Barry perfectly.

It should be simple: They want what I've got; I want what they've got. That's the basis of a great relationship. But nothing is simple in a relationship between art and commerce. For one thing, these days, the art is of secondary importance to the artist. Sometimes I think they don't want the art at all—they only want a marketable artist. And increasingly, of course, that is just what they're getting—kids so greedy for attention that they sell their pretty young images to front a product so banal that no one listens to it.

Which makes it tough when what you want to sell are songs to the greedy bastards who only want the singer.

And that is why, when Nash was staring at me from across the boardroom table with his little saurian eyes magnified by thick plastic lenses, even before he opened his greedy mouth to drop his bombshell, I wrote on my copy of the contract, "Up your bum, Nash Zalisky." Childish, undignified? Yes. Satisfying? Oh, absolutely.

"I always wanted Jack," he told me once, not mentioning music at all. Well, I'm not selling Jack. I'm not loaning him, leasing him, or giving him away, either. I have ten good songs and that was all I ever intended to sell. The rest? Well, call it my advertising campaign, if you like. It was never up for grabs.

The Antigua Movie? What was that but beautiful visual images packaged for a music industry which is willing to spend more on making a video than on cutting an album. It was beautiful visual images which got my back taxes paid, brought me to the bargaining table, and gave me a bank account with money in it.

Nash will want it all back, of course. But he can't have it. He'll have to let it go—the way I've had to let go of all those past royalties, the way Jack had to let go of a little dance number that went platinum in Brazil.

Obviously, Nash will say I scammed him. But he'll never be quite sure. Nor will Sasson, and nor will any of the other legal and financial advisors sitting at that table. After all, it was Nash who pulled out of the deal, Nash who said he didn't want to sign with me. Everyone at the table heard him. He said he'd prefer to sign with Jack. I was the innocent party in the rainbow dress who fainted from the shock.

He spent quite a lot of money on nothing. But even so, the price was small compared with what the industry owes Jack and me. He'll never pay that back. What he paid was the price for being a greedy little bastard who looked where he wasn't supposed to look—or rather, being Nash, sending his minions to look. It's the price he pays for looking when he should be listening, for listening when he has no right to listen, for stealing images I didn't want to show him, for corrupting kids like Alec who are primed from birth to want, want, want. But most of all, it's the price he pays for corrupting, with hope, innocent dreamers like my sister.

Her weakness was to love a man who didn't even see her. And Nash exploited her love. He said, "You can have him, but only if you betray him." You pay for that, Nash. I only wish I could've made you pay more.

Later, what Robin remembered most vividly of the horrible, frightening incident was teeth: the gleaming white teeth of snarling dogs and the yellow ocher teeth of a heavy smoker who mouthed the words "Fuck off" at her through mosquito netting.

The frenzied dogs clawed at the screen, rattling it, threatening to hurl their lean muscular bodies through it. She did not back off or

303

run away. She stood her ground and called through the din, "Anyone at home?"

And then the face appeared at a window curtained only by mosquito netting. It was a nightmare face, bearded with wiry salt and pepper hair. Leathery skin hung in corrugations from sharp cheekbones. One eye was missing and the eyelid sank into an empty socket like a withered petal.

"Jack?" she said uncertainly. "Is it you?" She tried in vain to make out the color of the surviving eye—willing it, like a prayer, to be gloriously blue. But the surviving eye was so narrow, so screwed up with enmity and spite, that she couldn't identify a trace of color in the hate-filled slit.

"Jack?" she said again, provoking the dogs to more insane rage. But the single slitty eye just poured cold contempt on her quaking heart. The ragged hair around the mouth parted, showing chipped yellow teeth, and the lips formed the words "Fuck off," but not a sound could be heard above the barking and snarling of the dogs. Then the face disappeared, leaving the black square of window bare.

She stood in front of his porch for fully ten minutes, waiting. She stood with tears pouring down her face, waiting for a stranger to come out and tell her that he wasn't Jack, that however long she waited he never would be Jack. Jack was gone. But the disfigured stranger didn't even return to the window. He left her standing in front of his porch while his dogs screamed and roared.

After a while, she wiped her eyes on the hem of her pretty summer dress and walked slowly back to the car.

"Well?" Barry asked, his cheeks wobbling with anticipation. "Well?"

"It wasn't him," Robin said, her throat sore from gulping tears.

"Wasn't? Wasn't?" Barry said. "Then why are you crying?"

"Because it might have been," she said, utterly defeated. "It might have been, but it wasn't."

"Are you sure?"

"Absolutely sure."

"Did you see his face? How can you be so certain? I don't know that I trust either of the Walker sisters."

304

"Go and look for yourself." Robin climbed wearily into the car. With silent sympathy, Alicia handed her a fistful of tissues and she buried her face in them, unable to prevent another wave of grief from shaking her drooping middle-aged body.

With the car door open, they could all hear the hysterical barking of the dogs. Barry got out and took a couple of steps toward the dark secret house. Then he turned and got back in again.

"If you're absolutely sure," he said.

To believe anything else, Robin would have had to accept that her bright angel had become an ugly monster. She would have accepted his ugliness. After all, she had kept the ugly blackened lump that had once been his gold ring. But she could not accept that the man who gave her barmy mother a house when he didn't have one himself could stare at her with such contempt and hatred. She couldn't believe the beautiful youth whose voice made her heart soar could set his dogs on her and stand there staring while she wept in front of his house. An ugly face and body she could accept as Jack's but not an ugly soul.

Therefore it was not Jack's face she saw at the window. Robin's bright angel was a charmed thing etched into eternity. She knew she might not recognize his face, but she could never be mistaken about his soul.

CODA

"You left your mark on me, it's permanent, a tattoo."
Lucinda Williams

I

On a gray, drizzly hillside in north Oxfordshire, the Hebbingdon Free Festival was in the middle of its noisy, gaudy first day. The damp grass was covered with groundsheets and polythene, and the groundsheets were covered by a sea of stoned kids, rocked into mindless paralysis by stacks of giant speakers from three stages.

Sheltering under the apron at the back of Stage Two were the five members of InnerVersions, Dram, Sapper, Corky, Karen, and their new drummer, Patsi Noble. It was their first festival—their first time playing on an outdoor stage, and they were nervous as hell.

"So many people," Sapper said. "There must be thousands."

There *were* thousands—the hillside was carpeted with kids. They weren't all waiting for InnerVersions, though. They were simply hanging and waiting for whatever happened next.

"The sound's horrible," Karen muttered. It *was* horrible—muddled and muddy. The only thing to be said for it was that it was loud. But no louder than the sounds from the other two stages which could be heard clearly from where the band shivered under the backstage. Every now and then, the wind blew across the faces of the open mikes, causing a thunderous roar.

InnerVersions was slotted in between The Rolling Clones and a club act called Doreen Doreen with only fifteen minutes for the stage crew to set up. There would be no time for a proper soundcheck.

They'd never played to such a large audience and to do so without a proper soundcheck reminded Karen of all those dreams of incompetence and unreadiness. Thousands and thousands of people, only a forty-minute set to make an impression on them, and no bleeding soundcheck.

Worse, the Clones were doing very well. They had the front of the crowd jumping and singing along to "Brown Sugar."

"If they like that," Dram said gloomily, " they'll fuckin' hate us. No one knows us. They want a sing-along, fuck it, and no one knows our material."

"They will after today," Ozzy Ireland said. He was getting used to InnerVersions' pernicious habit of bringing each other down. "Enjoy yourselves for once. Go up there and just belt it out."

"Easy for you to say," Corky said with a sly look at Patsi. "This isn't your first outing with a new drummer." He emphasized the word "outing." He still couldn't quite believe that Flambo had been replaced by a woman, a muscular woman who, it seemed, could count.

"Shut up and listen to this," Ozzy said. He folded back the flapping pages of *Mojo* magazine and began to read aloud. " 'In the studio this month: Birdie, self-styled widow of the more famous Jack, is overseeing production and remastering of the eagerly awaited ten lost tracks. The Hyde Voodoo studio in New Orleans was picked for its proximity to ex-Jack producer, Junior Moline. "We're going for a raw, live sound," says Moline, "something as close to the spirit of *Hard Candy* and *Hard Time* as we can get without too much overdubbing. We're calling the album *Hard On* at the moment, but I expect the label will have something to say about it.

" 'Surprisingly, the label is not Jack's old company, Dog Records, as was expected and, indeed, publicized. The prize, which is expected to go gold in its first week of release, has gone to Atlantic. After the aborted signing, a spokesman for Dog was tight-lipped about the loss. "We are releasing a Jack-In-The-Box set of our own in time for Christmas," was his only comment. But a little Birdie tells us that the rift was caused when conglomerate boss, Nash Zalisky, flipped his lid and started to believe in Jack sightings from as far afield as Acapulco, Miami, and Bali. "The ghosts of dead rock stars are always haunting us," she said with her familiar sexy laugh, "but you don't expect multimedia moguls to want to sign contracts with them." So, no *Hard On* for Dog this Christmas.' "

"Well that explains why we haven't seen her," Corky said, digging his elbow into Sapper's ribs. "Nothing personal, old fruit—she was just feathering her own nest."

II

It is finished and I'm holding in my hand the slim plastic box with a cover-picture of sunlit, windblown Jack. His face emerges like a specter's from a stormy sea. Or is it receding into the waves? Coming or going? Who knows—it's all down to individual interpretation, like everything else in rock music.

I'm holding in my hand the voice that can still make my loins ache. I haven't done it any harm. It rings out clear as a bell. It's warm and cold. It's angry, hard, sad, and sexy. It's funny and sly. It takes you places you've never been. It finds secret longings, corners of your soul and memory you never knew existed. It makes you get down and boogie. That voice. Remember it?

If I'd had a voice like that … ah, but I didn't. It was a gift, and it was not given to me. It was given to Jack. Jack had it and Jack used it. May God bless him and keep him. Beautiful Jack.

I didn't have a voice, but I had some music and I had some words. What could I do but give them to Jack? People wanted to listen to him. They didn't want to listen to me. Even if I'd had a voice, no one would have wanted to hear it. My young life was a performance before an audience of millions. It was a role thrust upon me by nature and my own youthful stupidity. But it was a non-speaking, non-singing role—which I suppose you could see as something of a tragedy for a woman who thought she had something to say.

But never mind. It's all over now, and at least sometimes I had Jack's voice to speak for me. I would never, never, *ever*, have harmed that voice. No. Jack did that all by himself when he burned his throat out with boiling, choking smoke and lost it forever. May God curse him for that. That voice could have lasted for decades if he'd taken care of it. But he didn't, and now all he has is fame—empty, resounding, eternal fame.

Here's another rock'n'roll story: this one's about the destructive

311

power of fame. Lethal fame and lethal longing. One dark night, a famous self-indulgent rock star is prowling around his mansion under the influence of reds, greens, blues. He's a famous rock star, so he has uppers and downers of all the colors of the rainbow. You name it, he's got it. He's got it, so he takes it. That's what rock stars are supposed to do. This rock star is playing at being a rock star, out of his skull in his lonely old mansion. He may be very famous, but he can also be quite banal at times.

Outside his gate, there's a hippie camp, a gathering of stoned kids who are playing at being besotted fans. They wait there, all day and all night, for a glimpse of the famous rock star. Whenever he comes out they crowd around his car, screaming, "Yeah, Jack! We love you, man."

And then, into this tableau walks the real thing—the truly besotted fan, the one who, when he isn't thinking he owns Jack and all his work, thinks he is Jack and all his work. He looks at the hippie camp. He looks at the gate. He looks at the wall. He sees no barrier. It's only God's little mistake that Jack is inside and he is outside. He is mad enough to think that he can rectify God's mistake. He can climb walls. He can cross lawns. He can walk straight into a lonely mansion on the hill. And when Jack sees him, Jack will recognize him as his brother, his twin, his other self. Because that is what Jack is to this crazy fan—his other self. So Jack will have to recognize him. There's no other way.

Except, of course, Jack doesn't recognize him. Jack sees him as a trippy nightmare figure creeping down the basement stairs with a kerosene lamp in his hand, like the robed figure of Death with empty eye sockets. Jack freaks. The mad other self freaks. The angel wrestles frantically with Death. Hell-fire laps around his ankles. The mansion on the hill burns to a crisp.

All Jack had to do was talk the guy down. All he had to do was hit the panic button. Wait for help. Ah yes, but you're forgetting all those yellows, reds, greens, and blues. And what about whatever the mad other self had dropped to help him on his crazy way?

We'll never know about that. He never even got the chance to tell Jack his name.

Anyway, I don't know how much of this is true. I'm making half of it up, and Jack couldn't remember properly the half I'm not making up. It was all a nightmare to him.

All I know for certain is that the charred bone fragments in the basement were not Jack's. And the ugly lump of gold which I wept such bitter tears over was not Jack's Egyptian ring.

When I saw Jack next, it was a week later and I nearly didn't recognize him. He came in the night to Robin's kitchen door. The right side of his face and his right hand were a mass of healing burns. The fire had scorched away every beautiful hair on his head. He could only speak in a hoarse whisper. He couldn't remember where he'd been or how he got home. And he thought he was a murderer.

Technically speaking, I don't suppose anyone else would have even called him a killer, let alone a murderer. But the mad other self left an indelible calling card on Jack's mind as well as on his body.

"Hide me," he whispered. "Help me. Hide me."

God help me, God hide me—that's exactly what I did. I thought I could heal him. Did I really think that? Did I really think at all? I know I thought I could help him find his voice again. I thought that when the burns closed, when his hair grew back, his mind would heal too. So much for the optimism of youth.

Youth and optimism faded together. Ah well—goodbye both. I was sorry to see you go, but you went—the way you always do.

And, fuck it, what was I supposed to do? Feed Jack—bald, burned, whispering Jack—to the tabloid vultures hanging around my sister's house? Are you insane?

No, I had a bolt-hole, a tiny cabin on a scruffy overgrown key on the Gulf Coast of Florida. I bought it with the proceeds from a shameful transaction in LA. Check out a certain pornographic web-site on your computer and you'll clearly see Birdie-the-whore accepting twenty-thousand dollars for unspeakable services rendered to a plump, powerful pig. You can check it out any time, night or day, courtesy of Nash Zalisky.

Unspeakable services, my arse! It was just a fuck, and it bought me a house. My house. Not the bank's, not the record company's, not Jack's. Mine. A little cedar shack on the beach. An old broken-down dock, just right for tying up an old broken-down outboard. My back door onto the mangroves—in the days when the mangroves were thick and plentiful.

In those days, you could only get to the key by boat across the bay. And the bay was teeming with pompano, and the mangroves were teeming with herons, egrets, and the elusive snook. Then, you could see ibis stalking the beach every morning and watch the sea eagles circling the trees. It was a safe place to hide out in.

Nowadays, you're lucky ever to see an ibis, and the key is linked to three other keys and the mainland by concrete bridges which bring rivers, floods, of holiday-makers like some infernal aqueduct. The little spit of sand and greenery is groaning under the weight of condominiums and golf clubs. No, this island is no longer even an island. I could sell my few acres of it tomorrow. And, believe me, I've had some very tempting offers. I could sell up and move Jack to another island without a backward glance. Except that Jack won't let me because that would leave his only friend, Mekong Marty, without a home.

Mute Mekong Marty is the only man on the island uglier, madder, and worse off than Jack. Jack is a peach compared to Marty, and maybe that's why Jack likes him. They built their houses together. Jack's house is right on the bay, Marty's is between Jack's house and the road. Marty and his dogs guard Jack from intruders. Marty will never leave. He'll shoot himself and his dogs—three bullets into three welcoming skulls—rather than be uprooted.

If I couldn't sell, I couldn't buy another place. The scruffy plot of land was the only thing I could call my own. So I had to watch while the road was paved, the bridges were built. More and more buildings went up and the water table went down. The ibis flew away.

Now, though, everything has changed. This slim box with Jack's bright picture on the cover has changed everything. I can move Jack and leave Mekong Marty where he wants to be. I can afford proper care for Jack and a good new outboard for me.

You'd think, wouldn't you, that I'd have told Robin. Who would be better to tell than her? She would've looked after Jack. She might have put our mother in a home for Jack's sake. Or she'd have brought

314

her along with her two little children. She'd have lived in isolation and secret with her entire family just for the privilege of looking after Jack. Hooray for the selfless heroine, the woman who would beggar herself and die for love.

She does love him, she always has. She loved him better and much more faithfully than I ever could. It's her nature to love that way. The poor deluded cow even loves *me*.

Well, that's why I never told her. I could kid you and say I kept silent to protect her and her children from the consequences of her sweet love. But no one would believe that. So I'll tell you instead that the one I want to protect from sweet love is Jack.

Obsessive love nearly killed him. He's had too much love to cope with—no one should have to suffer so much love. And Robin's sweet love would soften him and rot him to the core like sugar rots a tooth. He doesn't get that kind of love from me. Never has, never will. And he's better off without it.

I'll be with him in time for Christmas, and he'll come to the edge of the dock. He'll whisper, "Hey, babe. What's that you've got there? Have you brought me a present?"

And I'll say, "I've brought your stupid voice back, take it or leave it."

He'll take it. And maybe he'll laugh, or maybe he'll cry, you can never tell with Jack. But one thing's certain—he won't rot. And another thing's certain—he won't starve. Not now. And nor will I.

Acknowledgments

"KIND HEARTED WOMAN BLUES"
Robert Johnson, author
© (1978) 1990. 1991 King of Spades Music
All rights reserved. Used by permission.

"SHE JUST WANTS TO DANCE"
Words and music by Kevin Moore and Georgina Graper
© 1994 Playin' Possum Music and Keb' Mo' Music, USA
Warner/Chappell Music Ltd, London, W6 8BS
Reproduced by permission of IMP Ltd.

"MEMO FROM TURNER"
Written by Mick Jagger & Keith Richards
© 1969. Renewed 1997 ABKC0 Music Inc.
All rights reserved. Reprinted by permission.

Lyrics from "AWFUL"
(Love/Erlandson/Auf Der Maur/Schemel)
© 1998 by kind permission of Mother May I Music/
Polygram Music Publishing/MCA Music Ltd.

Lyrics from "ACROSS THE BORDERLINE"
(Dickinson/Hiatt/Cooder)
© 1982 by kind permission of
MCA Music Publishing/MCA Music Ltd.

"RIGHT IN TIME"
Words and music by Lucinda Williams
© 1998 Lucy Jones Music and Nomad-Norman Music USA
Warner/Chappell Music Ltd, London, W6 8BS
Reproduced by permission of IMP Ltd.